D1270888

DELTA'S
Key to the
Next Generation
TOEFL® Test

Essential Grammar for the iBT

by

Nancy Gallagher

TOEFL is a registered trademark of Educational Testing Service (ETS).
This publication is not endorsed or approved by ETS.

(cw)
Eng 2nd
PE
1128
.G35
2009
C.2

DELTA PUBLISHING COMPANY
A Division of
DELTA SYSTEMS CO., INC.

© 2009 by NANCY GALLAGHER

All rights reserved. No part of this publication may be reproduced or transmitted in any form or by any means, electronic or mechanical, including photocopying, recording, or any information storage and retrieval system, without permission in writing from the publisher.

Requests for permission to make copies of any part of the work should be sent to:

DELTA PUBLISHING COMPANY
A Divison of Delta Systems Co., Inc.
1400 Miller Parkway
McHenry, IL 60050 USA
(800) 323-8270 or (815) 363-3582
www.deltapublishing.com

WITHDRAWN

Editor: Patricia Brenner
Page Layout & Design: Linda Bruell
Cover Design: Damon Taylor
Audio Production: Jay Kenney and Audio Logic, Inc.

Text with Audio CD   978-1-934960-16-5

Printed in the United States of America

10 9 8 7 6 5 4 3 2 1

LOYOLA UNIVERSITY LIBRARY

CONTENTS

About this Book 1

About the TOEFL® 3

Diagnostic Test 4

Unit 1   Nouns 7

Unit 2   Verbs 21

Unit 3   Infinitives and Gerunds 41

            Quiz 1   Units 1–3 53

Unit 4   Clauses and Sentences 54

Unit 5   Conjunctions 64

Unit 6   Adverb Clauses 76

            Quiz 2   Units 4–6 89

Unit 7   Adjective Clauses 90

Unit 8   Noun Clauses 106

Unit 9   Conditional Sentences 115

            Quiz 3   Units 7–9 128

Unit 10   Singular and Plural 129

Unit 11   Articles 139

Unit 12   Subject–Verb Agreement 148

Unit 13   Pronoun Agreement 160

            Quiz 4   Units 10–13 175

Unit 14   Comparison 176

Unit 15   Prepositions 187

Unit 16   Word Order 198

Unit 17   Parallel Structure 210

            Quiz 5   Units 14–17 218

Unit 18   Word Form 219

Unit 19   Common Word Errors 228

Unit 20   Punctuation 237

            Quiz 6   Units 18–20 248

Review Test 249

Answer Key 252

Audio Scripts 275

Index 285

How to Score Speaking 296

How to Score Writing 298

Score Charts 300

ABOUT THIS BOOK

Delta's Key to the Next Generation TOEFL® Test: Essential Grammar for the iBT is designed for international students who wish to enter a program of study in an English–speaking institution. Although its chief focus is preparation for the Test of English as a Foreign Language® (TOEFL®), the book also provides a general review of English grammar. Content includes essential points of sentence structure, along with practice in reading, listening, speaking, and writing.

Essential Grammar for the iBT can be used in a number of ways:

- As practice for the TOEFL iBT, the TOEFL PBT, and other tests of English proficiency
- As the primary or secondary text in an English grammar course
- As a companion to other books in the **Delta's Key to the Next Generation TOEFL® Test** series
- As a resource for skill building in English for academic purposes

Diagnostic Test

The Diagnostic Test is a short, timed pre–test of grammar knowledge. It may be used to identify a student's particular areas of concern and to assist in forming an individual study plan.

Grammar Units

The chart below shows a breakdown of grammar topics in the book, by skill area. The units may be studied in the order given, or in any sequence that suits one's individual focus.

Unit	Grammar Topic	Skill Area			
		Reading	Listening	Speaking	Writing
1	Nouns	√	√	√	√
2	Verbs	√	√	√	√
3	Infinitives and Gerunds			√	√
4	Clauses and Sentences	√		√	√
5	Conjunctions	√			√
6	Adverb Clauses	√	√	√	√
7	Adjective Clauses	√	√	√	√
8	Noun Clauses	√		√	
9	Conditional Sentences	√	√	√	
10	Singular and Plural			√	√
11	Articles			√	√
12	Subject–Verb Agreement			√	√
13	Pronoun Agreement	√		√	√
14	Comparison	√	√	√	
15	Prepositions	√		√	
16	Word Order		√	√	
17	Parallel Structure				√
18	Word Form	√			√
19	Common Word Errors		√	√	
20	Punctuation	√			√

Each unit opens with an exercise to focus attention on a particular topic, followed by a study of grammar points with numerous examples. Practice exercises allow students to apply knowledge and build skills. Many exercises simulate TOEFL form and content. Extension exercises include pair and group activities, discussion topics, and ways to link the classroom with the real world.

Quizzes

The six timed quizzes review the grammar skills studied in the previous three or four units.

Review Test

The timed Review Test assesses grammar skills from all 20 units. The Review Test mirrors the Diagnostic Test. Just as the Diagnostic Test is a pre–test, the Review Test is a post–test of grammar proficiency.

Answer Key

The Answer Key gives the correct answer for each question, along with a brief explanation or a list of key points.

Audio Scripts

The Audio Scripts include complete transcripts for all listening material in the book. The scripts can be used for checking answers, for reading and listening practice, and for learning vocabulary in context.

How to Score Speaking and How to Score Writing

These charts provide criteria for evaluating responses to the TOEFL iBT speaking and writing tasks, with a description for each score level.

Score Charts

The Score Charts are a place to record scores on the quizzes and tests.

Audio Disk

The audio compact disk contains all of the audio texts for the TOEFL iBT exercises that involve listening, including integrated speaking and integrated writing tasks.

ABOUT THE TOEFL®

The TOEFL® iBT

The Internet–based TOEFL (iBT) has four sections that assess the language skills of reading, listening, speaking, and writing. Although the TOEFL iBT does not have a discrete grammar section, knowledge of English sentence structure is important throughout the test.

TOEFL® IBT			
Section	**Content**	**Number of Questions**	**Approximate Time**
Reading	3–5 passages (12–14 questions each)	36–70	60–100 minutes
Listening	2–3 conversations 4–6 lectures (5–6 questions each)	34–51	60–90 minutes
Break			10 minutes
Speaking	2 independent tasks 4 integrated–skills tasks	6	20 minutes
Writing	1 integrated–skills task 1 independent task	2	60 minutes

The content of the TOEFL iBT reflects the language that is used in real academic settings. Reading passages are similar to those in textbooks and various course materials. Conversations include office consultations, service interactions, and discussions of campus situations. Lectures and class discussions reflect those in college and university classrooms. The TOEFL iBT allows test takers to take notes during all sections of the test. Some tasks involve integrated skills. For example, one task requires reading, listening, and writing. Knowledge of grammar is tested indirectly in all four sections of the test.

The TOEFL® PBT

The paper–based TOEFL (PBT) is administered in parts of the world where the iBT is not available. It is also administered in the TOEFL Institutional Testing Program (TOEFL ITP), for use within academic institutions.

Unlike the TOEFL iBT, the TOEFL PBT *does* assess grammar knowledge directly in the Structure and Written Expression section. Therefore, students who are preparing for the paper–and–pencil test will find the material in this book directly applicable to their study. Many questions are similar to questions on the TOEFL PBT, including those in the Diagnostic Test, the Sentence Completion exercises in each unit, the six quizzes, and the Review Test.

TOEFL® PBT			
Section	**Content**	**Number of Questions**	**Approximate Time**
Listening	Conversations and lectures	50	35 minutes
Structure and Written Expression	Sentence completion, error identification	40	25 minutes
Reading	5 passges	50	55 minutes

DIAGNOSTIC TEST

Time – 30 minutes

Choose the word or phrase that best completes the sentence.

1. Humans ------- by what holds objects together.

   (A) always fascinated
   (B) have always fascinated
   (C) always has been fascinated
   (D) have always been fascinated

2. ------- slow changes in the distribution of Earth's magnetic field.

   (A) The
   (B) How the
   (C) Do the
   (D) There are

3. In eastern Canada ------- approaches two hundred inches in Quebec and Newfoundland.

   (A) where the seasonal rainfall
   (B) the seasonal rainfall
   (C) that the seasonal rainfall
   (D) the seasonal rainfall it

4. Large, fast–moving trucks have been known to create blasts of wind ------- a motorcyclist.

   (A) can startle
   (B) can they startle
   (C) that can startle
   (D) are startling

5. Bacteria have survived longer than any other organism, ------- the most abundant type of cell.

   (A) why they
   (B) and they are
   (C) also are
   (D) they are

6. Because of -------, mastiff bats require considerable space to take off in flight.

   (A) large in size
   (B) their large size
   (C) it's a large size
   (D) they are large size

7. The age of a white–tailed deer is determined not ------- but by its teeth.

   (A) only its antlers
   (B) it has antlers
   (C) by its antlers
   (D) all of its antlers

8. ------- on a two–lane road, you should pass only on the left side of the vehicle.

   (A) If you overtake another vehicle
   (B) Another vehicle is overtaken
   (C) Can you overtake another vehicle
   (D) You should overtake another vehicle

9. The hummingbird's agility in flight lets it ------- from flower to flower like an insect.

   (A) flit
   (B) flitting
   (C) to flit
   (D) flits

10. At ------- of sixty–five, workers become eligible to collect retirement benefits.

    (A) age
    (B) an age
    (C) ages
    (D) the age

11. ------- of deuterium and tritium are fused, they produce a nucleus containing two protons and three neutrons.

    (A) The nuclei
    (B) In the nuclei
    (C) When the nuclei
    (D) Which nuclei

12. ------- is a question that concerns the researchers who have been studying it.

    (A) Because the spotted owl's survival
    (B) Whether the spotted owl can survive
    (C) Can the spotted owl's survival
    (D) The spotted owl could survive

13. Most shrubs should be fertilized early in the summer ------- late fertilizing can damage some plants.

(A) . Only if
(B) ; in fact,
(C) , which
(D) : because

14. In the eighth century, the calendar used in Europe was not as ------- used by the Mayans in Central America.

(A) accurately as
(B) accurate than
(C) accurate as that
(D) accurate that was

15. ------- crude hydrocarbons into such products as gasoline and petrochemicals is at the heart of the petroleum industry.

(A) Refine
(B) Are refined
(C) By refining
(D) Refining

16. Claude Debussy started the harmonic revolution in France, ------- not without help from other musical impressionists.

(A) although it was
(B) because of
(C) since
(D) unless he did

17. Stores use computers to check inventory and to determine which products are selling well and which are -------.

(A) less popular
(B) less popularly
(C) little popularity
(D) least popularity

18. Everglades National Park, an area of ------- and saw grass, is rich in wildlife.

(A) mud is a solid pack
(B) solidly packed mud
(C) pack mud solidly
(D) solid mud is packed

One of the underlined parts in each sentence is incorrect. Circle the letter of the incorrect part.

19. Nettles <u>are</u> a good <u>source</u> of iron and silica, <u>whose</u> are important for <u>healthy</u> blood formation.
         A   B   C   D

20. The dogwood tree <u>tolerates</u> a wide <u>variety</u> of conditions, <u>such as</u> pollution, <u>sunny</u>, and shade.
            A   B   C   D

21. <u>During</u> the <u>eighth</u> century, the Mayan Empire <u>achieved</u> magnificent cultural <u>also</u> economic heights.
    A   B   C   D

22. <u>Because</u> of the short <u>growing</u> season, trees at high altitudes may <u>not have</u> enough time <u>produce</u> seeds.
    A   B   C   D

23. Tiles made of either clay <u>and</u> slate are popular roofing <u>materials</u> in areas <u>where</u> raw materials are
                A   B   C

easily <u>found</u>.
    D

24. <u>Between</u> 1914 and 1932, T. S. Eliot <u>taught</u> school, wrote poems, and <u>assistant</u> in editing a <u>literary</u>
    A   B   C   D
journal.

25. Earth is <u>divided to</u> several climatic <u>zones</u> that <u>are based</u> on average <u>annual</u> temperature and rainfall.
           A   B   C   D

26. Periods of <u>recession</u> and currency overvaluation <u>is when</u> countries are <u>likely</u> to establish <u>protective</u>
               A   B   C   D
tariffs.

27. In 1856 an English <u>chemistry</u> produced a <u>brightly</u> colored dye <u>while</u> he was trying <u>to make</u> a new drug.
                  A   B   C   D

28. <u>The</u> largest of the terrestrial <u>carnivore</u>, bears have massive <u>bodies</u>, moderate-sized heads, and tiny <u>tails</u>.
  A   B   C   D

29. If one <u>wants</u> to keep up with the rapid <u>advances</u> in workplace technology, <u>they</u> must plan <u>to take</u>
        A   B   C   D
frequent refresher courses.

30. <u>Alike</u> most other endangered animals, the world's <u>remaining</u> caribou populations face <u>an uncertain</u>
  A   B   C
future <u>due to</u> habitat loss.
      D

Answers to the Diagnostic Test are on page 252.

Record your score on page 300.

UNIT 1   NOUNS

1. **Noun Structures**
2. **Subjects**
3. **Objects**
4. **Appositives**
5. *It* and *There* **as False Subjects**
6. **Duplicate Subjects**
7. **Facts about Nouns**

 FOCUS

What does this sentence need?

------- of the water withdrawn by industry is used for cooling.

- ○ In ninety percent
- ○ Ninety percent is
- ○ How ninety percent
- ○ Ninety percent

The sentence needs a subject. The **subject** of a sentence performs the action of the verb. A subject must be a noun, a pronoun, or another noun structure. The fourth answer, *Ninety percent*, is a noun phrase that functions correctly as the subject. The other choices are not noun structures. The correctly formed sentence is:

Ninety percent of the water withdrawn by industry is used for cooling.

What does this sentence need?

The retina is the tissue at the back of the eye that sends ------- to the brain.

- ○ to the visual impulses
- ○ visual impulses
- ○ impulses are visually
- ○ they are visual impulses

The verb *sends* needs a direct object. A **direct object** receives the verb's action. A direct object must be a noun, a pronoun, or another noun structure. The second answer, *visual impulses*, is a noun phrase that functions correctly as the direct object of *sends*. The other choices are not noun structures. The correctly formed sentence is:

The retina is the tissue at the back of the eye that sends **visual impulses** to the brain.

 STUDY

1. Noun Structures

A *noun* is a word that identifies a person, place, thing, state, or quality. Nouns are content words; they are essential for conveying meaning. A *noun structure* may be a single word or a group of words.

Structure	What It Is	Examples
Noun	A word that names a person, place, thing, state, or quality	<u>Lenses</u> are very important in <u>devices</u> that use <u>light</u>. <u>Condensation</u> occurs when <u>humidity</u> is high enough.
Noun Phrase	A group of words including a noun and words that modify it	<u>Silicon Valley</u> provides <u>a good example</u> of <u>the electronics industry</u>. <u>The quickly forming clouds</u> were the cause of <u>a catastrophic flood</u>.
Pronoun	A word that replaces a noun	Bears are dangerous after <u>they</u> have lost their fear of people. When <u>I</u> was very young, my grandmother told <u>me</u> a lot of stories.
Infinitive	A verb that acts as a noun: *to* + base–form verb (See Unit 3.)	<u>To transform</u> public opinion is the goal of some writers. All North American canines tend <u>to travel</u> in packs.
Gerund	A verb that acts as a noun: base–form verb + *-ing* (See Unit 3.)	<u>Swimming</u>, <u>boating</u>, and <u>camping</u> are popular summer activities. Language is the primary means of <u>transmitting</u> culture.
Noun Clause	A subordinate clause with a subordinator + subject + verb (See Unit 8.)	<u>How people learn</u> is a major topic in cognitive psychology. We do not really understand <u>why cats purr</u>.

Noun structures perform various functions in sentences, acting as subjects or objects.

2. Subjects

Noun structures function as subjects. A **subject** identifies the doer of a verb's action. Every clause in every sentence must have a subject. The subject is always a noun structure.

Function	What It Is	Examples
Subject of a Sentence or an Independent Clause	Performs the action of the verb	After bathing, <u>elephants</u> coat their skin with dust for protection against insects. In the 1990s, <u>executive salaries</u> doubled or tripled, but <u>most workers' salaries</u> barely changed.
Subject of a Subordinate Clause	Performs the action of the verb in a subordinate clause	When <u>a child</u> starts school, his view of the world changes. River otters maintain holes in the ice through which <u>they</u> catch fish.
Subject Complement	Identifies or defines the subject and usually follows a form of the verb *be*	Yosemite is <u>a national park in California</u>. Andrew Jackson was <u>the first president</u> who came from the western frontier.
Passive Subject	Receives the action of a passive–voice verb	<u>The global temperature balance</u> is maintained by the movement of maritime air. In the nineteenth century, <u>meats</u> were salted or smoked.

The following pronouns function as subjects:

I	we	you	he	she	it	they

3. Objects

Noun structures function as objects. An *object* receives the effect of a verb or a preposition. An object can receive the action of a verb, either directly or indirectly. An object can be controlled by a preposition. Every preposition must have an object, and the object must be a noun structure.

Function	What It Does	Examples
Direct Object	Receives the action of a verb and usually follows the verb	Chemical reactions often involve <u>the production of heat</u>. Autumn transforms <u>a maple tree's leaves</u> into beautiful colors.
Indirect Object	Receives the effect of the verb and the direct object	Good parents teach <u>their children</u> the difference between right and wrong. The art critic Lawrence Alloway gave <u>us</u> the term "Pop Art" in the 1950s.
Object Complement	Identifies or defines a direct object	My brother calls his son <u>Tiger</u> because he wants the boy to be a golf star someday. In 1782 King George III appointed William Pitt <u>prime minister of Great Britain</u>.
Object of a Preposition	Follows a preposition and is controlled by the preposition	A star at <u>the end</u> of <u>its life</u> is called a white dwarf. The General Assembly of <u>the United Nations</u> first met in <u>London</u> in <u>1946</u>.

The following pronouns function as objects:

me	us	you	him	her	it	them

4. Appositives

An *appositive* is a noun structure that identifies, defines, describes, or gives information about another noun structure. An appositive is also called a *noun in apposition* because its position is near the other noun that it identifies. Appositives are placed either before or after the other noun and are separated from the rest of the sentence by commas, dashes, or parentheses.

<u>A proven man–eater</u>, the tiger shark is one of the most feared sharks in the world.

African–American dance—<u>a blend of elements from diverse traditions</u>—has attracted wide attention from the professional dance scene.

You should not operate machinery or drive a vehicle if you have taken a cold remedy containing codeine (<u>a narcotic</u>).

In the first example, *A proven man–eater* adds information about *the tiger shark*. In the second example, *a blend of elements from diverse traditions* defines *African–American dance*. In the third example, *a narcotic* gives information about *codeine*.

Tip: To check whether a structure between two commas is an appositive, try adding *who is*, *who are*, *which is*, or *which are* before the structure.

In the following sentence, *a cone–shaped organ* is an appositive because you can add *which is* before it.

> The heart, <u>a cone–shaped organ</u>, pumps blood throughout the body.
>
> The heart, <u>which is a cone–shaped organ</u>, pumps blood throughout the body.

5. *It* and *There* as False Subjects

Every clause must have a noun structure as the subject. Sometimes a clause has *it* or *there* as a "false" subject. The true subject will then follow the verb, which is usually a form of the verb *be*.

Each of the following sentences has a false subject. The true subject is underlined.

> *It* is <u>the boys</u> in a middle school classroom who demand more attention from the teacher.
>
> *There* were <u>several causes</u> for the ecological disaster known as the Dust Bowl.

Tip: You can rewrite each sentence without the false subject.

> <u>The boys</u> in a middle school classroom demand more attention from the teacher.
>
> <u>Several causes</u> existed for the ecological disaster known as the Dust Bowl.

6. Duplicate Subjects

A clause can have only one subject. A **duplicate subject** is incorrect because it incorrectly repeats or duplicates the subject.

Each of the following sentences has an incorrect duplicate subject, shown in *italics*. The correct subjects are underlined. In each example, the duplicate subject must be omitted for the sentence to be correct.

Incorrect	Correct
<u>The octopus</u> *it* makes its home in a hole or rock crevice in shallow water.	<u>The octopus</u> makes its home in a hole or rock crevice in shallow water.
<u>W. C. Handy</u>, an orchestra leader, *he* wrote a popular song called "The St. Louis Blues."	<u>W. C. Handy</u>, an orchestra leader, wrote a popular song called "The St. Louis Blues."
<u>The Nile Valley and the Indus Valley</u> *they* were important cultural hearths.	<u>The Nile Valley and the Indus Valley</u> were important cultural hearths.

Note: The third sentence has a **compound subject** connected by *and*. A subject is compound when two or more nouns perform the action of the verb. A compound subject is not the same as a duplicate subject. A compound sentence is correct, but a duplicate subject is incorrect.

7. Facts about Nouns

The word *noun* came from the Latin word *nomen*, which means "name."

Every noun is either proper or common. A ***proper noun*** is the name of a specific person, place, or thing. Proper nouns always begin with a capital letter.

Albert Einstein	South Africa	Jupiter	Oxford University

A ***common noun*** is the name for one or all of the members of a class of persons, places, things, states, or qualities.

scientist	mountain	school	happiness	truth

Nouns have singular and plural forms. (See Unit 10.)

Nouns can be countable or uncountable. (See Unit 10.)

In addition to subject and object forms, pronouns have possessive forms, as well as masculine, feminine, and neuter forms. (See Unit 13.)

A ***suffix***, or word ending, can indicate that a word is a noun. (See Unit 18.)

 PRACTICE

Exercise 1–A

Noun Structures. Name the function of the underlined noun structure in each sentence, using the abbreviations below.

S	subject	IO	indirect object
SC	subject complement	OP	object of a preposition
DO	direct object		

1. _____ When water evaporates, it absorbs <u>heat</u> and becomes steam.

2. _____ <u>How cells grow</u> is not the only process that cell biologists study.

3. _____ Except during rush–hour periods, commuter trains seldom run at <u>full capacity</u>.

4. _____ Mount Everest is <u>the highest mountain in the world</u>.

5. _____ Photographic prints may appear to have many colors, but <u>they</u> are made of only three colors arranged in layers.

6. _____ The Cooperative Education Office offers <u>students</u> several internship opportunities each semester.

7. _____ Sometimes in childhood there seems to be a war between <u>reality and imagination</u>.

8. _____ In a short and simple musical instrument, such as the recorder, <u>the fingers</u> can cover all the holes directly.

Exercise 1–B

Appositives. Identify the appositives in the following sentences. Underline each appositive and circle the noun that it identifies, defines, or describes.

1. The work of A. Y. Jackson, a Montreal artist, inspired a generation of Canadian painters.

2. To increase profits, supermarket chains are using a strategy that involves building bigger stores— super supermarkets.

3. Adhesion, the ability of paint to remain attached to the canvas, is one of the basic considerations of permanence.

4. An organ for breathing and smelling, the elephant's trunk is also an extra limb for picking up objects.

5. Modern technology would collapse without engineers, the problem solvers of the world.

6. Each of the gas giants—Jupiter, Saturn, Uranus, and Neptune—is a rapidly rotating sphere of gas surrounding a hot, dense core.

Exercise 1–C

Sentence Completion.   Choose the word or phrase that best completes the sentence.

1. Ocean currents are responsible for ------- around the planet Earth.

    (A) to move the water
    (B) the movement of water
    (C) the water is moving
    (D) have moved water

2. Because it decomposes violently when disturbed, ------- must be handled cautiously.

    (A) nitroglycerin
    (B) it's nitroglycerin
    (C) for nitroglycerin
    (D) nitroglycerin, it

3. Harvard, ------- in North America, was founded in 1636.

    (A) was the first college
    (B) it was the first college
    (C) the first college was
    (D) the first college

4. Water plants provide food for many animals, and ------- also supply oxygen to the water.

    (A) what they
    (B) do they
    (C) they
    (D) they are

5. Of all the senses, it is ------- that triggers the strongest memories and emotions.

    (A) the sense is to smell
    (B) by the sense of smell
    (C) the sense of smell
    (D) how the sense of smell

6. Allergic reaction to bee venom can be life threatening, so there are ------- for avoiding bee stings.

    (A) precautions that several
    (B) several precautions are
    (C) for several precautions
    (D) several precautions

7. Coal is classified as a fossil fuel because ------- is made from compressed plant fossils.

    (A) it
    (B) of its
    (C) is coal
    (D) coal it

8. In order to sustain a snowfall, there must be ------- to feed the growing ice crystals.

    (A) a constant inflow of moisture is
    (B) of a constant inflow of moisture
    (C) a constant inflow of moisture
    (D) moisture constantly flows in

9. -------, Edgar Allan Poe became known as the father of the modern detective story.

    (A) The son of actors was
    (B) He was the son of actors
    (C) The son of actors
    (D) Acted as the son of

10. While it is difficult for some people to change unhealthy habits, there are ------- for exercising frequently and eating fewer fatty foods.

    (A) an excellent reason
    (B) excellent reasons
    (C) reasons are excellent
    (D) because excellent reasons

Exercise 1–D

Sentence Editing.   In each sentence, one of the underlined words is incorrect and must be omitted. Cross out the incorrect word.

1. Rosa Bonheur <u>she</u> lived in Paris and was <u>one</u> of the most popular <u>artists</u> of her <u>day</u>.

2. <u>How</u> the diesel <u>engine</u> is similar to the gasoline engine, but <u>it</u> runs on a heavier grade of <u>fuel</u>.

3. Bayberries, small <u>trees</u> or shrubs with leathery leaves, <u>they</u> have berries that produce a <u>wax</u> used in making <u>candles</u>.

4. <u>Because</u> an elementary school girl who is proud of her athletic <u>ability</u> may face an <u>adjustment</u> by the time <u>she</u> enters high school.

5. The digital <u>camera</u>, which has computer abilities, <u>it</u> does not need <u>film</u> but records onto computer <u>memory</u>.

6. In addition to <u>pain</u> on swallowing, <u>with</u> a sore throat may be associated with <u>fever</u>, headache, and a stuffy <u>nose</u>.

7. The Puerto Rican <u>community</u> in the United States is a young and growing <u>population</u>, and Puerto Ricans <u>they</u> are becoming more politically <u>active</u>.

8. Ichthyology, <u>is</u> a branch of zoology dealing with fish, has made important <u>discoveries</u> about the <u>effects</u> of pollution on the world's fish <u>resources</u>.

9. It was <u>by</u> the failure of the stock <u>market</u> in <u>October</u> 1929 that led to the Great Depression of the <u>1930s</u>.

10. Although heat, water, or pressure <u>they</u> can affect the <u>formation</u> of a crystal, its <u>structure</u> will fall into <u>one</u> of seven groups.

Exercise 1–E

TOEFL iBT Reading.   Read the passages and choose the best answer to each question.

QUESTIONS 1–6

1   Dementia, a general decrease in intellectual abilities, involves impairment of memory, judgment, and social functioning. The two most frequent causes of dementia are Alzheimer's disease and multiple small strokes, but it can also be caused by depression, drug intoxication, alcohol abuse, head trauma, and advanced stages of AIDS.

2   Studies from China, Japan, Sweden, Italy, and the United States suggest that between 3 and 6 percent of all adults over age 65 show significant signs of dementia. The researchers concluded that as many as 47 percent of all adults 85 and older suffer from some level of dementia, and medical experts generally agree that the rate of dementia is highest in adults over 85.

3   The cause of approximately half of all cases of dementia, Alzheimer's disease involves specific processes in the brain, most prominently a kind of tangling of the fibers in the nerve cell bodies. This tangling, which contributes to a major loss of synapses, occurs mostly in the areas of the brain that regulate new learning and memory. While all aging adults appear to have some such tangling, those that show symptoms of Alzheimer's disease have far more. This tangling short–circuits many of the brain pathways, interfering with the person's ability to remember even well–learned skills, such as driving a car and using a fork.

1. The word impairment in paragraph 1 is closest in meaning to

   Ⓐ part
   Ⓑ growth
   Ⓒ study
   Ⓓ loss

2. The passage lists all of the following as causes of dementia EXCEPT

   Ⓐ depression
   Ⓑ heart attack
   Ⓒ AIDS
   Ⓓ alcohol abuse

3. What is the main purpose of paragraph 2?

   Ⓐ To list the symptoms of dementia
   Ⓑ To give rates of dementia in older adults
   Ⓒ To define the various types of dementia
   Ⓓ To explain how dementia progresses

4. The author mainly explains Alzheimer's disease as the result of

   Ⓐ tangling of the fibers in brain cells
   Ⓑ multiple small strokes or head trauma
   Ⓒ a major loss in sensory function
   Ⓓ changes that are a normal part of aging

5. What does the author say about tangling?

   Ⓐ It involves a decrease in a certain protein in brain cells.
   Ⓑ It affects areas of the brain that control memory.
   Ⓒ It is less evident in people with Alzheimer's disease.
   Ⓓ It has been a subject of controversy among researchers.

6. Why does the author mention driving a car and using a fork in paragraph 3?

   Ⓐ To argue that older adults can not learn new skills
   Ⓑ To point out tasks that most people perform every day
   Ⓒ To give examples of skills affected by Alzheimer's disease
   Ⓓ To suggest exercises for people with Alzheimer's disease

QUESTION 7

1   The jazz that was popular during the 1930s and 1940s was known as "big band" or "swing." A big band, or jazz orchestra, consisted of approximately 12 to 25 musicians and contained saxophones, trumpets, trombones, and a rhythm section. The music was highly arranged: prepared in advance and written on charts. Occasionally the arranger called for an improvised solo, a short piece of music created spontaneously by one of the players. In many bands, the arranger was also the bandleader.

2   Big band jazz was first and foremost dance music. The earliest bands played music characterized by a sweet and romantic melody, suitable for dancing. Later, the music acquired a "swing beat," a style of playing with a strong, driving rhythm. The "hot" rhythms of bandleaders such as Benny Goodman and Count Basie became the dominant form of popular music after 1935. From this joyous, swinging music came the energetic style of dancing called "jitterbug."

3   However, many younger jazz players felt that swing jazz was the music of an older generation and did not express their experiences. The younger musicians wanted jazz to progress. Thus, the style of jazz known as "bebop" arose. Bebop—later called simply "bop"—was a revolt against big bands and arrangements. A typical band consisted of five instruments: saxophone, trumpet, bass, drums, and piano. The "bopsters" rejected the traditional dance beat because they felt it prevented the free–flowing, improvisational expression of ideas. They viewed jazz not as dance music but as a form of art.

4   The musician who brought bop to the attention of the public was trumpeter Dizzy Gillespie. In the late thirties and early forties, while playing with the major jazz orchestras of the time, Gillespie experimented with new forms. He and a few friends worked out the ideas that were to become the essence of bop: fast tempos and improvisation based on harmonic structure rather than melody. In 1945 Dizzy Gillespie formed his own band and started collaborating with saxophonist Charlie Parker. The band made a number of first–rate records, including "Salt Peanuts" and "Hot House." Gillespie's popularity with jazz fans led to the gradual acceptance of bebop as an art form distinct from the jazz of the dance hall.

7. Select the appropriate phrases from the answer choices and match them to the form of jazz that they characterize. TWO of the answer choices will NOT be used.

Answer Choices
- (A) A band with five musicians
- (B) A strong, driving dance rhythm
- (C) Emphasis on harmonic structure
- (D) A slow melody
- (E) Musical arrangements on charts
- (F) A steady beat for marching
- (G) Jazz as a form of art

Big Band

•
•

Bebop

•
•
•

Exercise 1–F

TOEFL iBT Listening. Listen to the recordings. You may take notes as you listen. Do not look at the questions until the conversation or lecture has ended. When you hear the questions, look at the questions and choose the best answer to each.

 Audio Track 1

1. Why does the student speak to her professor?

   (A) She wants to know his philosophy of life.
   (B) She needs advice about an assignment.
   (C) She has a problem with her grandmother.
   (D) She needs more time to finish her project.

2. What is the student's idea for her project?

   (A) A survey of grandmothers
   (B) A handbook for host families
   (C) A story about a fourteen–year–old girl
   (D) A comparison of opinions

3. What does the professor suggest the student do?

   (A) Prepare a list of possible questions
   (B) Choose a more interesting topic
   (C) Express her opinion more clearly
   (D) Interview at least ten people

 Audio Track 2

4. What is the main idea of the lecture?

   (A) Young children have the ability to learn quickly.
   (B) It is important for children to play every day.
   (C) Children have a culture in which play is central.
   (D) The best games for children have clear rules.

5. Listen again to part of the lecture. Then answer the question.

   What does the professor imply about child culture?

   (A) Parents should tell children that child culture has rules.
   (B) Child culture involves the ability to keep a secret.
   (C) Children learn child culture from other children.
   (D) Older children often treat younger children unfairly.

6. Why does the professor say this:

   (A) To list important elements of child culture
   (B) To compare various types of communication
   (C) To explain why children need good teachers
   (D) To describe a typical preschool curriculum

7. What characterizes the play of preschool children?

   Choose two answers.

   [A] Physical activity
   [B] Team sports
   [C] Strict rules
   [D] Open games

8. How are the games of older children different from those of younger children?

   (A) They are more difficult to play.
   (B) They are the creation of teachers.
   (C) They are played on the computer.
   (D) They are more structured by rules.

Exercise 1–G

TOEFL iBT Speaking. In this integrated speaking task, you will listen to part of a lecture. You will then be asked to summarize important information from the lecture.

Cover the question while the lecture is playing. You may take notes, and you may use your notes to help you answer the question. After you hear the question, you may look at the question and prepare your response. You have 20 seconds to prepare your response and 60 seconds to speak.

 Audio Track 3

> Using points and examples from the lecture, explain how a bird's physical features contribute to its ability to fly.

 Stop

Preparation Time – 20 seconds
Response Time – 60 seconds

Answers to Exercises 1–A through 1–G are on pages 252–253.

Exercise 1–H

TOEFL iBT Writing. For this independent writing task, respond to the question by writing an essay in which you state and support your opinion on the topic. Your essay will be scored on the quality of your writing, including how well you organize and develop your ideas and how well you use language to express your ideas. An effective essay will have a minimum of 300 words.

Read the following question and make any notes that will help you plan your response. Then begin writing. You have 30 minutes to plan and write your essay.

> Do you agree or disagree with the following statement?
>
> **You can learn about the character of a country from the way that it treats animals.**
>
> Use specific reasons and examples to support your answer.

Time – 30 minutes

Answers to Exercise 1–H will vary.

 EXTENSION

1. **Sentence Analysis.** Outside class, look in a newspaper, magazine, or book for examples of sentences with various noun structures. Bring five examples to share in class. Write some of the sentences on the board. Your classmates must identify each noun structure and explain its function.

    a. Identify subjects, direct objects, indirect objects, objects of prepositions, and appositives.

    b. Identify proper nouns and common nouns.

2. **Sentence Writing.** Working in pairs, students write sentences about people or objects in the classroom. Add appositives to rename, define, explain, or provide information about the people or objects. Use commas or other punctuation around the appositives.

    Example: Ali, a businessman from Kuwait, is sitting next to Solomon,
                an engineering student from Ethiopia.

Write some of the sentences on the board. Your classmates must identify the appositives.

UNIT 2   VERBS

1. **Verbs and Verb Phrases**
2. **Principal Parts of Verbs**
3. **Auxiliaries**
4. **Tenses**
5. **Modals**
6. **Causatives**
7. **Active and Passive Voice**
8. **Facts about Verbs**

 FOCUS

What does this sentence need?

> People ------- with more than just words.
>
> ○ communication
> ○ to communicate
> ○ communicate
> ○ communicating

Every sentence must have a verb. Only the third answer, *communicate*, is a verb. The other choices are either not verbs or not complete verbs. The correctly formed sentence is:

> People **communicate** with more than just words.

What does this sentence need?

> Snowflakes ------- single ice crystals or multi–crystal aggregates.
>
> ○ composing
> ○ composing of
> ○ composed of
> ○ can be composed of

Every sentence must have a verb. The fourth answer, *can be composed of*, is correct in this sentence. The other choices are not complete verbs or do not complete the sentence. The correct choice is a passive–voice verb phrase. The correctly formed sentence is:

> Snowflakes **can be composed of** single ice crystals or multi–crystal aggregates.

 STUDY

1. Verbs and Verb Phrases

A *verb* is a word that expresses existence, action, or possession. Every sentence must have at least one verb. Verbs are content words; like nouns, verbs are essential for conveying meaning.

A *verb phrase* is a group of words that contains a verb and closely related words, such as auxiliaries and adverbs.

Structure	What It Is	Examples
Verb	A word that expresses existence, action, or possession	The escallonia plant <u>is</u> especially popular because of the many varieties available. The forests of British Columbia <u>produce</u> about half of Canada's marketable wood.
Verb Phrase	A group of words containing a verb and related words	Thunderstorms <u>frequently occur</u> in the afternoon. Although they <u>are not often seen</u>, coyotes <u>have been living</u> among humans for centuries.
Auxiliary Verb	A special verb that helps the main verb in a verb phrase	The gypsy moth, which <u>is</u> spreading across North America, <u>has</u> eaten the leaves of 13 million acres of trees. Some species of trees <u>do</u> not bear fruit for several years.
Modal Verb	An auxiliary verb that expresses mood	The ocean <u>can</u> store great amounts of heat. Every home <u>should</u> have an emergency kit in an accessible location.

2. Principal Parts of Verbs

Verbs have five forms, or *principal parts*. The principal parts of *regular verbs* have regular forms, in which *–ed* or *–ing* is added to the base form. Below are the principal parts of some frequently used regular verbs.

Base Form	Present Form	Past Form	Present Participle	Past Participle
call	call/calls	called	calling	called
cry	cry/cries	cried	crying	cried
die	die/dies	died	dying	died
open	open/opens	opened	opening	opened
start	start/starts	started	starting	started
walk	walk/walks	walked	walking	walked

The principal parts of *irregular verbs* do not have regular forms. Below are the principal parts of some frequently used irregular verbs.

Base Form	Present Form	Past Form	Present Participle	Past Participle
be	am/is/are	was/were	being	been
build	build/builds	built	building	built
come	come/comes	came	coming	come
do	do/does	did	doing	done
eat	eat/eats	ate	eating	eaten
fly	fly/flies	flew	flying	flown
go	go/goes	went	going	gone
have	have/has	had	having	had
make	make/makes	made	making	made
speak	speak/speaks	spoke	speaking	spoken
take	take/takes	took	taking	taken
write	write/writes	wrote	writing	written

3. Auxiliaries

An *auxiliary verb* is a special verb that accompanies another verb and "helps" the verb. Auxiliaries help the main verb by expressing:

- person: first, second, third
- number: singular, plural
- tense: present, past, future

The most common auxiliaries are *be*, *have*, and *do*.

> The two largest national chains <u>are</u> opening new restaurants in the suburbs.
>
> By the age of twenty, Elvis Presley <u>had</u> recorded several songs.
>
> When I was in high school, I <u>did</u> not like getting up early.

Adverbs are words that modify verbs. Adverbs usually follow the first auxiliary. In the following sentences, the adverbs are in *italics*.

> This factory <u>has</u> *never* <u>had</u> any serious accidents among the workers.
>
> I <u>had</u> *not* <u>been speeding</u>, so I <u>do</u>*n't* <u>know</u> why I got a traffic ticket.
>
> The restaurant <u>has</u> *recently* <u>been inspected</u> for adherence to the health code.

4. Tenses

The *tense* of a verb shows the time of the verb's action, possession, or state of being. Verbs have several tenses to indicate present, past, and future time.

The *simple tenses* take either the present form or the past form of the verb.

simple present:	present form
simple past:	past form
simple future:	*will* + present form

The *progressive tenses*—also called the *continuous tenses*—express continuous action. The progressive tenses take a form of the auxiliary *be* followed by the present participle.

present progressive:	*am/is/are* + present participle
past progressive:	*was/were* + present participle
future progressive:	*will be* + present participle

The *perfect tenses* take a form of *have* followed by the past participle.

present perfect:	*have/has* + past participle
past perfect:	*had* + past participle
future perfect:	*will have* + past participle

The *perfect progressive tenses* take a form of *have* + *been* followed by the present participle.

present perfect progressive:	*have/has been* + present participle
past perfect progressive:	*had been* + present participle
future perfect progressive:	*will have been* + present participle

Note: The past and present participles are never used alone as verbs. They must have an auxiliary when they function as verbs.

Tense	Examples
Simple Present	Thunderstorms <u>form</u> when an air parcel <u>becomes</u> buoyant and <u>rises</u>.
Present Progressive	Astronomers <u>are</u> now <u>looking</u> for planets beyond our solar system.
Present Perfect	Sophisticated detection devices <u>have brought</u> the extent of pollution to the public's attention.
Present Perfect Progressive	For more than thirty years, Anna Deavere Smith <u>has been writing</u> and <u>performing</u> one–woman plays.

Tense	Examples
Simple Past	Each time the moneychangers of ancient Greece <u>made</u> an exchange, they <u>charged</u> a fee.
Past Progressive	Between 1945 and 1980, the federal government <u>was spending</u> 75 percent of its transportation budget on highways.
Past Perfect	Before the two Germanys reunited, East Germany <u>had built</u> the Berlin Wall to keep East Berliners from crossing into the West.
Past Perfect Progressive	Humans <u>had been dreaming</u> of flight for centuries before the Wright brothers built their glider.
Simple Future	Global warming <u>will cause</u> flooding, windstorms, and killer heat waves.
Future Progressive	The number of teenagers <u>will be</u> steadily <u>increasing</u> for the next decade.
Future Perfect	Millions of children <u>will have experienced</u> famine or war by the time they reach their teens.
Future Perfect Progressive	When I enter graduate school, I <u>will have been studying</u> foreign languages for twelve years.

UNIT 2

Some words and phrases function as ***time markers***. Time markers indicate whether the action is in present, past, or future time.

Present	Past	Future
today	yesterday	tomorrow
at present	in the past	in the future
now	ago	from now
usually	formerly	next week
every time	in the 1980s	by 2050
in the current period	in the former period	in the coming period
currently	during the sixth century	during the next decade

Tip: When you write sentences, use the correct tense for the meaning you want to convey. Beware of using a tense that does not make sense with a time marker or with other parts of the sentence.

Incorrect	Correct
In the sixteenth century, Leonardo da Vinci <u>studies</u> many topics and <u>makes</u> important discoveries.	In the sixteenth century, Leonardo da Vinci <u>studied</u> many topics and <u>made</u> important discoveries.
I believe that art teaches us how to live, so art <u>was</u> a necessary part of a good education.	I believe that art teaches us how to live, so art <u>is</u> a necessary part of a good education.

5. Modals

A *modal* is a type of auxiliary verb that modifies the main verb. A modal expresses mood or attitude. A modal shows that the main verb's action is certain, possible, probable, advisable, necessary, or habitual. A modal can also express intention, make a suggestion, or state a preference.

Modals can indicate present, future, and past time. Modals can show progressive or continuous action.

present and future:	modal + base–form verb
past:	modal + *have* + past participle
progressive:	modal + *be* + present participle

Below are some modals and examples of verb phrases with modals.

Modal	What It Shows	Examples
will	present or future certainty	A baby <u>will cry</u> when it is hungry or frightened.
	intention	The dean <u>will announce</u> a new policy soon.
be going to	future probability	It looks like it<u>'s going to</u> rain.
	intention	The committee <u>is going to study</u> emerging technologies.
shall	intention	We <u>shall work</u> hard to accomplish our goals.
can	present or future possibility	The vampire bat <u>can infect</u> farm animals with the deadly rabies virus.
	present ability	Many children <u>can ride</u> a bicycle by the age of six.
could	past possibility	I <u>couldn't go</u> to the game because I had a physics test at eight o'clock the next day.
	past ability	Wolfgang Mozart <u>could compose</u> elaborate symphonies and operas at the age of sixteen.
	advisability	You <u>could ask</u> the librarian to help you find the book.
may	present or future possibility	In summer, the tiger shark <u>may follow</u> warm water currents as far south as New Zealand.
	continuous possibility	Diet sodas <u>may actually be causing</u> people to gain weight.
might	present or future possibility	A cougar <u>might not eat</u> for several days at a time.
	past possibility	Some form of primitive life <u>might once have developed</u> on Mars.
	continuous possibility	My brother <u>might be living</u> in Australia next year.
had better	present or future advisability	You<u>'d better register</u> early, before enrollment closes in the more popular classes.

Modal	What It Shows	Examples
need to	present or future advisability	I think you <u>need to see</u> your dentist before that tooth gets worse.
ought to	present or future advisability	We're lost. We <u>ought to stop</u> and ask someone for directions.
should	present or future advisability	Hikers <u>should carry</u> extra food and clothing when hiking in the mountains.
	past advisability	They <u>should have left</u> the demonstration before the violence started.
	present or future expectation	When the first frost occurs, we <u>should see</u> the beginning of the fall colors.
have/has to	present or future necessity	I <u>have to talk</u> to my professor about my research project.
had to	past necessity	Last semester I <u>had to hire</u> a tutor to help me with calculus.
have/has got to	present or future necessity	The government <u>has got to develop</u> a better plan for dealing with epidemics.
must	present or future necessity	Students <u>must pay</u> all tuition and fees on time.
	present probability	The birds are singing, so it <u>must be</u> spring.
	past probability	Tony got an A in physics, so he <u>must have worked</u> hard.
	continuous probability	My roommate isn't back yet. She <u>must be having</u> a good time at the beach.
would	past habit	In the early twentieth century, people <u>would ride</u> the trolley to work.
used to	past habit	My mother <u>used to take</u> us to the library every Saturday.
would rather	preference	I'<u>d rather play</u> tennis than go swimming.

6. Causatives

A *causative* is a verb that causes a certain action. A causative verb can require, request, persuade, enable, or allow someone to do something. A verb phrase with a causative always has an indirect object.

> causative + indirect object + base–form verb

In the following examples, the indirect object is shown in *italics*.

Causitive	What It Means	Examples
make	require	Our apartment manager <u>makes</u> *everyone* <u>follow</u> the rules.
have	request	Professor Jones always <u>has</u> *us* <u>work</u> with a partner in class.
get	persuade	My cat <u>gets</u> *me* <u>to open</u> doors for him all day long.
help	enable	The new program <u>helps</u> *children* <u>appreciate</u> art.
		The new program <u>helps</u> *children* <u>to appreciate</u> art.
let	allow, permit	Some dog owners always <u>let</u> *their dogs* <u>run loose</u>.

Causative *get* takes an infinitive: *to* + base–form verb. Causative *help* takes either a base–form verb or an infinitive.

Causatives can be in past time.

> His supervisor <u>made</u> him <u>correct</u> the errors in the monthly report.
>
> Doctor Armstrong <u>had</u> her assistant <u>prepare</u> the handouts.
>
> We should <u>have gotten</u> someone <u>to give</u> us a ride home.

Causatives can be in future time.

> I hope my roommate <u>will help</u> me <u>clean</u> the apartment.
>
> Next year the university <u>will let</u> students <u>register</u> for courses online.

7. Active and Passive Voice

Sentences can be in the active voice or the passive voice. *Voice* refers to the relationship between the subject and verb.

In an *active–voice* sentence, the subject is the doer of the verb's action. The emphasis is on who or what performs the action. In the following sentence, the emphasis is on the doer of the action, *William Herschel*. The verb *discovered* is in the active voice, and *Uranus* is the direct object.

> <u>William Herschel</u> <u>discovered</u> <u>Uranus</u> in 1781.
>   S   V   O

In a *passive–voice* sentence, the subject is the receiver of the verb's action. The emphasis is on the receiver rather than the doer of the action. The doer of the action follows the verb or may be omitted. When the sentence is in the passive voice, *Uranus* is the passive subject. The emphasis is on *Uranus* rather than *William Herschel*. The verb *was discovered* is in the passive voice.

Uranus <u>was discovered</u> by William Herschel in 1781.
  S   V

A passive subject is actually the direct or indirect object of the verb. For this reason, only *transitive verbs*, verbs that have an object, can be written in the passive voice.

Sentences in the passive voice occur frequently in written English, especially scientific, technical, business, and government publications. Writers use the passive voice when they want the action or the object of the action to be the focus of the sentence.

Passive–voice verbs are formed with the auxiliary *be* and the verb's past participle. The passive voice can be used in many tenses. The tense of the auxiliary *be* varies with tense.

simple tenses:	*am/is/are/was/were/will be* + past participle
progressive tenses:	*am/is/are/was/were + being* + past participle
perfect tenses:	*have/has/had/will have + been* + past participle

Tense	Examples
Simple Present	A language <u>is considered</u> "dead" when it <u>is</u> no longer <u>used</u> for oral communication.
Present Progressive	Algebra and physical science <u>are</u> now <u>being taught</u> in the eighth grade.
Present Perfect	Cats <u>have been kept</u> as domestic animals ever since humans started harvesting grains.
Simple Past	The first thermometer <u>was invented</u> by the great Italian astronomer Galileo.
Past Progressive	Theories of logic and binary numbers <u>were being developed</u> by Gottfried Leibniz in the 1600s.
Past Perfect	By the seventeenth century, chemistry <u>had been recognized</u> as a science.
Simple Future	The course Human Development <u>will be offered</u> only during the fall term.
Future Perfect	When the average worker retires, he <u>will have been promoted</u> at least twice.
Infinitive	An innovative group of painters working in New York came <u>to be known</u> as "abstract expressionists."

Note: The present perfect progressive, past perfect progressive, future progressive, and future perfect progressive tenses are not used in the passive voice.

Passive–voice verbs can take modals, such as *will, can, may, might, should,* and *must.*

present:	modal + *be* + past participle
past:	modal + *have/has been* + past participle
future:	modal + *be* + past participle

Generalizations are scientific statements that <u>can be verified</u> with data.

Stonehenge <u>must have been built</u> to serve a scientific or religious purpose.

Any changes to the program <u>will be announced</u> before the first speaker begins.

Adverbs usually come after the modal and before other auxiliaries. In the following sentences, the adverbs are in *italics.*

Jupiter's smaller satellites <u>can</u> *not* <u>be seen</u> without a telescope.

Some medications <u>must</u> *always* <u>be taken</u> with food.

Tip: In many cases, sentences in the active voice make your writing stronger. You can rewrite most passive sentences in the active voice. When the doer of the action is not named, you must infer who or what performs the action.

Passive Voice	Active Voice
Ocean tides <u>are caused</u> by the moon.	The moon <u>causes</u> ocean tides.
A constant body temperature <u>can be maintained</u> by some animals.	Some animals <u>can maintain</u> a constant body temperature.
Paper <u>is made</u> from wood pulp.	We <u>make</u> paper from wood pulp.
Radar maps of several planets <u>have been produced</u>.	Scientists <u>have produced</u> radar maps of several planets.

8. Facts about Verbs

— The word *verb* came from the Latin word *verbum*, which means "word."

— Verbs have singular and plural forms. (See Unit 12.)

— A *suffix*, or word ending, can indicate that a word is a verb. (See Unit 18.)

 PRACTICE

Exercise 2–A

Verb Phrases.   Underline the verbs and verb phrases in the following sentences. A verb phrase can include auxiliaries, modals, causatives, and adverbs. Some sentences have more than one verb.

1. Central Oregon has experienced a large earthquake once every ten thousand years.

2. Each cubic meter of rock can store the equivalent of one firecracker.

3. Lava Butte was formed seven thousand years ago when magma erupted violently.

4. At first, geologists did not fully understand where the magma had originated.

5. Changes in the caldera floor have presumably accompanied each eruption.

6. The lava blocked the Deschutes River in many places and permanently altered its course.

7. Scientists think that the next eruption might occur within the next thousand years.

8. The article about Lava Butte helped the students understand how natural processes work.

Exercise 2–B

Verb Tenses.   Fill in the blanks with a correct form of the verb **build**. If there is an adverb in parentheses before the sentence, use the adverb with the verb.

1.   Many birds _____ nests so far this year.

2. (not)   Some species _____ a new nest every year.

3.   Throughout the coming summer, birds _____ nests.

4.   Last year several birds _____ their nests in the barn.

5. (already)   Before spring began, some birds _____ their nests.

6. (now)   Three different species _____ nests in the pine tree.

7. (probably)   The birds _____ their nests in the same tree next year.

8. (still)   A few of the birds _____ nests when the first snow fell.

Exercise 2–C

Active and Passive Voice. The following sentences are in the passive voice. Identify the doer of the verb's action. In some cases, you must infer who or what performs the action. Then rewrite each sentence in the active voice, with the doer as the subject of the verb.

1. Most oil spills are caused by accidents involving tankers or pipelines.

   _____

2. The state of Texas was annexed by the United States in 1845.

   _____

3. A wrench is used for turning nuts and bolts.

   _____

4. Foreign languages are being taught to children as young as five.

   _____

5. Some health problems may be alleviated by stress management.

   _____

6. Peas, eggs, and other foods can be dried.

   _____

7. Venus, the second planet from the sun, is covered with a dense atmosphere.

   _____

8. New marketing techniques have recently been developed.

   _____

9. The idea that everything is made up of elements was first studied by the ancient Greeks.

   _____

   _____

10. Steps should have been taken to control the pests before the plants were damaged.

   _____

   _____

Exercise 2–D

Sentence Completion.   Choose the word or phrase that best completes the sentence.

1. A lockout occurs when management ------- workers from returning to work.

    A prevents
    B preventing
    C prevention
    D prevented

2. Many paints ------- after the plant, rock, or place from which they come.

    A named
    B be named
    C have named
    D are named

3. Dixieland jazz ------- from military music, blues, and the French influence in New Orleans.

    A a development
    B developing
    C developed
    D it developed

4. In a retail store, consumers ------- the merchandise and compare brands.

    A they can inspect
    B can they inspect
    C can inspect
    D can be inspected

5. Radio waves traveling at the speed of light ------- their discoveries to Earth.

    A have brought
    B are brought
    C bringing
    D is bringing

6. Each word in our mental dictionaries must ------- with its unique sound and meaning.

    A store
    B be stored
    C have stored
    D to be stored

7. Ammonia ------- as the refrigerant in the first practical refrigerator, made by Karl von Linde in 1876.

    A used
    B had used
    C is used
    D was used

8. The first punk rock of the 1960s ------- the aggressive response of the American garage bands to the more refined British bands.

    A being
    B did
    C was
    D would

9. A robot may ------- an action such as paint spraying by guiding its hand through the movements.

    A is taught
    B taught
    C been taught
    D be taught

10. The production of a practical hydrofoil first ------- in Italy, where it was developed during the first decade of the twentieth century.

    A takes place
    B took place
    C is taking place
    D will take place

Exercise 2–E

Sentence Editing. One of the underlined parts in each sentence is incorrect. Cross out the incorrect part and write the correction above it.

1. A <u>healthy</u> river bank <u>creation</u> a lot of cover and <u>shade</u> for fish and other <u>wildlife</u>.

2. In 1800 the northwest <u>coast</u> of North America <u>is</u> one <u>of</u> the world's least explored <u>areas</u>.

3. Solar <u>cells</u>, which are often <u>call</u> photovoltaic cells, are <u>composed</u> of single crystals of <u>silicon</u>.

4. <u>The</u> monarch butterfly begins <u>its life</u> in the northern United States and then <u>flew</u> two thousand miles <u>to</u>

   spend the winter in Mexico.

5. Many psychologists <u>belief</u> that <u>it is</u> not middle age but young adulthood <u>that is</u> the most stressful <u>period</u>

   of adult life.

6. Autumn is an excellent <u>time</u> to plant trees, but there <u>were</u> several points to consider as <u>you</u>

   determine which tree best <u>fits</u> the landscape.

7. <u>During</u> the Jurassic Period, which <u>extended</u> from 180 million to 135 <u>million</u> years ago, reptiles <u>reach</u>

   fantastic sizes.

8. Old–growth forests are <u>define</u> as being at least 250 <u>years</u> old, though some forests <u>are</u> actually

   far older, with a few that are <u>approaching</u> one thousand years.

9. When Karl Marx <u>was living</u> in London, he <u>published</u> the first volume of *Das Kapital*, which <u>become</u>

   the fundamental <u>written</u> work of world socialism.

10. The road test for the first Ford automobile had to <u>been</u> postponed <u>because</u> the finished car <u>was</u> wider

    than the door of the shed in which it was <u>built</u>.

Exercise 2–F

TOEFL iBT Reading. Read the passages and choose the best answer to each question.

QUESTIONS 1–6

1   Real estate agents are employed by real estate agencies that sell or rent property or manage, appraise, or develop real estate. Most real estate agents sell private homes. Some specialize in commercial property, such as apartment buildings, stores, and office buildings. Others specialize in undeveloped land sites for commercial or residential use. Real estate agents spend a great deal of time on the telephone, locating property for sale and negotiating with clients and property owners. They spend time in the field, where they look for and investigate new properties and show real estate to prospective buyers.

2   In any sale, an agent must negotiate with both the seller and the buyer. Many sellers begin by asking more for their property than buyers are willing to pay for it. The agent must persuade the seller to set a realistic price. However, most of the agent's effort focuses on the buyer. The agent tries to learn what will motivate the buyer to make a purchase. The agent has to convince the buyer that the property suits his needs and is a good buy. Buyers generally offer less for a property than the seller asks. The agent helps negotiate the final price and may help the buyer arrange a bank loan. The agent is generally present at the closing, when the final contract of a sale is signed.

1. According to the passage, real estate agents do all of the following EXCEPT

   (A) own car rental agencies
   (B) manage rental property
   (C) develop real estate
   (D) sell land for commercial use

2. The phrase specialize in in paragraph 1 is closest in meaning to

   (A) write about
   (B) approve of
   (C) focus on
   (D) refer to

3. The word investigate in paragraph 1 is closest in meaning to

   (A) sell
   (B) examine
   (C) buy
   (D) improve

4. In paragraph 2, the author states that the seller

   (A) does not understand real estate law
   (B) should speak directly to the buyer
   (C) is more important than the buyer is
   (D) may initially ask a price that is too high

5. Which sentence below best expresses the essential information in the highlighted sentence in paragraph 2?

   (A) The agent has a strong argument for why the property is valuable.
   (B) The buyer can ask the agent to look for a more suitable property.
   (C) The agent must make the buyer see the purchase as fair and desirable.
   (D) The buyer should clearly communicate his requirements to the agent.

6. It can be inferred from paragraph 2 that in negotiating the final price of a property, a real estate agent must

   (A) seek the advice of an insurance agency
   (B) persuade the buyer and the seller to agree
   (C) find a similar property in order to set a fair price
   (D) let the buyer look at other properties

QUESTION 7

1   The solar nebula theory states that the sun, the planets, and related debris all came from a huge interstellar gas cloud called a nebula. According to the theory, the solar system formed when parts of the nebula condensed and eventually collapsed. The explosion of a nearby star may have triggered the collapse by sending shock waves into the nebula. As it collapsed, three physical processes shaped the nebula: it became hotter, it started to spin, and it flattened into a disk.

2   At first, the nebula was large and diffuse, and it rotated slowly. Gradually, the gas and dust began to condense. The densest, hottest part was at the center, where all matter existed in a gaseous state. As the gas became hotter, its atomic particles moved faster and collided more frequently, converting kinetic energy into more heat. The hot mass collected in the nebula's center. Gradually, the forces of gravity, pressure, and magnetism caused the nebula to flatten into a spinning disk. At its core was a hot, dense protostar, surrounded by cooler regions of gas and dust. Over 50 million years, the heat and pressure at the center of the protostar became so great that hydrogen began to fuse into helium, creating an internal source of energy. At this point, the protostar "turned on" and became the sun, a main sequence star.

3   The planets formed from the gas and dust left over from the sun's formation. The planets fall into two groups that are very different in density and composition. The inner planets, including Earth, are those in smaller orbits that are closer to the sun. They formed from heavy elements that condensed into clumps, which in turn collided with others to form larger bodies and eventually, rocky planets. The outer planets, Jupiter and those beyond, are mainly composed of gases. Hence, they are known as the gas giants: rotating spheres of gas surrounding hot, dense cores. Although the outer planets are so unlike the inner planets, they all evolved from the same cloud of gas and dust.

7. Read the first sentence of a summary of the passage. Complete the summary by selecting the THREE answer choices that express the most important ideas in the passage. Some sentences do not belong in the summary because they express ideas that are not presented in the passage or are minor ideas in the passage.

The solar nebula theory explains how the solar system formed from a huge gas cloud.

•
•
•

Answer Choices

(A) An exploding star near the nebula emitted energy in the form of a shock wave.

(B) The nebula condensed, grew very hot, flattened into a disk, and started to spin.

(C) In the nebula's center was a hot, dense protostar that eventually became the sun.

(D) Main sequence stars derive their energy from the fusion of hydrogen into helium.

(E) Nebular material formed the rocky inner planets and the outer gas giants.

(F) After the planets had formed, the solar wind carried away all remaining gas.

Exercise 2–G

TOEFL iBT Listening. Listen to the recording. You may take notes as you listen. Do not look at the questions until the lecture has ended. When you hear the questions, look at the questions and choose the best answer to each.

 Audio Track 4

1. How does the professor develop the topic of the violin family?

   Choose two answers.

   [A] She compares the instruments in the family.
   [B] She traces the history of violin making.
   [C] She describes the violin's role in an orchestra.
   [D] She explains how a violin creates sound.

2. What point does the professor make about the instruments in the violin family?

   (A) They can be played by people of any age.
   (B) They were the first musical instruments with strings.
   (C) They sound best when mixed with other instruments.
   (D) They are all built and played in the same way.

3. How do the other members of the family differ from the violin?

   (A) They have a greater number of strings.
   (B) They play a lower range of notes.
   (C) They are made of different kinds of wood.
   (D) They are not part of a typical orchestra.

4. Listen again to part of the lecture. Then answer the question.

   Why does the professor mention a room with mirrors on all the walls?

   (A) To identify the ideal place for playing a violin
   (B) To show how mirrors reflect the sounds in a room
   (C) To explain how sound increases inside the violin
   (D) To describe the violin from many different angles

5. The professor briefly explains what happens when a violin is played. Indicate whether each sentence below is part of the process.

   For each sentence, check the correct box.

	Yes	No
The strings vibrate, causing the bridge to vibrate.		
A piston valve is pressed to lower the pitch of the sound.		
The sound increases as the air inside the instrument vibrates.		
The instrument's bell shape projects sound outward.		
Sound comes out through two f–shaped holes in the belly.		

UNIT 2

Exercise 2–H

TOEFL iBT Speaking. In the independent speaking tasks below, use appropriate verb tenses in your responses. For each task, allow 15 seconds to prepare your response and 45 seconds to speak.

1. Describe a person who helped you accomplish an important goal. Explain what this person did to help you. Include details and examples in your explanation.

2. What will you do during your next vacation from school or work? Explain why you will do this. Include details and examples to support your explanation.

Preparation Time – 15 seconds
Response Time – 45 seconds

Exercise 2–I

TOEFL iBT Speaking. In this integrated speaking task, you will listen to a conversation. You will then be asked to talk about the information in the conversation and to give your opinion about the ideas presented.

Cover the question while the conversation is playing. You may take notes, and you may use your notes to help you answer the question. After you hear the question, you may look at the question and prepare your response. You have 20 seconds to prepare your response and 60 seconds to speak.

 Audio Track 5

> The students discuss possible solutions to the man's problem. Describe the problem.
> Then state which of the solutions you prefer and explain why.

 Stop

Preparation Time – 20 seconds
Response Time – 60 seconds

Exercise 2–J

TOEFL iBT Writing. In this integrated writing task, you will write a response to a question about a reading passage and a lecture. Your response will be scored on the quality of your writing and on how well you connect the points in the lecture with points in the reading. Typically, an effective response will have 150 to 225 words.

Reading Time – 3 minutes

For plants to grow and develop properly, they need a constant supply of chemical nutrients. The primary nutrients in soil are nitrogen, phosphorus, and potassium. These three nutrients must be replenished often because crops use them in large quantities. A chemical fertilizer with these nutrients will increase the productivity of croplands. The best fertilizer for all types of soils is a balanced 20–20–20 fertilizer containing 20 percent each of nitrogen, phosphorus, and potassium.

Nitrogen is the key element in plant growth. Soil nitrogen stimulates stem and leaf growth, resulting in lush, full plants. Plants use nitrogen to make chlorophyll molecules, so a high level of nitrogen is required for greener, healthier plants. Nitrogen dissolves in water, and plants look greener after being watered because they have absorbed nitrogen from the soil. When plants lack sufficient nitrogen, their leaves turn yellow and eventually die.

Phosphorus, which helps plants hold and transfer energy for metabolism, moves within the plant to wherever cell division is taking place. Phosphorus accelerates plant growth. It makes plants bloom faster and produce more seeds. Insufficient phosphorus causes reduced growth and seeds that will not develop. Because phosphorus is so vital to agriculture, most soils must be enriched with phosphorus–bearing minerals called phosphates, which are mined from the earth and used as chemical fertilizers.

Potassium is necessary for plant metabolism, respiration, transpiration, and cell division. When potassium–rich fertilizer is applied, plants produce strong, erect stems. Potassium is important in the plant's manufacture of carbohydrates (sugars and starches) and oils, which contribute to the improved flavor, color, and texture of fruits, vegetables, and nuts.

Now listen to the lecture. You may take notes, and you may use your notes to help you write your response. After you hear the question, you have 20 minutes to plan and write your response. You may look at the reading passage during the writing time.

 Audio Track 6

Summarize the points in the lecture, explaining how they cast doubt on points made in the reading.

 Stop

Time – 20 minutes

Answers to Exercises 2–A through 2–J are on pages 253–255.

 EXTENSION

1. **Sentence Analysis.** In reading done outside class, look for sentences with various verb forms and tenses. Bring five examples to share in class. With a small group of classmates:

    a. Underline the verb phrases in your sentences.

    b. Identify the time and tense of each verb.

    c. Identify auxiliaries, modals, causatives, direct objects, and indirect objects.

2. **Modals.** Outside class, ask three people for advice. Then listen to their advice and notice whether they use any modals. Write down what people say. Report your findings to your class.

Examples of how to ask for advice:

    I have to ____. What do you think I should do?

    I'm looking for a ____. What do you suggest?

    I need to buy a ____. Can you give me any advice?

Expressions you might hear people say:

    You should ____.   You could ____.

    You need to ____.   Couldn't you ____?

    You'd better ____.   Why don't you ____?

3. **Passive Voice.** Outside class, look in a newspaper, magazine, or book for examples of sentences with passive verbs. Bring examples to share in class. With your classmates and teacher:

    a. Discuss why the writer probably used the passive voice.

    b. Rewrite the sentences in the active voice. Do you have to infer who or what the active subject is?

    c. Decide which sentence is better—passive voice or active voice? In what context is passive voice better? In what context is active voice better?

Unit 3   Infinitives and Gerunds

1. **Verbals**
2. **Infinitives**
3. **Infinitives as Objects**
4. **Infinitives after Adjectives**
5. **Gerunds**
6. **Gerunds as Objects**
7. **Infinitives or Gerunds as Objects**
8. *Use* **with Infinitives and Gerunds**

 FOCUS

What is wrong with this sentence?

> The cougar likes hunt under the cover of darkness, when it uses its keen night vision to find prey.

The cougar likes something. What does it like? The cougar likes *hunt*? The verb *likes* must have a noun object, but *hunt* is a verb, not a noun. *Hunt* is incorrect and must be changed. One possible solution is the infinitive *to hunt*. Another solution is the gerund *hunting*. Two correct ways to write the sentence are:

> The cougar likes **to hunt** under the cover of darkness, when it uses its keen night vision to find prey.

> The cougar likes **hunting** under the cover of darkness, when it uses its keen night vision to find prey.

What is wrong with this sentence?

> Many chefs use fruit for add color and texture to familiar dishes made of meats and grains.

Many chefs use fruit for something—but what? The structure *for add* is incorrect because the preposition *for* must have a noun object, but *add* is a verb. One solution is to omit *for add* and put *to add* in its place. Another solution is to change *add* to *adding*. Two correct ways to write the sentence are:

> Many chefs use fruit **to add** color and texture to familiar dishes made of meats and grains.

> Many chefs use fruit for **adding** color and texture to familiar dishes made of meats and grains.

 STUDY

1. Verbals

Infinitives and *gerunds* are verbals. A **verbal** is a word form that comes from a verb and looks like a verb, but does not act like a verb. Infinitives and gerunds function not as verbs but as other parts of speech. Both infinitives and gerunds can be nouns. Infinitives can also be adjectives or adverbs.

Infinitives	Gerunds
to do	doing
to feel	feeling
to swim	swimming
to trade	trading

Although infinitives and gerunds are not verbs, they share some characteristics with verbs. For example, like verbs, they can have modifiers and direct objects.

An infinitive with modifiers or objects is called an **infinitive phrase**. In the following sentence, the infinitive *to represent* has a direct object, *numbers*. *To represent numbers* is an infinitive phrase.

The Roman abacus used pebbles <u>to represent</u> <u>numbers</u>.
Infin.   DO

A gerund with modifiers or objects is called a **gerund phrase**. The sentence below has two gerund phrases. The gerund *checking* has an adverb modifier, *frequently*, and a direct object, *your rearview mirror*. The gerund *driving* has an adjective modifier, *safe*.

<u>Frequently</u> <u>checking</u> <u>your rearview mirror</u> is a good tip for <u>safe</u> <u>driving</u>.
Adv.   Ger.   DO   Adj. Ger.

Infinitive phrases and gerund phrases are frequently used structures.

Infinitive Phrases	Gerund Phrases
to think creatively	wearing sunglasses
to speak Korean	clear writing
not to ask a question	freely deciding
to walk to the bus stop	the mining of silver

2. Infinitives

An **infinitive** is formed with *to* and the base form of a verb.

to + base–form verb

An infinitive phrase can function as a noun, an adjective, an adjective complement, or an adverb. An infinitive can *not* be the object of a preposition.

DELTA'S KEY TO THE NEXT GENERATION TOEFL® TEST

Function	Examples
Subject	To dance professionally requires years of training.
	To own a home has always been part of the American dream.
Subject Complement	The purpose of a committee is to study an issue.
	The main purpose of the Federal Reserve System is to control the money supply.
Direct Object	Some babies begin to walk at the age of nine months.
	Jane Addams tried to put her education to use in social work.
Adjective	A cougar has the ability to see in the dark.
	Comedians have the power to make people laugh.
Adjective Complement	Many people find it convenient to shop online.
	It is becoming common to see office workers dressing casually on Fridays.
Adverb	Sensors are designed to detect the presence of specific substances.
	To focus on an image, a photographer looks through the camera's viewfinder.

When an infinitive is negative, *not* comes before the infinitive.

> I've decided *not* to apply for the job in the library.
>
> That sign warns people *not* to park cars or bicycles in the loading zone.

When there are two infinitives in a list, *to* can be omitted from the second infinitive. When there are three or more infinitives in a list, *to* can either be included or omitted from the second and successive infinitives.

> Marine biologists are attempting to monitor and control the krill populations.
>
> The liver manages to process proteins, to produce bile, and to cleanse the blood.
>
> The liver manages to process proteins, produce bile, and cleanse the blood.

Infinitives are used after causative verbs such as *get* and *help*. After causative *help*, you may either include *to* or omit it.

> My uncle always *gets* me to laugh at his corny jokes.
>
> The World Bank *helps* member nations to develop their economies.
>
> The World Bank *helps* member nations develop their economies.

Infinitives can be in the passive voice.

Most teenagers want <u>to be taken</u> seriously by adults.

<u>To be seen</u> at night by drivers, bicyclists should wear reflective clothing.

---

3. Infinitives as Objects

An infinitive can be a direct object after the following verbs.

Verb + Infinitive				
advise*	claim	fail	need	seem
afford	come	forbid*	neglect	serve
agree	command*	force*	offer	strive
allow*	compel*	get	order*	struggle
appear	consent	help	permit*	teach*
appoint*	convince*	hesitate	persuade*	tell*
arrange	dare	hire*	plan	tend
ask	decide	hope	prepare	threaten
attempt	demand	instruct*	pretend	try
be	deserve	intend	proceed	urge*
beg	direct*	invite*	promise	wait
care	enable*	learn	prove	want
cause*	encourage*	manage	refuse	warn*
challenge*	endeavor	mean (intend)	remind*	wish
choose	expect	motivate*	require*	work

Do you *care* <u>to comment</u> on the lecture?

Please do not *hesitate* <u>to call</u> if you have any questions.

We *need* <u>to use</u> wind, water, and solar power as alternative energy sources.

Shrubs *tend* <u>to have</u> several stems branching out from the main stem near the ground.

Note: In the table above, verbs marked * must have an indirect object: verb + indirect object + infinitive. In the following examples, the indirect object is shown in *italics*.

President Jefferson <u>appointed</u> *Meriwether Lewis* <u>to lead</u> the expedition.

Adaptations <u>enable</u> *some organisms* <u>to live</u> outside their ideal temperature range.

My grandfather <u>taught</u> *my uncle* <u>to drive</u> a tractor when he was twelve years old.

---

4. Infinitives after Adjectives

An infinitive can be an adjective complement after the following adjectives.

Adjective + Infinitive				
able	delighted	glad	necessary	sad
afraid	determined	good	pleased	shocked
amazed	difficult	happy	possible	sorry
careful	disappointed	hesitant	prepared	strange
common	eager	honored	proud	surprised
content	easy	important	ready	usual
dangerous	essential	motivated	relieved	willing

> Computers are *able* to perform increasingly sophisticated functions.
>
> Project plans must include the steps that are *necessary* to achieve success.
>
> I was *sorry* to hear about your accident.

Sometimes *for* + noun comes between an adjective and an infinitive.

> It is *dangerous* for backpackers to hike in the wilderness alone.
>
> It is very *important* for everyone to remember the rules of the game.

5. Gerunds

A **gerund** is formed with the base form of a verb and *-ing*.

> base–form verb + *-ing*

A gerund functions as a noun.

Function	Examples
Subject	Drawing the human face is a challenge for artists. Adapting to change is necessary for survival.
Subject Complement	The most common pastime is watching television. An important part of a speech is getting the audience's attention.
Direct Object	Teachers recommend writing an outline for an essay. Marian Anderson began singing opera to help support her mother and sisters.

Function	Examples
Object of a Preposition	We know about past climate by <u>looking at the geological record</u>.
	The raccoon is known for <u>washing its food</u> before <u>eating</u>.

Note: Gerunds are uncountable nouns and do not usually take an article (see Unit 11). One exception is gerund + *of* + noun, which takes the definite article *the*.

> Historically, responsibility for *the* <u>rearing of children</u> belonged to the parents.

6. Gerunds as Objects

A gerund can be a direct object after the following verbs.

		Verb + Gerund		
admit	consider	imagine	object to	report
aid in	count on	insist on	postpone	resent
anticipate	delay	involve	practice	resist
appreciate	deny	keep/keep on	prevent	resume
approve of	depend on	look forward to	put off	risk
avoid	discuss	mean (intend)	recall	succeed in
believe in	enjoy	mention	recollect	suggest
call for	finish	mind	recommend	think about/of
complete	give up	miss	rely on	tolerate

> Most professors do not *approve of* <u>using</u> mobile telephones in class.
>
> The committee chairman *will consider* <u>adding</u> two items to the agenda.
>
> We *look forward to* <u>visiting</u> you during spring break.
>
> After a six–month delay, the company *resumed* <u>importing</u> raw materials.

7. Infinitives or Gerunds as Objects

Either an infinitive or a gerund can be a direct object following these verbs:

		Verb + Infinitive or Gerund		
advise	begin	forbid	prefer	start
allow	continue	forget*	regret*	stop*
attempt	dislike	like	remember*	try

The following sentences have the same meaning.

> People *started* <u>to build</u> skyscrapers in the nineteenth century.
>
> People *started* <u>building</u> skyscrapers in the nineteenth century.

After verbs marked *, infinitives and gerunds convey a different meaning. The following sentences have a different meaning.

> Dave must *remember* <u>to feed the dog</u>.
>
> Dave must *remember* <u>feeding the dog</u>.

In the first sentence, the dog has not been fed; Dave is supposed to feed the dog. In the second sentence, the dog has been fed, and Dave probably remembers this.

8. *Use* with Infinitives and Gerunds

In discussions of tools, materials, and methods, the verb *use* is often followed by an infinitive phrase. *Use* may also be followed by the gerund phrase *for* + gerund, in which the gerund is the object of the preposition *for*. In the following pairs of sentences, both sentences have the same meaning.

> A surgeon *uses* a lancet <u>to make</u> small incisions.
>
> A surgeon *uses* a lancet <u>for making</u> small incisions.
>
> A centrifuge *is used* <u>to separate</u> particles from a liquid.
>
> A centrifuge *is used* <u>for separating</u> particles from a liquid.
>
> Many designers *have used* natural objects <u>to decorate</u> rooms.
>
> Many designers *have used* natural objects <u>for decorating</u> rooms.

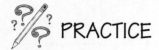 PRACTICE

Exercise 3–A

Function of Verbals. Underline the infinitive phrases and gerund phrases in each sentence. Some sentences have more than one. Above each underlined phrase, name its function, using the following abbreviations:

S	subject	OP	object of a preposition
SC	subject complement	AC	adjective complement
DO	direct object	ADV	adverb

1. One of the biggest decisions we ever make is buying a home.

2. Geologists are now able to predict when earthquakes might occur.

3. Treating mental illness has become an art as well as a science.

4. Deforestation is caused by cutting down trees.

5. To keep seafood from spoiling, it should be refrigerated.

6. It is possible to discourage squirrels from eating food set out for wild birds.

7. When men first learned to hunt in groups and to use stone axes, they started to dominate the other creatures on Earth.

8. Electrons may be freed from atoms to flow through a conductor in an electrical current or move through a vacuum in an electron beam.

Exercise 3–B

Infinitives and Gerunds. Underline the infinitives and *for* + gerund structures. Above each underlined part, change infinitives to gerunds, and change gerunds to infinitives. Add or omit *for* as necessary.

1. A scalpel is used to cut tissue during surgery and dissection.

2. Chemists frequently use computers for analyzing the results of soil tests.

3. Young people often use fashion to make a political statement.

4. There are several methods for converting geothermal energy into electricity.

5. Chimpanzees have used sticks and other tools to obtain food.

6. Solar energy has great potential for providing electricity in many regions of the world.

Exercise 3–C

Sentence Completion. Choose the word or phrase that best completes the sentence.

1. Salts can be prepared by ------- an acid with a base or a metal.

   (A) mix
   (B) mixing
   (C) mixed
   (D) to mix

2. Traffic signs are used ------- the flow of traffic.

   (A) the control
   (B) control
   (C) to control
   (D) for control

3. Gorillas have a wide range of calls that help them ------- information.

   (A) convey
   (B) conveyed
   (C) are conveying
   (D) to be conveyed

4. Human language puts a number of sounds together -------

   (A) form words
   (B) to form words
   (C) words are formed
   (D) word formation

5. The computer's mouse permits the computer operator ------- the cursor on the video display.

   (A) move
   (B) moving
   (C) to move
   (D) is moving

6. In 1954 Dr. Jonas Salk began ------- a killed–virus vaccine for polio.

   (A) tested
   (B) had tested
   (C) test
   (D) testing

7. There are many machines ------- one form of movement into another.

   (A) to convert
   (B) to be converted
   (C) the conversion of
   (D) are converting

8. Motivation is a difficult subject ------- because so many different factors influence the inclination to act.

   (A) analyze
   (B) analyzing
   (C) be analyzed
   (D) to analyze

9. Beginning around 1830, the Underground Railroad helped thousands of escaped slaves ------- their way north to freedom.

   (A) to find
   (B) were finding
   (C) found
   (D) to be found

10. We cannot understand the life of someone without ------- of the world in which he or she lived.

   (A) have knowledge
   (B) to have knowledge
   (C) having knowledge
   (D) be having knowledge

Exercise 3–D

Sentence Editing. One of the underlined parts in each sentence is incorrect. Cross out the incorrect part and write the correction above it.

1. Beavers <u>use</u> small logs, sticks, and mud for <u>build</u> dams that can <u>last</u> for many <u>years</u>.

2. In <u>make</u> cheese, the main goal is <u>getting</u> the milk to <u>separate</u> into the liquid and solid <u>portions</u>.

3. <u>Not</u> only does personality <u>affect</u> specific life events, but it also helps <u>shaping</u> the emotional fabric of adult <u>life</u>.

4. <u>Increasing</u> physical activity can <u>help</u> people with normal blood pressure <u>lower</u> their risk of <u>develop</u> high blood pressure.

5. A nation can <u>have</u> a major <u>impact</u> on its economic performance through its economic policies: regulation, <u>spending</u>, taxing, and <u>change</u> the money supply.

6. On very hot days, <u>the keeping</u> cool for <u>just a few</u> hours in an air–conditioned <u>building</u> can result in <u>saving</u> lives.

7. To <u>become</u> airborne and begin <u>soar</u>, a glider is <u>pulled</u> behind a motor vehicle by a cable <u>attached</u> to a tow hook.

8. Some linguists <u>believe</u> that women <u>use</u> conversation to <u>creating</u> equality between the speakers, while men use it to <u>establish</u> hierarchy.

9. The purpose of a screwdriver's handle is <u>to</u> allow one to <u>hold</u> the screwdriver and to <u>amplify</u> the force with which one turns it <u>for</u> drive a screw.

10. Polar bears <u>appear</u> bow–legged, but the purpose of this strange walk is <u>enable</u> these massive animals to <u>maintain</u> their balance without <u>slipping</u>.

Answers to Exercises 3–A through 3–D are on pages 255–256.

Exercise 3–E

TOEFL iBT Speaking. In the independent speaking tasks below, use infinitives and gerunds in your responses. For each task, allow 15 seconds to prepare your response and 45 seconds to speak.

1. Describe a tool or instrument that is used in your chosen field of work. Explain its purpose and give examples of how it is used.

2. Some people like going to a store to buy things. Others prefer to shop online or from a catalog. Which way of shopping do you prefer, and why? Include details and examples in your explanation.

Preparation Time – 15 seconds
Response Time – 45 seconds

Exercise 3–F

TOEFL iBT Writing. For this independent writing task, respond to the question by writing an essay in which you state and support your opinion on the topic. Your essay will be scored on the quality of your writing, including how well you organize and develop your ideas and how well you use language to express your ideas. An effective essay will have a minimum of 300 words.

Read the following question and make any notes that will help you plan your response. Then begin writing. You have 30 minutes to plan and write your essay.

> Some people learn best by reading or observing. Others learn best by listening to a teacher. Still others learn best by doing or acting. Which is the best way for you to learn? Use specific reasons and examples to support your answer.

Time – 30 minutes

Answers to Exercises 3–E and 3–F will vary.

 EXTENSION

1. **Sentence Writing.** Choose five verbs or five adjectives from each table on pages 44–46. Write a sentence with each chosen word, using infinitives or gerunds. Write some of your sentences on the board. Your classmates must identify the infinitives and gerunds.

2. **Sentence Completion.** Look in a book or a magazine for examples of sentences with infinitives and gerunds. Bring five sentences to class. Write a sentence on the board, but omit the infinitive or gerund and leave a blank line where it should be. Your classmates must complete the sentence with a correct infinitive or gerund. Would both an infinitive and a gerund be correct in the sentence? Why or why not?

3. **What is the Difference?** Write a sentence using each of the following phrases:

   a. forgot + infinitive

   b. forgot + gerund

   c. regret + infinitive

   d. regret + gerund

   e. stop + infinitive

   f. stop + gerund

For sentences with the same verb, discuss with your teacher the difference in meaning between sentences with infinitives and sentences with gerunds.

QUIZ 1   UNITS 1 – 3

Time – 10 minutes

Choose the word or phrase that best completes the sentence.

1. Volcanoes sometimes throw ------- and gases sideways.

   (A) of the hot rocks
   (B) hot rocks
   (C) the rocks are hot
   (D) are hot rocks

2. The ancient Egyptians used papyrus, ------- that they dried and glued together to form a sheet.

   (A) a type of grass
   (B) it was a type of grass
   (C) as if a type of grass
   (D) of a type of grass

3. Millions of office workers ------- most of their time sitting in front of computer screens.

   (A) spending
   (B) to spend
   (C) spend
   (D) are spent

4. A virus is harmful because ------- reproduces by killing the host cell.

   (A) it
   (B) it is
   (C) can it
   (D) it can

5. Two epic poems, the *Iliad* and the *Odyssey*, ------- by the blind poet Homer.

   (A) probably wrote
   (B) were probably written
   (C) probably writing
   (D) probably to be written

6. Driver inattention is a factor contributing to ------- of all auto accidents.

   (A) by half
   (B) causes half
   (C) it causes half
   (D) half

One of the underlined parts in each sentence is incorrect. Cross out the incorrect part and write the correction above it.

7. <u>Because</u> of their high rate of predation, <u>it is</u> not unusual for rabbits <u>producing</u> more than six <u>litters</u> of young per year.

8. As a source of <u>power</u>, electricity <u>had</u> no rival because it is <u>clean</u>, silent, and <u>can</u> be turned on and off instantly.

9. <u>Gorillas</u> can communicate with a wide <u>variety</u> of vocal calls, but they <u>could</u> not use language <u>to speak</u>.

10. <u>Invest</u> money means putting it into some business <u>project</u> such as <u>building</u> a housing complex or doing medical <u>research</u>.

Answers to Quiz 1 are on page 256.

Record your score on page 301.

UNIT 4   CLAUSES AND SENTENCES

1. **Clauses**
2. **Sentences**
3. **Subordinate Clauses**
4. **Functions of Subordinate Clauses**
5. **More about Clauses**

 FOCUS

What does this sentence need?

When two primary colors are added together, ------- a secondary color.

○ to form
○ forming
○ they form
○ for forming

The sentence has two clauses. A **clause** is a group of words with a subject and a verb. The first clause is *When two primary colors are added together*. The second clause is incomplete. Only the third answer, *they form*, is a subject + verb structure that will complete the clause. The other choices do not complete the clause. The correctly formed sentence is:

When two primary colors are added together, **they form** a secondary color.

What does this sentence need?

People enjoy dance because ------- the power to express the deepest human emotions.

○ it has
○ having
○ to have
○ has had

The sentence has two clauses. The first clause is *People enjoy dance*. The second clause, beginning with *because*, needs a subject and a verb. Only the first answer, *it has*, is a subject + verb structure. The other choices are other types of structures. The correctly formed sentence is:

People enjoy dance because **it has** the power to express the deepest human emotions.

STUDY

1. Clauses

A **clause** is a group of words containing a subject and a verb. Every sentence has at least one clause. Some sentences have two or more clauses.

One Clause	<u>Scientists</u> <u>are exploring</u> new uses of corn and soybeans. S V
Two Clauses	Before <u>she</u> <u>was</u> nineteen, <u>Billie Holiday</u> <u>had sung</u> with several bands. S V S V

Three Clauses	<u>The jaguar</u> <u>has</u> a reputation as a man-eater, but <u>many people</u> <u>tell</u>
	    S V S V
	stories in which <u>a jaguar</u> <u>followed</u> them for hours without attacking.
	               S V

There are two types of clauses: independent and subordinate. An **independent clause** can stand alone as a complete sentence. A **subordinate clause**, or **dependent clause**, cannot stand alone as a complete sentence.

Independent Clause	Some early cultures left no written records for us to discover.
Subordinate Clause	Because he wrote bleak plays about human fate

2. Sentences

A **sentence** is a grammatical unit that expresses a complete thought. A sentence must have at least one independent clause. Sentences can be simple, compound, or complex.

A **simple sentence** has one independent clause.

A **compound sentence** has two or more independent clauses joined with a conjunction such as *and*, *but*, or *so*.

A **complex sentence** has at least one independent clause and one subordinate clause. The subordinate clause begins with a subordinator such as *although* or *before*.

Simple Sentence	Charles Parsons invented the steam turbine in 1884. In some forests, the soils are shallow and poor in nutrients.
Compound Sentence	Erika likes modern art, *but* she never goes to art museums. An electric bulb produces light, *and* a radio emits sound energy.
Complex Sentence	*Although* dogs are primarily carnivores, many will eat fruits and grains. The electric trolley had dominated city streets *before* buses took over.

3. Subordinate Clauses

A *subordinate clause* has a subject and a verb but does not express a complete idea. Subordinate clauses are incomplete sentences, or *fragments*.

Subordinate Clauses	because it is hollow
(fragments)	if two lines in the same plane are parallel
	that a boat displaces water
	unless it stops raining

A subordinate clause depends on another clause to express a complete idea. For this reason, subordinate clauses are also called *dependent clauses*. A subordinate clause must be joined to an independent clause. Together, the two clauses form a complex sentence. The independent clause is the *main clause* of the sentence.

A subordinate clause is joined to a main clause by a *subordinating conjunction*, or *subordinator*. The words below function as subordinators.

after	before	since	until	whether
although	even if	so that	when	which
as	if	that	whenever	while
as if	just as	though	where	who
because	once	unless	whereas	whose

Note: Because subordinators signal the start of a clause, they are also called *clause markers*.

4. Functions of Subordinate Clauses

A subordinate clause can function as an adverb, an adjective, or a noun.

Adverb Clause	Our minds remain active while we are sleeping. As the Yellowstone River moves eastward, it picks up the waters of three other rivers.
Adjective Clause	A zoologist is a scientist who studies animals. The discovery of fire, which happened about a million years ago, provided humans with heat for cooking and warmth.
Noun Clause	Scholars have long debated how the universe began. What predicts life satisfaction in middle adulthood has been the subject of much research on young adults.

Adverb clauses, adjective clauses, and noun clauses are covered in Unit 6, Unit 7, and Unit 8.

5. **More about Clauses**

In clauses with *there* as the "false" subject, the verb is usually a form of *be*.

> There <u>is</u> a thick wall of cellulose surrounding every plant cell.
>
> In Canada <u>there</u> <u>are</u> two official languages: English and French.

A clause can contain another clause. Conversely, a clause can be part of another clause. For example, in the following sentence, the main clause contains two subordinate clauses.

> In a dry steam reservoir, the steam is piped to where it can spin turbines that generate electricity.

Main Clause	the steam is piped to where it can spin turbines that generate electricity
Subordinate Clauses	where it can spin turbines that generate electricity where it can spin turbines that generate electiricity

 PRACTICE

Exercise 4–A

Sentence Type. Classify each sentence by writing **simple**, **compound**, or **complex** next to it.

1. _____ A rainbow may be visible when water drops refract light rays.

2. _____ My history professor requires everyone to lead a class discussion.

3. _____ Hamburgers are the most popular fast food, yet some people never eat them.

4. _____ Money plays a large part in war because it pays for the necessary weapons and soldiers.

5. _____ As electronic technology developed, the transistor gave way to the integrated circuit.

6. _____ Gabriel Fahrenheit invented the first mercury thermometer, and the Fahrenheit temperature scale bears his name.

Exercise 4–B

Subordinate Clauses. Underline the subordinate clauses. Circle the subordinator that introduces each subordinate clause.

1. Sunglasses are absolutely essential for snow travel because they filter light.

2. Whenever you use oil paints, you need turpentine to clean your brushes.

3. It is important that each hiker carry extra food and clothing, even if only a day hike is planned.

4. People who speak to animals believe that the animal understands what is being said.

5. Because its young are vulnerable, the black rosy finch builds its nest in a rocky crevice so that predators cannot reach it.

6. Deltas are formed when tidal currents are unable to disperse all of the sediment that reaches the river mouth.

7. After a spill has occurred, many animals swallow oil when they try to clean themselves, which can poison them.

8. Economists believe that investment takes place when investors decide that the economy will have more consumption tomorrow if it sacrifices consumption today.

Exercise 4–C

Sentence Completion. Choose the word or phrase that best completes the sentence.

1. Banknotes are only paper, ------- represent value.

   - (A) why they
   - (B) but they
   - (C) they can
   - (D) they always

2. During the Jurassic period, ------- the dominant animals on land.

   - (A) dinosaurs
   - (B) while dinosaurs
   - (C) dinosaurs were
   - (D) when dinosaurs were

3. ------- the ability of birds to move through the air using wings and feathers.

   - (A) Flight
   - (B) It is flight
   - (C) As if flight
   - (D) Flight is

4. Dams are costly, but once they have been built, ------- electricity very cheaply.

   - (A) producing
   - (B) they produce
   - (C) production of
   - (D) and produce

5. ------- the commercial sewing machine was introduced, thousands of women found jobs in the textile industry.

(A) When
(B) Later
(C) Then
(D) How

6. ------- many types of building stone, from tough granite to soft sandstone.

(A) The
(B) Because
(C) There are
(D) So

7. Fixed bridges do not have moving parts, ------- either lift or swing open.

(A) movable bridges
(B) do movable bridges
(C) movable bridges are
(D) while movable bridges

8. ------- in 1980, Pierre Trudeau proposed a new constitution for Canada.

(A) His return to power
(B) After he had returned to power
(C) Who was returning to power
(D) His power was returned

9. In any environment ------- a limit to the resources that are available for any particular species.

(A) there is
(B) where
(C) by which
(D) maybe

10. The Harvest Moon, the full moon nearest the autumn equinox, ------- a period of several days when the moon rises soon after sunset.

(A) it brings
(B) which brings
(C) and brings
(D) brings

Exercise 4–D

TOEFL iBT Reading. Read the passages and choose the best answer to each question.

QUESTION 1

Look at the four squares, **A**, **B**, **C**, and **D**, which indicate where the following sentence could be added to the passage. Where would the sentence best fit?

> **Although these scientists believed that the planet was very old, they had no means of determining its exact age.**

In the past, there were a number of scientists who attempted to determine the age of Earth. In the eighteenth century, James Hutton recognized that time was an element in all geological processes. **A** He argued that geological changes did not happen in a short period of time as a result of catastrophe. Instead, processes that were still happening had caused them. **B** In the nineteenth century, Sir Charles Lyell studied the composition of rock layers. **C** He concluded that Earth had experienced several periods of mountain formation and erosion, which must have occurred over great lengths of geologic time. **D** Until modern dating methods were devised, geologists could only wonder whether Earth was many millions, or even billions of years old.

QUESTIONS 2–5

The human heart is enclosed in a sac with a two-layered wall. A lubricating fluid fills the space between the two walls, enabling them to slide past each other as the heart pulsates. The heart is mostly cardiac muscle tissue divided into four chambers, two atria and two ventricles. The atria have relatively thin walls and function as collection chambers for blood. The ventricles have thicker walls and are much more powerful than the atria, especially the left ventricle, which must pump blood to all organs of the body. **A** When the heart beats, the ventricles contract and pump blood. As the heart relaxes after a contraction, the atria fill with blood. **B** One complete sequence of pumping and filling is called the cardiac cycle. **C** In an average adult at rest, the cycle takes about 0.8 second. The number of times the heart beats each minute is the heart rate, which can be measured by taking the pulse. **D** On average, a healthy adult at rest has a heart rate of about 70 beats per minute. An individual's heart rate will vary, depending on the level of activity.

2. The word pulsates in the passage is closest in meaning to

   Ⓐ pumps
   Ⓑ grows
   Ⓒ weakens
   Ⓓ divides

3. Why does the left ventricle have thick walls?

   Ⓐ It produces fluid to lubricate the heart.
   Ⓑ It stores a large amount of blood.
   Ⓒ It pumps blood through the body.
   Ⓓ It helps the heart fight infection.

4. What happens during the cardiac cycle?

   Ⓐ The atria pump blood to the ventricles.
   Ⓑ The heart contracts and relaxes.
   Ⓒ The heart rate decreases.
   Ⓓ The body shifts from rest to activity.

5. Look at the four squares, **A**, **B**, **C**, and **D**, which indicate where the following sentence could be added to the passage. Where would the sentence best fit?

   The pulse is the rhythmic stretching of the arteries caused by the pressure of the blood when the ventricles contract.

QUESTION 6

1   Communication between children and parents starts very early. A baby's cry is designed to get adult attention. Babies cry when they are upset, and their voices cause stress in adults. Babies recognize their parents' voices. When parents talk to babies, they tend to give their voice a happy singsong that grabs the baby's attention and says, "I'm talking to you." The rising and falling of a parent's voice helps a baby interpret the strange sounds of language. The more talk that babies hear, the better, so it is beneficial for parents to narrate what happens around a baby. It is one of the ways that parents help children accomplish a major goal of the first two years: identifying sounds with experience.

2   At around six months old, they start to babble, and the sounds they produce include the sounds of human languages. Research suggests that it is during the babbling stage that children start to distinguish between the sounds of their native language and the sounds of other languages. Babies are extraordinary language generalists and can easily pick up two or three languages. However, they start to specialize in their native tongue by the age of three years.

3   The earliest age that children start to speak is ten months. However, most do not talk until the age of 12 or 13 months. Others wait as long as 19 months, although almost all children who lag behind eventually catch up. When children have learned that sounds are related to meanings, they produce their first words. Most children go through a "one word equals one sentence" stage. Between 18 and 24 months, they may begin learning as many as nine new words each week. This spurt in vocabulary occurs after children have accumulated between 30 and 100 words. By then, children can produce two-word utterances like "hi mommy" and "all gone." After that, they quickly learn to string words together in longer "sentences."

6. Read the first sentence of a summary of the passage. Complete the summary by selecting the THREE answer choices that express the most important ideas in the passage. Some sentences do not belong in the summary because they express ideas that are not presented in the passage or are minor ideas in the passage.

A child's first few years are an important period in language learning.

•
•
•

Answer Choices

(A) Babies can understand almost everything that their parents say.

(B) Parents play an essential role in teaching children language.

(C) Young children are proficient language learners.

(D) Some children start to talk much earlier than others do.

(E) Children learn nine words each week at age 24 months.

(F) Children go through stages as they develop language ability.

Exercise 4–E

TOEFL iBT Speaking. In this integrated speaking task, you will read a short passage, listen to a lecture on the same topic, and then speak in response to a question about what you have read and heard. Do not look at the question until the lecture has ended. Do not look at the reading passage while you are speaking.

Reading Time – 45 seconds

MICROPHONING

Microphoning is the art and science of deciding which kinds of microphones to use, how many to use, and where to put them. The goal of microphoning, or "micing," is to get a recording that sounds most like the live performance. Different microphones can "hear" in different ways, a characteristic known as polar pattern. Polar pattern indicates how sensitive the microphone is to sounds arriving from different directions. Two common polar patterns are "unidirectional" and "omnidirectional." A unidirectional microphone picks up sounds fromonly one direction. An omnidirectional microphone picks up sounds equally from all directions.

Now cover the passage and listen to the lecture. You may take notes, and you may use your notes to help you answer the question. After you hear the question, begin preparing your response. You may look at the question, but NOT at the passage. You have 30 seconds to prepare your response and 60 seconds to speak.

 Audio Track 7

> The professor describes unidirectional and omnidirectional microphones. Explain how their polar pattern makes these microphones appropriate for recording specific performances.

 Stop

Preparation Time – 30 seconds
Response Time – 60 seconds

Answers to Exercises 4–A through 4–E are on pages 256–257.

Exercise 4–F

TOEFL iBT Writing. For this independent writing task, respond to the question by writing an essay in which you state and support your opinion on the topic. Your essay will be scored on the quality of your writing, including how well you organize and develop your ideas and how well you use language to express your ideas. An effective essay will have a minimum of 300 words.

Read the following question and make any notes that will help you plan your response. Then begin writing. You have 30 minutes to plan and write your essay.

> Some people think that the primary responsibility for educating children belongs to the government. Others believe that education is mainly the responsibility of parents. Which position do you agree with? Use specific reasons and examples to support your opinion.

Time – 30 minutes

Answers to Exercise 4–F will vary.

 EXTENSION

1. **Sentence Analysis.** Outside class, look in a newspaper, magazine, or book for examples of sentences with more than one clause. These sentences will be either compound or complex. Bring five examples to share in class. Write some of the sentence on the board. For each sentence, the class must perform the following tasks:

   a. Classify the sentence as compound or complex.

   b. Identify conjunctions in compound sentences.

   c. Identify subordinators in complex sentences.

   d. Identify the subjects and verbs in every clause.

2. **Sentence Writing.** Practice writing sentences using the subordinators in the list below. Make sure that each subordinate clause has a subject and a verb.

after	because	if	unless	where
although	before	since	when	while

UNIT 5 CONJUNCTIONS

1. **Coordination**
2. **Correlation**
3. **Conjunctive Adverbs**
4. **Subordination**

 FOCUS

What does this sentence need?

Early carpenters developed several ways of joining pieces of wood, ------- some of those are still used today.

- ○ why
- ○ also
- ○ with
- ○ and

The sentence has two independent clauses; it needs a conjunction to join the two clauses. **Conjunctions** are words that connect other words, phrases, or clauses. The fourth answer, *and*, is a conjunction. The other choices are not conjunctions. The correctly formed sentence is:

Early carpenters developed several ways of joining pieces of wood, **and** some of those are still used today.

What does this sentence need?

Rice needs either plains ------- terraces that can be flooded during the growing season.

- ○ but
- ○ or
- ○ are
- ○ to

The sentence needs a conjunction to join the nouns *plains* and *terraces*. The word before *plains* is *either*, the first part of a conjunction. When *either* is paired with *or*, it is a two–part conjunction. The second answer, *or*, completes the structure by joining the two nouns. The correctly formed sentence is:

Rice needs either plains **or** terraces that can be flooded during the growing season.

 STUDY

1. Coordination

Coordination is the joining of similar structures. *Conjunctions* are words that join other words, phrases, or clauses. *Coordinating conjunctions* connect structures of the same value: words, phrases, or independent clauses. Coordinating conjunctions express a relationship of addition, alternative, contrast, or cause and result between the joined structures.

Addition	Alternative	Contrast	Result
and	or	but yet	so

Structure	Examples
Words	The flower known as baby's–breath starts to bloom in <u>June</u> *or* <u>July</u>. In the classic fable, the tortoise crawled <u>slowly</u> *but* <u>steadily</u> to win the race with the hare.
Phrases	A jet engine <u>takes in air at the front</u> *and* <u>ejects it from the back</u>. The first agents of socialization are <u>the child's parents</u> *or* <u>the other adults</u> who take care of the child.
Independent Clauses	<u>Churchill is icebound eight months a year</u>, *yet* <u>its harbor has a long history</u>. <u>Reptiles cannot regulate body temperature physiologically</u>, *so* <u>they must regulate it behaviorally</u>.

2. Correlation

Correlation is the joining of structures that are in a parallel or complementary relationship. *Correlative conjunctions* connect structures of the same value: single words, phrases, or independent clauses. Because correlative conjunctions have two parts, they are also called *two–part conjunctions* or *paired expressions*.

Addition	Alternative	Exclusion/Inclusion
and…as well as both…and not only…but also	either…or neither…nor	not…but

UNIT 5

Structure	Examples
Words	Thomas Jefferson was <u>a farmer</u> *and* <u>architect</u>, *as well as* <u>a statesman</u>. An animal in a state of torpor is *neither* <u>active</u> *nor* <u>responsive</u>.
Phrases	Rats are *both* <u>agricultural pests</u> *and* <u>carriers of disease</u>. Many people learn about job openings *not* <u>by reading the newspaper</u> *but* <u>by talking to people who work</u>.
Independent Clauses	*Either* <u>a society changes through innovation and contact with other societies</u>, *or* <u>it remains stagnant and isolated</u>.

As well as is usually paired with *and* or *both...and*. However, *as well as* can be used by itself as a conjunction that is not part of a paired expression.

The Salish people developed their wood arts <u>as well as</u> their mythology.

Also can be omitted from *not only...but also* and replaced by *as well* or *too* at the end of the clause.

Astronomers are beginning to understand <u>not only</u> the physical make–up of stars, <u>but</u> their origins and life cycles <u>as well</u>.

Kobe is <u>not only</u> a major industrial city, <u>but</u> a center of culture <u>too</u>.

Not...but makes the structure after *not* false and the structure after *but* true. According to the following sentence, it is not true that a groundhog is a hog; it is true that a groundhog is a large rodent.

A groundhog is actually <u>not</u> a hog <u>but</u> a large rodent.

---

3. Conjunctive Adverbs

Conjunctive adverbs connect two independent clauses and express a relationship between the ideas in the clauses. Conjunctive adverbs are ***transitions*** between clauses. They may express addition, illustration, contrast, cause and result, condition, or time relationships.

When two independent clauses are joined in a single sentence, the conjunctive adverb comes between them. A semicolon comes after the first clause, and a comma comes after the conjunctive adverb. When a conjunctive adverb is a transition between two sentences, it comes at the beginning of the second sentence, followed by a comma.

Addition	also	furthermore	in fact
	besides	in addition	moreover

Many herbal remedies are not safe; <u>besides</u>, their effectiveness has not been proven scientifically.

Computer graphics contribute to creativity and productivity. <u>In fact</u>, they are a vital part of the computer–human interface.

Illustration	for example	for instance

The field of nursing reaches beyond medicine; <u>for instance</u>, nurses may study how nonmedical factors affect the delivery of health care.

Contrast	however	instead	on the contrary
	in contrast	nevertheless	on the one hand...on the other hand

Traditional authority is based on custom and habit. <u>In contrast</u>, legal authority rests on elections and laws.

Some people with hepatitis have no symptoms; <u>nevertheless</u>, they might develop liver failure.

On the one hand...on the other hand is a paired expression. *On the one hand* must be used with *on the other hand*. However, *on the other hand* can be used alone.

<u>On the one hand</u>, the majority of North Americans take their vacation in July or August. <u>On the other hand</u>, a number of people prefer a winter vacation.

Most North Americans take their vacation in the summer; <u>on the other hand</u>, many prefer a winter vacation.

Cause/Result	accordingly	consequently	therefore
	as a result	hence	thus

A black pigment absorbs all three primary colors; <u>consequently</u>, it appears black.

Global cooling occurs over hundred of years. <u>Hence</u>, ice ages are very long in developing.

Condition	otherwise

> A pidgin develops as a contact language among people who speak different languages; <u>otherwise</u>, communication would be impossible.

Time	afterward	later	next
	beforehand	meanwhile	then

> A cognitive shift occurs around the age of seven; <u>afterward</u>, the child has a deeper understanding of shape, volume, and quantity.
>
> I was on the telephone for almost an hour; <u>meanwhile</u>, the meeting started without me.

A comma is not necessary after the conjunctive adverbs *later*, *next*, and *then*, but may be used.

> We played chess all afternoon; <u>next</u> we went for a walk. <u>Later</u>, we cooked a delicious meal.
>
> Life began in the sea; <u>then</u> organisms evolved capabilities to live on land.

4. Subordination

Subordination is the joining of a subordinate clause and a main clause. ***Subordinating conjunctions*** connect the clauses and express a relationship between the ideas in them, such as cause and result, contrast, or time order. Also called ***subordinators***, subordinating conjunctions come at the beginning of a subordinate clause.

Cause/Result	as	since	so…that
	because	so that	such…that

> <u>Because</u> glacial erosion occurs very slowly, it is difficult to view in action.
>
> The disk plate is exposed to the air <u>so that</u> heat generated by braking is released.
>
> My professor's explanation was <u>so</u> confusing <u>that</u> I could barely take notes.

Contrast	although	though	while
	even though	whereas	

> Rice is the staple food in southern China, <u>whereas</u> wheat is the staple in the North.
>
> <u>While</u> some artists have readily accepted computers, others refuse to work with them.

Time	after	before	when
	as	since	while

An airplane makes an explosive noise <u>as</u> it breaks through the sound barrier.

<u>When</u> fertilizer is added to soil, the natural phosphorus cycle is disrupted.

Subordinating conjunctions are also discussed in Unit 4, Unit 6, Unit 7, and Unit 8.

 PRACTICE

Exercise 5–A

Conjunctions. Circle the conjunctions, and underline the structures that are connected. Identify the type of structure by writing **W** for words, **P** for phrases, or **C** for clauses next to each sentence.

1. _____ A planet's ring system is a collection of ice, rocks, and dust circling the planet in a belt.

2. _____ The exterior of Hagia Sophia is not elaborately decorated, so nothing distracts from the building's basic form.

3. _____ The poetry of Emily Dickinson focused on values that were both material and spiritual.

4. _____ Neither the cat's teeth nor its digestive system is suited for anything except an all–meat diet.

5. _____ The scorpion's poison is not in its bite but in the sting of its tail.

6. _____ Global warming will interfere with the North Atlantic currents; furthermore, it may disrupt the entire system of ocean currents.

Exercise 5–B

Sentence Completion. Choose the word or phrase that best completes the sentence.

1. Combustion produces ------- heat.

   (A) and light of
   (B) both light and
   (C) light also
   (D) as light as

2. Two–thirds of the land in Australia is either semiarid -------.

   (A) but is desert
   (B) or is it desert
   (C) or desert
   (D) nor desert

3. Birds not only bring song, color, and activity to a garden ------- are vitally needed by plants.

   (A) but also
   (B) as well as
   (C) and
   (D) and they

4. Some economists call for a return to the gold standard, ------- others urge a more broadly based standard.

   (A) in fact
   (B) the
   (C) nor
   (D) while

5. ------- Mother Teresa and Martin Luther King won the Nobel Peace Prize.

   (A) Either
   (B) As
   (C) Both
   (D) Besides

6. The expression in dance arises from the physical experience; -------, mental preparation is equally important.

   (A) so
   (B) however
   (C) for instance
   (D) while

7. ------- Millard Fillmore nor Franklin Pierce is a well–known ex–president.

   (A) Not
   (B) Not only
   (C) Never
   (D) Neither

8. Columbia University includes schools of journalism, mining, and international affairs, ------- a geological laboratory.

   (A) in addition
   (B) as a result
   (C) as well as
   (D) instead

9. Along the California coast the chaparral shrubs are ------- hot fires burn the area every few decades.

   (A) in fact dry
   (B) so dry that
   (C) as dry as
   (D) either dry or

10. Five thousand years ago a new kind of civilization emerged, based not on superior agricultural lands ------- superior location for trade.

    (A) but on
    (B) yet having
    (C) based on
    (D) but also

Exercise 5–C

Sentence Editing.   One of the underlined parts in each sentence is incorrect. Cross out the incorrect part and write the correction above it.

1. Not only <u>are</u> rhododendrons known for <u>their</u> dramatic, colorful flowers, <u>and</u> they are also valuable <u>as</u> landscape plants.

2. In summer, the tiger shark <u>may</u> follow warm water currents <u>as</u> far south as New Zealand <u>or</u> north to Japan <u>nor</u> the northern United States.

3. The Muses were the nine Greek goddesses of the arts <u>and</u> sciences; <u>instead</u>, schools <u>devoted</u> to the study of art and science <u>were</u> called Music Schools.

4. <u>Unlike</u> early capitalism, modern capitalism <u>depends</u> on the state, <u>and</u> the government is expected to fight <u>either</u> unemployment and inflation.

5. On the one hand, Earth <u>was</u> lifeless for its first two <u>billion</u> years; <u>otherwise</u>, it was a seething mass of volcanic <u>and</u> geologic activity.

6. The "baby boomers" are the <u>largest</u> generation in recent history; <u>consequently</u>, they had <u>more</u> impact on the birth rate than did <u>neither</u> the prior or the successive generation.

7. Examples of minimal art <u>are the</u> structures of <u>such</u> sculptors as Carl Andre <u>also</u> Donald Judd, <u>as well as</u> the paintings of Frank Stella.

8. <u>Many</u> astronomers agreed <u>with</u> Shapley's big galaxy hypothesis; <u>therefore</u>, others disputed the idea <u>and</u> found it unlikely.

Exercise 5–D

TOEFL iBT Reading.   Read the passage and choose the best answer to each question.

QUESTIONS 1–5

1 The number of insect species on Earth exceeds that of all other life forms combined. Entomologists estimate that there are well over one million different known species of insects, or possibly as many as 10 million. Insects live in almost every habitat on land and in fresh water, as well as in the air. Even in the frozen extremes of the Arctic and Antarctic some insects are active during the summer months. The oldest insect fossils date from the Devonian period, which began 400 million years ago. Later, when insect flight evolved during the Carboniferous and Permian periods, there was a rapid expansion in insect variety.

2 The adult insect body has three pairs of walking legs and a body segmented into three regions: head, thorax, and abdomen. Many species have one or two pairs of wings emerging from the thorax. The wings are not true legs; therefore, insects can fly without sacrificing any walking legs. In contrast, the wings of birds are one of their two pairs of walking legs modified for flight. Consequently, birds are relatively clumsy on the ground.

3 The evolution of flight is one key to the tremendous success of insects. Flying enables insects to escape from predators, find food and mates, and move quickly to new habitats. Some entomologists believe that wings first evolved to help the insect body absorb heat and later became organs for flight. Others think that wings allowed the insects to glide from plants to the ground, or possibly served as gills for aquatic insects to breathe. Still others hypothesize that wings first evolved not for flying but for swimming. Insects called stoneflies still use their tiny wings to skip across the surface of streams. The fossil record shows that dragonflies, with two pairs of wings, were among the first insects to fly. Several insects that evolved later have modified flight equipment. For example, bees and wasps hook their wings together and move them as a single pair. Beetles have rear wings that are used for flight and front wings modified as covers that protect the flight wings when the beetle is on the ground or burrowing.

4 Because insects are so numerous, diverse, and widespread, they affect the lives of all other terrestrial organisms, including humans. **A** On the one hand, insects have an essential role in pollinating many of our crops and orchards. **B** On the other hand, they are carriers for many diseases, including malaria, Lyme disease, and African sleeping sickness. Insects that eat plant leaves have defoliated forests, killed trees, and created nuisances in urban areas. **C** In some parts of the world, insects claim over half of the grain crops. **D** In the United States, farmers who try to minimize their losses spend billions of dollars each year on pesticides, spraying crops with massive doses of poison.

5 Despite all of our efforts, we are not able to challenge the preeminence of insects on Earth. In fact, global warming will lead to an increase in the number of insects worldwide, with serious consequences for humans. New research shows that insect species in warmer regions are more likely to undergo rapid population growth because they have high metabolic rates and they reproduce frequently. A surge in populations of beetles, locusts, and other crop eaters will require the use of more pesticides, a solution that will be not only very costly but also hazardous to other organisms. Rising temperatures will cause a widening of areas habitable for mosquitoes, and a surge in mosquito populations will mean more infections of mosquito–borne diseases such as malaria. Researchers have already observed that new cases of malaria have appeared in previously unaffected areas.

1. In paragraph 1, the author states that insects

   (A) evolved 10 million years ago
   (B) live in a wide variety of places
   (C) cannot survive in the ocean
   (D) were the first animals to fly

2. The word sacrificing in paragraph 2 is closest in meaning to

   (A) growing
   (B) feeling
   (C) changing
   (D) using

3. Which sentence below best expresses the essential information in the highlighted sentence in paragraph 3?

   (A) One view is that the first wings enabled insects to swim rather than to fly.
   (B) Some insect wings evolved for flying, and others were used for swimming.
   (C) Not only did insects develop the ability to fly, but they could also swim.
   (D) Some scientists think that insect wings are not strong enough for flying.

4. Look at the four squares, **A**, **B**, **C**, and **D**, which indicate where the following sentence could be added to paragraph 4. Where would the sentence best fit?

   Moreover, insects that eat crops compete with us for food.

5. Read the first sentence of a summary of the passage. Complete the summary by selecting the THREE answer choices that express the most important ideas in the passage. Some sentences do not belong in the summary because they express ideas that are not presented in the passage or are minor ideas in the passage.

   Insects are the most numerous and diverse of all life forms on Earth.

   -
   -
   -

   Answer Choices

   (A) The ability to fly is an important factor in the variety and abundance of insects.
   (B) The insect body is composed of the head, the thorax, and the abdomen.
   (C) Dragonflies may have been the first insects to evolve the ability to fly.
   (D) The preeminence of insects greatly influences humans and other organisms.
   (E) Global warming will benefit insects and negatively impact humans.
   (F) Mosquitoes breed in salt marshes and floodwaters as well as artificial containers.

UNIT 5

Exercise 5–E

TOEFL iBT Writing. In this integrated writing task, you will write a response to a question about a reading passage and a lecture. Your response will be scored on the quality of your writing and on how well you connect the points in the lecture with points in the reading. Typically, an effective response will have 150 to 225 words.

Reading Time – 3 minutes

The term "invasive species" loosely describes a non–native species that, when introduced into a new habitat, adversely affects that habitat. Most introduced species of plants and animals do not become invasive. However, a combination of several mechanisms will cause an invasive situation to occur.

Invasion is more likely if the new habitat is similar to the one in which the introduced species evolved. Invasive species may proliferate quickly in a new ecosystem with favorable conditions, especially if the habitat lacks the natural competitors and predators with which the invader evolved. Ecosystems are prone to invasion if they have "open" niches, or if their native species have faced few strong competitors or predators during their evolution, and therefore lack the adaptations necessary for dealing with introduced species.

An introduced species might become invasive if it overwhelms native species in the competition for resources, such as nutrients, light, water, or physical space. While all species compete to survive, invasive species have traits that allow them to outcompete. Sometimes invaders just have the ability to grow and reproduce more rapidly than native species. They may experience early sexual maturity, have a high reproductive output, or be able to disperse their seeds or offspring widely. Invasive species may also be able to tolerate a broad range of environmental conditions.

Non–native species are introduced through several means, both natural and human, but most of the species considered invasive are associated with human activity. Invaded ecosystems have often experienced a change or disturbance that is human–induced. This disturbance may give invasive species an opportunity to establish themselves. Because they have not evolved within the ecosystem, invasive species may face little competition from native species.

Now listen to the lecture. You may take notes, and you may use your notes to help you write your response. After you hear the question, you have 20 minutes to plan and write your response. You may look at the reading passage during the writing time.

 *Audio Track 8*

Summarize the points made in the lecture, explaining how they support points made in the reading.

 Stop

Time – 20 minutes

Exercise 5–F

TOEFL iBT Writing. For this independent writing task, respond to the question by writing an essay in which you state and support your opinion on the topic. Your essay will be scored on the quality of your writing, including how well you organize and develop your ideas and how well you use language to express your ideas. An effective essay will have a minimum of 300 words.

Read the following question and make any notes that will help you plan your response. Then begin writing. You have 30 minutes to plan and write your essay.

> Do you agree or disagree with the following statement?
>
> **A good education includes both arts and sciences.**
>
> Use specific reasons and examples to support your answer.

Time – 30 minutes

Answers to Exercises 5–A through 5–E are on pages 257–258.

Answers to Exercise 5–F will vary.

 EXTENSION

1. **Sentence Analysis.** In reading done outside class, look for examples of sentences with various types of conjunctions. Bring five examples to share in class. Write some of the sentences on the board. Your classmates must identify the conjunctions and the structures that are connected.

2. **Sentence Completion.** In a variation on Exercise 1, write some of the sentences on the board, but omit the conjunctions. Leave blank spaces where the conjunctions should be. Your classmates must complete the sentences with appropriate conjunctions.

3. **Sentence Writing.** Practice writing sentences with conjunctive adverbs. Use the words in the list below. Make sure to use correct punctuation.

as a result	in addition	on the contrary
for instance	in contrast	otherwise
furthermore	instead	then
however	moreover	therefore

UNIT 6   ADVERB CLAUSES

1. Adverb Clauses
2. Subordinators
3. Position of Adverb Clauses
4. Adverb Phrases
5. Active and Passive Voice

 FOCUS

What does this sentence need?

> The Great Depression began ------- in 1929.
>
> ○ that the stock market crash
> ○ the stock market had crashed
> ○ the stock market to crash
> ○ after the stock market crashed

The verb *began* needs a modifier or object. Only the fourth answer, *after the stock market crashed*, will correctly complete the sentence. It is an **adverb clause**, a subordinate clause that functions as an adverb. In this case, the adverb clause modifies *began*. The correctly formed sentence is:

> The Great Depression began **after the stock market crashed** in 1929.

What does this sentence need?

> ------- to within thirty feet of its prey, the Siberian tiger pounces and grabs its meal.
>
> ○ Creeping
> ○ How creeping
> ○ Creeps
> ○ It creeps

The main clause, *the Siberian tiger pounces and grabs its meal*, needs a modifier. Only the first answer, *Creeping*, forms a modifier, the adverb phrase *Creeping to within thirty feet of its prey*. An **adverb phrase** is a group of words that functions as an adverb. In this case, the adverb phrase modifies the main clause. The correctly formed sentence is:

> **Creeping** to within thirty feet of its prey, the Siberian tiger pounces and grabs its meal.

 STUDY

1. Adverb Clauses

An *adverb* is a word that modifies a verb. An *adverb clause* is a subordinate clause that functions as a single–word adverb. An adverb clause can modify a verb or an independent clause. Like all subordinate clauses, adverb clauses must have a subject and a verb.

> subordinator + subject + verb (+ rest of clause)

An adverb clause cannot stand alone as a complete sentence. It must be connected to an independent (main) clause to form a complete sentence.

> The dog walked to the intersection and waited, <u>just as</u> <u>it</u> <u>had been trained</u> to do.
>   sub.   S   V

Main Clause   The dog walked to the intersection and waited

Adverb Clause   just as it had been trained to do

2. Subordinators

Adverb clauses begin with a *subordinating conjunction*, or *subordinator*. The subordinator expresses the relationship between the adverb clause and the main clause. Various subordinators express relationships of time, place, cause, purpose, contrast, manner, or condition.

Time				
	after	as soon as	once	when
	as	before	since	whenever
	as long as	by the time	until	while

> Children learn their culture from their parents <u>as they listen to family stories</u>.
>
> <u>By the time his autobiography was published</u>, Malcolm X had been assassinated.
>
> Our brain is busy sorting and storing information <u>while we are sleeping</u>.

Place	where	wherever

> <u>Wherever a bit of soil collects in a sidewalk crack</u>, a seed is likely to germinate.

Cause	as	because	now that	since

I will not be answering e–mail next week, <u>as I will be away from my computer</u>.

<u>Now that spring has arrived</u>, the days are longer than the nights.

Purpose	so that	so…that	such...that	in order that

Martin Luther King was <u>such</u> a powerful orator <u>that his speeches continue to inspire people today</u>.

Contrast	although	even though	whereas	despite the fact that
	even if	though	while	in spite of the fact that

<u>Even though it helps some people</u>, doctors disagree on the safety of melatonin.

Some students prefer lecture classes, <u>while others like small group discussions</u>.

Manner	as	as if	as though	just as

The raccoon rubs and tears its food underwater, <u>as if the food needed washing</u>.

Condition	as long as	if	only if	unless
	even if	in case	provided that	whether or not

Dogs are allowed in city parks <u>only if they are on a leash</u>.

<u>Unless fish is properly preserved</u>, it will spoil in just a few days.

Sentences with adverb clauses expressing condition are called ***conditional sentences***. (See Unit 9.)

3. Position of Adverb Clauses

In a sentence, the position of the adverb clause and the main clause can be reversed, with no change in meaning. The adverb clause can come either before or after the main clause. When the adverb clause comes first, a comma separates it from the main clause.

<u>When I was six years old</u>, my grandmother taught me how to bake a pie.

My grandmother taught me how to bake a pie <u>when I was six years old</u>.

When the adverb clause comes after the main clause, a comma is not required but may be used to indicate a pause in speaking or a separation of ideas. The comma is often used when the adverb clause expresses contrast.

> Cats rarely meow at other cats, <u>although they often meow at humans</u>.
>
> Schools continue to use intelligence tests, <u>even if they are of limited value</u>.

4. Adverb Phrases

Some adverb clauses can be reduced to adverb phrases, with no change in meaning. An ***adverb phrase*** is a group of words that functions as an adverb.

An adverb clause can be reduced to an adverb phrase only when the subject of the adverb clause is the same as the subject of the main clause. Adverb clauses that express time are often reduced to phrases.

Adverb phrases take the present or past participle of a verb. For this reason, adverb phrases are also called ***participial phrases***.

In reducing an adverb clause to an adverb phrase:

- The subject of the clause is omitted.
- Auxiliary verbs, if any, are omitted.
- The verb is changed to its present or past participle.

Adverb Clause	You should plan your route carefully <u>before you leave home</u>.
Adverb Phrase	You should plan your route carefully <u>before leaving home</u>
Adverb Clause	<u>While he was working as a printer</u>, Benjamin Franklin invented many things.
Adverb Phrase	<u>While working as a printer</u>, Benjamin Franklin invented many things.
Adverb Clause	<u>When students were told that tuition would increase</u>, they organized a protest rally.
Adverb Phrase	<u>When told that tuition would increase</u>, students organized a protest rally.

When an adverb clause beginning with *as* or *because* is reduced to an adverb phrase at the beginning of a sentence, the subordinator is omitted.

Adverb Clause	<u>As we watched the night sky</u>, we saw seven satellites pass by.
Adverb Phrase	<u>Watching the night sky</u>, we saw seven satellites pass by.
Adverb Clause	<u>Because it was once considered a dangerous predator</u>, the wolf has been hunted to near–extinction.
Adverb Phrase	<u>Once considered a dangerous predator</u>, the wolf has been hunted to near–extinction.

Note: An adverb clause *cannot* be reduced if the adverb clause and main clause have different subjects. The following sentences cannot be reduced. The subject of each clause is shown in *italics*.

> When the *cat* is away, the *mice* will play.
>
> Wherever ornamental *grasses* are used, the *garden* will have a finished look.

5. Active and Passive Voice

Adverb phrases can be in active voice or passive voice. *Active–voice* adverb phrases take the *-ing* form (present participle) of the verb.

Adverb Clause	When a substance undergoes a slow oxidation, the substance can burst into flame.
Adverb Phrase	When undergoing a slow oxidation, a substance can burst into flame.
Adverb Clause	Frank Sprague developed the elevator after he had improved the electric motor.
Adverb Phrase	Frank Sprague developed the elevator after improving the electric motor.

Passive–voice adverb phrases take the *-ed* form (past participle) of the verb.

Adverb Clause	Dogs cannot compete in shows until they are properly trained.
Adverb Phrase	Dogs cannot compete in shows until properly trained.
Adverb Clause	Since it was discovered, penicillin has been used to treat many bacterial infections.
Adverb Phrase	Since discovered, penicillin has been used to treat many bacterial infections. *or* Since being discovered, penicillin has been used to treat many bacterial infections.

 PRACTICE

Exercise 6–A

Adverb Clauses. Underline the adverb clauses. Circle the subordinator that introduces each adverb clause.

1. Photovoltaic cells are used to power satellites because they are sturdy and lightweight.

2. Before he was cast in his first film, Rudolph Valentino worked as a tango dancer.

3. All homes should have an emergency kit, in case there is a natural disaster.

4. Mario attended law school, as his father and grandfather had done before him.

5. Artists are advised to buy a variety of brushes so that the right brush is always on hand.

6. People continued to pour into the auditorium, in spite of the fact that all seats were taken.

Exercise 6–B

Adverb Phrases. Underline the subordinator, subject, and verb in each adverb clause. Reduce the underlined part to an adverb phrase, writing the adverb phrase above the clause. In some adverb phrases, the subordinator may be omitted.

1. You should turn on the headlights when you drive through mountainous terrain.

2. My grandfather has not seen his native land since he immigrated to Canada.

3. While we were walking across campus, we noticed a crowd in front of the library.

4. Jack McAuliffe had been the undefeated amateur boxing champion before he became the professional

champion.

5. Until they reach the age of six, children retain their deciduous "baby" teeth.

6. As technicians build scenes on screen, technicians use the computer to draw and animate screen models.

7. After fruit is infected with brown rot, fruit develops soft brown spots that grow and rot.

8. Because they are encouraged by success, students perform better when they are given opportunities

to succeed.

Exercise 6–C

Sentence Completion. Choose the word or phrase that best completes the sentence.

1. -------, small substances pass through the cell membrane.

    (A) How a cell eats
    (B) A cell will eat
    (C) When a cell eats
    (D) A cell is eating

2. An architect usually makes drawings ------- any construction begins.

    (A) earlier
    (B) before
    (C) during
    (D) then

3. Brasses are musical instruments that produce tones ------- the mouthpiece.

    (A) lips vibrating
    (B) lips are vibrating
    (C) lips vibrate
    (D) when lips vibrate

4. Customers are entitled to receive additional credit services ------- maintain their account in good standing.

    (A) they can
    (B) do they
    (C) as long as
    (D) as long as they

5. The spider called "daddy longlegs" is omnivorous, ------- plant fluids, animal tissue, and other spiders.

    (A) feeding on
    (B) is fed on
    (C) feeds on
    (D) to feed on

6. ------- common usage among economists, the term "natural rate" is misleading.

    (A) It has gained
    (B) That it has gained
    (C) Has it gained
    (D) Although it has gained

7. ------- Becquerel's discovery of radioactivity, Marie Curie began to study uranium.

    (A) Following
    (B) Was following
    (C) Followed
    (D) She followed

8. ------- golf became increasingly accessible, the game attained popularity with both ordinary people and professional players.

    (A) So
    (B) As
    (C) As if
    (D) That

9. ------- to a surgeon in 1811, sixteen–year–old John Keats soon met the writer Leigh Hunt and gave up surgery for poetry.

    (A) To be apprenticed
    (B) Apprenticed
    (C) He was apprenticed
    (D) Apprenticeship

10. Prehistoric men hunted the hairy mammoth with spears and axes, later ------- the animal's body to a variety of uses.

    (A) put
    (B) to be put
    (C) putting
    (D) their putting

Exercise 6–D

TOEFL iBT Reading.   Read the passages and choose the best answer to each question.

QUESTION 1

Which sentence below best expresses the essential information in the highlighted sentence in the passage?

> According to the principle of allocation, each animal has a limited amount of energy that can be used for obtaining food, escaping from predators, regulating body temperature, and other basic maintenance needs. Whenever energy is used for coping with environmental fluctuations, it is not available for other functions. Small birds such as wrens must use 99 percent of their energy just to stay warm and active. Because their maintenance costs are so high, wrens have little energy for allocating to other functions, such as growth and reproduction.

- (A) Wrens have so much energy that they are active 99 percent of the time.
- (B) It is difficult for wrens to stay warm because they need so much energy.
- (C) When wrens use energy for growth, they have none left over for reproduction.
- (D) Wrens use much energy for maintenance, so they have little for other purposes.

QUESTION 2

Look at the four squares, **A**, **B**, **C**, and **D**, which indicate where the following sentence could be added to the passage. Where would the sentence best fit?

> **The herding of cattle is a trait in many cultures, although different cultures view cattle differently.**

> While more than one culture may show a particular culture trait, each will consist of a different combination of traits. **A** The Masai of East Africa herd their cattle throughout the year, consuming blood and milk as the basis of their diet. **B** Since cattle are essential to survival, they occupy a central position in Masai culture. **C** In Europe, cattle are kept for their milk, though dairy products are consumed as part of a diet that is very different from that of the Masai. **D** In India, cattle plow fields and pull carts, and in most states they are protected from slaughter because they are considered sacred.

QUESTION 3

Look at the four squares, **A**, **B**, **C**, and **D**, which indicate where the following sentence could be added to the passage. Where would the sentence best fit?

After the flower has bloomed, the leaves gradually die back.

Even when it is dormant, a bulb holds the life of a whole plant. Because each bulb is a self–contained storehouse, the plant can survive for months in the ground without moisture. As the soil warms in the spring, the bulb draws on its food reserves to push up shoots, followed immediately by the flower stem. **A** By the time the flower reaches its peak, the bulb has exhausted its entire food store. **B** It then starts to split, forming two or more new bulbs at its base. **C** The plant gathers nutrients from the fading leaves so that the new bulbs have food. **D** Finally, the plant goes into its dormant state, where it remains until the cycle begins again.

QUESTIONS 4–7

1   Early in life Martha Graham learned that "movement never lies." When she was a little girl, her father warned her never to lie because he would always know it by the tensions in her body. Later, while studying dance as a young woman, Graham remembered her father's warning. She tried to tell the truth in her dances, even if the truth was unpleasant.

2   Inventing a new language of movement, Graham used the human body to express the passion and ecstasy of the human experience. Just as many modern dancers had before her, Graham invented her style as she went along. Her early technique was notorious for its nervous jerking and trembling. However, it was not irrational because it was aligned with a fundamental fact of life: breathing. Studying the bodily changes that occur during inhalation and exhalation, she developed the principles known as contraction and release. She experimented with the dynamics of the process, allowing contractions to take on a whip–like intensity. Whereas classical ballet attempted to conceal effort, Graham sought to reveal it because she believed that life required exertion. Graham's characteristic percussive style enabled her to express emotional extremes.

3   Always a vehicle for human passion, Graham's immense body of work prompted both praise and controversy. Although critics faulted her for obscurity or obscenity, Graham's audiences were enthralled. Perhaps her defining work was "Chronicle," a 1936 dance drama that portrayed the darkness and isolation of the Great Depression and the Spanish Civil War. Her later productions were so rich in terms of music and design that they left audiences spellbound.

4. What aspect of Martha Graham's work had roots in her childhood?

(A) An ability to amuse others
(B) An attempt to be truthful
(C) An interest in power and strength
(D) A focus on darkness and isolation

5. All of the following characterized Graham's work EXCEPT

(A) creation of a new system of movement
(B) a technique based on breathing
(C) an attempt to appear effortless
(D) expression of human emotions

6. The word enthralled in paragraph 3 is closest in meaning to

(A) frightened
(B) disgusted
(C) confused
(D) fascinated

7. Which sentence below best expresses the essential information in the highlighted sentence in paragraph 3?

(A) Graham's later dances amazed audiences because they were so elaborate.
(B) Audiences did not always appreciate Graham's later productions.
(C) Although Graham's later work was popular, it was expensive to produce.
(D) Graham's music and design appealed mostly to wealthy audiences.

Exercise 6–E

TOEFL iBT Listening. Listen to the recording. You may take notes as you listen. Do not look at the questions until the lecture has ended. When you hear the questions, look at the questions and choose the best answer to each.

 Audio Track 9

1. What is the main idea of the lecture?

(A) Some people are biased toward using their left brain more than the right.
(B) Positive and negative emotions are linked to different sides of the brain.
(C) Humans and animals have different ways of expressing emotions.
(D) A recent study reveals an interesting feature of dog body language.

2. What point does the professor make about the two sides of the brain?

(A) Both sides of the brain are important in learning and memory.
(B) Only humans show a difference between the two sides of the brain.
(C) The left brain probably evolved earlier than the right brain.
(D) Each side of the brain controls the opposite side of the body.

3. Why does the professor say this:

(A) To illustrate a difference between chimpanzees and humans
(B) To explain why humans think chimpanzees are amusing
(C) To give an example of left–right bias in an animal brain
(D) To describe an evolutionary change in chimpanzee behavior

4. What does the professor imply by this statement:

(A) A dog has negative feelings when it sees an unfriendly dog.
(B) Some dogs' tails wag to the left, while others wag to the right.
(C) Most dogs would rather fight another dog than run away.
(D) A dog's behavior is unpredictable when its owner is absent.

5. Indicate whether each behavior is associated with the left brain or the right brain.

For each sentence, check the correct box.

	Left Brain	Right Brain
A bird uses its left eye to watch for predators.		
A dog's tail wags to the right side of its rump.		
The muscles in a person's face express happiness.		
An animal runs away because it senses danger.		

Exercise 6–F

TOEFL iBT Speaking. In this integrated speaking task, you will read a short passage, listen to a lecture on the same topic, and then speak in response to a question about what you have read and heard. Do not look at the question until the lecture has ended. Do not look at the reading passage while you are speaking.

Reading Time – 45 seconds

SPATIAL INTELLIGENCE

Spatial intelligence, a highly developed understanding of space, is important when we are locating ourselves in various settings. Spatial intelligence probably emerged very early in human evolution, since survival depended on having a keen understanding of the landscape, such as being able to recall distances and angular relationships among landmarks. Spatial intelligence involves the ability to create mental imagery and to remember and use that imagery when needed. We use spatial abilities when working with graphic models of real–world scenes and with symbols such as maps, diagrams, or geometrical forms.

Now cover the passage and listen to the lecture. You may take notes, and you may use your notes to help you answer the question. After you hear the question, begin preparing your response. You may look at the question, but NOT at the passage. You have 30 seconds to prepare your response and 60 seconds to speak.

 *Audio Track 10*

> The professor talks about the movement of people through different spaces. Explain how these examples illustrate spatial intelligence.

 Stop

Preparation Time – 30 seconds
Response Time – 60 seconds

Exercise 6–G

TOEFL iBT Writing. In this integrated writing task, you will write a response to a question about a reading passage and a lecture. Your response will be scored on the quality of your writing and on how well you connect the points in the lecture with points in the reading. Typically, an effective response will have 150 to 225 words.

Reading Time – 3 minutes

> At the beginning of the twenty–first century, the family is more rootless and less stable than it was a century ago. In the past, children grew up in the same town as their grandparents, usually in their grandparents' house, along with several other relatives. Extended families were linked with other families, forming networks throughout the community. Today, people move from job to job, following career paths that take them from one single–family home to another. The mobility of families leaves them with no neighborly networks. As a result, families are more isolated from the larger community.
>
> Contemporary families have lost touch with extended family networks. Starting in the 1950s, "family values" have focused on the nuclear family: a husband, a wife, and their children. Married couples broke free of the extended family, becoming emotionally and economically self–sufficient. They established single–family homes in the suburbs, away from the influence of the elder generation.
>
> Today, the nuclear family is in trouble. Parent–child bonds have lapsed so much that parents have little control over their children. While divorce used to be uncommon, it is now a fact of life, and highly disruptive to families. Half of all children spend some of their childhood in a single–parent home because their parents have divorced. Single–parent homes are difficult for everyone. Often the parent is chronically tired from working "double shifts" at a job and at home. In such circumstances, it is difficult for parents to make decisions about children. When they must discipline children, there is no spouse to back them up. Conversely, children in single–parent homes have no one else to turn to when their one parent is too tired or too busy for them.

Now listen to the lecture. You may take notes, and you may use your notes to help you write your response. After you hear the question, you have 20 minutes to plan and write your response. You may look at the reading passage during the writing time.

 Audio Track 11

> Summarize the points made in the lecture, explaining how they contradict points made in the reading.

 Stop

Time – 20 minutes

Answers to Exercises 6–A through 6–G are on pages 258–259.

EXTENSION

1. **Sentence Analysis.** In reading done outside class, look for examples of sentences with adverb clauses and phrases. Bring five examples to share in class. Write some of the sentences on the board. With your teacher and classmates, answer the following questions about each sentence.

    a. How many clauses does the sentence have? Count both independent and subordinate clauses.
    b. Identify the adverb clauses. What subordinator marks the beginning of each adverb clause? What relationship between the adverb clause and the main clause does the subordinator express? Identify the subject and the verb of the adverb clause. Can the adverb clause be reduced to an adverb phrase?
    c. Identify the adverb phrases. What word marks the beginning of the adverb phrase? Is the adverb phrase in the active or passive voice?

2. **Sentence Writing.** Practice writing sentences with adverb clauses. Use the subordinators in the list below. Make sure that every clause in every sentence has a subject and a verb.

after	because	even though	when
although	before	since	while (time)
as if	by the time	so that	while (contrast)

QUIZ 2   UNITS 4 – 6

Time – 10 minutes

Choose the word or phrase that best completes the sentence.

1. Cardiac muscle is found only in the heart, where ------- that organ's thick walls.

   (A) it forms
   (B) forms
   (C) forming
   (D) formation of

2. ------- limits on the dollar amount of contributions taxpayers can deduct on their income tax return.

   (A) There
   (B) There may be
   (C) Maybe there
   (D) Why there may

3. The seeds of the peanut are eaten fresh or roasted, ------- is used for industrial purposes.

   (A) the oil
   (B) while the oil
   (C) the oil that
   (D) the oil, it

4. The first use of the principle of the airfoil was ------- but in water.

   (A) in air
   (B) neither air
   (C) either in air
   (D) not in air

5. Charcoal moves over paper easily, ------- good for making quick sketches.

   (A) it is
   (B) so it is
   (C) it also
   (D) so that

6. ------- a living plant, animal, or bacterial cell, they make use of the host cell's chemical energy.

   (A) Viruses enter
   (B) Viruses entering
   (C) Do viruses enter
   (D) When viruses enter

7. ------- in a high voice, Little Richard became a key figure in the birth of rock and roll.

   (A) Pounding the piano and singing
   (B) To be pounding the piano and singing
   (C) He pounded the piano and sang
   (D) The piano was pounded and he sang

8. ------- its nest in a tree cavity, but a mated pair may also perch in trees.

   (A) If the wood duck can build
   (B) Because the wood duck will build
   (C) How does the wood duck build
   (D) The wood duck builds

One of the underlined parts in each sentence is incorrect. Cross out the incorrect part and write the correction above it.

9. <u>When she</u> was a girl, novelist Lucy Maud Montgomery <u>found</u> comfort in <u>reading</u> and writing <u>as well in</u>

   the colorful landscape of Prince Edward Island.

10. After <u>determine</u> how much the money of one country <u>is worth</u> in another, banks <u>help</u> people from both

    places <u>exchange</u> money.

Answers to Quiz 2 are on page 260.
Record your score on page 301.

QUIZ 2

UNIT 7 ADJECTIVE CLAUSES

1. **Adjectives**
2. **Adjective Clauses**
3. **Subordinators**
4. **Necessary and Unnecessary Clauses**
5. **Adjective Phrases**
6. **Active and Passive Voice**
7. **Participial Adjectives**

 FOCUS

What does this sentence need?

> Some plants ------- add to their diet by feeding on insects.
>
> ◯ live in poor soil
> ◯ that live in poor soil
> ◯ are living in poor soil
> ◯ have lived in poor soil

The sentence needs a modifier between the subject *plants* and the verb *add*. Only the second answer, *that live in poor soil*, is a modifier. It is an **adjective clause**, a subordinate clause that functions as an adjective. In this case, the adjective clause modifies *plants*. The correctly formed sentence is:

Some plants **that live in poor soil** add to their diet by feeding on insects.

What does this sentence need?

> An element is a substance ------- only one kind of atom.
>
> ◯ contains
> ◯ it contains
> ◯ containing
> ◯ is containing

The sentence needs a modifier after the noun *substance*. Only the third answer, *containing*, will complete an **adjective phrase**, a group of words that functions as an adjective. The phrase *containing only one kind of atom* modifies *substance*. The correctly formed sentence is:

An element is a substance **containing** only one kind of atom.

 STUDY

1. Adjectives

An *adjective* is a word or structure that modifies a noun. An adjective limits, qualifies, specifies, or describes a noun. An adjective may be a single word or a group of words.

Structure	What It Is	Examples
Adjective	A word that modifies a noun	The <u>average</u> seagull feeds on a <u>wide</u> range of <u>prey</u> species. Dancers are usually <u>elegant</u>, <u>graceful</u>, and <u>strong</u>.
Adjective Clause	A subordinate clause that modifies a noun	A child <u>who rides a bicycle</u> will develop strong leg muscles. Estuaries, <u>where rivers meet the sea</u>, are home to an abundance of plants and animals.
Adjective Phrase	A group of words that modifies a noun	Winds <u>blowing in from the ocean</u> are warm and moist. The toga <u>worn by the Etruscan kings</u> was decorated with embroidered designs.
Participial Adjective	A verb participle that functions as an adjective	All of the large sports stores carry <u>climbing</u> gear. The main sources of typhoid fever are <u>contaminated</u> water, milk, and food.

Single–word adjectives usually come before the nouns they modify. When adjectives follow the verb *be*, they modify the subject of *be*. Adjective clauses and adjective phrases come after the noun they modify. Participial adjectives come before the noun they modify.

2. Adjective Clauses

An *adjective clause* is a subordinate clause that functions as an adjective. Adjective clauses are modifiers; they modify nouns. Like all subordinate clauses, adjective clauses must have a subject and a verb. Adjective clauses may also have objects.

> subordinator + subject + verb (+ rest of clause)

An adjective clause comes after the noun it modifies. In the following sentences, the modified nouns are shown in *italics*.

> A bird's primary habitat is the *one* <u>where</u> <u>most people</u> <u>observe</u> <u>it</u>.
>   sub.   S   V   O
>
> Robert Frost was a *poet* <u>whose</u> <u>work</u> <u>changed</u> <u>American poetry</u>.
>   sub.   S   V   O

Adjective clauses occur frequently in spoken and written English. A sentence can contain several adjective clauses. An adjective clause can contain other adjective clauses. In the following sentence, the modified nouns are shown in *italics*.

> The *musician* <u>who popularized bop</u> was *Dizzy Gillespie*, <u>whose performance elicited</u> a *delight* <u>that audiences had never known before</u>.

Adjective Clauses	<u>who popularized</u> bop S V
	whose <u>performance elicited</u> a delight S V
	that <u>audiences had never known</u> before S V
Main Clause	<u>The musician</u>… <u>was</u> Dizzy Gillespie S V

3. Subordinators

Adjective clauses begin with subordinators called *relative pronouns*. For this reason, adjective clauses are also called *relative clauses*. The relative pronouns below function as subordinators in adjective clauses.

that	which	who	whom	whose

Relative pronouns refer to a noun that has previously been mentioned. *That* can refer to nouns for people, animals, and things. *Which* refers only to animals and things. *Who* and *whom* refer only to people. *Whose*, the possessive form, can refer to people, animals, and things.

In the following sentences, the noun referent of the relative pronoun is shown in *italics*.

> Grass belongs to a group of *plants* <u>that have long, narrow leaves</u>.
>
> A climatologist is a *scientist* <u>who studies weather trends to determine patterns</u>.

Adjective clauses can also begin with a subordinating conjunction.

when	where	whereby

> Spring is the *season* <u>when snow melts and flowers bloom</u>.
>
> The dean explained the *process* <u>whereby scholarships would be rewarded</u>.

Relative pronouns come after their noun referent. However, sometimes other modifiers come between the noun and the relative pronoun introducing an adjective clause. In the following sentences, the noun referent is shown in *italics*.

> The minnow belongs to the *family* of fish <u>that includes carp and goldfish</u>.
>
> Mass *migrations* during the twentieth century, <u>which affected countless people</u>, were driven by political factors.

Within an adjective clause, the relative pronoun can serve various functions. The relative pronoun can be the subject of an adjective clause.

Subject of Adjective Clause	The general <u>who</u> <u>led</u> the Union Army to victory was Ulysses S. Grant.
	                 S V
	
	 The chimpanzee has a genetic make–up <u>that</u> closely <u>resembles</u> our own.
	                         S V

The relative pronoun can be the direct object of the verb in an adjective clause.

Direct Object in Adjective Clause	The cat is the animal <u>that most apartment dwellers choose</u> as their pet.
	            DO S V
	
	 Shakespeare is the playwright <u>whom many actors consider</u> the greatest.
	                 DO S V

Note: When *that* or *whom* is the direct object of the verb in an adjective clause, the relative pronoun can be omitted, with no change in meaning.

> The cat is the animal <u>most apartment dwellers choose as their pet</u>.
>
> Shakespeare is the playwright <u>many actors consider the greatest</u>.

The relative pronoun can be the object of a preposition. The preposition is part of the adjective clause.

Object of Preposition	Bermuda is an area of islands and coral rocks *to* <u>which tourists are attracted</u>.

In the above sentence, the verb *are attracted* needs the preposition *to*, so *to* must come before *which*.

> an area … *to* <u>which</u> thousands of tourists *are attracted*

However, in informal usage, the preposition *to* comes at the end of the sentence.

> Bermuda is an area of islands and coral rocks which tourists are attracted *to*.

The above sentence can be written in another way:

> Tourists *are attracted to* an area of islands and coral rocks, Bermuda.

The object forms *which* and *whom*, and the possessive *whose*, can follow a preposition. However, *who*, *that*, *when* and *where* never follow a preposition at the beginning of an adjective clause.

Incorrect	Correct
A child's best friend is the person <u>in who</u> she confides her most personal dreams.	A child's best friend is the person <u>in whom</u> she confides her most personal dreams.
Twenty–seven is the median age <u>at when</u> American men marry for the first time.	Twenty–seven is the median age <u>at which</u> American men marry for the first time. Twenty–seven is the median age <u>when</u> American men marry for the first time.

4. Necessary and Unnecessary Clauses

Some adjective clauses are essential to the identification of a noun and to the meaning of a sentence. *Necessary adjective clauses*, also called *restrictive clauses*, are necessary for identifying, limiting, or restricting the noun that they modify. Necessary adjective clauses do not have commas.

> People <u>who live in glass houses</u> should not throw stones.
>
> Conifers are trees <u>that produce seed–bearing cones</u>.

Some adjective clauses are not essential to the meaning of a sentence. *Unnecessary adjective clauses*, also called *nonrestrictive clauses*, give information that is not necessary for identifying or restricting the noun that they modify. Unnecessary clauses require commas to separate them from the rest of the sentence. Commas are a signal that the adjective clause provides extra, nonessential information about the noun.

> Eugene O'Neill, <u>who wrote over thirty plays</u>, won the Nobel Prize in 1936.
>
> The Cretaceous period, <u>which spanned 70 million years</u>, was a time of intense volcanic activity.

Unnecessary adjective clauses cannot begin with *that*.

Incorrect	Correct
The saxophone, <u>that</u> was created for the marching band, is now an important jazz instrument.	The saxophone, <u>which</u> was created for the marching band, is now an important jazz instrument.

5. Adjective Phrases

Some adjective clauses can be reduced to adjective phrases, with no change in meaning. An *adjective phrase* is a group of words that functions as an adjective.

An adjective clause can be reduced to an adjective phrase only when the relative pronoun *who*, *which*, or *that* is the subject of the adjective clause.

Adjective phrases take the present or past participle of a verb. For this reason, adjective phrases are also called *participial phrases*.

In reducing an adjective clause to an adjective phrase:

- The relative pronoun is omitted.
- Auxiliary verbs, if any, are omitted.
- The verb is changed to its present or past participle.

Adjective Clause	A pediatrician is a doctor <u>who specializes</u> in the care of children.
Adjective Phrase	A pediatrician is a doctor <u>specializing</u> in the care of children.
Adjective Clause	The results of the study, <u>which were released last year</u>, surprised nearly everyone.
Adjective Phrase	The results of the study, <u>released last year</u>, surprised nearly everyone.
Adjective Clause	Lava <u>that is thrown</u> from a volcano travels great distances.
Adjective Phrase	Lava <u>thrown</u> from a volcano travels great distances.

If the adjective clause is unnecessary, and therefore needs commas, the adjective phrase derived from it is also unnecessary and needs commas.

Crater Lake, <u>which was formed by a volcano</u>, is a superb setting for day hikes.
Crater Lake, <u>formed by a volcano</u>, is a superb setting for day hikes.

Adjective clauses with *which* or *who* and a form of *be* as the verb can be reduced to appositives. An *appositive* is a noun structure placed near another noun and separated from it by commas. (See pages 10–11.) In forming an appositive, the relative pronoun and verb are omitted.

Adjective Clause	One application of the laser is holography, <u>*which is* the production of three–dimensional images</u>.
Appositive	One application of the laser is holography, <u>the production of three–dimensional images</u>.
Adjective Clause	Currier and Ives, <u>*who were* American lithographers</u>, produced popular hand–colored prints.
Appositive	Currier and Ives, <u>American lithographers</u>, produced popular hand–colored prints.

6. Active and Passive Voice

Adjective phrases can be in active voice or passive voice. *Active–voice* adjective phrases take the *-ing* form (present participle) of the verb.

Adjective Clause	Animals <u>that live</u> in alpine zones have thick coats.
Adjective Phrase	Animals <u>living</u> in alpine zones have thick coats.

Passive–voice adjective phrases take the *-ed* form (past participle) of the verb.

Adjective Clause	Yellowstone, <u>which was authorized by Congress in 1872</u>, is the oldest national park.
Adjective Phrase	Yellowstone, <u>authorized by Congress in 1872</u>, is the oldest national park.

7. Participial Adjectives

Participial adjectives are adjectives formed from the present or past participle of a verb. Participial adjectives are extreme reductions of adjective clauses.

Adjective Clause	Toes <u>that are frozen by sub–zero temperatures</u> must sometimes be amputated.
Adjective Phrase	Toes <u>frozen by sub–zero temperatures</u> must sometimes be amputated.
Participial Adjective	<u>Frozen</u> toes must sometimes be amputated.

Participial adjectives usually come before the nouns they modify.

<u>Freezing</u> <u>temperatures</u> cause a lot of damage to fingers and toes.
  Adj   N

When a participial adjective comes after *be* or *become*, it usually modifies the subject of the verb.

<u>China</u> is ideally <u>suited</u> for growing tea.
  S   Adj

Note: Participial adjectives can be modified by adverbs. In the above sentence, the adverb *ideally* modifies the participial adjective *suited*.

Active participial adjectives describe the doer or cause of an action. Active participial adjectives come from active–voice verbs. They take the *-ing* form (present participle) of the verb.

A <u>magnifying</u> glass makes objects appear larger than they really are.
Human behavior is an <u>interesting</u> topic to psychologists.

In the first sentence above, *a glass* performs the action; a glass *magnifies* objects. In the second sentence, the *topic* of human behavior *interests* psychologists.

Passive participial adjectives describe the receiver or result of an action. Passive participial adjectives come from passive–voice verbs. They take the *-ed* form (past participle) of the verb.

> The history professor gave his students a list of six <u>required</u> books.
>
> <u>Dried</u> fruit weighs much less than an equivalent volume of <u>canned</u> fruit.

In the first sentence above, *books* receives the action; books are *required* by the professor. In the second sentence, *fruit* receives the action; fruit is *dried* and fruit is *canned* by someone.

Irregular verbs have irregular past participles, so the participial adjectives derived from them are also irregular.

bent	forbidden	kept	spoken
broken	forgotten	known	stolen
chosen	frozen	lost	worn
fallen	hidden	mistaken	written

> After the storm, there were many <u>broken</u> windows and <u>fallen</u> branches.
>
> *Romeo and Juliet* is Shakespeare's <u>best–known</u> play.
>
> Idioms are used frequently in both <u>spoken</u> and <u>written</u> English.

 PRACTICE

Exercise 7–A

Adjective Clauses.   Underline all adjective clauses and circle the nouns that they modify.

1. Samuel Barber, who wrote the popular *Adagio for Strings*, won two Pulitzer Prizes.

2. In 1924 Congress passed the Johnson–Reed Act, which severely restricted immigration.

3. An organization of producers whose purpose is to restrict competition is called a cartel.

4. First–time homebuyers are the group toward which many lending institutions direct their message.

5. For today's astronomers, constellations are simply areas of the sky in which there are interesting

   objects that await our observation.

6. Microscopes, which upgrade the lenses in our eyes, reveal the extraordinary amount of fine detail

   that actually is present in light rays.

7. There are many social situations where people who give information are higher in status than those who need information.

8. Biologists who study the South Pacific have made the important discovery that huge snails, which are aided by bacteria in their gills, feed off the metal–rich compounds that surround hydrothermal vents.

Exercise 7–B

Adjective Phrases. Underline the subject and verb in each adjective clause. Reduce the clause to an adjective phrase, writing the adjective phrase above the clause.

1. Astronauts who live in space for long periods must adjust to weightlessness.

2. A cut diamond is designed to reflect most of the light that falls on its front.

3. Bobsleds, which are driven by two– or four–person crews, have a metal brake with several teeth.

4. The technology that impacts us most is what we use in our homes.

5. A movable device that is attached to a guitar neck, the capo is used to raise the pitch of the strings.

6. A proton is one of two kinds of particles that make up the nucleus of an atom.

7. Gravity dams, which are usually made of concrete, use their weight to provide resistance to the

pressure of water.

8. Homeostasis, which means "steady state," is the process that enables the body to maintain balance.

Exercise 7–C

Sentence Completion. Choose the word or phrase that best completes the sentence.

1. Chinooks are warm winds ------- off the
   mountains and across the plains in winter.

   (A) that come
   (B) come from
   (C) they come
   (D) are coming

2. When we breathe, oxygen is passed to special
   molecules in the blood, ------- it to the muscles.

   (A) is carried
   (B) carried
   (C) which carry
   (D) will carry

3. Hammurabi, ------- his capital at Babylon,
   issued a code of laws for the management of
   his large empire.

   (A) whose
   (B) had
   (C) he had
   (D) who had

4. Genes are the biological instructions -------
   in every cell.

   (A) are found
   (B) found
   (C) find
   (D) finding

5. A lot of unemployment is the simple turnover
   of people either ------- for the first time or
   reentering it.

   (A) enter the labor force
   (B) entered the labor force
   (C) are entering the labor force
   (D) entering the labor force

6. Tarragon has long been cultivated for its leaves,
   ------- for flavoring vinegar, sauces, and soups.

   (A) that are used
   (B) been used
   (C) which are used
   (D) they are used

7. The principles of Dada, ------- to New York by
   Max Ernst and Marcel Duchamp, eventually
   became the basis of Surrealism.

   (A) carried
   (B) were carried
   (C) they were carried
   (D) carried them

8. The fat–soluble vitamins are stored in body
   fat and may therefore accumulate in quantities
   -------.

   (A) can be toxic
   (B) they can be toxic
   (C) can they be toxic
   (D) that can be toxic

9. A patient's health history is a collection of
   ------- from the patient and other sources.

   (A) information is obtained
   (B) information obtained
   (C) obtain the information
   (D) obtained the information

10. Maurice Ravel based some of his finest works
    on the Oriental scales ------- he was introduced
    at the Paris Exhibition of 1889.

    (A) that
    (B) which
    (C) to which
    (D) and which

UNIT 7

Exercise 7–D

Sentence Editing.   One of the underlined parts in each sentence is incorrect. Cross out the incorrect part and write the correction above it.

1. The Gulf Stream, <u>what</u> is located just off the Atlantic Coast, <u>brings</u> a temperate <u>climate</u> to the coastlines <u>it passes</u>.

2. Tourists <u>traveled</u> abroad should carry a debit card <u>as well as</u> a credit card because automatic teller machines <u>are</u> available in airports and <u>other</u> locations.

3. *Hosta* is the name <u>given</u> to a genus of <u>flowering</u> plants, all of <u>whose</u> thrive in the <u>shade</u>.

4. The vacuum coffee maker is a <u>complicated</u> device in <u>where</u> steam is <u>generated</u> in a glass bowl <u>connected</u> to a container of coffee grounds and hot water.

5. <u>Although</u> he is not the scientist <u>who</u> invents the new process, the innovator is the one <u>which</u> successfully <u>introduces</u> it to the public.

6. Lipids, one of the <u>principal</u> components of <u>living</u> cells, have a <u>specialize</u> role as the main <u>structural</u> component of membranes.

7. The Tarascans, <u>they</u> were traditionally <u>known</u> for their hummingbird–feather mosaics, are still noted for their <u>lacquered</u> bowls and <u>woven</u> cloth.

8. Sam Cooke's <u>appealing</u> image and clear vocals, <u>that</u> were widely imitated, <u>influenced</u> the style of singing <u>that</u> dominated the next two decades.

9. One of the best <u>known</u> and lavishly <u>praising</u> architectural projects of the twentieth century was Habitat, the experimental <u>housing</u> complex <u>created</u> for Montreal's Expo 67.

10. The belief <u>who</u> a man in his early twenties <u>ought</u> to have a firm occupational choice reflects the <u>prevailing</u> view <u>that</u> development is complete by the end of adolescence.

Exercise 7–E

TOEFL iBT Reading. Read the passages and choose the best answer to each question.

QUESTIONS 1–2

The first Europeans to visit southwestern Colorado were the Spanish, who sought gold, animal skins, and other riches. Under orders from the Spanish governor in Santa Fe, Juan Maria Antonio Rivera led a prospecting and trading party into the region in 1765. Rivera found little of commercial value that would interest his superiors, but he did open up a route that soon led to the establishment of the Old Spanish Trail. This expedition and others that followed left an abundance of Spanish place names, which are the only evidence we have today that the Spanish once explored the region.

1. It can be inferred that Rivera's expedition

   (A) did not find gold and other riches
   (B) was part of a military invasion
   (C) did not have any effect on the region
   (D) used a route through the mountains

2. Which of the following remains as a sign of the Spanish exploration of southwestern Colorado?

   (A) Trade with the native people
   (B) The development of agriculture
   (C) Spanish names for places
   (D) A new form of government

QUESTIONS 3–6

1   Permafrost occurs in areas where the mean annual temperature is at or below minus nine degrees Celsius. In Canada, where over fifty percent of the land area is permanently frozen, the depth of the permafrost ranges from two meters at the southern edge to as many as 300 meters in the far north. Almost all of the soil moisture occurs in the form of ground ice, which creates a challenge for the plants and animals that must survive in the North.

2   Temperature changes take a long time to penetrate the ground, and deep layers that froze during the last Ice Age remain insulated from current surface conditions. A thin surface layer may thaw if air temperatures rise above freezing in the summer. However, a brief thaw promotes the growth of sparse vegetation, which acts as an insulating layer for the lower levels, keeping them frozen.

3. The term permafrost in paragraph 1 is used to describe

   (A) a very cold temperature range
   (B) ground that remains frozen
   (C) water that is deep underground
   (D) organic matter in the soil

4. It can be inferred from the passage that a large area of Canada has

   (A) an annual temperature at or below minus nine degrees
   (B) no large animals and very few species of plants
   (C) land that is rich in oil and mineral resources
   (D) soil that will remain frozen during global warming

5. According to the passage, what challenge faces plants and animals in the North?

   (A) No species can survive the cold winter.
   (B) Soil moisture takes the form of ice.
   (C) Human activities have destroyed habitat.
   (D) The growing season is very short.

6. Why do the deep layers of ground remain frozen even when temperatures rise above freezing?

   (A) Small variations in temperature do not affect surface conditions.
   (B) Climate change in the North is contributing to a new Ice Age.
   (C) The ground thaws only when the temperature rises and falls rapidly.
   (D) Vegetation insulates the deep layers from surface temperatures.

Exercise 7–F

TOEFL iBT Listening. Listen to the recording. You may take notes as you listen. Do not look at the questions until the discussion has ended. When you hear the questions, look at the questions and choose the best answer to each.

 Audio Track 12

1. What is the discussion mainly about?

   (A) The schedule of an average business day
   (B) Factors that make meetings successful
   (C) Different ways to develop policy
   (D) People who participate in meetings

2. What point does the professor make about the person who calls a meeting?

   (A) That person should bring coffee and snacks.
   (B) That person is usually the meeting leader's supervisor.
   (C) That person knows the outcome of the meeting in advance.
   (D) That person is responsible for the meeting's success.

3. According to the discussion, what are some factors that should be considered in planning a meeting?

   Choose two answers.

   A The number of participants
   B The leader's experience
   C The equipment needed
   D The permission required

4. What does the professor mean by this statement:

   (A) It is appropriate for the leader to have help in planning a meeting.
   (B) The leader may not really mean everything that he or she says.
   (C) A successful meeting usually has more than one leader.
   (D) Everything that happens in a meeting is the leader's responsibility.

5. Why does the professor say this:

   (A) To stress the importance of dealing with problems right away
   (B) To introduce the sequence of events in a typical meeting
   (C) To state the reasons that some meetings are unsuccessful
   (D) To identify the problems in a specific company's policy

6. The class talks about what usually happens during a business meeting. Put the events in the order in which they occur.

   Put the letter of each answer in the correct space.

   (A) Participants state relevant facts and opinions.
   (B) The group plans how to put the solution into action.
   (C) A decision is made about the best solution.
   (D) The leader calls attention to a current problem.

1	
2	
3	
4	

Exercise 7–G

TOEFL iBT Speaking. In this integrated speaking task, you will listen to part of a lecture. You will then be asked to summarize important information from the lecture.

Cover the question while the lecture is playing. You may take notes, and you may use your notes to help you answer the question. After you hear the question, you may look at the question and prepare your response. You have 20 seconds to prepare your response and 60 seconds to speak.

 Audio Track 13

Using points and examples from the talk, describe qualitative research, explaining some of the methods that researchers use.

 Stop

Preparation Time – 20 seconds
Response Time – 60 seconds

Exercise 7–H

TOEFL iBT Writing. For this independent writing task, respond to the question by writing an essay in which you state and support your opinion on the topic. Your essay will be scored on the quality of your writing, including how well you organize and develop your ideas and how well you use language to express your ideas. An effective essay will have a minimum of 300 words.

Read the following question and make any notes that will help you plan your response. Then begin writing. You have 30 minutes to plan and write your essay.

Do you agree or disagree with the following statement?

The people that we love are the ones who can hurt us the most.

Use specific reasons and examples to support your answer.

Time – 30 minutes

Answers to Exercises 7–A through 7–G are on pages 260–261.

Answers to Exercise 7–H will vary.

 EXTENSION

1. **Sentence Analysis.** In reading done outside class, look for examples of sentences with adjective clauses and phrases. Bring five examples to share in class. Write some of the sentences on the board. With your teacher and classmates, answer the following questions about each sentence.

    a. How many clauses does the sentence have? Count both independent and subordinate clauses.

    b. Identify the adjective clauses. What relative pronoun marks the beginning of each adjective clause? What noun does the adjective clause modify? Identify the subject and the verb of the adjective clause.

    c. Identify the adjective phrases. What word marks the beginning of each adjective phrase? What noun does the adjective phrase modify? Is the adjective phrase in the active or passive voice?

2. **Participial Adjectives.** In reading done outside class, look for examples of sentences with participial adjectives. Bring examples to share in class, and write some on the board. Are the participial adjectives active or passive? What nouns do they modify?

3. **Sentence Writing.** Practice writing sentences with adjective clauses. Use the subordinators in the list below. Make sure that every clause in every sentence has a subject and a verb. In some sentences, the subordinator may be the subject of the adjective clause.

that	where	in which	whom
when	which	who	whose

UNIT 8 NOUN CLAUSES

> 1. **Noun Clauses**
> 2. **Subordinators**
> 3. **Noun Clauses as Subjects**
> 4. **Noun Clauses as Objects**
> 5. **Reduction of Noun Clauses**

 FOCUS

What does this sentence need?

------- has interested both artists and scientists throughout history.

- ◯ Why we dream
- ◯ Often we dream
- ◯ Do we dream
- ◯ We can dream

The sentence needs a subject. A subject must be a noun structure. The first answer, *Why we dream*, is a noun structure. It is a **noun clause**, a type of subordinate clause that functions as a noun. The other choices are not noun structures. The correctly formed sentence is:

Why we dream has interested both artists and scientists throughout history.

What does this sentence need?

Effective journalists can predict ------- to a story.

- ◯ will their readers respond
- ◯ their readers how to respond
- ◯ how their readers will respond
- ◯ of their readers' response

The verb *can predict* needs a direct object. A direct object must be a noun structure. The third answer, *how their readers will respond*, is a noun clause. The other choices are not noun structures. The correctly formed sentence is:

Effective journalists can predict **how their readers will respond** to a story.

STUDY

1. Noun Clauses

A **noun clause** is a type of subordinate clause. Like all subordinate clauses, noun clauses must have a subject and a verb. Noun clauses may also have objects or modifiers.

subordinator + subject + verb (+ rest of clause)

<u>What</u> <u>one person</u> <u>considers</u> <u>a wildflower</u> may be a weed to another.
sub.　　S　　　　V　　　　O

Psychiatrists have concluded <u>that</u> <u>stress</u> <u>impacts</u> <u>health</u> <u>negatively</u>.
　　　　　　　　　　　　　sub.　S　　V　　　O　　modifier

A noun clause functions as a noun. Like all noun structures, noun clauses serve as subjects and objects.

Function	What It Does	Examples
Subject	Performs the action of a verb	<u>How life began</u> has been debated for many centuries.
Subject Complement	Identifies or defines the subject and usually follows a form of the verb *be*	A little mass gives a lot of energy, and this is <u>why nuclear power is so abundant</u>.
Direct Object	Receives the action of a verb	In 1978 scientists discovered <u>that the planet Pluto has a satellite</u>.
Object of a Preposition	Follows and is controlled by a preposition	Microeconomics is concerned with <u>how some prices rise while others fall</u>.

2. Subordinators

Noun clauses generally begin with a **subordinating conjunction**, or **subordinator**. The words and phrases below function as subordinators in noun clauses.

how	if	where	who
how long	that	wherever	whoever
how many	what	whether	whom
how much	whatever	whether or not	whomever
how often	when	which	whose
how soon	whenever	whichever	why

UNIT 8

A subordinator signals the start of a noun clause. The usual pattern is subordinator + noun + verb.

> You may bring <u>whomever</u> <u>you</u> <u>like</u> to the class picnic.
>   sub.   S   V

Sometimes the subordinator itself is the subject of the noun clause. In the following sentences, the subordinator, shown in *italics*, is the subject of the noun clause.

> *What* <u>goes up</u> must come down.
>
> Mr. Brooks did not know *who* <u>left the mysterious message</u>.
>
> *Whoever* <u>bothers to read junk mail</u> is probably wasting a lot of time.

3. Noun Clauses as Subjects

Noun clauses can function as the subject of another clause. When a noun clause is the subject of another clause, a verb must follow the noun clause.

The examples below have two clauses: a noun clause and a main clause. The noun clause is the subject of the main clause. Both clauses have a subject and a verb.

> That humans cause global warming is generally accepted among scientists.

Noun Clause	That <u>humans</u> <u>cause</u> global warming
	S V

Main Clause	<u>That humans cause global warming</u> <u>is</u> generally accepted among scientists.
	S V

> How long patients have to wait influences their decision to seek medical care.

Noun Clause	How long <u>patients</u> <u>have to wait</u>
	S V

Main Clause	<u>How long patients have to wait</u> <u>influences</u> their decision to seek medical care.
	S V

Tip: In your own writing, check that all clauses—both main clauses and subordinate clauses—have a subject and a verb.

In sentences with *it* as the "false" subject, the true subject is sometimes a noun clause.

> It has been shown <u>that secondhand smoke can cause serious health problems</u>.
>
> It is not clear <u>whether climate change will have an impact on mental health</u>.

Tip: You can rewrite each sentence without the false subject.

> That secondhand smoke can cause serious health problems has been shown.
>
> Whether climate change will have an impact on mental health is not clear.

4. Noun Clauses as Objects

Noun clauses can function as the direct object of a verb. When a noun clause is the direct object, the main clause must have a subject and a verb.

The examples below have two clauses: a noun clause and a main clause. The noun clause is the direct object of the verb in the main clause. Both clauses have a subject and a verb.

> I don't know if I can finish this book before Friday.

Noun Clause   if I can finish this book before Friday
                         S   V

Main Clause   I don't know if I can finish this book before Friday.
                     S   V   O

> Children usually imitate whatever their parents do.

Noun Clause   whatever their parents do
                              S   V

Main Clause   Children usually imitate whatever their parents do.
                        S   V   O

When a noun clause beginning with *that* is the direct object of a verb, *that* can be omitted, with no change in meaning. Both of the following sentences are correct.

> Most astronomers believe *that* some form of life must exist on other planets.
>
> Most astronomers believe some form of life must exist on other planets.

5. Reduction of Noun Clauses

Sometimes a noun clause can be reduced to an infinitive phrase. An *infinitive phrase* takes the following form:

> subordinator + *to* + base-form verb (infinitive)

Infinitive Phrases   how to dance   when to stop
                            how many to buy   whether or not to go

In reducing a noun clause to an infinitive phrase:

  ✐ The subject is omitted.

  ✐ The verb is changed to the infinitive.

Because the subject is omitted, a noun clause can be reduced to an infinitive phrase only when the identity of the subject is obvious.

Noun Clause	How members of a society should behave is often codified in a society's laws.
Infinitive Phrase	How to behave is often codified in a society's laws.
Noun Clause	In children's games, the leader tells the others what they must do.
Infinitive Phrase	In children's games, the leader tells the others what to do.

 PRACTICE

Exercise 8–A

Noun Clauses. Underline the noun clause in each sentence. Name the function of the noun clause, using the abbreviations below.

S	subject	DO	direct object
SC	subject complement	OP	object of a preposition

1. _____ Soil tests determine what nutrients are present in the soil.

2. _____ Whoever arrives early will have the best choice of seating.

3. _____ Please let me know how many people will be coming to your party.

4. _____ Scholars disagree over who really wrote some of Shakespeare's sonnets.

5. _____ The biggest question about the American eel is why its numbers are decreasing.

6. _____ The Counseling Center will tell students where they can find resources in the community.

7. _____ The new laboratory procedure differs from what our instructor required us to do last semester.

8. _____ That standardized tests discriminate against certain types of students has been argued since the 1970s.

Exercise 8–B

Infinitive Phrases. Underline the subordinator, subject, and verb in each noun clause. Reduce the underlined part to an infinitive phrase. Write the infinitive phrase above the noun clause.

1. Professor Park advised me on where I might look for information.

2. The directions failed to mention how much ointment should be applied.

3. Do you have any suggestions for what I should read next?

4. Many people are unable to express any opinion about what they would change in their lives.

5. Perhaps our most important challenge is how we will control the effects of global warming.

6. Unemployed workers often have a strong sense of whom they ought to blame for their economic hardship.

Exercise 8–C

Sentence Completion. Choose the word or phrase that best completes the sentence.

1. ------- has always fascinated biologists.

    (A) Fish are swimming
    (B) The fish can swim
    (C) How fish swim
    (D) Could fish swim

2. A good college history textbook includes ------- about history.

    (A) every student to know
    (B) should every student know
    (C) in which every student knows
    (D) what every student should know

3. When changing lanes, a driver should use the turn signal to let other drivers know -------.

    (A) which lane he is entering
    (B) he is entering which lane
    (C) which is the lane entering
    (D) is entering which lane

4. How vines climb, -------, and what special needs they have all make a big difference when deciding where to put vines.

    (A) they can be planted
    (B) when they plant
    (C) can they be planted
    (D) when they can be planted

5. There are a number of organizations and books that can help you learn more about ------- indoor air quality.

    (A) to improve
    (B) how to improve
    (C) improve the
    (D) how improve

6. Before paper was invented, people wrote on ------- could obtain: silk, palm leaves, or clay tablets.

   (A) what
   (B) whatever
   (C) whatever they
   (D) they

7. It is thought ------- of seasonal variation is the change in the wind patterns of the Northern and Southern Hemispheres.

   (A) what the principal cause
   (B) of the principal cause
   (C) that the principal cause
   (D) the principal cause is

8. The architects of the grand Palace at Fontainebleau did not know ------- with the building's exterior.

   (A) what doing
   (B) to do what
   (C) they did what
   (D) what to do

9. ------- Abraham Lincoln was the greatest American president was the unanimous vote of a group of prominent historians.

   (A) He was
   (B) As
   (C) That
   (D) Because

10. Sharks were once thought to be instinctive killing machines, but it is now believed -------.

    (A) they learn to hunt by experience
    (B) learn to hunt by experience
    (C) learning to hunt by experience
    (D) that learning to hunt by experience

Exercise 8–D

TOEFL iBT Reading. Read the passage and choose the best answer to each question.

QUESTIONS 1–4

1   The field of economics studies the basic problems that every economy must face: what goods will be produced and for whom they will be produced. The underlying assumptions of the field are that resources are scarce, or at least limited, and that not all human needs and desires can be met. How to allocate limited resources in the fairest and most efficient way is a principal concern of economists.

2   Two major branches of economics are macroeconomics and microeconomics. Macroeconomics is concerned with how a national or regional economy behaves as a whole. It analyzes aggregate data in such areas as the gross national product, general price levels, and total employment. Macroeconomists examine how national income, output, consumption, inflation, and investment influence each other, and try to determine why any imbalance among them occurs. They develop models to explain the interplay of forces and to make economic forecasts. Governments use macroeconomic models to guide the creation and evaluation of economic policy. Large corporations use macroeconomic models in developing their business strategy.

3   Microeconomics is mainly focused on economic activity in the individual case, whether it is a single firm, commodity, or group of consumers. It studies how individuals, households, and companies make decisions to allocate limited resources. It is especially interested in what determines the price levels of goods and services in specific markets. Moreover, it analyzes market failure by examining where and why markets fail to produce efficient results.

1. The passage states that economics is primarily concerned with

  (A) why people like to have new things
  (B) who should make decisions about money
  (C) how a society allocates scarce resources
  (D) why some goods are more expensive than others

2. Macroeconomics deals with all of the following EXCEPT

  (A) what determines the price levels of particular goods
  (B) the performance of an economy as a whole
  (C) how output, consumption, and investment are related
  (D) why imbalances occur among various economic forces

3. Microeconomics differs from macroeconomics in its emphasis on

  (A) the relationship between government and business
  (B) how individual behavior affects specific markets
  (C) the structure and behavior of the global economy
  (D) which sectors of the national economy will grow

4. It can be inferred from the passage that the field of economics

  (A) has developed models that can be used in other fields
  (B) considers nations to be more important than individuals
  (C) looks at patterns in production and consumption
  (D) assumes that all human behavior can be explained

Exercise 8–E

TOEFL iBT Speaking. In this integrated speaking task, you will listen to a conversation. You will then be asked to talk about the information in the conversation and to give your opinion about the ideas presented.

Cover the question while the conversation is playing. You may take notes, and you may use your notes to help you answer the question. After you hear the question, you may look at the question and prepare your response. You have 20 seconds to prepare your response and 60 seconds to speak.

 *Audio Track 14*

> The students discuss a problem that the man has. Briefly summarize the problem. Then state what you think the man should do, and explain why.

 Stop

Preparation Time – 20 seconds
Response Time – 60 seconds

Answers to Exercise 8–A through 8–E are on pages 261–262.

 **EXTENSION**

1. **Sentence Analysis.** Outside class, look in a newspaper, magazine, or book for examples of sentences with noun structures. Bring five examples to share in class. Write some of the sentences on the board. With your teacher and classmates, answer the following questions about each sentence.

   a. How many clauses does the sentence have? Count both independent and subordinate clauses.
   b. Does the sentence contain any noun clauses? If so, what subordinator introduces the noun clause?
   c. Can any of the noun structures be changed to a noun clause?
   d. Can any of the noun clauses be reduced to an infinitive phrase?

2. **Sentence Writing.** Practice writing sentences with noun clauses as subjects and objects. Use the subordinators in the list below. Make sure that every clause in every sentence has a subject and a verb.

how	how soon	what	where	who
how often	that	when	whether	why

UNIT 9 CONDITIONAL SENTENCES

1. **Conditions**
2. **Subordinators**
3. **Present and Future Real**
4. **Past Real**
5. **Present and Future Unreal**
6. **Past Unreal**
7. **Passive Voice**
8. **Wishes**

 FOCUS

What does this sentence need?

> If the goal of education is societal development, then schools ------- learning communities.
>
> ○ be
> ○ were
> ○ should be
> ○ should have been

The first clause states a condition: *If the goal of education is societal development....* The second clause (main clause) states a result of the condition, and it needs a verb. Only the third answer, *should be*, is a correctly formed verb for expressing the result of a present condition. The correctly formed sentence is:

> If the goal of education is societal development, then schools **should be** learning communities.

What does this sentence need?

> The bubonic plague might not ------- so many people in the fourteenth century if the germ theory of disease had been known.
>
> ○ kill
> ○ be killing
> ○ killed
> ○ have killed

The main clause needs a verb. The second clause, *if the germ theory of disease had been known*, states a condition that did not happen in the past. The germ theory of disease was *not* known in the fourteenth century. Only the fourth answer, *have killed*, is a verb in the correct tense for expressing the unreal result of an unreal past condition. The correctly formed sentence is:

> The bubonic plague might not **have killed** so many people in the fourteenth century if the germ theory of disease had been known.

UNIT 9

 STUDY

1. Conditions

A *condition* is a situation or set of circumstances. A *conditional sentence* expresses a condition that leads to, or does not lead to, a specific result. Conditional sentences are used for expressing:

        scientific facts

        general truths

        predictions

        advice

        mistakes and regrets

        wishes and dreams

A conditional sentence is a *complex sentence* with a subordinate clause and an independent clause. The subordinate clause is an adverb clause that expresses a condition. The independent clause expresses a result and is the main clause of the sentence.

Like all subordinate clauses, the condition clause must have a subordinator, a subject, and a verb.

> subordinator + subject + verb (+ rest of clause)

> If <u>water</u> <u>flows</u> over loose rock, it will eventually transport most of the rock.
> sub. S   V

Condition (Subordinate Clause)	If water flows over loose rock
Result (Main Clause)	it will eventually transport most of the rock

Because the condition clause is a subordinate clause, it cannot stand alone as a sentence. It must be connected to a result clause to form a complete sentence.

The order of the condition clause and the result clause can be reversed, with no change in meaning. When the condition clause comes first, a comma comes after it. When the result clause comes first, a comma is optional.

> <u>If a submarine's ballast tanks are flooded with water</u>, its weight increases.
>
> The weight of a submarine increases <u>if its ballast tanks are flooded with water</u>.

Different types of conditional sentences express differences in time (present, future, past) and differences in degree of reality or truth. The various types of conditional sentences use a different combination of verb tenses and modals.

2. Subordinators

In conditional sentences, the condition clause begins with a **subordinator**, a word or phrase that connects the condition clause to the result clause. The most common subordinator is *if*. Thus, the condition clause is sometimes called the *if*–clause. However, other subordinators can also introduce conditions.

as long as	if	only if	unless
even if	in case	provided (that)	whether or not

> <u>As long as</u> the planet keeps spinning, the sun will rise in the east.
>
> Professor Wood does not accept late papers, <u>even if</u> you have a good excuse.
>
> <u>In case</u> students need enrollment advice, counselors will be available.
>
> Banks make a profit <u>provided that</u> they collect more interest than they pay out.
>
> Music will always be a part of my life, <u>whether or not</u> I go to music school.

The subordinator *unless* has a negative meaning. *Unless* + an affirmative verb has the same meaning as *if* + a negative verb. In the two sentences below, the condition clauses have the same meaning, and the result is also the same.

> *Unless* the eggs <u>are kept</u> warm, the young alligators will die.
>
> *If* the eggs <u>are not kept</u> warm, the young alligators will die.

When a condition clause with the subordinator *only if* comes first, the subject and verb in the result clause are inverted, as in question word order. When the result clause comes first, the subject and verb have normal word order.

> *Only if* you submit it by the deadline <u>will your application be considered</u>.
>
> <u>Your application will be considered</u> *only if* you submit it by the deadline.

3. Present and Future Real

A situation is **real** if it is certain, probable or possible. **Present real** conditional sentences express scientific facts and general truths.

	Condition Clause	Result Clause
If +	simple present present progressive present perfect present perfect progressive	simple present

> If the volume of an object <u>expands</u>, the buoyancy of the object <u>increases</u>.
>
> If something <u>is vibrating</u> faster than twenty times a second, it <u>is</u> audible to us.
>
> If students <u>have eaten</u> breakfast, they <u>are</u> more attentive in class.
>
> If it <u>has been raining</u> for several days, the soil <u>becomes</u> saturated.

In present real conditional sentences, *if* can sometimes be changed to *when* with little change in meaning.

> Today, *if* Canadians <u>are traveling</u> cross–country, they usually <u>choose</u> to fly.
>
> Today, *when* Canadians <u>are traveling</u> cross–country, they usually <u>choose</u> to fly.

Future real conditional sentences express situations that will certainly, probably or possibly happen. The future real is used to state scientific facts and general truths. It is also used to make predictions and to give advice.

	Condition Clause	Result Clause	
If +	simple present present progressive present perfect present perfect progressive	*will* *can* *may* *might* *must* *should* *have to*	+ base–form verb

> If we <u>hurry</u>, we <u>might catch</u> the bus.
>
> If you <u>are studying</u> a foreign language, you <u>have to learn</u> vocabulary and grammar.
>
> If the usual treatment <u>has had</u> no effect, the patient <u>may need</u> to consult an allergist.
>
> If a project <u>has been making</u> money, the investors <u>should receive</u> some of the profits.

4. Past Real

Past real conditional sentences express general truths or regular occurrences in the past.

	Condition Clause	Result Clause	
If +	simple past past progressive past perfect past perfect progressive	simple past *would* *could* *might* *had to*	+ base–form verb

> In the twelfth century, if you <u>owned</u> land, you <u>were</u> a wealthy person.
>
> If Canadians <u>were traveling</u> cross–country before 1900, they <u>had to take</u> the train.
>
> Even if a man <u>had been working</u> ten hours, he <u>would receive</u> no dinner break.

5. Present and Future Unreal

A situation is **unreal** if it is untrue, unlikely, or impossible. **Present unreal** and **future unreal** conditional sentences express situations that are not real or are unlikely to happen.

In present and future unreal conditional sentences, the condition clause has a past–tense verb. The result clause has a verb with a past–tense modal. Together, the past–tense verbs in both clauses indicate that the situation is unreal, untrue, unknowable, or unlikely.

	Condition Clause	Result Clause	
If +	simple past past progressive	*would* *could* *might* *had to*	+ base–form verb

Present/Future Unreal	Meaning
If you <u>lived</u> on another planet, the conditions for life <u>might be</u> very different.	You do *not* live on another planet; you cannot know about the conditions there.
If energy <u>decreased</u> as machines <u>worked</u>, then the machines <u>would</u> eventually <u>slow down</u>.	Energy does *not* decrease as machines work; thus, the machines will not slow down.
If the trains <u>were running</u> on time, more people <u>might take</u> the train.	The trains are *not* running on time; it is unlikely that more people will take the train.

When *be* is the verb or auxiliary in the condition clause, *were* is the correct form of the verb with subjects in the first person, second person, and third person.

If *I* <u>were</u> a better swimmer, I'd try out for the swim team.
If *you* <u>were going</u> to the same college, I would ask you to be my roommate.
If *the patient* <u>were</u> overweight, he could have a heart attack in the next five years.

Speakers often use the condition clause *if I were you* to make suggestions or give advice.

Present/Future Unreal	Meaning
If I were you, <u>I'd buy</u> the bigger one.	I suggest that you buy the bigger one.
If I were you, I <u>might wait</u> a while before calling him back.	I advise you to wait a while before calling him back.

UNIT 9

6. Past Unreal

Past unreal conditional sentences express situations that did not happen in the past. The past unreal is used to express mistakes and regrets.

	Condition Clause	Result Clause	
If +	past perfect past perfect progressive	*would* *could* *might* *should*	+ *have* + past participle

Past Unreal	Meaning
If we <u>had hurried</u>, we <u>could have caught</u> bus.	We did *not* hurry, and we missed the bus.
If their supply ship <u>had arrived</u> on time, the Roanoke colonists <u>might not have perished</u>.	Their supply ship did *not* arrive on time, and the colonists perished.
If you <u>had been listening</u>, you <u>should have heard</u> what the teacher said.	You were *not* listening; you did *not* hear what the teacher said.

7. Passive Voice

Real and unreal conditional sentences can be in the passive voice. The condition clause, the result clause, or both clauses may be in the passive voice.

Real Conditional Sentence	If a sore throat <u>is accompanied</u> by a fever and swollen neck glands, then the cause may be the streptococcus bacteria. If you buy this product, you <u>will be satisfied</u>. If a mural <u>is to be painted</u> inside a building, it <u>must be planned</u> to fit into the architectural design.
Unreal Conditional Sentence	If language <u>were not spoken</u>, then pronunciation <u>would not have to be learned</u>. If only the book <u>had been read</u>, it might have changed public opinion.

8. Wishes

Conditional structures can express wishes and dreams, especially in spoken English. Such expressions of desire or longing are similar to unreal conditional sentences, in which past–tense verbs and modals indicate unreality. Wishes express things that are not real or not yet true, but which the speaker wants to be true.

Wish Clause		Result Clause	
wish +		would	
if +	simple past	could	+ base–form verb
if only +		might	

Wish	**Meaning**
I *wish* I <u>knew</u> where to find a reliable used car.	I do *not* know where to find a reliable car, but I want to find one.
My brother *wishes* he <u>had</u> my musical ability.	My brother does *not* have the same musical ability as I have, but he desires musical ability.
If I <u>had</u> an apartment on the top floor, I <u>could</u> see the lighthouse.	I do *not* have an apartment on the top floor, and I *cannot* see the lighthouse, but I want an apartment on the top floor.
If only the room <u>weren't</u> so noisy, I <u>might hear</u> myself think.	The room *is* noisy, and I *cannot* hear myself think. I want the room to be less noisy.
I'm in the mood for Indian food. *If only* this town <u>had</u> an Indian restaurant!	I want to eat Indian food, but this town does *not* have an Indian restaurant.

UNIT 9

 PRACTICE

Exercise 9–A

Sentence Completion. Choose the word or phrase that best completes the sentence.

1. If plants are to grow, they ------- nitrogen

   Ⓐ have to
   Ⓑ had
   Ⓒ having
   Ⓓ must have

2. Soil–covered lava lands usually support a normal forest ------- enough water.

   Ⓐ is there
   Ⓑ if there is
   Ⓒ there has been
   Ⓓ there is also

3. Adults should have regular physical examinations ------- have no sign of illness.

   Ⓐ they may
   Ⓑ might they
   Ⓒ as if they
   Ⓓ even if they

4. If thunder is the atmosphere's noisiest production, lightning ------- its most dazzling.

   Ⓐ is certainly
   Ⓑ certainly
   Ⓒ certainly to be
   Ⓓ was certainly

5. ------- a predator approaches, the plover performs a distraction display by pretending to have a broken wing.

(A) There
(B) Why
(C) In case
(D) Only

6. If all of the ice in Antarctica and Greenland ------, sea level could rise 65 to 80 meters.

(A) to melt
(B) melted
(C) melting
(D) is melting

7. ------- information is encoded effectively in the memory, it may not be easily recalled when necessary.

(A) This
(B) Unless
(C) That
(D) As if

8. A balloon ------- as long as the weight of the balloon and the air inside is less than the upthrust of the air it displaces.

(A) will rise
(B) to rise
(C) rising
(D) has risen

9. Unless skill standards ------- as the basis for hiring employees, they will serve no role in helping people move from school to work.

(A) accepted
(B) been accepted
(C) were accepted
(D) are accepted

10. ------- the negative feedback loop works properly, thermoregulation prevents small changes in body temperature from becoming too large.

(A) That provided
(B) Provided that
(C) If that provided
(D) If it provides

Exercise 9–B

Sentence Editing. One of the underlined parts in each sentence is incorrect. Cross out the incorrect part and write the correction above it.

1. If you drink three or more sodas per day, you were at higher risk for developing diabetes.

2. A seedling will grow into a large, healthy tree as long it can extend its roots to a nearby soil pocket in the rocky landscape.

3. If a skydiver was not attached to a static line, which will automatically open the parachute, he can free–fall before pulling the rip cord.

4. If you are living on a large comet in the Kuiper Belt, you would see another large comet passing by once a month.

5. Unless you have already planted your vegetable garden, you can still making changes that will benefit your vegetables.

6. <u>Passed</u> by New York State in 1838, the Free Banking Act allowed anyone <u>to start</u> a bank <u>as long as</u> that

person <u>will make</u> certain promises.

7. We <u>could</u> see how various <u>factors</u> cause periods of global warming and cooling <u>only if</u> we combine

past data <u>with</u> current knowledge.

8. If <u>the</u> principle of conservation of energy were <u>erased</u> from the rules <u>governing</u> machines, then nothing

<u>will</u> work.

9. If <u>teachers</u> communicate the expectation <u>that</u> certain students will <u>behave</u> in a certain manner, those

students actually <u>did</u> behave in that manner.

10. Even if a disease <u>had</u> not destroyed the Irish potato <u>crop</u> in the 1840s, <u>thousands</u> of people would

probably <u>emigrate</u> because of political and social factors.

Exercise 9–C

TOEFL iBT Reading.   Read the passages and choose the best answer to each question.

QUESTIONS 1–2

Boaters will see advance warning of a storm if they know what to look for in the clouds. If there is a high cloud formation with a dirty bottom and a tall, stringy top, a storm is on the way. In that case, it is important not to try and outrun the storm but to head for a protected area. If a boat does get caught in a storm, a bucket or any kind of drag should be attached to the anchor line. As long as the occupants sit or lie on the bottom of the boat, they should be safe. Many people have fallen overboard and drowned because they stood up, swung their arms, and shouted for help.

1. What is the main purpose of the passage?

   (A) To describe a frightening experience
   (B) To explain how boating is dangerous
   (C) To warn boaters that storms are unpredictable
   (D) To advise boaters on what to do in a storm

2. During a storm, what should people in a boat do?

   (A) Try to outrun the storm
   (B) Keep low in the boat
   (C) Jump overboard and swim
   (D) Stand up and call for help

QUESTIONS 3–5

1   The majority of advertising used to be aimed at the traditional family: breadwinner father, non–working mother, and two children. However, if advertisers still focused on that segment of the population, they would put themselves out of business. Only about ten percent of American families fit the stereotype, and households with working mothers and singles are on the rise. If advertising is to be successful, it has to identify the potential users of a product and aim its message toward that group.

2   An advertising agency can decide on the best way of reaching potential buyers only if it conducts market research to understand who they are. Are they homemakers or professional people? Are they young or old? Do they live in the city, the country, or the suburbs? Unless the agency obtains detailed data and marketing expertise, the advertising campaign will face failure.

3. Why does the author say they would put themselves out of business in paragraph 1?

   (A) To explain what advertisers did in the past
   (B) To complain about false advertising
   (C) To identify the main fear of advertisers
   (D) To show that advertisers have changed what they do

4. The author believes that advertisers today should do all of the following EXCEPT

   (A) focus on the traditional family
   (B) identify potential buyers
   (C) conduct research
   (D) obtain marketing expertise

5. Which sentence below best expresses the essential information in the highlighted sentence in paragraph 2?

   (A) Before doing any research, advertisers must decide who the buyers are.
   (B) The best way to reach potential buyers is to find out where they live and work.
   (C) Advertisers must know their potential buyers in order to reach them effectively.
   (D) There are many creative ways for conveying a message to potential buyers.

Exercise 9–D

TOEFL iBT Listening.   Listen to the recording. You may take notes as you listen. Do not look at the questions until the conversation has ended. When you hear the questions, look at the questions and choose the best answer to each.

 Audio Track 15

1. Why does the student talk to his adviser?

   (A) He needs advice about which course to take in the summer.
   (B) He wants to take a course and its prerequisite at the same time.
   (C) He needs information about careers in oceanography.
   (D) He wants permission to graduate without a required course.

2. What does the adviser mean when she says this:

   (A) The oceanography course requires a strong background in mathematics.
   (B) It is useless to study mathematics before oceanography.
   (C) Many students avoid oceanography because it is too difficult.
   (D) It is difficult to find a job in oceanography.

3. Listen again to part of the conversation. Then answer the question.

What does the adviser imply?

(A) Taking both courses at the same time is a good idea.
(B) He must talk to the professor as soon as possible.
(C) The professor will not allow him to take both courses.
(D) He can do well in both courses only if he works very hard.

Exercise 9–E

TOEFL iBT Speaking. In this integrated speaking task, you will read a short passage about a campus situation, listen to a conversation, and then speak in response to a question about what you have read and heard. Do not look at the question until the conversation has ended. Do not look at the reading passage while you are speaking.

Reading Time – 45 seconds

LINKED COURSE IN GREEK DRAMA AND PHILOSOPHY

Study the plays of Aristophanes and Sophocles, and ponder the ideas of Socrates, Plato, and Aristotle. This linked course combines two courses: Introduction to Drama and Introduction to Philosophy. By enrolling in both courses, you will explore drama and its traditions as a distinctive form of creative expression in ancient Greece. You will investigate problems such as the nature of human knowledge, free will, morality, and the individual and the state. You will develop strategies for reading, analysis, and interpretation. Students who enroll in Introduction to Drama must also enroll in Introduction to Philosophy.

Now cover the passage and listen to the conversation. You may take notes, and you may use your notes to help you answer the question. After you hear the question, begin preparing your response. You may look at the question, but NOT at the passage. You have 30 seconds to prepare your response and 60 seconds to speak.

 Audio Track 16

The man expresses his opinion about the linked course. State his opinion and explain the reasons he gives for holding that opinion.

 Stop

Preparation Time – 30 seconds
Response Time – 60 seconds

Exercise 9–F

TOEFL iBT Speaking. In this integrated speaking task, you will listen to a conversation. You will then be asked to talk about the information in the conversation and to give your opinion about the ideas presented.

Cover the question while the conversation is playing. You may take notes, and you may use your notes to help you answer the question. After you hear the question, you may look at the question and prepare your response. You have 20 seconds to prepare your response and 60 seconds to speak.

 *Audio Track 17*

> The students discuss possible solutions to a problem that the woman has. Describe the problem. Then state what you think the woman should do, and explain why.

 Stop

Preparation Time – 20 seconds
Response Time – 60 seconds

Answers to Exercises 9–A through 9–F are on pages 262–263.

 EXTENSION

1. **Sentence Analysis.** In reading and listening outside class, look and listen for conditional sentences. Bring examples to share in class. Write some of the sentences on the board. With your teacher and classmates, answer the following questions about each sentence.

    a. Identify the condition clause. What is the subordinator?
    b. Look at the verb tenses and modals. Is the situation real or unreal?
    c. Is the situation certain, probable, possible, untrue, unlikely, or impossible?
    d. What is the purpose of the sentence?

2. **Oral Exercise:** Advice. Practice using conditional sentences to give advice.

    Examples: If you _____, you should/have to _____.

                             If I were you, I would _____.

3. **Oral Exercise:** Mistakes and Regrets. Practice using conditional sentences to express mistakes and regrets.

Examples: If I had _____, I would/could/might/should have _____.

If _____ had _____, then _____ would/might _____.

4. **Conditional Chain.** Work in a group of four students. The group builds conditional sentences and changes their meaning from real to unreal.

   a. Each person starts with a piece of paper. On your paper, write a condition clause with a present–tense verb. Then pass the paper to the person on your left.
   b. You now have a condition clause. Finish the sentence with a result clause. Then pass the paper to the person on your left.
   c. You now have a present real conditional sentence. Below that sentence, write the sentence in the present unreal. Then pass the paper to the person on your left.
   d. You now have two conditional sentences. Below the present unreal sentence, write the sentence in the past unreal. Then take turns reading the sentences aloud to your group. As a group, make any necessary corrections. Choose one set of sentences to read aloud to the whole class.

Example: If I go to New York

If I go to New York, I will see a play.

If I went to New York, I would see a play.

If I had gone to New York, I would have seen a play.

Suggestion: Use various verbs, such as *buy*, *feel*, *find*, *get*, *hear*, *make*, *see*, and *take*.

QUIZ 3 UNITS 7 – 9

Time – 10 minutes

Choose the word or phrase that best completes the sentence.

1. The heart is a striated muscle ------- contract as quickly as the skeletal muscles.

   (A) it does not
   (B) does not
   (C) that does not
   (D) who does not

2. An ionizing smoke detector contains a chamber ------- a low electric current flows.

   (A) that
   (B) that is
   (C) which
   (D) in which

3. The aurora borealis ------- as a soft glow along the northern horizon if the base of its arc is beneath the horizon.

   (A) which appears
   (B) may appear
   (C) appeared
   (D) would have appeared

4. A study found that men in discussion groups spent a lot of time finding out ------- about politics and current events.

   (A) who was best informed
   (B) the best informed that
   (C) whose best informed
   (D) the best informed is

5. That all ------- is made up of cells is a unifying concept in modern biology.

   (A) living material
   (B) material is living
   (C) material has lived
   (D) which material lives

6. Companies buy information from marketing analysts to help characterize their customers and learn -------.

   (A) finding more of them
   (B) that finding more of them
   (C) they find more of them
   (D) how to find more of them

7. If farmers ------- so much of the prairie, the dust storms of the 1930s would not have been so severe.

   (A) do not plow
   (B) have not plowed
   (C) had not plowed
   (D) will not plow

8. ------- at Lake Geneva, the Montreux International Jazz Festival showcases leading jazz artists and jazz–rock performers.

   (A) Held
   (B) Holding
   (C) It is held
   (D) By holding

One of the underlined parts in each sentence is incorrect. Cross out the incorrect part and write the correction above it.

9. If the front <u>teeth</u> of a rodent <u>do</u> not continue <u>growing</u>, they would be <u>worn</u> away.

10. <u>Benefits</u> of a credit account, <u>what</u> may change from time to time, typically <u>include</u> certain <u>kinds</u> of

    insurance coverage.

Answers to Quiz 3 are on page 263.

Record your score on page 301.

UNIT 10 SINGULAR AND PLURAL

1. **Countable Nouns**
2. **Irregular Plurals**
3. **Uncountable Nouns**
4. **Expressions of Quantity**
5. **Expressions of Class**
6. **Adjectives and Numeric Terms**

 FOCUS

What is wrong with this sentence?

> Most airlines allow no more than two carry–on luggages for each passenger.

It is incorrect to say *two carry–on luggages* because *luggage* is a noun that does not have a plural form. However, it would be correct to say *two pieces of carry–on luggage*. The correctly formed sentence is:

Most airlines allow no more than **two pieces of carry–on luggage** for each passenger.

What is wrong with this sentence?

> The pygmy rabbit is the smallest of the North American member of the rabbit family.

In this sentence, *member* is incorrect because *member* is a singular noun where a plural noun is needed. The pygmy rabbit is not the only North American member of the rabbit family, but it is the smallest of the members. The correctly formed sentence is:

The pygmy rabbit is the smallest of the North American **members** of the rabbit family.

 STUDY

1. Countable Nouns

Nouns that can be counted are called ***countable nouns***, or ***count nouns***. Countable nouns are either singular or plural in ***number*** and have different forms to denote the number. The ***singular*** form denotes a number of one. The ***plural*** form denotes a number of two or more.

Most plurals are formed by adding *-s* or *-es* to the singular form.

bird—birds	day—days	match—matches	wish—wishes

For nouns ending in a consonant + *y*, the *y* changes to *i* before adding *-es*.

country—countries	family—families	party—parties

For many nouns ending in the *f* sound, the spelling changes from *f* to *v* before adding *-es*.

knife—knives	life—lives	shelf—shelves
leaf—leaves	loaf—loaves	wife—wives

2. Irregular Plurals

Many nouns have irregular plurals. An ***irregular plural*** is a plural that is *not* formed by adding *-s* or *-es* to the singular form.

Some nouns for people and animals have irregular plurals.

child—children	louse—lice	ox—oxen
deer—deer	man—men	person—people
fish—fish	moose—moose	sheep—sheep
goose—geese	mouse—mice	woman—women

Some nouns for body parts have irregular plurals.

foot—feet	tooth—teeth	vertebra—vertebrae

Some academic and scientific nouns have irregular plurals.

analysis—analyses	genus—genera	series—series
basis—bases	medium—media	species—species
crisis—crises	nucleus—nuclei	stimulus—stimuli
criterion—criteria	phenomenon—phenomena	thesis—theses

Note: The plural of *fish* is normally *fish* when it names individuals. However, the plural form *fishes* is used in a scientific context when naming more than one group or species.

> There are thirty–five <u>fish</u> in my aquarium.
>
> Global warming will have a tremendous impact on the world's <u>fishes</u>.

Note: The noun *people* is normally plural and means "more than one person." However, when *people* refers to a specific group of humans, it has the plural form *peoples*, which refers to groups of humans.

> The American <u>people</u> elect a president every four years.
>
> Several different <u>peoples</u> have immigrated to the United States.

3. Uncountable Nouns

Nouns that cannot be counted are called ***uncountable nouns***, or ***noncount nouns***. Uncountable nouns are words that name activities, abstractions, conditions, phenomena, substances, or classes of things. Uncountable nouns have only one form, instead of different forms for singular and plural.

Nouns that name activities and fields of study are uncountable.

applause	dentistry	laughter	research
biology	golf	medicine	teaching
chess	genetics	poetry	work

Nouns that name abstractions, conditions, ideas, and qualities are uncountable.

beauty	importance	leisure	peace
capitalism	insomnia	love	safety
enjoyment	knowledge	luck	violence

Nouns that name natural phenomena are uncountable.

darkness	heat	rain	thunder
energy	moisture	snow	wind

Nouns that name substances are uncountable. Substances are viewed as wholes that are made up of parts.

beef	dust	rice	sugar
bread	gold	sand	tea
calcium	meat	smoke	water

Nouns that name whole classes of things are uncountable.

advice	furniture	livestock	music
baggage	gear	luggage	news
cash	homework	machinery	postage
clothing	information	mail	scenery
equipment	jewelry	money	traffic

Uncountable nouns do not have plural forms. For example, *research* and *machinery* do not have plural forms. Therefore, it is incorrect to say *two researches* or *several machineries*.

Some uncountable nouns can be expressed as a limited or defined quantity by using the uncountable noun as an adjective before a countable noun.

a golf game	a news item	a research study
a homework assignment	a raindrop	a snowflake

Some uncountable nouns can be expressed as a limited or defined quantity by putting a countable noun + *of* before the uncountable noun. In such phrases, the countable noun can be pluralized.

Limited Quantity	Plural Quantity
a word of advice	words of advice
an article of clothing	articles of clothing
a bit of information	bits of information
a piece of jewelry	pieces of jewelry
a grain of sand	grains of sand
an act of violence	acts of violence
a glass of water	glasses of water
a gust of wind	gusts of wind

UNIT 10

Some nouns that are normally uncountable are countable when they name a class or a portion. For example, *food* and *coffee* are usually uncountable, but they are countable in the following sentences.

> Most large supermarkets carry a wide variety of ethnic <u>foods</u>.
>
> I'll ask the waiter to bring us four <u>coffees</u>.

4. Expressions of Quantity

Different expressions of quantity are used with singular countable nouns, plural countable nouns, and uncountable nouns.

Singular Countable Nouns	Plural Countable Nouns	Uncountable Nouns
a/an	—	—
one	two, three, four	—
a single	multiple	—
another	other	other
—	both	—
—	few, a few	little, a little
—	fewer	less
—	some	some
—	many	much
—	a lot of, lots of	a lot of, lots of
—	several	—
—	various	—
—	most	most
each	—	—
every	all	all
—	number of, quantity of	amount of, quantity of
any	any	any
no	no	no

Singular Countable Nouns	Professor Duncan will schedule <u>a conference</u> with <u>each student</u> during the term.
	Geologists predict <u>another</u> volcanic <u>eruption</u> will occur within the next century.
Plural Countable Nouns	Having no more than <u>a few</u> important <u>goals</u> is a good way to manage your life.
	The interior of Florida has the greatest average <u>number of thunderstorms</u> each year.
Uncountable Nouns	With <u>a little luck</u>, the weather will be nice this weekend.
	A large <u>quantity of e–mail</u> is actually unwanted advertising known as "spam."

5. Expressions of Class

Expressions of class or type can be used with both countable and uncountable nouns.

category of class of	genre of kind of	sort of species of	type of variety of

Singular Countable Nouns	Which <u>sort of person</u> are you—an early bird or a night owl? A single <u>species of beetle</u> has caused extensive damage to pine forests.
Plural Countable Nouns	Humorist Mark Twain said there are three <u>kinds of lies</u>: lies, damned lies, and statistics. There are several <u>varieties of sparrows</u> living in North America.
Uncountable Nouns: singular meaning	My favorite <u>genre of music</u> is Latin jazz. Currency is a <u>type of money</u> that bears no interest.
Uncountable Nouns: plural meaning	Biography and history are <u>categories of nonfiction</u>. A giggle and a chuckle are two <u>kinds of laughter</u> that mean quite different things.

The following superlative structures are frequently used with plural countable nouns.

one of the	the --- of the

Edward Hopper's *Nighthawks* is <u>one of the best examples</u> of American realism.
The Siberian tiger is <u>the fiercest of the world's big cats</u>.

6. Adjectives and Numeric Terms

Adjectives do not have plural forms, even when they modify plural nouns or are combined with numbers greater than one.

Incorrect	**Correct**
Diamonds come in many <u>beautifuls</u> colors.	Diamonds come in many <u>beautiful</u> colors.
Early societies had <u>elaborates</u> rituals to mark the seasons.	Early societies had <u>elaborate</u> rituals to mark the seasons.
The condor has a <u>nine–feet</u> wing span.	The condor has a <u>nine–foot</u> wing span.
That swimming class is for <u>six–months–old</u> babies.	That swimming class is for <u>six–month–old</u> babies.

Numeric terms such as *hundred*, *thousand*, and *million* are adjectives when they follow a number and precede a plural noun. Because they are adjectives, the numeric terms do not have plural forms.

Incorrect	Correct
More than <u>four hundreds students</u> came to the meeting.	More than <u>four hundred students</u> came to the meeting.
<u>Two millions people</u> lost their jobs last year.	<u>Two million people</u> lost their jobs last year.

Numeric terms are plural nouns when they are followed by *of* + plural noun.

Incorrect	Correct
We sold <u>hundred of books</u> at our yard sale.	We sold <u>hundreds of books</u> at our yard sale.
<u>Ten of thousand of years</u> ago, forests covered the planet.	<u>Tens of thousands of years</u> ago, forests covered the planet.

The term *percent* is a noun meaning "one part in a hundred." It does not have a plural form, even when it follows a number.

Incorrect	Correct
The flood affected <u>fifty percents</u> of the town's inhabitants.	The flood affected <u>fifty percent</u> of the town's inhabitants.

 PRACTICE

Exercise 10–A

Singular and Plural. Fill in the blanks with the correct singular or plural form of the given noun.

1. thesis   The library contains original copies of all masters' _____ completed at the university.

2. phenomenon   Physicists study _____ such as heat, light, magnetism, and gravity.

3. crisis   The success or failure of a government is often decided during an economic _____.

4. species   Scientists add several _____ of plants and animals to the endangered list every year.

5. criterion   The essential _____ for managers are courage, energy, and effective communication.

6. analysis   The president requests both statistical and descriptive _____ of the data.

Exercise 10–B

Sentence Completion.   Choose the word or phrase that best completes the sentence.

1. ------- ring in the wood of a tree trunk indicates one year of growth.

   (A) Some
   (B) Each
   (C) All
   (D) Several

2. There are ------- of bird species in the Americas.

   (A) thousand
   (B) the thousand
   (C) thousands
   (D) by the thousands

3. ------- state in the United States has a governor who is the state's chief administrator.

   (A) Every
   (B) All
   (C) Most
   (D) Always

4. Alabaster, a kind of -------, is often made into jars, vases, and ornaments.

   (A) soft white stone
   (B) soft white the stone
   (C) soft white stones
   (D) its soft white stones

5. When Rip Van Winkle came out of the forest after sleeping for twenty years, ------- news awaited him in his native village.

   (A) a
   (B) many
   (C) much
   (D) several

6. The Miocene Period lasted from 25 to 11 ------- ago.

   (A) million year
   (B) million years
   (C) millions year
   (D) millions years

7. Dark colors trap many light rays; thus, a great ------- light is transformed into heat.

   (A) many
   (B) most of
   (C) number of
   (D) amount of

8. In the 1940s, Langston Hughes published the first of the ------- that later were collected in five volumes.

   (A) satirical story
   (B) another satirical story
   (C) satirical stories
   (D) stories were satirical

9. Once you have finished an article and identified its main ideas, it may not be necessary to read ------- word again.

   (A) many
   (B) some
   (C) all
   (D) every

10. Adding a bicycle lane along the freeway has resulted in ------- bicycle traffic on the two main routes through town.

   (A) a few
   (B) fewer
   (C) less
   (D) lesser

Exercise 10–C

Sentence Editing. One of the underlined parts in each sentence is incorrect. Cross out the incorrect part and write the correction above it.

1. The rattlesnake injects <u>poison</u> into its <u>prey</u> through fangs, <u>which</u> are hollow <u>tooth</u>.

2. The formation of <u>proteins</u> is one of the most important <u>function</u> of the <u>genes</u> in a <u>cell</u>.

3. <u>Every</u> furniture on display in the central <u>mall</u> is on sale for thirty <u>percent</u> off the regular <u>price</u>.

4. <u>Alliances</u> are joint business <u>ventures</u> formed by <u>companies</u> in different <u>country</u>.

5. Florida, <u>always</u> a popular tourist <u>destination</u>, is well known for its <u>abundance</u> of beautiful <u>sceneries</u>.

6. Northern Canada is a <u>home</u> for some of North America's largest <u>animal</u>, such as polar <u>bears</u> and <u>moose</u>.

7. In the 1800s, there <u>were</u> about 1,000 <u>million</u> people on Earth, and until recently, there was <u>few</u> increase

   in world <u>population</u>.

8. A flashing yellow traffic <u>signal</u> means one must slow down and proceed with <u>caution</u>, watching for

   <u>vehicles</u>, pedestrians, or other <u>hazard</u>.

9. <u>Research</u> has shown that <u>less</u> boys than girls are socialized to seek <u>jobs</u> in which they can help <u>others</u>,

   such as nursing.

10. <u>Much</u> of the worst tropical storms and <u>hurricanes</u> are likely to occur in the late <u>summer</u> along the

    Atlantic and Gulf of Mexico <u>coasts</u>.

Answers to Exercises 10–A through 10–C are on page 264.

Exercise 10–D

TOEFL iBT Speaking. In the independent speaking tasks below, use correct singular and plural nouns. For each task, allow 15 seconds to prepare your response and 45 seconds to speak.

1. Describe a natural or geographic feature for which your country is well known. Explain why this feature is famous. Include details and examples in your explanation.

2. Some schools require students to follow a strict course of study determined by the school. Other schools allow students to choose which classes they will take. Which system do you think is better for students, and why? Include details and examples in your explanation.

Preparation Time – 15 seconds
Response Time – 45 seconds

Exercise 10–E

TOEFL iBT Writing. For this independent writing task, respond to the question by writing an essay in which you state and support your opinion on the topic. Your essay will be scored on the quality of your writing, including how well you organize and develop your ideas and how well you use language to express your ideas. An effective essay will have a minimum of 300 words.

Read the following question and make any notes that will help you plan your response. Then begin writing. You have 30 minutes to plan and write your essay.

> Some people think that employers should expect the same performance from male and female employees. Others believe that employers should accept that men and women have different work styles. Which view do you agree with? Use specific reasons and examples to support your answer.

Time – 30 minutes

Answers to Exercises 10–D and 10–E will vary.

 EXTENSION

1. **Expressions of Quantity.** With your classmates, make a list of five countable nouns and five uncountable nouns. For each countable noun, include both the singular and the plural form. Then decide which expressions of quantity from the list below would be correct with each noun. Practice writing sentences with some of the nouns from your list and the expressions of quantity.

all	each	less	much	other
amount of	every	little	number of	several
another	few	many	one of the	some

2. **Uncountable Nouns.** With your classmates and teacher, discuss exceptions to the rule that uncountable nouns do not have singular and plural forms.

Examples:	*a* sugar	*foods* from Mexico	the spring *rains*
	a tea	the *teas* of China	take the *waters*
	a water	a selection of *meats*	*works* of art

In what context do these exceptions occur? Outside class, look for other examples. Report your findings in class.

UNIT 11   ARTICLES

1. **The Indefinite Articles:** *a* **and** *an*
2. **The Definite Article:** *the*
3. **Noun Structures with** *the*
4. **Categories of Nouns with** *the*
5. **Nouns with No Article**

FOCUS

What is wrong with this sentence?

> Searching the Internet is the fastest way to find an information about international sports.

The noun phrase *an information* is incorrect. The uncountable noun *information* does not have a singular form. Therefore, it does not take the article *an*, which is used only with singular nouns. No article is needed here. The correctly formed sentence is:

> Searching the Internet is the fastest way to find **information** about international sports.

What is wrong with this sentence?

> A hailstorm is product of the updrafts and downdrafts that develop inside the clouds of a thunderstorm.

The singular countable noun *product* needs an article. The sentence defines *a hailstorm* as the specific result of given conditions. Therefore, the definite article *the* is needed. The correctly formed sentence is:

> A hailstorm is **the product** of the updrafts and downdrafts that develop inside the clouds of a thunderstorm.

STUDY

1.   The Indefinite Articles: *a* and *an*

An *article* is a word that signals a noun. The presence or absence of an article indicates whether a noun is singular or plural, specific or non–specific. There are two types of articles: indefinite and definite.

The *indefinite articles*, *a* and *an*, denote a single but unspecified noun. They are used with singular countable nouns. They are never used with plural nouns or with uncountable nouns.

The indefinite articles are used with indefinite nouns. **Indefinite nouns** are non–specific; they do not name a particular person, place, or thing. The indefinite articles are also used with **generic nouns**, which represent a whole class or type of person, place, or thing.

Singular Countable Nouns	When <u>an object</u> moves around in <u>a circle</u>, it is always changing direction.
	Leaves can be <u>an important aid</u> to identifying <u>a wildflower</u>.
Generic Nouns	<u>An ophthalmologist</u> is <u>a doctor</u> who specializes in the structure and diseases of the eye.
	The chill of <u>a winter storm</u> can be felt inside as well as outside.

The article *a* comes before a consonant sound and before sounds that are spelled with a vowel but pronounced as a consonant.

a box	a student	a university
a European	a wild animal	a useful example
a hurricane	a year ago	a utility vehicle

The article *an* comes before a vowel sound and before sounds that are spelled with a consonant but pronounced as a vowel.

an American	an honor	an oil derrick
an economics test	an hourly wage	an unusual request
an elephant	an invention	an uprising

2. The Definite Article: *the*

The **definite article**, *the*, denotes a definite noun. A **definite noun** refers to a person, place, or thing that is specific and known. The definite article is used with singular and plural countable nouns and with uncountable nouns.

Singular Countable Nouns	Please set <u>the box</u> on <u>the table</u> in <u>the hall</u>.
	<u>The process</u> of homeostasis underlies <u>the ability</u> of an animal to maintain balance.
Plural Countable Nouns	<u>The creatures</u> that live in caves are often extraordinarily delicate.
	<u>The folktales</u> that children love most are based on <u>the actions</u> of real people.
Uncountable Nouns	It was four o'clock before <u>the police</u> received <u>the information</u> about the suspect.
	Good teachers care about <u>the progress</u> made by their students.

An indefinite noun can be made definite in a conversation or text. A noun may be indefinite the first time it is mentioned and later become definite. After a noun is mentioned, it is then specific and known to the listener and reader. In the following sentence, *a perennial border* is changed to *the border* because it becomes definite.

> The size of <u>a perennial border</u> can vary, but if the garden is large, <u>the border</u> should also be large.

3. Noun Structures with *the*

The definite article is used with noun structures containing a comparative or superlative adjective.

> There are two trains this evening; you'd better take the earlier one.
>
> The great gray owl is the largest owl in North America.

The definite article is used with plural nouns following *one of*.

> My friend Carlos was one of the students mentioned in the newspaper article.
>
> A ripe apricot is one of the most pleasurable rewards from an orchard.

Gerunds and gerund phrases are indefinite and uncountable, and therefore take no article, with one notable exception. A gerund + *of* + noun structure takes the definite article.

> Copper mining is a very important industry in Chile.
>
> The mining of copper accounts for a large proportion of Chile's export revenues.

4. Categories of Nouns with *the*

The definite article is used with various categories of definite nouns.

Species of Plants and Animals	The pussy willow was named for the catlike fur on its flowers. Despite its tiny size, the hummingbird migrates great distances every year.
Body Parts	Asthma attacks cause the lungs to constrict and the linings of the windpipe to swell.
Instruments, Inventions, and Models	Composers in many musical genres have used the mandolin. The elevator was invented just in time to lend itself to the new architecture of the industrial age, the skyscraper.
Machine Parts	The gearbox of a gasoline engine lies between the clutch and the differential.
Public Places	I'll meet you in the cafeteria after I take this package to the post office.
Time Periods	New types of art were being created in the late 1940s. Leonardo da Vinci was the most versatile genius of the Renaissance.

The definite article is used with proper nouns for large bodies of water, geographical regions, and groups of mountains, islands, and lakes.

the Arctic Ocean	the Panama Canal	the Himalayas
the Caribbean	the West	the Philippines
the Ganges	the Pacific Rim	the Great Lakes

The definite article is used with nouns that name someone or something unique: the only one of a person, place, or thing.

Lucy Larcom was <u>the seventh daughter</u> of ten children in a seafaring family.

Infrared photographs show variations in surface temperature across <u>the moon</u>.

Hydropower has become <u>the leading source</u> of renewable energy.

---

5. Nouns with No Article

In general statements, the following nouns take no article: indefinite plural nouns, indefinite uncountable nouns, gerunds, and nouns after an expression of class.

Indefinite Plural (Countable) Nouns	Capitol Reef National Park is a rock wilderness of massive <u>domes</u>, <u>cliffs</u>, and <u>canyons</u>. In <u>headlights</u> and <u>flashlights</u>, a concave mirror is located behind the light bulb.
Indefinite Uncountable Nouns	<u>Land</u>, <u>labor</u>, and <u>capital</u> are essential for the production of goods. Admissions counselors will be there to provide <u>advice</u> and <u>information</u>.
Gerunds	<u>Linking</u> a store's computer to that of the supplier helps automate <u>ordering</u>, <u>shipping</u>, and <u>billing</u>.
Nouns after an Expression of Class	A blizzard is a category of <u>snowstorm</u> with high–speed winds. The robin is the most common species of <u>thrush</u>.

Nouns that are modified by a possessive adjective—such as *my*, *his*, or *their*—take no article. Nouns that are modified by a demonstrative adjective—*this*, *that*, *these*, or *those*—take no article.

Nouns with a Possessive Adjective	Abraham Lincoln delivered <u>his famous Gettysburg address</u> at the dedication of a cemetery.
Nouns with a Demonstrative Adjective	Many engineers obtain a master's degree, which is desirable for promotion in <u>this field</u>. <u>These packages</u> and <u>that one</u> over there are ready to ship.

PRACTICE

Exercise 11–A

Articles.   Write the correct article in the blank space. If no article is needed, write X.

1. _____ blue whale is _____ largest of _____ marine mammals.

2. John Steinbeck, _____ American writer, won _____ Nobel Prize for _____ literature in 1962.

3. Economics is _____ study of _____ money, _____ capital, and _____ wealth.

4. _____ huge release of energy from _____ large star at _____ end of its life is called

   _____ supernova.

5. _____ woodchuck has traditionally been called _____ "groundhog" because it lives in _____

   underground den.

6. James Cotton began playing _____ blues harmonica after leaving _____ home at _____ age

   of nine.

7. Because so much news is available on _____ Internet, some experts predict _____ decrease in

   _____ number of _____ newspapers.

8. _____ remains of buildings are _____ our principal sources of _____ information about

   _____ many early cultures.

9. Soybeans are _____ valuable subsistence crop, and they are used as _____ source of protein for

   _____ humans and animals.

10. _____ number of hair cells that are stimulated in _____ ear depends on _____ loudness of

    _____ sound.

Exercise 11–B

Sentence Completion. Choose the word or phrase that best completes the sentence.

1. Some engineers prefer having -------.

   (A) outdoor job
   (B) a outdoor job
   (C) an outdoor job
   (D) the outdoor job

2. When the first gummed postage stamp was introduced, some people called ------- a "lick–and–stick."

   (A) stamps
   (B) their stamps
   (C) stamp
   (D) this stamp

3. Nimbus clouds generally have ------- and a shapeless appearance.

   (A) an uniformly dark color
   (B) uniformly the dark color
   (C) a uniformly dark color
   (D) uniformly dark in color

4. Individuals purchase a lot of technology for the home because ------- has become so inexpensive.

   (A) of electronic equipment
   (B) the equipment's electronic
   (C) an electronic equipment
   (D) electronic equipment

5. The first writing ink was made from a pigment found in -------.

   (A) ink sac of octopus
   (B) the ink sac of the octopus
   (C) an ink sac of octopus
   (D) this ink sac of an octopus

6. The Altamira cave paintings show several animals and some men in the act of -------.

   (A) the hunting
   (B) a hunting
   (C) hunting
   (D) an hunting

7. Edgar Varese was ------- major composers to embrace the possibilities of electronic music.

   (A) first
   (B) one of the first
   (C) the first
   (D) first one of

8. Identical twins have ------- blood types, eye and skin colors, and fingerprints.

   (A) identical
   (B) an identical
   (C) the identical
   (D) that identical

Exercise 11–C

Sentence Editing. One of the underlined parts in each sentence is incorrect. Cross out the incorrect part and write the correction above it.

1. Most retailers now use the computers for making sales presentations in stores.

2. Issues surrounding the distribution of income are among most controversial in economics.

3. After plow was introduced in the Middle East, it freed some people from having to grow their food.

4. Over half of all mammal species are rodents, and the nearly three thousand species of rodents form

   a largest mammalian order.

5. The Columbia River begins in the high meadows of western Canada, flows through the mountains,

   and then joins Snake River in Washington.

6. If an astronomer looks at star that is one hundred light years away, the light that can be seen is one

   hundred years old.

7. Many of greatest floods occur when excessive rain falls over river basins that are already saturated

   because of previous wet periods.

8. Human blood has a chemical composition similar to a seawater from which our ancestors first emerged.

9. Sometimes an English word is derived from an association with a place; for example, the kind of

   the cheese we know as cheddar originated in Cheddar, England.

10. There is an evidence that the formation of life is not an accident but a process that takes place

    whenever a planet exists under the right conditions.

UNIT 11

Exercise 11–D

TOEFL iBT Speaking. In this integrated speaking task, you will read a short passage, listen to a lecture on the same topic, and then speak in response to a question about what you have read and heard. Do not look at the question until the lecture has ended. Do not look at the reading passage while you are speaking.

Reading Time – 45 seconds

MUTUALISM

Mutualism is a biological interaction in which two different species live together as partners. Both species benefit in a mutualistic relationship. For example, both may experience increased survival and reproductive success. Mutualism plays a key role in ecology and evolutionary biology. Mutualistic relationships require the evolution of adaptations in both species because changes in either species are likely to affect the survival and reproduction of the other. Mutualism can be contrasted with competition, which has a negative effect on both species, and exploitation, in which one species benefits at the expense of the other.

Now cover the passage and listen to the lecture. You may take notes, and you may use your notes to help you answer the question. After you hear the question, begin preparing your response. You may look at the question, but NOT at the passage. You have 30 seconds to prepare your response and 60 seconds to speak.

 *Audio Track 18*

> The professor describes the relationship between the acacia tree and the stinging ant. Explain how their interaction is an example of mutualism.

 Stop

Preparation Time – 30 seconds
Response Time – 60 seconds

Answers to Exercises 11–A through 11–D are on pages 264–265.

Exercise 11–E

TOEFL iBT Writing. For this independent writing task, respond to the question by writing an essay in which you state and support your opinion on the topic. Your essay will be scored on the quality of your writing, including how well you organize and develop your ideas and how well you use language to express your ideas. An effective essay will have a minimum of 300 words.

Read the following question and make any notes that will help you plan your response. Then begin writing. You have 30 minutes to plan and write your essay.

Do you agree or disagree with the following statement?

The most important lessons in life are not learned in school.

Use specific reasons and examples to support your answer.

Time – 30 minutes

Answers to Exercise 11–E will vary.

 EXTENSION

1. **Proper Nouns.** In reading done outside class, look for proper nouns with the definite article *the* and proper nouns that have no article. Bring examples to share in class. With your teacher and classmates, discuss why some of the nouns have the article and some do not.

2. **Sentence Analysis.** Outside class, look in a newspaper or magazine for a short passage of one to three paragraphs. Make a copy of the passage and bring it to class. In class, exchange papers with a classmate. Your classmate must underline all of the nouns and circle all of the articles in the passage. Write some of the sentences on the board. With your classmates, identify whether the nouns are (a) singular or plural, (b) countable or uncountable, and (c) definite or indefinite. Discuss why some of the nouns have no article.

UNIT 12 SUBJECT–VERB AGREEMENT

1. **Agreement**
2. **Singular Verbs**
3. **Special Nouns with Singular Verbs**
4. **Pronouns with Singular Verbs**
5. **Plural Verbs**
6. **Verb Agreement with Other Sentence Parts**
7. **Expressions of Necessity or Importance**

 FOCUS

What is wrong with this sentence?

> The slender bristles on the stems of cotton grass is actually the tiny petals of the plant's flowers.

The subject and verb do not match in number. The subject, *the slender bristles*, is plural. It must have a plural verb. However, the verb—*is*—is singular. Because the singular verb does not agree with the plural subject, the verb must be changed to *are*. The correctly formed sentence is:

> The slender bristles on the stems of cotton grass **are** actually the tiny petals of the plant's flowers.

What is wrong with this sentence?

> Haze from pollen and forest fires have always been present in the Grand Canyon, but the recent increase comes from outside the national park.

Like the first sentence above, the second sentence also lacks agreement. The subject, *haze*, is an uncountable noun. An uncountable noun takes a singular verb. However, *have always been* is a plural verb. To agree with *haze*, the verb must be changed to *has always been*. The correctly formed sentence is:

> Haze from pollen and forest fires **has always been** present in the Grand Canyon, but the recent increase comes from outside the national park.

STUDY

1. Agreement

Agreement is a correct match between parts of a sentence. In every clause, the subject and the verb must agree in number. A singular subject must have a singular verb; a plural subject must have a plural verb. *Subject–verb agreement* occurs when the form of the subject and the form of the verb match correctly.

Singular Subject and Verb	An amplifier increases the voltage of a signal from a microphone. S V
Plural Subject and Verb	Elephants eat a wide variety of grasses, foliage, and fruits. S V

Agreement is necessary when the verb is in any of the present tenses, the past progressive tense, or the passive voice. Whether a subject is singular or plural determines the form of the verb.

Modifiers that come between a subject and a verb do not change the subject's number. Modifying phrases and clauses are part of the subject, but they do not affect whether the subject is singular or plural. Only the subject noun matters in subject–verb agreement.

Singular Subject and Verb	Invasion of the lungs by plague bacteria causes a fatal disease. S V
Plural Subject and Verb	All devices that are powered by electricity contain a circuit. S V

Tip: To check subject–verb agreement in your writing, look at the subject noun only, disregarding its modifiers. Then check the verb. If the noun and verb agree in number, you have subject–verb agreement.

Both singular and plural subjects can have a ***compound verb***, two or more verbs joined by *and* or *or*. Each part of a compound verb must agree with the subject.

Singular Subject and Compound Verb	The pituitary gland secretes hormones *and* controls body processes. S V V
Plural Subject and Compound Verb	Herbicides kill plants *or* inhibit their growth. S V V

UNIT 12

2. Singular Verbs

A singular verb is used when the subject is a singular noun, an uncountable noun, a gerund, or a noun clause.

Singular Noun	A hydrangea produces blue flowers when it grows in acid soil.
Uncountable Noun	Research shows that men speak more in meetings than women do.
Gerund	Preparing a budget translates planned activities into monetary terms.
Noun Clause	How animals interact with each other interests their trainers.

The verb *be* has irregular singular forms: *am, is, was*. These forms are used when *be* is a simple–present main verb or when *be* is auxiliary to another verb in the present progressive tense, the past progressive tense, or the passive voice.

> The polar bear is one of the largest carnivores in the world.
>
> I'm looking for an apartment near the train line.
>
> In the last four years of his life, Mozart was writing his best operas.
>
> Emily Carr is regarded as one of the best artists in Canadian history.

In the simple present tense, a third–person singular subject takes a verb with the *-s* or *-es* ending.

> An element contains only one kind of atom.
>
> When one catches a cold, the best treatment includes plenty of rest.

When a modal is used with a simple–present verb, the verb has no *-s* or *-es* ending.

> The hepatitis B virus may increase the risk of liver cancer.
>
> In order to survive, an organism must adapt to changes in its environment.

In the present perfect and present perfect progressive tenses, a third–person singular subject takes a verb with the auxiliary *has*.

> After a child has learned to read, he may have new interests.
>
> The human population has been increasing rapidly over the past four decades.

3. Special Nouns with Singular Verbs

Some nouns appear to be plural but actually are singular and take singular verbs.

diabetes	genetics	news	politics
economics	mathematics	physics	statistics

> Economics <u>is</u> concerned with production, employment, and prices.
>
> Mathematics <u>illustrates</u> many ideas that words cannot describe.

A ***collective noun*** denotes a collection of people, animals, or things. Collective nouns are usually regarded as a unit or a whole. Therefore, they are singular and take singular verbs.

class	company	family	group
clergy	corporation	flock	public
committee	enemy	government	team

> Professor Hart's <u>class</u> <u>is studying</u> population ecology.
>
> My <u>family</u> <u>owns</u> a business that specializes in wedding photography.
>
> The <u>government</u> <u>has established</u> a new educational policy.

The following collective nouns take a singular verb, even when the noun is followed by *of* + a plural noun.

collection of	flock of	group of	pair of
colony of	genus of	herd of	team of

> A <u>pair</u> *of electrodes* <u>conducts</u> the current in a battery.
>
> A <u>team</u> *of graduate students* <u>is analyzing</u> soil samples from the spill site.

Note: In British English, collective nouns are usually treated as plurals and take plural verbs.

> The <u>government</u> <u>have established</u> a new educational policy.

4. Pronouns with Singular Verbs

An ***indefinite pronoun*** replaces a non–specific noun. When an indefinite pronoun functions as a subject, it takes a singular verb. The following pronouns take singular verbs, even though they may seem to have plural meanings.

anybody	each	everyone	nobody	somebody
anyone	either	everything	no one	someone
anything	everybody	neither	nothing	something

> I can't find my keys. <u>Has</u> <u>anyone</u> <u>seen</u> them?
>
> <u>Everyone</u> <u>has</u> an equal chance of winning the lottery.
>
> <u>Everything</u> alive on our planet <u>is composed</u> of cells.
>
> <u>Nothing</u> <u>prevents</u> an earthquake from happening.

An **indefinite pronoun** takes a singular verb, even when the pronoun is followed by *of* + a plural noun.

> <u>Each</u> *of the climate zones* <u>has</u> a different pattern of weather.
>
> <u>Neither</u> *of the proposals* <u>satisfies</u> the requirements of the project engineers.

Note: *Each, either*, and *neither* can also function as adjectives modifying a singular noun. The singular noun takes a singular verb.

> <u>Each</u> *climate zone* <u>has</u> a different pattern of weather.
>
> <u>Neither</u> *proposal* <u>satisfies</u> the requirements of the project engineers.

5. Plural Verbs

A plural verb is used when the subject is a plural noun, a compound subject of two or more nouns, or a plural pronoun. Plural verbs in the simple present tense do *not* have the *-s* or *-es* ending.

Plural Noun	<u>Scientists</u> <u>predict</u> that winter storms will become more severe.
Compound Subject	<u>Antarctica and Greenland</u> <u>contain</u> the two largest masses of land–based ice on Earth.
Plural Pronoun	Because <u>they</u> <u>have</u> difficulty making friends, shy children often feel lonely.

The verb *be* has irregular plural forms: *are* and *were*. The plural forms are used when *be* is a simple–present main verb or when *be* is auxiliary to another verb.

> <u>Substances</u> containing nitrogen <u>are</u> potential sources of nitrate.
>
> <u>Laurel and Hardy</u> <u>were</u> famous comedians of films made in the 1920s.
>
> <u>Floods</u> <u>are caused</u> by excessive rain and poor drainage.

In the present perfect and present perfect progressive tenses, a plural subject takes a verb with the auxiliary *have*.

> <u>We</u> <u>have</u> not yet <u>discovered</u> a cure for the common cold.
>
> <u>Humans</u> <u>have been migrating</u> across Earth for several millennia.

A **compound subject** has two nouns joined by a conjunction. A compound subject joined by *and* or *both...and* takes a plural verb.

> <u>Chipmunks, mice, *and* squirrels</u> <u>belong</u> to the order *Rodentia*.
>
> *Both* <u>Spain</u> *and* <u>France</u> <u>were</u> major colonial powers of the Americas.

When the following pronouns function as subjects, they take plural verbs.

both	a few	few	many	others	several

> Only <u>a few</u> of the club's members <u>are coming</u> on the field trip.
>
> Of all fifty states, <u>few</u> <u>have</u> as much open space as Montana does.
>
> Some birds build their nests in trees; <u>others</u> <u>build</u> them on the ground.
>
> <u>Several</u> of my professors <u>believe</u> that life exists on other planets.

6. Verb Agreement with Other Sentence Parts

Sometimes parts of a sentence other than the subject will determine whether the verb is singular or plural.

When some pronouns function as subjects, they take either a singular or a plural verb, depending on the noun to which they refer. The following pronouns take a singular verb if the noun is uncountable; they take a plural verb if the noun is plural.

all	any	most	none	some

> <u>None</u> of the *information* in that almanac <u>is</u> current. <u>None</u> of it <u>is</u> current.
>
> <u>None</u> of the *students* <u>are</u> in the laboratory. <u>None</u> <u>are</u> in the laboratory.
>
> <u>Some</u> of the *news* on television <u>distorts</u> the truth. <u>Some</u> <u>distorts</u> the truth.
>
> <u>Some</u> of the most prominent *reporters* <u>distort</u> the truth. <u>Some</u> <u>distort</u> the truth.

When a compound subject is joined by any of the following conjunctions, the verb agrees with the subject that is closer to it.

either...or	neither...nor	not only...but also

> *Either* work references *or* a school <u>certificate</u> <u>is</u> necessary to get a job.
>
> *Not only* the grizzly bear *but also* many <u>bird species</u> <u>are</u> endangered.

In sentences with the "false" subject *there*, the verb agrees with the true subject, which comes after the verb.

> Until 1977, *there* <u>was</u> <u>no Department of Energy</u> at the federal level. (singular)
>
> *There* <u>were</u> <u>creatures</u> on Earth long before humans arrived. (plural)

Both *a number of* and *the number of* are used with plural countable nouns. *A number of* expresses an indefinite quantity and takes a plural verb. *The number of* expresses a definite quantity and takes a singular verb, even though a plural noun follows it.

A number of <u>department stores</u> <u>are developing</u> a specialty–store look. (plural)

The number of <u>people</u> who go to college <u>has risen</u> since the 1960s. (singular)

In an adjective clause with a relative pronoun as the subject, the verb agrees with the noun referred to by the relative pronoun.

Workers must pick and destroy any <u>fruit</u> *that* <u>shows</u> signs of brown rot.

<u>Students</u> *who* <u>register</u> early usually get into the most popular classes.

A hiker can go to <u>places</u> in Sequoia National Park *that* <u>are</u> far from any road.

In the first sentence above, the verb in the adjective clause, *shows*, agrees with *fruit*, the noun to which it refers. In the second sentence, the verb in the adjective clause, *register*, agrees with *students*. In the third sentence, the verb in the adjective clause, *are*, agrees with *places*, the noun to which it refers.

7. Expressions of Necessity or Importance

Some expressions of necessity or importance have special rules for subject–verb agreement.

After the following verbs of importance, noun clauses with *that* + subject + verb take the base form of the verb. This rule applies even when the subject of the noun clause is third person singular.

ask	insist	propose	request	suggest
demand	prefer	recommend	require	urge

Professor Blake *asks that* <u>each student</u> <u>submit</u> an outline for the term paper.

Doctors *recommend that* <u>an adult</u> <u>have</u> at least seven hours of sleep every night.

Note: When the noun clause is in the passive voice, the verb takes the base form of *be*.

The company *requires that* <u>every employee</u> <u>be evaluated</u> once a year.

The guidelines *suggest that* <u>the air pressure</u> in your tires <u>be checked</u> regularly.

With certain adjectives of importance, noun clauses following *It is* + adjective + *that* take the base form of the verb, even when the subject is third person singular.

essential	important	necessary	recommended	required

It is essential that <u>a manager</u> <u>have</u> good communication skills.

It is important that <u>everyone</u> <u>be</u> on time for the budget meeting.

It is necessary that <u>the mining industry</u> <u>enforce</u> its safety regulations.

 PRACTICE

Exercise 12–A

Subjects and Verbs. In the following sentences, underline the subjects and verbs. Write **S** above singular subjects and verbs. Write **P** above plural subjects and verbs. Some sentences have more than one subject and verb.

1. Both Latvia and Lithuania are members of the European Union.

2. Chemical oceanographers search for ways to remove valuable compounds from seawater.

3. A sensor detects the presence of something and often measures it.

4. There are many types of lichens that grow on the tundra.

5. Studies have linked laughter with increased pain tolerance, possibly because it triggers the release of endorphins.

6. Some grizzly bears are almost black, others are reddish brown, and still others have white–tipped brown hair.

7. In a capitalist economy, what will be produced is determined by the marketplace, which is considered the center of the system.

8. In an escalator, the descending half of the stairs acts as a counterweight to the ascending half, and the motor moves only the weight of the people who are riding.

Exercise 12–B

Sentence Completion. Choose the word or phrase that best completes the sentence.

1. Physics, one of the natural sciences, ------- energy and matter.

    (A) deal with
    (B) are dealing with
    (C) deals with
    (D) dealing with

2. For more than two centuries, Washington ------- the site of political demonstrations.

    (A) is
    (B) were
    (C) have been
    (D) has been

3. Many of the world's endangered species
------- altogether.

   (A) disappears
   (B) is disappearing
   (C) are disappearing
   (D) has disappeared

4. *The Book of Changes*, a classic Chinese book
of wisdom, ------- of eight trigrams that
correspond to the powers of nature.

   (A) consist
   (B) consists
   (C) it consists
   (D) to consist

5. The finch family of birds ------- sparrows and
grosbeaks.

   (A) includes
   (B) including
   (C) is included
   (D) include

6. The physical environment where educational
activities take place ------- learning.

   (A) affected
   (B) affect
   (C) to affect
   (D) affects

7. Why a person has no friendships -------
something that a survey cannot adequately
explain.

   (A) is
   (B) there is
   (C) are
   (D) they are

8. Both strip mining and quarrying -------
exposure to the earth's surface.

   (A) maintain
   (B) maintaining
   (C) maintains
   (D) is maintained

9. Everyone who reads the newspaper or watches
the news ------- that health care is changing.

   (A) know
   (B) who knows
   (C) knows
   (D) have known

10. None of the other poisonous snakes of the
Americas ------- as deadly as the brightly–
colored coral snake.

   (A) be
   (B) are
   (C) is
   (D) was

Exercise 12–C

Sentence Editing. One of the underlined parts in each sentence is incorrect. Cross out the incorrect part and
write the correction above it.

1. Ocean currents, <u>wind</u>, and air temperature <u>contributes</u> to rainfall, <u>which is</u> one of the primary <u>factors</u>

   of climate.

2. A <u>number</u> of important services <u>are provided</u> by a bank, which <u>are more</u> than just a safe place

   <u>to store</u> money.

3. <u>Much</u> information <u>about</u> cross–cultural facial expressions <u>have</u> been published recently in

   psychological <u>journals</u>.

4. Archaeologists <u>have</u> found records over two <u>thousand</u> years old that <u>shows</u> the amount of precious

    metal <u>deposited</u> in a temple in Babylon.

5. A college graduate who <u>is trained</u> in one of the natural <u>sciences</u> or mathematics usually <u>qualify</u> for a

    beginning–level engineering <u>job</u>.

6. Forensic scientists, who <u>work</u> in crime laboratories, <u>conduct</u> testing that <u>help</u> law enforcement

    agencies <u>solve</u> crimes.

7. The number of <u>women</u> who <u>enter</u> nontraditional fields <u>have</u> been <u>increasing</u> steadily since the 1970s.

8. If you <u>want</u> to start an exercise program, <u>remember</u> that either aerobics or cycling <u>are</u> excellent

    <u>for</u> conditioning.

9. Many health care <u>specialists</u> recommend that a forty–year–old man <u>consumes</u> no more than twenty

    <u>percent</u> of his daily caloric <u>intake</u> in the form of fat.

10. Adding extra passengers <u>cause</u> a boat to settle more <u>deeply</u> in the water, but the boat must not <u>be</u>

    so loaded that the watermarks on its side <u>go</u> below the water's surface.

Exercise 12–D

TOEFL iBT Speaking. In the independent speaking tasks below, use correct subject and verb forms in your responses. For each task, allow 15 seconds to prepare your response and 45 seconds to speak.

1. Describe a sport or game that is popular in your country. Explain why many people enjoy this sport or game. Include details and examples in your explanation.

2. Some teachers require students to work with other students in small groups in class. Other teachers request that students work independently. Which type of class work do you think is better for students, and why? Include details and examples in your explanation.

Preparation Time – 15 seconds
Response Time – 45 seconds

Exercise 12–E

TOEFL iBT Writing. In this integrated writing task, you will write a response to a question about a reading passage and a lecture. Your response will be scored on the quality of your writing and on how well you connect the points in the lecture with points in the reading. Typically, an effective response will have 150 to 225 words.

Reading Time – 3 minutes

The growth of the suburbs was a direct result of the rise of the automobile. Suburban housing developments allow car owners to live farther away from their workplace than ever before. Before the automobile, commuters relied on trains and buses, whose service was generally restricted to urban areas. The convenience of the private automobile and an extensive system of highways have virtually eliminated the restrictions on travel that characterize public transportation. Because every suburban household owns at least one car, public transit has become unnecessary.

Crowding in the central city and a consequent deterioration of living conditions there have provided an incentive for people to move to suburbia. Many suburban developments are primarily residential districts close to the city. The suburban lifestyle is very appealing because it evokes an ideal of an "urban" society living graciously in a "country" setting of single–family houses on large, private lots. Suburban neighborhoods are built for the automobile. They are separated from the city's problems yet are within driving distance of the city's employment opportunities and cultural attractions.

The shift of population out of the central city has had the effect of attracting industry and commerce to the suburbs. Many suburbs are built around a single purpose of economic activity and are particularly successful in attracting shopping centers or high–technology industries. Large areas of suburban land have been zoned primarily for office space, leading to the rise of the suburban business park. Much commercial activity has moved to large suburban centers that rival the central city's downtown, providing further incentive for people to migrate to the suburbs.

Now listen to the lecture. You may take notes, and you may use your notes to help you write your response. After you hear the question, you have 20 minutes to plan and write your response. You may look at the reading passage during the writing time.

 Audio Track 19

> Summarize the points made in the lecture, explaining how they differ from points made in the reading.

 Stop

Time – 20 minutes

Exercise 12–F

TOEFL iBT Writing. For this independent writing task, respond to the question by writing an essay in which you state and support your opinion on the topic. Your essay will be scored on the quality of your writing, including how well you organize and develop your ideas and how well you use language to express your ideas. An effective essay will have a minimum of 300 words.

Read the following question and make any notes that will help you plan your response. Then begin writing. You have 30 minutes to plan and write your essay.

Do you agree or disagree with the following statement?

Online courses and distance learning should replace traditional classroom study at universities.

Use specific reasons and examples to support your answer.

Time – 30 minutes

Answers to Exercises 12–A through 12–C and 12–E are on pages 265–266.

Answers to Exercises 12–D and 12–F will vary.

 EXTENSION

1. **Sentence Analysis.** Outside class, look in a newspaper, magazine, or book for a short passage of one or two paragraphs. Copy and bring the passage to class. Working in a group of three or four students, identify all subjects and verbs in the passage. With your classmates, answer the following questions:

   a. Are the subjects singular or plural?
   b. Are the verbs singular or plural?
   c. How do you know that the verbs are singular or plural?
   d. Do you see any errors in subject–verb agreement in the passage?

2. **Sentence Writing.** Practice writing sentences in which the subject is a pronoun from the list below. Is the subject pronoun singular or plural? Make sure the verb agrees in number with the subject.

all	both	few	most	nothing
anything	everyone	many	none	someone

UNIT 13 PRONOUN AGREEMENT

1. **Pronoun Function**
2. **Personal Pronouns**
3. **Person and Number**
4. **Gender**
5. **Relative Pronouns**
6. **Demonstratives**
7. **Indefinite Pronouns**
8. **Other Pronouns**

FOCUS

What is wrong with this sentence?

> Bracket mushrooms usually remain above the snow line in winter because their grow on trees.

The subject of a clause must be a subject form. In the second clause, *their* is incorrect because it is not a subject form. The correct form is *they*, a subject pronoun referring to *mushrooms*. The correctly formed sentence is:

Bracket mushrooms usually remain above the snow line in winter because **they** grow on trees.

What is wrong with this sentence?

> Orville and Wilbur Wright were the first Americans which achieved flight.

The pronoun *which* is incorrect because *which* can refer to things or animals, but never to people. Because the pronoun refers to *the first Americans*, it should be changed to *who*. The correctly formed sentence is:

Orville and Wilbur Wright were the first Americans **who** achieved flight.

What is wrong with this sentence?

> If one is planning to travel in a foreign country, you should learn about the nonverbal communication of that culture.

The subject of the first clause is the indefinite pronoun *one*. The subject of the second clause is the definite pronoun *you*. Because the parts of the sentence must agree, one pronoun must be changed. Two correct ways to write the sentence are:

If one is planning to travel in a foreign country, **one** should learn about the nonverbal communication of that culture.

If **you are** planning to travel in a foreign country, you should learn about the nonverbal communication of that culture.

STUDY

1. Pronoun Function

A *pronoun* substitutes for a noun or refers to a noun. A pronoun can replace a *proper noun*, which names a specific, individual person, place, or thing, or it can replace a *common noun*, which names any of a class of person, place, or thing.

The noun to which a pronoun refers is called the *referent* or the *antecedent* of the pronoun.

Pronouns can be definite or indefinite. A *definite pronoun* replaces a noun that has been mentioned and whose identity is clear. An *indefinite pronoun* refers to a non–specific or unidentified noun.

In spoken English, both the speaker and the listener know the identity of a definite pronoun's noun referent. In written English, the identity of the referent is given in the text, usually before the pronoun, but sometimes after it. The referent may be in the same sentence as the pronoun, or it may be in another sentence.

In the following passage, all underlined pronouns refer to the proper noun *Willa Cather*.

> Willa Cather was born in Virginia but grew up in Nebraska. After working as a teacher and a journalist, Cather later devoted <u>herself</u> to writing novels. Like other realists before <u>her</u>, <u>she</u> wrote about human nature. In <u>her</u> poems, stories, novels, and essays, <u>she</u> portrayed the people and places that <u>she</u> loved. While many of Cather's contemporaries attained financial success, <u>hers</u> was a personal success.

2. Personal Pronouns

Personal pronouns are definite pronouns that replace nouns for known or previously mentioned nouns. A personal pronoun must agree with its noun referent in form, person, number, and gender.

- Form: subject, object, possessive, reflexive
- Person: first, second, third
- Number: singular, plural
- Gender: masculine, feminine, neuter

A pronoun's form depends on its function in a sentence. A pronoun can function as a subject, an object, or a possessive. A *possessive adjective* agrees with its noun referent, not the noun it modifies. A *reflexive pronoun* is the direct object of a verb whose subject is the referent of the pronoun.

Person/ Number/ Gender	Subject Pronoun	Object Pronoun	Possessive Adjective	Possessive Pronoun	Reflexive Pronoun
First/singular	I	me	my	mine	myself
First/plural	we	us	our	ours	ourselves
Second/singular	you	you	your	yours	yourself
Second/plural	you	you	your	yours	yourselves
Third/singular /m.	he	him	his	his	himself
/f.	she	her	her	hers	herself
/n.	it	it	its	–	itself
Third/plural	they	them	their	theirs	themselves

In the following sentences, the referent for each underlined pronoun or possessive adjective is shown in *italics*.

Form	Examples
Subject Pronoun	Because few *people* are perfect, they may have invisible faults.
Object Pronoun	If you asked them to speak honestly, some *people* would feel uncomfortable.
Possessive Adjective	Honest *people* are able to examine their own faults.
Possessive Pronoun	Some people find your *mistakes* more forgivable than theirs.
Reflexive Pronoun	Wise *people* are able to view themselves honestly.

3. Person and Number

A personal pronoun must agree with its noun referent in person, number, and gender.

Person denotes one of three categories of nouns and pronouns. *First person* means the person or people who speak. *Second person* means the person or people who are spoken to. *Third person* means the person, people, or thing(s) that are spoken about.

Number denotes how many there are. The number can be singular or plural. *Singular* means there is one. *Plural* means there are two or more.

First Person	My roommate and I both have new vehicles; mine is a pickup truck.
	Our instructor gives us a quiz every Monday, and we have a lab report due every Thursday.
Second Person	If you want to speak in class, please raise your hand.
	You are all encouraged to tell your friends about the job fair.
Third Person	When a man is laid off from his job, he is likely to experience depression and anxiety.
	Early movie audiences showed that they liked feature films and preferred to see them in one sitting.

4. Gender

Gender refers to the sex of the pronoun's referent, which can be masculine (m.), feminine (f.), or neuter (n.). First– and second–person pronouns do not have special forms for gender. Only third–person pronouns have different forms for each gender.

Masculine and feminine pronouns refer to people and sometimes to animals. *Masculine* pronouns refer to men, boys, and male animals. *Feminine* pronouns refer to women, girls, and female animals.

	Subject Pronoun	Object Pronoun	Possessive Adjective	Possessive Pronoun
Masculine Singular	he	him	his	his
Feminine Singular	she	her	her	hers
Plural	they	them	their	theirs

Neuter pronouns refer to things and ideas: inanimate objects and abstractions that are neither male nor female. Neuter pronouns can also refer to animals. However, masculine and feminine pronouns are often used for pets and familiar animals.

	Subject Pronoun	Object Pronoun	Possessive Adjective	Possessive Pronoun
Neuter Singular	it	it	its	–
Neuter Plural	they	them	their	theirs

In the following sentences, the referent for each underlined pronoun is shown in *italics*.

Masculine	*Mr. Lee* won the contest, but it was a long time before <u>he</u> realized the money was really <u>his</u>. *Tom* was very young when <u>his</u> mother took <u>him</u> on a trip to Egypt.
Feminine	When *Golda Meir* was seventy years old, <u>she</u> became prime minister of Israel. *Sheba* was weak after <u>her</u> surgery, so the veterinarian kept <u>her</u> in the hospital for two days.
Neuter	*The honeybee* has come to represent summer, but sometimes <u>it</u> can be seen flying in January. As *airplanes* travel, <u>they</u> push the air in front of <u>them</u>, compressing the air into waves.

UNIT 13

5. Relative Pronouns

Relative pronouns introduce adjective clauses. A relative pronoun must agree with its referent, the noun modified by the adjective clause. Different relative pronouns refer to people, animals, and things.

	Subject	**Object**	**Possessive**
People	who, that	whom, that	whose
Animals and Things	which, that	which, that	whose

Who and *whom* refer only to people.

> *Archimedes*, <u>who</u> defined the principle of levers, also developed the pulley.
>
> Judges are *professionals* in <u>whom</u> fairness is an essential quality.

Which refers only to animals and things.

> My sister raises *basset hounds*, <u>which</u> are among the most popular family pets.
>
> The *thyroid gland*, <u>which</u> regulates metabolism, is part of the endocrine system.

That can refer to people, animals, and things.

> *Workers* <u>that</u> are analytical and sociable often make good supervisors.
>
> A constrictor is a *snake* <u>that</u> wraps and squeezes its prey.
>
> A delta plain has *areas* of shallow water <u>that</u> separate its many channels.

Whose, the possessive form, can refer to people, animals, and things.

> Sonja Henie was a *figure skater* <u>whose</u> skill brought her three Olympic medals.
>
> There are hundreds of *species* of fish <u>whose</u> survival depends on krill.
>
> *Electrons*, <u>whose</u> movement causes electricity, are the smallest atomic particles.

6. Demonstratives

Demonstrative pronouns and *demonstrative adjectives* specify, single out, or point to a noun. A demonstrative pronoun must agree in number with the noun it replaces. A demonstrative adjective must agree in number with the noun it modifies.

Singular	**Plural**	**Meaning**
this	these	present; nearby; just mentioned
that	those	past; farther; previously mentioned

In the following sentences, the referent for each demonstrative pronoun is shown in *italics*, and the noun modified by each demonstrative adjective is shown in *italics*.

Singular Demonstrative Pronoun	When a plane flies faster than the speed of sound, *a huge noise* can be heard. <u>This</u> is known as a "sonic boom." *The range* of the gray wolf is greater than <u>that</u> of the red wolf.
Plural Demonstrative Pronoun	<u>These</u> need to be checked regularly in your car: *oil, other fluids, brakes, and tires*. Western *maples* do not turn as red in autumn as <u>those</u> in eastern North America do.
Singular Demonstrative Adjective	<u>This</u> *book* changed my life. Scientists predicted the melting of polar ice, and <u>that</u> *phenomenon* has already started.
Plural Demonstrative Adjective	Stomach, liver, pancreas—<u>these</u> *organs* are all part of the digestive system. My little dog thinks he's just as fierce as <u>those</u> big *dogs* over there.

Note: Demonstrative adjectives are the only adjectives that agree in number with the nouns they modify.

7. Indefinite Pronouns

An *indefinite pronoun* replaces or refers to an indefinite, general, or unidentified person or thing. Indefinite pronouns either do not have a referent or do not have a specific referent.

The following indefinite pronouns refer only to people.

anybody	everybody	nobody	somebody
anyone	everyone	no one	someone

Note: Pronouns ending in *–body* are more informal than those ending in *–one*.

<u>Everyone</u> in the anatomy class usually applies to medical school.

There was a knock on the door, but when I looked, <u>nobody</u> was there.

The following indefinite pronouns refer only to things, ideas or abstractions.

anything	everything	nothing	something

My grandfather always said that <u>anything</u> was possible under the sun.

When used as indefinite pronouns, the following words can refer to people, animals, or things. In the following sentences, the referent for each underlined pronoun is shown in *italics*.

all	both	few/a few	neither	others
another	each	many	none	several
any	either	most	one	some

> One *branch* of geography is physical geography; <u>another</u> is cultural geography.
>
> *Thomas Ahearn* and *John Wright* worked with electricity. <u>Both</u> were Canadian.
>
> Some *elements* are gases at 15 degrees C, <u>others</u> are solids, and <u>a few</u> are liquids.
>
> Most *daisies* are perennials, but <u>some</u> bloom for only one or two seasons.

8. Other Pronouns

The following phrases often function as definite pronouns, replacing nouns or other types of structures that have recently been mentioned.

the first	the last	the former	the latter	the other

> The flood had three *causes*, <u>the first</u> being massive deforestation in the hills.
>
> Students can live in a dormitory or *off campus*; most senior students choose <u>the latter</u>.

 PRACTICE

Exercise 13–A

Pronouns and Referents. Underline all pronouns and demonstratives. Circle their referents.

1. The cat keeps itself clean with its paws and barbed tongue.

2. Rivers are truly remarkable in their ability to erode and shape our planet.

3. Driving while intoxicated is illegal, but this is not the only reason to avoid it.

4. The stories of Mark Twain were more widely read than were those of any other humorist of his time.

5. Creative people tend to be more independent than others, and they also have a higher degree of

   self–acceptance.

6. Despite the vampire bat's tiny size—its body is no larger than that of a mouse—this blood–sucking

   creature is a threat to cattle.

7. Studies show that men who are successful in their careers are not much happier than are those who

are less successful.

8. Because of its lower pitch, the bassoon has a tonal quality that is less rasping than that of the oboe.

Exercise 13–B

Sentence Completion.   Choose the word or phrase that best completes the sentence.

1. Desert trees such as the giant cactus guard
------- internal moisture with sharp spikes.

   (A) their
   (B) theirs
   (C) they
   (D) these

2. Some people are practical and down–to–earth,
while ------- are dreamers.

   (A) another
   (B) others
   (C) them
   (D) their

3. The thymus gland, ------- is located in the
upper part of the chest, produces cells that
help fight infection.

   (A) it
   (B) who
   (C) that
   (D) which

4. There are several differences between the
composition of river water and ------- of
seawater.

   (A) that
   (B) some
   (C) those
   (D) both

5. A master of watercolor was John Marin,
------- used the medium to portray the city as
a mighty organism.

   (A) he
   (B) who
   (C) his
   (D) which

6. Bicycle messengers have existed for a hundred
years in New York, and ------- number reached
a peak in the 1990s.

   (A) its
   (B) his
   (C) they
   (D) their

7. Eugene O'Neill's plays have been compared
to ------- of the ancient Greeks.

   (A) their
   (B) whose
   (C) they
   (D) those

8. If you want to observe Venus and Mars together,
------- should look in the southwestern sky after
sunset in December.

   (A) they
   (B) one
   (C) you
   (D) he

9. In 1609 Galileo built the first telescope, -------
he used to discover the four largest satellites
of Jupiter.

   (A) this
   (B) that
   (C) which
   (D) whom

10. ------- in the grammar and vocabulary of
Standard American English conveys where a
speaker comes from.

   (A)   No one
   (B)   Nothing
   (C)   Nobody
   (D)   Neither

Exercise 13–C

Sentence Editing. One of the underlined parts in each sentence is incorrect. Cross out the incorrect part and write the correction above it.

1. Memory begins to diminish in <u>some</u> people as early as <u>their</u> forties, but <u>this</u> does not mean <u>he</u> will develop Alzheimer's disease.

2. The flavor of a salad oil is <u>usually</u> enhanced by the foods <u>that</u> are preserved in it, and <u>this</u> improves the taste of <u>yours</u> salads.

3. During the Civil War, the <u>North's</u> population, industrial capacity, and financial <u>resources</u> were <u>much</u> greater than <u>that</u> of the South.

4. Mary Pickford, <u>an</u> actress known as "America's Sweetheart," <u>was</u> most famous for <u>his</u> roles in <u>films</u> such as *The Poor Little Rich Girl* and *Rebecca of Sunnybrook Farm*.

5. When a chimpanzee is frightened, <u>it</u> touches <u>another</u> chimpanzee, just like a child <u>who</u> is watching a scary movie takes <u>their</u> mother's hand.

6. Gutzon Borglum, <u>his</u> first work <u>was</u> a statue of Abraham Lincoln, is famous for the figures <u>he</u> carved on mountainsides, especially <u>those</u> on Mount Rushmore.

7. <u>We</u> laugh during moments of anxiety because we <u>feel</u> a loss of control, and <u>our</u> laughter reassures <u>ours</u> that we can cope with the situation.

8. When students <u>apply</u> for admission to a university, <u>they</u> generally must submit transcripts of all of <u>your</u> previous college–level <u>work</u>.

9. The Hurons, <u>whom</u> numbered about twenty <u>thousand</u> in the 1600s, <u>were</u> a confederation of Native American groups <u>that</u> spoke Wyandot, an Iroquoian language.

10. Although <u>both</u> are similar in size and behavior, the red squirrel can be identified by <u>its</u> coat, <u>which</u> is brighter and redder than <u>those</u> of its cousin, the Douglas squirrel.

Exercise 13–D

TOEFL iBT Reading. Read the passages and choose the best answer to each question.

QUESTION 1

Whether true bulb, rhizome, or tuberous root, all bulbs produce flowers year after year. The true bulbs are the daffodils and tulips. Rhizomes produce the calla lily; tuberous roots produce the dahlia and begonia. Some bulbs are hardy, able to stay in the ground all winter. Others are tender and must be dug up and stored when temperatures drop.

1. The word Others in the passage refers to

(A) rhizomes
(B) tuberous roots
(C) dahlia and begonia
(D) bulbs

QUESTIONS 2–3

The causes of most disease, parasites such as viruses, bacteria, and fungi, all specialize in breaking into cells, either to eat them, as fungi and bacteria do, or, like viruses, to subvert their genetic machinery for the purpose of making new viruses. Either way, parasites must get into cells. To do that, they employ protein molecules that bind to other molecules on cell surfaces. The struggle between parasites and their hosts is all about these binding procedures.

2. The word them in the passage refers to

(A) parasites
(B) viruses
(C) cells
(D) bacteria

3. The word they in the passage refers to

(A) parasites
(B) viruses
(C) cells
(D) molecules

QUESTIONS 4–5

An essential part of the marketing process, advertising can be tremendously influential in selling products. Not only does advertising help people recognize a particular brand, but it also aims to keep them loyal to it. Brand loyalty is one of the most important goals of consumer advertising. Whether manufacturers produce cars, canned foods or cosmetics, they want their customers to make repeated purchases. The quality of the product will encourage this, of course, but so will effective advertising.

4. The word them in the passage refers to

(A) products
(B) people
(C) goals
(D) manufacturers

5. The word this in the passage refers to

(A) brand loyalty
(B) consumer advertising
(C) producing cars, canned foods or cosmetics
(D) making repeated purchases

QUESTIONS 6–7

Saturn, the farthest planet visible to the unaided eye, is almost twice as far from the sun as Jupiter is. Although Saturn is second in size only to Jupiter, its mass is significantly smaller. With a diameter of approximately 114,000 kilometers at the equator, Saturn's rotational speed spins it completely around in a little more than ten hours. Either Saturn is composed entirely of gas, or it has a small dense center surrounded by a layer of liquid and a deep atmosphere. Saturn's atmosphere is much like that of Jupiter, except that the temperature at the top of its cloud layer is at least 38 degrees C. lower.

6. The word its in the passage refers to

- (A) Saturn
- (B) eye
- (C) sun
- (D) Jupiter

7. The word that in the passage refers to

- (A) gas
- (B) center
- (C) atmosphere
- (D) temperature

QUESTIONS 8–10

1   After the United States purchased Louisiana from France, President Jefferson called for an expedition to explore the new territory. Jefferson's secretary, Meriwether Lewis, led the expedition, along with army officer William Clark. The Lewis and Clark expedition would discover an abundance of natural wealth, about which the two young explorers would return to tell the world. When the expedition departed in 1804, there were twenty–nine members, including a few Frenchmen and several frontiersmen from Kentucky. Along the way they picked up an interpreter named Toussant Charbonneau and his wife Sacajawea, the Shoshone "Bird Woman," who aided them as guide and peacemaker.

2   During the long journey, the explorers met friendly Otos and hostile Teton Sioux. They discovered giant buffalo herds and the bones of a forty–five–foot dinosaur. They encountered antelope so innocent of human contact that they tamely approached the men. Both Lewis and Clark kept detailed journals, cataloging an astonishing array of new plants and animals.

8. The word which in paragraph 1 refers to

- (A) the new territory
- (B) Lewis and Clark
- (C) an abundance of natural wealth
- (D) the expedition

9. The word who in paragraph 1 refers to

- (A) Frenchmen
- (B) frontiersmen
- (C) Toussant Charbonneau
- (D) Sacajawea

10. Which sentence below best expresses the essential information in the highlighted sentence in paragraph 2?

- (A) The antelope walked up to the men because they did not fear humans.
- (B) Lewis and Clark killed the antelope that came too close to the men.
- (C) The antelope were beautiful, and the men wanted to touch them.
- (D) The men were surprised because they had never seen antelope before.

QUESTION 11

Look at the four squares, **A**, **B**, **C**, and **D**, which indicate where the following sentence could be added to the passage below. Where would the sentence best fit?

The Romans built many in Europe, as did the Chinese at around the same time.

Early bridges were built on the principle of the pillar and beam. Vertical pillars and horizontal beams stretched from one side of a river to the other. However, with beam construction, the span had to be short. **A** Long crossings required many pillars, which would impede river traffic. **B** The arch, a relatively late development, provided a much more elegant solution. The arch could reach high above the river, leaving shipping lanes unobstructed. **C** When constructed of stone, the arch could bear a tremendous load. Stone arch bridges were suitable for carrying roads over rivers and for carrying aqueducts. **D** The tradition of building stone arch bridges continued for nearly two thousand years.

QUESTION 12

Look at the four squares, **A**, **B**, **C**, and **D**, which indicate where the following sentence could be added to the passage below. Where would the sentence best fit?

With the completion of the first transcontinental railroad, they had access to those of the West as well.

Historians who have examined the intellectual origins of the national park system have discovered the essential role of the railroads in promoting the American West. **A** Tourists in search of spectacular scenery had always traveled to the natural wonders of the East, such as Niagara Falls in New York. **B** Without the railroads, the natural beauty of the West might never have been preserved. The railroads did everything possible to stimulate interest in the West. **C** The Southern Pacific Railroad founded *Sunset*, a monthly magazine supporting artists, photographers, and journalists who chronicled the wonders of the region. The Santa Fe Railway displayed paintings of the Grand Canyon and other southwestern landscapes in its stations. **D** By emphasizing the imposing features of the West, the railroads helped inspire the government to preserve these wild lands as national parks.

QUESTION 13

Look at the four squares, **A**, **B**, **C**, and **D**, which indicate where the following sentence could be added to the passage below. Where would the sentence best fit?

In some studies, it is measured by such criteria as marital status and frequency of contact with friends and relatives.

Adults face different sets of changes as they move through the normal role acquisitions and losses of adulthood. **A** At every age, high levels of life changes, particularly those involving emotional losses, are linked to higher rates of depression and physical illness. However, there are personal and social resources that may buffer the individual from the potential impact of stress. **B** Such resources are collectively referred to as resistance resources. **C** Central among these is the availability of social support, which can be defined as the receipt of aid and affirmation from others. **D** Researchers have concluded that one's perception of the adequacy of social support is a reliable measure of one's well being.

Exercise 13–E

TOEFL iBT Speaking. In the independent speaking tasks below, use correct pronouns in your responses. For each task, allow 15 seconds to prepare your response and 45 seconds to speak.

1. Describe a person who helped you make a decision that was important in your life. Explain how he or she helped you. Include details and examples in your explanation.

2. Some families spend most of their time together in one room when they are at home. In others, individual family members spend most of their time in their own rooms. Which situation do you think is better, and why? Include details and examples in your explanation.

Preparation Time – 15 seconds
Response Time – 45 seconds

Exercise 13–F

TOEFL iBT Speaking. In this integrated speaking task, you will read a short passage about a campus situation, listen to a conversation, and then speak in response to a question about what you have read and heard. Do not look at the question until the conversation has ended. Do not look at the reading passage while you are speaking.

Reading Time – 45 seconds

NOTICE OF CHANGES AT THE COUNSELING CENTER

We regret to inform you that the Counseling Center will no longer be open five days a week. Starting on March 15, the Center will be open only on Mondays, Wednesdays, and Thursdays, from 8:00 a.m. to 4:00 p.m. Another change is the new fee of $25 for our special workshops. These workshops, which were formerly free of charge, include evening and weekend courses in career planning, stress management, and test preparation. The above changes are due to budget cuts and increased costs throughout the college. Despite these changes, however, we will continue to provide our students with high–quality counseling services.

Now cover the passage and listen to the conversation. You may take notes, and you may use your notes to help you answer the question. After you hear the question, begin preparing your response. You may look at the question, but NOT at the passage. You have 30 seconds to prepare your response and 60 seconds to speak.

 Audio Track 20

The woman expresses her opinion about the changes at the Counseling Center. State her opinion and explain the reasons she gives for holding that opinion.

 Stop

Preparation Time – 30 seconds
Response Time – 60 seconds

UNIT 13

Exercise 13–G

TOEFL iBT Writing. For this independent writing task, respond to the question by writing an essay in which you state and support your opinion on the topic. Your essay will be scored on the quality of your writing, including how well you organize and develop your ideas and how well you use language to express your ideas. An effective essay will have a minimum of 300 words.

Read the following question and make any notes that will help you plan your response. Then begin writing. You have 30 minutes to plan and write your essay.

Do you agree or disagree with the following statement?

The differences between young people and old people are greater today than they were in the past.

Use specific reasons and examples to support your answer.

Time – 30 minutes

Answers to Exercises 13–A through 13–D and 13–F are on pages 266–267.

Answers to Exercises 13–E and 13–G will vary.

 EXTENSION

1. **Pronoun Form.** In reading done outside class, look for sentences with pronouns. Bring five sentences to share in class. Write a sentence on the board, but omit the pronouns and leave blank lines where they should be. Your classmates must complete the sentence. How many pronouns would be correct in the sentence?

2. **Pronoun Gender.** Discuss why some nonliving things are referred to by masculine or feminine pronouns. For example, some people call their car or boat *she*. What other examples can you think of? Why do you think animals are sometimes referred to with neuter pronouns and sometimes with *he, she,* or *who*?

3. **Sentence Writing.** Practice writing sentences using the pronouns in the list below. Make sure pronouns agree with their referents in form, person, number, and gender.

him	its	them	those	who	the former
it	she	they	which	whose	the latter

QUIZ 4   UNITS 10 – 13

Time – 10 minutes

Choose the word or phrase that best completes the sentence.

1. In its gaseous state, water ------- invisible vapor.

   (A) is a
   (B) are
   (C) is the
   (D) is an

2. Some people stay in a single occupation for their entire working life, but the majority make at least ------- job changes.

   (A) the few
   (B) a few
   (C) fewer
   (D) a little

3. A demonstration of the link between long life and health practices ------- study in California.

   (A) are coming from
   (B) come from the
   (C) comes from a
   (D) it came from the

4. In addition to international banking and -------, Panama is also known for growing bananas.

   (A) oil refining
   (B) an oil refining
   (C) the oil refining
   (D) type of oil refining

One of the underlined parts in each sentence is incorrect. Cross out the incorrect part and write the correction above it.

5. A hurricane is a tropical storm in whom the wind reaches speeds of greater than 75 miles per hour.

6. Like many realist writers before he, novelist Theodore Dreiser told stories about ordinary people

   who struggle with moral issues.

7. The films of the early Italian filmmakers had larger casts and were more lavish than that made by

   the French.

8. The best known mimosa is the sensitive plant, whose leaves fold up and collapses under such

   stimuli as touch, darkness, or drought.

9. Several studies in the Netherlands have shown that there is a lower risk of heart disease among fish

   eaters than among people which eat no fish.

10. Enforcing minimum wages are the economic responsibility of the government, which also has the

    duty to regulate business and protect the environment.

Answers to Quiz 4 are on page 267.
Record your score on page 301.

UNIT 14 COMPARISON

1. **Degree Forms**
2. **The Equative**
3. **The Comparative**
4. **Double Comparatives**
5. **The Superlative**

FOCUS

What does this sentence need?

In North America, household water consumption is slightly ------- than it is in Europe.

- ○ high
- ○ as high
- ○ higher
- ○ highest

The sentence needs a comparative adjective. The word *than* indicates that two things are being compared: household water consumption in North America and household water consumption in Europe. The third answer, *higher*, is an adjective in the **comparative degree**. The correctly formed sentence is:

In North America, household water consumption is slightly **higher** than it is in Europe.

What does this sentence need?

Canvas is ------- surface for oil paintings.

- ○ the most common
- ○ more commonly
- ○ common than
- ○ almost as common

The sentence needs an adjective to modify *surface*. Only the first answer, *the most common*, is correct in the sentence. It is an adjective in the **superlative degree**. The correctly formed sentence is:

Canvas is **the most common** surface for oil paintings.

STUDY

1. Degree Forms

Adjectives and adverbs have different forms to express different levels, or *degrees*, of comparison. The *base form*, the simple form of an adjective or adverb, is also called the *positive degree*. The *comparative degree* is the intermediate level, and the *superlative degree* is the highest level of comparison.

Base Form	Comparative	Superlative
big	bigger	biggest
dark	darker	darkest
easy	easier	easiest
few	fewer	fewest
great	greater	greatest
hot	hotter	hottest
nice	nicer	nicest
old	older	oldest
small	smaller	smallest
ugly	uglier	ugliest

Some common adjectives have irregular forms for the comparative and superlative degrees.

Base Form	Comparative	Superlative
bad	worse	worst
good	better	best
little	less	least
many	more	most
much	more	most

Some common adverbs have irregular forms for the comparative and superlative degrees.

Base Form	Comparative	Superlative
badly	worse	worst
far	farther	farthest
far	further	furthest
well	better	best

Note: Far/farther/farthest usually refer to physical distance. *Far/further/furthest* refer to distance in a nonphysical dimension, such as time or degree.

2. The Equative

The *equative degree* of an adjective or adverb expresses an equal degree of comparison. The equative indicates equality between two things; it shows how two things are alike.

The equative degree takes the base form of the adjective or adverb, along with *as...as*. The equative form is the same for short and long adjectives and adverbs.

Short Adjective or Adverb *as...as*	Long Adjective or Adverb *as...as*
as fast as	as adequately as
as large as	as consistently as
as many as	as frustrated as
as often as	as interesting as
as tall as	as professional as
as well as	as successfully as

> A banana contains <u>as many</u> calories <u>as</u> a half–cup of noodles.
>
> A growing puppy eats <u>as often as</u> six times a day.
>
> Mr. Lee speaks <u>as eloquently</u> in person <u>as</u> he does in front of a television camera.
>
> Older workers have shown that they are <u>as productive as</u> younger workers are.

Equative adjectives can be modified by the adverb *not*, which changes the meaning to negative equality, or inequality.

> Quinine is *not* <u>as effective as</u> the newer anti–malarial drugs.
>
> The feathers of a female bird are *not* <u>as colorful as</u> those of a male.

Equative adjectives can have other modifiers, such as *almost*, *just*, and *twice*.

> A liquid quart holds *almost* <u>as much</u> water <u>as</u> a liter.
>
> The North American cougar is *just* <u>as fierce as</u> the Siberian tiger.
>
> A smoker's risk of heart attack is *twice* <u>as high as</u> that of a nonsmoker.

When two adjectives in an equative structure are joined by *and*, the first adjective is not followed by *as*.

> A cyclone is usually <u>as powerful</u> *and* <u>destructive as</u> any other tropical storm.

The equative degree can be used to show *complex equalities*, in which two things are compared.

> The *song* of the lark is just <u>as beautiful as</u> its *color* is <u>dull</u>.
>
> *Crater Lake* is seven times <u>as deep as</u> the *Giant Sequoia Tree* is <u>tall</u>.

3. The Comparative

The **comparative degree** expresses an unequal degree of comparison between two things. The comparative indicates that one thing has more or less of a quality than the other.

The comparative form is different for short and long adjectives and adverbs. Those with two or more syllables usually take the long form, with a few exceptions.

Short Adjective or Adverb *-er than*	Long Adjective or Adverb *more…than / less…than*
bigger than	more expensive than
earlier than	more important than
fewer than	more often than
lighter than	less frequently than
softer than	less interesting than
wider than	less successful than

> An apple contains <u>fewer</u> calories <u>than</u> a candy bar.
>
> The storm arrived <u>earlier than</u> we had expected.
>
> Puerto Rico has <u>higher</u> average January temperatures <u>than</u> Hawaii does.
>
> Quinine is <u>less effective than</u> the newer anti–malarial drugs.
>
> A parsnip is <u>more flavorful than</u> a potato.
>
> Some people work <u>less efficiently</u> under stress <u>than</u> others do.

4. Double Comparatives

A **double comparative** occurs when two comparatives are used together in a sentence. A double comparative often indicates a cause–result relationship. The first comparative shows cause, and the second comparative shows result.

Each part of a double comparative takes *the* + the comparative form.

> Mountaineers know that <u>the higher</u> you climb, <u>the colder</u> it gets.
>
> <u>The longer</u> the treatment for snakebite is delayed, <u>the more</u> one risks losing a limb.

In the first sentence above, the cause is the *higher you climb*; the result is *the colder it gets*. In other words, if you climb higher, it gets colder. In the second sentence, the cause is *the longer the treatment for snakebite is delayed*. The result is *the more one risks losing a limb*. In other words, if the treatment for snakebite is delayed too long, the risk of losing a limb increases.

In some double comparatives, the verb can be omitted from one or both comparatives as long as the meaning is clear.

> <u>The farther</u> a car moves away from a speed trap, <u>the lower</u> the frequency of the radar signal.
>
> <u>The higher</u> the elevation, <u>the colder</u> the temperature.

UNIT 14

In conversation, speakers often omit the verbs in double comparatives.

> The sooner, the better. (If something happens sooner, the result will be better.)
>
> The more, the merrier! (If more people come, the occasion will be merrier.)

5. The Superlative

The *superlative degree* expresses an unequal degree of comparison among three or more things. The superlative indicates that one thing has the most or least of a quality, compared to all others.

The superlative form is different for short and long adjectives and adverbs. Those with two or more syllables usually take the long form, with a few exceptions.

Short Adjective or Adverb *the -est*	Long Adjective or Adverb *the most... / the least...*
the earliest	the most confused
the fastest	the most daring
the fewest	the most frequently
the highest	the least complex
the largest	the least helpful
the shortest	the least independent

> The winning horse ran <u>the fastest</u> throughout the race.
>
> February has <u>the fewest</u> days of all the months.
>
> For four decades, the Empire State Building was <u>the tallest</u> building in the world.
>
> Many people think the swan is <u>the most elegant</u> bird.
>
> Mark Twain is probably <u>the most frequently</u> quoted American humorist.
>
> <u>The least successful</u> nests are those that are found by predators.

Superlative adjectives sometimes follow *one of*, *some of*, and *many of*.

> The grizzly is *one of* <u>the strongest</u> land mammals.
>
> Jamaica produces *some of* <u>the finest</u> coffees in the world.
>
> *Many of* <u>the most beautiful</u> beaches are difficult to reach.

With many superlative adverbs, *the* is omitted.

> <u>Most importantly</u>, organisms must be able to adapt to change.
>
> Studies show that accidents occur <u>most often</u> because of driver distraction.
>
> Companies function <u>least productively</u> when morale among workers is low.

When a possessive noun or adjective comes before a superlative adjective, *the* is omitted.

> With eleven million inhabitants, Ontario is *Canada's* <u>most populous</u> province.
>
> *His* <u>biggest</u> contribution was the graphic design for our web site.

 PRACTICE

Exercise 14–A

Degree Structures. Underline the degree structure in each sentence. Name the degree by writing **E** for equative, **C** for comparative, or **S** for superlative next to the sentence.

1. _____ Tariffs and quotas are the most visible trade barriers.

2. _____ In most species of seal, the females are not as large as the males.

3. _____ It was not until 1947 that someone actually traveled faster than the speed of sound.

4. _____ Inadequate support in young adulthood can be just as damaging as poor parenting in childhood.

5. _____ Some of the earliest records of money usage came from Africa, where coins were issued over two thousand years ago.

6. _____ People are more likely to see the need for health insurance than for life insurance.

Exercise 14–B

Sentence Completion. Choose the word or phrase that best completes the sentence.

1. Warm water is ------- cold water.

   (A) as less dense
   (B) less dense to
   (C) of less density
   (D) less dense than

2. The barn owl is twice ------- the pygmy owl.

   (A) taller than
   (B) as tall as
   (C) the tallest
   (D) as it is tall

3. Apartments are ------- to be built in cities than in suburban or rural areas.

   (A) more likely
   (B) as likely
   (C) the most likely
   (D) likely

4. Teacups have changed ------- in design over the years than have teapots.

   (A) less
   (B) lesser
   (C) little
   (D) a little

5. The folk paintings of Grandma Moses were ------- the works of the trained artists of her time.

   (A) more popular
   (B) as popular as
   (C) almost popular
   (D) the most popular

6. The more light energy an object absorbs, ------- the object becomes.

   (A) as warm as
   (B) warmer than
   (C) the warmer
   (D) the warmest

UNIT 14

7. Many people think the collie is as beautiful -------.

    (A) that the bulldog is ugly
    (B) as ugly as the bulldog
    (C) more than the ugly bulldog
    (D) as the bulldog is ugly

8. Dinah Washington's style of blues was ------- complex than that of Chicago blues singers.

    (A) the most
    (B) much
    (C) much more
    (D) as much

9. Semiprecious stones are ------- precious stones such as diamonds.

    (A) less valuable than
    (B) the least valuable
    (C) valuable than less
    (D) at least as valuable

10. Chippewa National Forest in Minnesota has one of ------- bald eagle populations outside Alaska.

    (A) larger
    (B) larger than
    (C) largest
    (D) the largest

Exercise 14–C

Sentence Editing. One of the underlined parts in each sentence is incorrect. Cross out the incorrect part and write the correction above it.

1. Australia is the flattest and dry of the continents, as well as the oldest and most isolated.

2. A tree's height will be stunted by the wind if it grows high than the protective snow pack.

3. The crocodile is slightly smaller and least bulky than the alligator, and it has a larger but narrower snout.

4. The Byzantine Empire was almost as large and just as powerful than the Roman Empire had been.

5. When an object is heated, the molecules move faster, and the faster they move, the hottest the object becomes.

6. The corporation is the formalest business arrangement, and the sole proprietorship is the least complex.

7. There is much cross–cultural misunderstanding about facial expressions, and this is likely to be

more greater for subtle expressions.

8. The longest river in the world, the Nile nourished most successful of the great ancient civilizations and

now supports agriculture in Egypt and Sudan.

9. The cat's eyes, perhaps the animal's most distinctive feature, can function just as well in darkness as if

they can in bright daylight.

10. The political revolutions of the eighteenth century had an immense impact on architecture, while the

effect of the Industrial Revolution was lesser direct.

Exercise 14–D

TOEFL iBT Reading. Read the passages and choose the best answer to each question.

QUESTIONS 1–4

1   The three energy–yielding food nutrients are carbohydrates, proteins, and fats. The amount of energy a food provides depends on how much of each nutrient it contains. When broken down in the body, a gram of carbohydrate and a gram of protein each yield about four kilocalories of energy. A gram of fat yields nine kilocalories; therefore, fat has a greater energy density than either protein or carbohydrates. Foods with a high energy density provide more kilocalories per gram than foods with a low energy density.

2   Different meals may deliver the same number of kilocalories but varying amounts of food energy. For example, a 450–gram breakfast of cereal, milk, fruit, egg, turkey sausage, toast, and jam and a 150–gram breakfast of doughnuts both deliver 500 kilocalories. However, the first breakfast, which is higher in protein, has a lower energy density than the doughnuts and supplies three times as much food energy.

3   During a meal, as food enters the digestive tract, hunger decreases and the body reaches satiation, the signal to stop eating. The nutrient composition of a meal affects the level of satiation the meal provides. Foods low in energy density are more satiating than foods high in energy density. Of the three energy–yielding nutrients, protein is the most satiating and fat is the least satiating. High–fat foods are flavorful, which encourages people to eat more, but they are also energy–dense and deliver more kilocalories per bite. Therefore, eating meals high in fat may lead to overconsumption.

1. It can be inferred from paragraph 1 that foods high in protein are

   (A) broken down slowly in the body
   (B) higher in calories than foods high in fat
   (C) more flavorful than foods high in fat
   (D) less energy–dense than foods high in fat

2. Which sentence below best expresses the essential information in the highlighted sentence in paragraph 2?

   (A) Although the first breakfast is higher in protein, the doughnuts are higher in food energy.
   (B) The high–protein, less energy–dense breakfast provides three times as much energy as the doughnuts.
   (C) The doughnuts provide more food energy than the first breakfast, which is lower in energy density.
   (D) Because the doughnuts are higher in fat, they contain three times as much food energy as the other breakfast.

3. What is the relationship between food nutrients and satiation?

   (A) Some nutrients have no effect on satiation.
   (B) Foods that taste better are more satiating.
   (C) High–fat foods give the highest level of satiation.
   (D) Satiation is lower in energy–dense foods.

4. The passage supports which of the following statements about food nutrition?

   (A) The nutrients in food determine its energy yield and level of satiation.
   (B) All foods with the same number of kilocalories are equally nutritious.
   (C) The most nutritious foods are those that are high in energy density.
   (D) Too many protein–rich foods will lead to overeating and weight gain.

QUESTIONS 5–6

Our perception that social support is available is related to our attachment to other people. The more secure the attachment, the greater the sense of social support. Adults with adequate support have a lower risk of disease and depression than do those with weaker social networks. This is especially clear when an individual is under high stress. The negative effect of stress is smaller for individuals with adequate social support than for those whose social support is weak. For example, one study showed that the link between severe life changes and depression in women was significantly weaker when the woman had a close, intimate relationship with a husband or friend. The women who had no close relationship were four times as likely to become depressed after a major change as were those who had a close confidant.

5. It can be inferred from the passage that one's perception of social support is

(A) not equal to the actual level of support
(B) not as stressful as one's desire to help others
(C) stronger when one feels a sense of security
(D) lower than the risk of disease and depression

6. Which sentence below best expresses the essential information in the highlighted sentence in the passage?

(A) Depression after a major change was four times as likely in women without close social support.
(B) Women who have close relationships are four times as confident as women with no relationships.
(C) Major life changes occurred four times as often to women who had no close confidant.
(D) Women are four times as likely as men are to form close relationships with other people.

Exercise 14–E

TOEFL iBT Listening. Listen to the recording. You may take notes as you listen. Do not look at the questions until the discussion has ended. When you hear the questions, look at the questions and choose the best answer to each.

 Audio Track 21

1. What does the professor mean by this statement: 🎧

(A) The shallow ocean is more interesting than the deep ocean.
(B) It is fair to say that water in the deep ocean does not circulate.
(C) There is more water in the ocean's shallow areas than in its deep areas.
(D) Scientists know relatively little about deep–water circulation.

2. According to the discussion, what factors influence the movement of water in the ocean?

Choose two answers.

[A] Wind blowing across the surface
[B] The addition of chemical pollutants
[C] Movement of the sea bottom
[D] A change in the water's density

3. How is the ocean's deep water different from the water at the surface?

- (A) It is warmer, cleaner, and saltier.
- (B) It is warmer, less dense, and less salty.
- (C) It is colder, heavier, and slower moving.
- (D) It is colder, denser, and faster moving.

4. Why does the professor say this:

- (A) To explain why oceanography is a challenging field
- (B) To emphasize a property of the ocean's lower layers
- (C) To point out that visibility is poor in the deep ocean
- (D) To imply that the course will become more difficult

Exercise 14–F

TOEFL iBT Speaking. In the independent speaking tasks below, use correct comparative structures in your responses. For each task, allow 15 seconds to prepare your response and 45 seconds to speak.

1. Compare two different subjects that you have studied. Which subject did you like better, and why? Include details and examples to support your explanation.

2. Some people like to attend live sports events at a stadium or park. Others think that sports are more enjoyable when seen on television. Which do you think is a better way to watch sports, and why? Include details and examples in your explanation.

Preparation Time – 15 seconds
Response Time – 45 seconds

Exercise 14–G

TOEFL iBT Speaking. In this integrated speaking task, you will listen to part of a lecture. You will then be asked to summarize important information from the lecture.

Cover the question while the lecture is playing. You may take notes, and you may use your notes to help you answer the question. After you hear the question, you may look at the question and prepare your response. You have 20 seconds to prepare your response and 60 seconds to speak.

 Audio Track 22

> Using points and details from the talk, explain some of the differences between the mass wasting processes of mudflow and creep.

 Stop

Preparation Time – 20 seconds
Response Time – 60 seconds

Answers to Exercises 14–A through 14–G are on pages 267–268.

EXTENSION

1. **Sentence Analysis.** In reading done outside class, look for examples of sentences with equative, comparative, and superlative structures. Bring examples to share in class. Write some of the sentences on the board. With your teacher and classmates, answer the following questions about each sentence.

    a. Identify the degree structure. Is it equative, comparative, or superlative? Is it an adjective or adverb?

    b. Rewrite the sentence, changing the degree structure to a different degree. For example, change an equative to a comparative, or change a comparative to a superlative.

2. **Pair Exercise.** Work with a partner to create a list of ten adjectives. Write down only the base form of the adjective. Exchange lists with another pair of classmates. Then follow the steps below.

    a. Work with your partner to list the comparative and superlative forms of each adjective on your new list. Be careful to spell correctly when adding *–er* and *–est*. Some adjectives may take the long form of comparative and superlative.

    b. Work with your partner to write ten sentences, using five of the comparative adjectives and five of the superlative adjectives on your list. You may divide the work any way you wish.

    c. Choose one sentence with a comparative and one with a superlative to read aloud to the whole class.

UNIT 15 PREPOSITIONS

1. **Prepositional Phrases**
2. **Function of Prepositional Phrases**
3. **Meaning of Prepositions**
4. **Paired Expressions**
5. **Compound Prepositions**
6. **Verbs with Prepositions**
7. **Adjectives with Prepositions**

 FOCUS

What is wrong with this sentence?

> The first animals to live on land were amphibians, which lived part of their lives from water and part on land.

The sentence has an incorrect preposition. A ***preposition*** is a word that shows how a noun is related to other words in a sentence. In this case, the preposition *from* is incorrect because it does not show the correct relationship between *lived part of their lives* and *water*. Amphibians lived part of their lives *in* water, not *from* water. The correctly formed sentence is:

> The first animals to live on land were amphibians, which lived part of their lives **in** water and part on land.

What is wrong with this sentence?

> Supermarkets depend high volume and low overhead to keep prices below the average for retail stores.

The verb *depend* must be followed by a preposition, usually the preposition *on*. *Depend on* is a common verb + preposition structure. The correctly formed sentence is:

> Supermarkets depend **on** high volume and low overhead to keep prices below the average for retail stores.

UNIT 15

 STUDY

1. Prepositional Phrases

A *preposition* is a word that shows how a noun is related to another part of the sentence. The preposition comes before the noun and controls the noun. The noun is the *object of the preposition*, and the preposition + noun structure is a *prepositional phrase*.

> preposition + noun

The following structures are prepositional phrases.

> by a doctor   for making   from the Ohio Valley   with hot water

The object of a preposition must be a noun structure.

Structure	Example
Noun	The cause *of* <u>malnutrition</u> is a lack *of* <u>vitamins</u>, <u>minerals</u>, and <u>proteins</u>.
Noun Phrase	Civil conflict characterized much of Asia *in* <u>the mid–twentieth century</u>.
Pronoun	Most energy waves pass *by* <u>us</u> or *through* <u>us</u> without having any harmful effect *on* <u>us</u>.
Gerund	Bank tellers are responsible *for* <u>recording</u> all of the transactions they perform.
Noun Clause	Physical health has a definite effect *on* <u>how people cope with emotional crises</u>.

Note: The object of a preposition can *not* be an infinitive. In the infinitive form, *to* is not a preposition. For example, in the infinitives *to plan* and *to control*, *to* is not a preposition; it is part of the infinitive.

2. Function of Prepositional Phrases

Prepositional phrases are *modifiers*, structures that change the meaning of other structures. In sentences, prepositional phrases can function as either adjectives or adverbs.

When a prepositional phrase functions as an *adjective*, it modifies a noun. The prepositional phrase comes after the noun that it modifies. In the following sentences, the modified nouns are shown in *italics*.

> The *rise* <u>of science</u> challenged the *authority* <u>of the old order</u>.
>   PP   PP
>
> There has been much *speculation* <u>about the *effects*</u> <u>of global warming</u>.
>   PP   PP

When a prepositional phrase functions as an **adverb**, it modifies a verb or a clause. The prepositional phrase can come at different places in a sentence. In the following sentences, the modified structures are shown in *italics*.

Many capitalist institutions *originated* <u>in ancient times</u>.
                                              PP

Musicians *traveled* <u>from every continent</u> <u>for the folk festival</u>.
                       PP   PP

<u>Until the 1920s</u>, *there were very few paved highways*.
   PP

---

3. Meaning of Prepositions

Prepositions are small words, but they are important in conveying meaning. Prepositions express various relationships between their noun objects and the words that come before the preposition. They can indicate relationships of space, time, direction, status, inclusion, or exclusion.

Space	about	at	beyond	on
	above	behind	by	outside
	across	below	from	over
	along	beneath	in	under
	among	beside	inside	upon
	around	between	near	within
Time	after	before	in	throughout
	around	beyond	on	till
	at	during	since	until
Direction	around	in	on	to
	down	into	out	toward
	from	off	through	up
Status/Position	against	between	from	throughout
	among	by	like	under
	as	despite	of	unlike
	behind	for	over	with
Inclusion	about	in	of	with
Exclusion	except	out	without	

UNIT 15

> The dog walked <u>across</u> the lawn and sat <u>under</u> the tree <u>beside</u> his master.
>
> The economy soared <u>throughout</u> most <u>of</u> the decade, <u>until</u> crashing <u>in</u> 1999.
>
> <u>Like</u> the Hawaiian Islands, the undersea mountains <u>off</u> the Oregon coast grew <u>from</u> the ocean floor.
>
> <u>Despite</u> problems <u>during</u> his college years, John is now working <u>toward</u> his Ph.D.
>
> All <u>of</u> my classmates were <u>in</u> the play <u>except</u> Tracy and Ben.

Between shows a relationship of two things. *Among* shows a relationship of three or more things.

> The esophagus is <u>between</u> the *mouth* and the *stomach*.
>
> Tom Thomson is <u>among</u> the most influential *Canadian artists*.

When the preposition *by* follows a passive–voice verb, its noun object is the doer of the verb's action.

> The common cold is <u>caused by</u> *a viral infection* of the upper respiratory track.
>
> The gas stove was <u>invented by</u> *James Sharp* in 1826.

Despite and *despite the fact that* are often confused, but they perform different functions.

> <u>Despite</u> his strong qualifications, Michael was not selected for the position.
>
> He did not get the job, <u>despite the fact that</u> he had experience and training.

In the first sentence above, the preposition *despite* has a noun object, *his strong qualifications*. In the second sentence, the subordinator *despite the fact that* introduces a clause, *he had experience and training*.

4. Paired Expressions

Some prepositions are used frequently as ***paired expressions***, structures with two parts.

Expression	What It Does	Examples
between…and	Shows a span of space, time, or status	The main entrance is in the block <u>between</u> Broadway <u>and</u> Third Avenue. <u>Between</u> 1940 <u>and</u> 1945, scientists in Britain developed radar. "Choice" is the grade of beef <u>between</u> "prime" <u>and</u> "select."
from…to	Shows a span of space or time	Funds can be transferred automatically <u>from</u> one bank account <u>to</u> another. Adolescence is the physical and mental transition <u>from</u> childhood <u>to</u> adulthood.

5. Compound Prepositions

Compound prepositions are prepositions that have two or more words.

Compound Prepositions				
according to	aside from	except for	in favor of	out of
across from	because of	in addition to	in front of	prior to
ahead of	contrary to	in back of	in spite of	regardless of
along with	down from	in case of	instead of	such as
as a result of	due to	in contrast to	next to	together with

> <u>According to</u> a recent poll, a vast majority of students own a cell phone.
>
> An ammonia detergent should never be used <u>along with</u> chlorine bleach.
>
> <u>Due to</u> rapid deforestation, timber towns have experienced economic depression.
>
> <u>In case of</u> fire, use the stairs <u>instead of</u> the elevator.
>
> The parking spaces <u>next to</u> the courthouse are reserved for the judges.
>
> Institutions <u>such as</u> schools, hospitals, and public transit define a society.

Because of and *because* are often confused, but they perform different functions.

> Immunization for measles is recommended <u>because of</u> the risk of secondary infection.
>
> Measles is a serious disease <u>because</u> it can lead to secondary infection.

In the first sentence above, the preposition *because of* has a noun object, *the risk of secondary infection.* In the second sentence, the subordinator *because* introduces a clause, *it can lead to secondary infection.*

Tip: To check whether a word is a preposition, look for its noun object. If it has a noun object, it is probably a preposition.

6. Verbs with Prepositions

Some verbs are usually followed by a preposition, particularly when a noun object receives the verb's effect. The noun is the object of the verb + preposition structure.

The following verb + preposition structures are common in written and spoken English. Such structures are also called *phrasal verbs*.

Verb + Preposition				
allude to	differ from	keep on/up	prepare for	succeed in
approve of	divide in/into	lay off	refer to	take over
bring about	figure out	listen to	rely on	think about/of
come up with	find out	look for	remove from	turn into
consist of	give up	look up	reply to	turn off/on
deal with	hand in	object to	respond to	use up
depend on	keep from	point out	run out of	worry about

UNIT 15

> A political cartoon may <u>allude to</u> a famous event from history or literature.
>
> The Steller's jay <u>differs from</u> the eastern bluejay mainly in appearance.
>
> Managers <u>rely on</u> their staff to perform the organization's daily operations.

Many verb + preposition structures are *idiomatic*: they have a meaning that is different from the meaning of the individual words.

> I would like to <u>point out</u> that there is a flaw in your argument.
>
> The speaker <u>ran out of</u> time before she could cover all of the material.
>
> Mr. Peterson <u>took over</u> the family business after his uncle retired.

7. Adjectives with Prepositions

Some adjectives are usually followed by a preposition. The following adjective + preposition structures are common in written and spoken English.

Adjective + Preposition

associated with	capable of	confused about	interested in	qualified for
attractive to	common in/to	conscious of	made (out) of	related to
aware of	composed of	different from	pleased with	satisfied with
based on	confined to	equal to	prejudiced against	similar to

> Diabetes is <u>associated with</u> high blood sugar and altered protein metabolism.
>
> Artificial selection is <u>common to</u> both plant and animal breeding.
>
> Oil varnishes are <u>made out of</u> hard gum or resin dissolved in oil.
>
> Flowers in the lily family are <u>related to</u> onions, leeks, and garlic.

 PRACTICE

Exercise 15–A

Prepositional Phrases. Circle all prepositions and underline their noun objects.

1. *Romeo and Juliet* was written by William Shakespeare around 1595.

2. A new multivitamin is based on decades of research into using vitamins and minerals as immunity

   boosters.

3. Before 1779 people did not know about photosynthesis, the process by which plants use light to

   make food.

4. Through the use of a simple genre like the folktale, teachers can point out ways to solve moral problems.

5. Environmental temperature is an important factor in the distribution of organisms because of its effect on biological processes.

6. For the study, the team analyzed the ratio of older adults to younger adults in dental samples from successive time periods.

Exercise 15–B

Sentence Completion. Choose the word or phrase that best completes the sentence.

1. Dinosaurs did not exist ------- the early years of life on Earth.

   (A) during
   (B) beneath
   (C) while
   (D) into

2. ------- the nature of rock, coasts come in a variety of shapes.

   (A) Because
   (B) Because of
   (C) Although
   (D) Although it

3. Sensory cells ------- impulses by producing electrical signals.

   (A) respond to
   (B) to respond
   (C) responding
   (D) by responding

4. Earthquakes cause vibrations to pass ------- around the ground in the form of waves.

   (A) throughout
   (B) through the
   (C) through and
   (D) to through

5. Psychologists believe that women are not very ------- men in their ability to develop skills.

   (A) different
   (B) different to
   (C) different from
   (D) different of

6. A flower ------- many tiny parts, such as the petal, pistil, and sepal.

   (A) consists
   (B) consists on
   (C) consists in
   (D) consists of

7. Amelia Earhart was the first person to fly alone ------- to California.

   (A) to Hawaii
   (B) from Hawaii
   (C) of Hawaii
   (D) that Hawaii

8. Research into the chemical complexities of the human body may yield insights ------- variety of diseases.

   (A) a
   (B) into a
   (C) except a
   (D) that a

UNIT 15

9. A range manager helps ranchers increase livestock production ------- the kind of animals to raise.

   (A) determine
   (B) in which determined
   (C) when to determine
   (D) by determining

10. A man of twenty is ------- his physical vigor and is ready to take his place in the society of adults.

   (A) the height
   (B) of height that
   (C) at the height of
   (D) that the height

Exercise 15–C

Sentence Editing. One of the underlined parts in each sentence is incorrect. Cross out the incorrect part and write the correction above it.

1. Estuaries <u>are</u> rivers <u>at</u> the border between <u>salt</u> water <u>to</u> fresh water.

2. A mirage occurs when a layer <u>of</u> warm air <u>next</u> the ground is trapped <u>by</u> cooler air that is <u>above</u> it.

3. The edelweiss is found <u>at</u> high altitudes <u>in</u> the mountains <u>for</u> Europe, Asia, <u>and</u> South America.

4. Moonquakes are <u>similar</u> the smaller tremors <u>that</u> are felt <u>during</u> earthquakes <u>on</u> Earth.

5. <u>In</u> the 1500s, civil unrest led <u>to</u> the breakup <u>of</u> Vietnam <u>for</u> several smaller states.

6. The science <u>of</u> psychology was founded <u>from</u> the psychiatrists Sigmund Freud <u>and</u> Carl Jung <u>in</u> the early twentieth century.

7. The force that makes objects fall <u>down</u> the ground is also the force <u>that</u> keeps the planets <u>in</u> their orbits <u>around</u> the sun.

8. A few saltbox houses <u>that</u> were built <u>in</u> the seventeenth century can still be found <u>to</u> the northeastern part <u>of</u> the United States.

9. Immanuel Kant never left the town of his birth and <u>taught at</u> the university <u>of there</u>, where he became professor <u>of logic</u> and metaphysics <u>in 1770</u>.

10. Agricultural economists deal <u>of</u> problems related <u>to</u> producing and marketing farm products, and they provide data <u>about</u> the financial aspects <u>of</u> the industry.

Exercise 15–D

TOEFL iBT Reading. Read the passages and choose the best answer to each question.

QUESTIONS 1–4

1   While single women had a long history of working outside the home, married women in the United States did not work outside the home in great numbers until the twentieth century. Between 1900 and 1930 there was a steady rise in the employment of married women. Then, during the Great Depression of the 1930s, many women sought work as their husbands were laid off or forced to take wage cuts. However, women faced barriers to employment. Federal laws discouraged the hiring of married women and required that they be the first to be laid off. Twenty–six states passed laws prohibiting the employment of married women altogether. Despite such discrimination, the proportion of married women who worked for pay increased to more than 15 percent. Instead of taking men's jobs in industry, as opponents feared, women worked primarily as domestics, typists, and clerks.

2   Many women chose not to enter the labor force because of gender stereotypes in pay and promotion. The long–standing difference in male and female earnings increased from 20 percent in 1900 to 55 percent in 1940. This was mostly due to business policies that tried to bind male employees to the company through pay raises and promotions but excluded women from advancement, however productive they may have been. Consequently, few women earned enough to give them any options other than marriage. Moreover, most women who did have jobs still depended on men for "extras" such as leisure and entertainment.

1. According to the passage, the number of working married women in the United States

   (A) has risen throughout history.
   (B) increased after 1900.
   (C) did not change during the 1930s.
   (D) rose by 55 percent in 1940.

2. Why does the author mention domestics, typists, and clerks in paragraph 1?

   (A) To distinguish "women's" and "men's" jobs
   (B) To identify jobs that women took from men
   (C) To explain why women should not work
   (D) To give examples of well–paying jobs

3. The phrase due to in paragraph 2 is closest in meaning to

   (A) equal to
   (B) in spite of
   (C) caused by
   (D) different from

4. According to the passage, women faced all of the following problems EXCEPT

   (A) discriminatory laws
   (B) lower pay than men
   (C) unsafe working conditions
   (D) lack of advancement

UNIT 15

QUESTIONS 5–6

Palpitations are usually reported as a fluttering in the chest or a feeling that the heart has jumped. A person may experience palpitations during times of stress, such as after several days with less sleep than normal, or before a test or an important meeting. Caffeine, nicotine, and medications such as cold tablets may be factors in bringing on the attacks. Another factor is a sudden change of position, such as getting out of bed too quickly or jumping up to answer the telephone. With palpitations, the heartbeat regulator has trouble adjusting to the quick switch from a circulatory system that is horizontal to one that is vertical. The pulse rate must be changed, and because of this, the heart may skip a few beats, similar to the way in which a car motor misses a beat as it goes from driving on a flat road to climbing a hill.

5. According to the passage, palpitations may result from all of the following EXCEPT

    (A) anxiety before a test
    (B) a change in occupation
    (C) cold medicine
    (D) standing up quickly

6. The author compares the heartbeat regulator to

    (A) an important meeting
    (B) getting out of bed
    (C) the telephone
    (D) the motor of a car

Exercise 15–E

TOEFL iBT Speaking. In this integrated speaking task, you will listen to part of a lecture. You will then be asked to summarize important information from the lecture.

Cover the question while the lecture is playing. You may take notes, and you may use your notes to help you answer the question. After you hear the question, you may look at the question and prepare your response. You have 20 seconds to prepare your response and 60 seconds to speak.

 Audio Track 23

> Using points and examples from the lecture, explain how the government studies the labor force and unemployment.

 Stop

Preparation Time – 20 seconds
Response Time – 60 seconds

Answers to Exercises 15–A through 15–E are on pages 268–269.

 EXTENSION

1. **Sentence Analysis.** In reading done outside class, look for examples of sentences with various types of prepositions. Bring examples to share in class. Write some of the sentences on the board. Your classmates must identify the prepositional phrases. With your teacher and classmates, answer the following questions about each prepositional phrase.

      a. Does the prepositional phrase function as an adjective or an adverb?
      b. What noun, verb, or clause does the prepositional phrase modify?
      c. Does the preposition indicate a relationship of space, time, direction, status, inclusion, exclusion, or something else?
      d. Would a different preposition also be correct in the sentence? If so, would it change the meaning of the sentence?

2. **Opposite Pairs.** With your classmates, make a list of preposition pairs that have opposite meanings, such as *in/out* and *up/down*.

3. **Phrasal Verbs.** In reading done outside class, look for examples of verb + preposition structures, or use the list of structures on page 191. Which verb + preposition structures are idiomatic? An ***idiom*** has a different meaning from the meaning of its individual words. Look for each structure in a dictionary of idioms and phrasal verbs. What other phrasal verbs have the same base verb?

4. **Sentence Writing.** Practice writing sentences with compound prepositions. Use the prepositions in the list below.

according to	due to	in spite of
as a result of	in addition to	instead of
because of	in contrast to	next to
contrary to	in favor of	such as

UNIT 15

UNIT 16 WORD ORDER

1. **Adjectives**
2. **Adverbs**
3. ***Enough*** **and** ***Too***
4. ***Only*** **and** ***Very***
5. **Subject–Verb Word Order**
6. **Introductory Prepositions of Location**
7. **Introductory Negative Adverbs**
8. ***So, Neither*****, and** ***Only if***

 FOCUS

What is wrong with this sentence?

> A steppe is a grassland temperate of Eurasia, but sometimes the term is applied to the pampas of South America and the high veldt of South Africa.

The phrase *grassland temperate* has incorrect word order. *Temperate* is an adjective, and single–word adjectives come before the nouns they modify. The order should be changed so that *temperate* is before *grassland*. The correctly formed sentence is:

> A steppe is a **temperate grassland** of Eurasia, but sometimes the term is applied to the pampas of South America and the high veldt of South Africa.

What is wrong with this sentence?

> In the Cascade Range the mountain bluebird lives, which can be seen hovering over the grass in open areas.

The first clause has incorrect word order. The introductory phrase, *In the Cascade Range*, is a prepositional phrase that expresses location. After prepositional phrases of location, the order of the subject and verb is reversed. The correctly formed sentence is:

> In the Cascade Range **lives the mountain bluebird**, which can be seen hovering over the grass in open areas.

STUDY

1. Adjectives

In standard word order, an adjective comes before the noun it modifies. If there is an article, it comes before the adjective.

(article) + adjective + noun

> Floods claim <u>an</u> <u>annual</u> <u>toll</u> of <u>two hundred</u> <u>lives</u>.
>   art.   Adj.   N   Adj.   N

A noun can have more than one adjective. A comma separates the adjectives.

> The warbler lays its eggs in a <u>loose</u>, <u>shallow</u>, <u>grass–lined</u> <u>nest</u>.
>   Adj.   Adj.   Adj.   N

When an adjective comes after a form of the verb *be* or *become*, the adjective may not always precede a noun. In such cases, the adjective modifies the noun that is the subject of the verb.

> As it ripens, the <u>fruit</u> of an eggplant *becomes* <u>purple</u>, <u>white</u>, or <u>striped</u>.
>   N   Adj.   Adj.   Adj.

No can function as an adjective. When *no* is an adjective, it means *not any* or *not one*.

> <u>No</u> <u>smoking</u> is allowed in airports and train stations.
> Adj.   N
>
> There have been <u>no</u> <u>accidents</u> on campus in the past six months.
>   Adj.   N

Adjective phrases and clauses come after the nouns they modify.

> The <u>winds</u> <u>blowing around mountain ridges</u> are a form of dust devil.
>   N   Adj. phrase
>
> The <u>winds</u> <u>that blow inland from the ocean</u> usually carry moisture.
>   N   Adj. clause

2. Adverbs

An adverb can come before or after the verb or independent clause that it modifies.

> <u>Always</u> <u>read</u> the directions <u>carefully</u>.
> Adv.   V   Adv.
>
> My boss <u>seriously</u> <u>considers</u> every suggestion from the staff.
>   Adv.   V
>
> Children who <u>act</u> <u>impulsively</u> or <u>talk</u> <u>excessively</u> may be hyperactive.
>   V   Adv.   V   Adv.
>
> <u>Occasionally</u>, <u>drought conditions lead to dust storms and forest fires</u>.
>   Adv.   Independent clause

If a verb has one or more auxiliaries, the adverb usually follows the first auxiliary.

> Crows <u>have</u> <u>recently</u> <u>been filmed</u> using tools in the wild.
>   aux.   Adv.   V
>
> If you look at the night sky, you <u>will</u> <u>probably</u> <u>see</u> the meteor shower.
>   aux.   Adv.   V

Not and *never* are adverbs that come after the first auxiliary and before the verb.

> Nitrates <u>do</u> *not* <u>evaporate</u>, so they are likely to remain in water.
>   aux.   V
>
> Some people think we <u>may</u> *never* <u>discover</u> evidence of life on other planets.
>   aux.   V

Adverbs can also modify adjectives. The standard word order is:

> (article) + adverb + adjective + noun

> <u>Electronically</u> <u>controlled</u> <u>robots</u> are <u>a</u> <u>fairly</u> <u>recent</u> <u>invention</u>.
>   Adv.   Adj.   N   art. Adv. Adj.   N
>
> The standard language is <u>the</u> <u>most widely</u> <u>understood</u> <u>variety</u> in a society.
>   art.   Adv.   Adj.   N

After a form of *be* or *become*, an adverb + adjective structure may not always precede a noun. In such cases, the structure modifies the noun that is the subject of the verb.

> The jackrabbit's <u>ears</u> *are* <u>characteristically</u> <u>long</u>.
>   N   Adv.   Adj.

The following negative expressions are adverb + adjective structures that modify nouns.

not all	not every	not much
not any	not many	not one

Not all valleys on Mars have a tectonic origin.

There are not any poisonous snakes that are native to New Zealand.

There was not much useful information in the article.

The following "almost negative" expressions are adverb + adjective structures that modify nouns.

| barely any | hardly any | scarcely any |

Women in the United States had barely any civil rights until the 1860s.

3. *Enough* and *Too*

When the modifiers *enough* and *too* are used with adjectives and infinitives, there are special rules for word order.

adjective + *enough* + infinitive

The water should be hot *enough* to steep the tea leaves.
      Adj.   Infin.

Such structures express a cause–result relationship. The adjective and *enough* indicate cause, and the infinitive indicates result. In the sentence above, the cause is *hot enough*, and the result is *to steep the tea leaves*.

Sometimes *for* + noun comes between *enough* and the infinitive.

adjective + *enough* + *for* + noun + infinitive

The specimens must be thin *enough for* a light beam to penetrate them.
      Adj.   N   Infin.

Sometimes *enough* functions as an adjective before a noun and an infinitive.

enough + noun + infinitive

There is *enough* work to keep everyone busy all week.
         N   Infin.

When *too* comes before an adjective, it means *excessively* and indicates a negative result.

too + adjective + infinitive

Some systems for checking blood glucose levels are *too* inaccurate to be reliable.
                                                   Adj.   Infin.

Sometimes *for* + noun comes between the adjective and the infinitive.

too + adjective + *for* + noun + infinitive

It was *too* windy on the hillside *for* trees to establish roots.
        Adj.   N   Infin.

4. *Only* and *Very*

The modifier *only* can function as an adjective or an adverb. *Only* comes immediately before the word or structure it modifies.

Noun	The bat is the *only* <u>mammal</u> that can fly.
Adjective	*Only* <u>seven</u> metals were familiar to the ancient world.
Prepositional Phrase	Most bears hunt *only* <u>at night</u>.
Verb	Arthritis pain will *only* <u>increase</u> if it is not treated properly.
Adverb Clause	Asters flourish *only* <u>where the sun shines all afternoon</u>.

The modifier *very* can function as an adjective or an adverb. *Very* comes immediately before the word it modifies.

When *very* is an adjective, it means *precise* or *absolute*.

> At the *very* <u>moment</u> the lightning flashed, the thunderclap sounded.
>
> Cajun music forms the *very* <u>heart</u> and soul of French Louisiana.

When *very* is an adverb, it means *truly*, *extremely*, or *excessively*.

> It was *very* <u>cold</u> when I went jogging this morning.
>
> The singer did not perform *very* <u>well</u> without her usual backup band.

5. Subject–Verb Word Order

The standard word order of a sentence is:

> subject + verb + (object)

Standard word order is used in statements and in independent clauses. It is also used in subordinate clauses that begin with question words such as *when*, *where*, and *why*.

> <u>Many companies</u> <u>release</u> their annual report in January.
>   S   V
>
> When <u>the bear</u> <u>hibernates</u>, <u>its temperature</u> <u>drops</u>.
>   S   V   S   V

In direct questions, an auxiliary verb comes before the subject. This is sometimes called ***question word order***.

> When <u>does</u> <u>the bear</u> <u>hibernate</u>?
>   aux.   S   V

If the verb has more than one auxiliary, the subject comes after the first auxiliary.

> Why <u>has</u> <u>the bee population</u> <u>been decreasing</u> so rapidly over the past decade?
>   aux.   S   V

With certain words and expressions, there are special rules for the word order of subjects and verbs. The subject and verb have a different order after:

- introductory prepositions of location
- introductory negative adverbs
- some uses of *so*, *neither*, and *only if*

6. Introductory Prepositions of Location

When a statement begins with a prepositional phrase of location, the subject and verb are inverted. Usually, the verb is *be*, *lie*, *live*, or some other verb expressing existence.

Prepositions of Location

above	around	beneath	in	on
across	at	beside	inside	outside
along	behind	between	near	over
among	below	beyond	next to	under

> <u>Along the Mississippi</u> <u>are</u> <u>forty–one dams</u> that regulate the flow of the river.
>   PP   V   S
>
> <u>At the North Pole</u> <u>lies</u> <u>a massive sheet</u> of permanent ice.
>   PP   V   S
>
> <u>Next to a car's wheel axles</u> <u>are</u> <u>the shock absorbers</u>.
>   PP   V   S

Sometimes an introductory prepositional phrase expresses position or status rather than physical location.

> <u>Among the best–loved fairy tales</u> <u>are</u> <u>"Cinderella" and "Snow White."</u>
>   PP   V   S

When *there* is the "false" subject, the true subject follows the verb.

> <u>Beneath the connective tissue</u> *there* <u>is</u> <u>a wall of smooth muscle</u>.
>   PP   V   S

The sentence above can be rewritten without *there*. The following sentences have the same meaning.

> Beneath the connective tissue is a wall of smooth muscle.
>
> A wall of smooth muscle is beneath the connective tissue.

UNIT 16

7. Introductory Negative Adverbs

When a sentence begins with certain negative or "almost negative" adverbs, question word order is used.

at no time	not often	on no account
hardly ever	not once	rarely
neither…nor	not only…but also	scarcely
never	not until	seldom
no sooner…than	nowhere	under no circumstances

> *Hardly ever* <u>does the black bear attack</u> humans.
>
> *No sooner* <u>had the baseball game started</u> *than* it started to rain.
>
> *Not only* <u>does the rule affect</u> individuals, *but* it *also* challenges the organization.
>
> *Not until* the 1840s <u>could women own</u> property in the United States.
>
> *Seldom* <u>are there any people</u> in the building on the weekend.

If the verb has more than one auxiliary, the verb's subject comes after the first auxiliary.

> *Never* <u>had</u> <u>the submarine</u> <u>been used</u> so effectively until the First World War.
>   aux.   S   V

8. *So, Neither,* and *Only if*

When the adverbs *so* and *neither* are used to compare two things, special word order will avoid unnecessary repetition.

> The gull is a cliff dweller, and *so* <u>is the common murre</u>.
>
> I don't like getting up early. *Neither* <u>does my roommate</u>.

When an introductory subordinate clause begins with *only if* or another of the *only* adverbs below, the subordinate clause has standard word order, but the main clause has question word order.

only if	only before	only when
only after	only since	only where

> *Only if* <u>there</u> <u>is</u> adequate snowfall <u>will</u> <u>there</u> <u>be</u> enough water in the spring.
>   S   V   aux.   S   V
>
> *Only when* <u>you</u> <u>see</u> no oncoming traffic <u>should</u> <u>you</u> <u>make</u> a left turn.
>   S   V   aux.   S   V

 PRACTICE

Exercise 16–A

Sentence Completion. Choose the word or phrase that best completes the sentence.

1. Spray cans produce an aerosol, which is -------.

   (A) very a fine spray
   (B) spray very fine
   (C) a very fine spray
   (D) a fine spray very

2. The coyote prefers to hunt at night, and so -------.

   (A) the leopard also
   (B) the leopard hunts
   (C) is the leopard
   (D) does the leopard

3. In the very center of a flower -------.

   (A) the pistil
   (B) is the pistil
   (C) the pistil there
   (D) the pistil is at

4. Nowhere in the United States ------- grizzly bear attacks than in Glacier National Park.

   (A) are there more
   (B) more than
   (C) there are more
   (D) more of

5. The sea fig's scientific name means "blooming at midday," and seldom ------- without full sun.

   (A) it blooms
   (B) does bloom
   (C) is blooming
   (D) does it bloom

6. Kites come in all shapes and sizes, some ------- a person.

   (A) large enough carrying
   (B) carrying large enough
   (C) large enough to carry
   (D) large to carry enough

7. Of all the planets of the solar system, ------- known to support life.

   (A) only Earth is
   (B) Earth only
   (C) is Earth only
   (D) Earth is only the

8. Under no circumstances ------- without looking carefully to the rear.

   (A) should one back up a motor vehicle
   (B) a motor vehicle should back up
   (C) one should back up a motor vehicle
   (D) should back up a motor vehicle

9. The chewable substance called chicle had ------- until Thomas Adams added licorice and sold it as gumballs.

   (A) hardly flavored
   (B) any flavor hardly
   (C) flavor hardly none
   (D) hardly any flavor

10. Although sometimes there is ------- before an avalanche, there are some basic signs of avalanche danger.

    (A) any warning
    (B) warning none
    (C) no warning
    (D) warning neither

UNIT 16

Exercise 16–B

Sentence Editing. One of the underlined parts in each sentence is incorrect. Cross out the incorrect part and write the correction above it.

1. When <u>the sun</u> is setting in Shanghai, New York <u>is just</u> emerging <u>into sunlight</u> on the <u>side opposite</u> of the world.

2. The tall <u>stone buildings</u> of the nineteenth century required <u>walls very thick</u> in the <u>lower stories</u>, which limited <u>the amount</u> of floor space.

3. Among central Asia's oldest cities <u>Tashkent is</u>, the <u>cultural capital</u> and <u>economic heart</u> of Uzbekistan, <u>as well as</u> its center of learning.

4. Water particles carried to a <u>great height</u> will freeze into <u>ice particles</u> and be swept upward and refrozen <u>repeatedly</u> until they are <u>enough heavy</u> to fall as hail.

5. Only after the <u>Civil War</u> had started <u>Lincoln issued</u> the Emancipation Proclamation, <u>which ended</u> slavery <u>in the South</u>.

6. The <u>widely popular</u> entertainment <u>known as</u> vaudeville consisted of <u>unrelated songs</u>, dances, magic acts, and <u>skits humorous</u>.

7. On the Galapagos Islands <u>half live</u> of the forty thousand <u>breeding pairs</u> of the blue–footed booby, a seabird whose <u>natural habitat</u> is tropical and <u>subtropical islands</u>.

8. Trenches in the ocean floor are of <u>great interest</u> because they are <u>lines where</u> the earth's crust is often <u>so weak</u> to resist the impact of <u>frequent earthquakes</u>.

Exercise 16–C

TOEFL iBT Listening. Listen to the recording. You may take notes as you listen. Do not look at the questions until the conversation has ended. When you hear the questions, look at the questions and choose the best answer to each.

 Audio Track 24

1. Why does the student speak with the man?

   (A) She wants to report a problem about her room.
   (B) She does not understand something on her bill.
   (C) Her bill includes a charge that she already paid.
   (D) Her roommate broke the closet door in their room.

2. Why does the student say this:

   (A) She wants to know what happened in her room
   (B) She is apologizing for a problem in her room.
   (C) She denies that anything happened in her room
   (D) She regrets not knowing of a problem in her room.

3. What does the student imply when she says this:

   (A) She and her roommate would not damage university property.
   (B) She is concerned about what happens to her roommate.
   (C) She and her roommate respect one another's property.
   (D) She respects university property, but her roommate does not.

4. What does the man suggest the student do?

   (A) Pay the charge for repairing the closet door
   (B) Ask her roommate about the closet door
   (C) Request a refund from the Housing Director
   (D) Describe the problem on a complaint form

5. Listen again to part of the conversation. Then answer the question.

   What does the student mean?

   (A) She agrees to work on the problem as soon as possible.
   (B) She does not have enough money to pay her bill.
   (C) She is concerned about the problem with her roommate.
   (D) She hopes the charge will be removed from her bill.

UNIT 16

Exercise 16–D

TOEFL iBT Speaking. In this integrated speaking task, you will read a short passage about a campus situation, listen to a conversation, and then speak in response to a question about what you have read and heard. Do not look at the question until the conversation has ended. Do not look at the reading passage while you are speaking.

Reading Time – 45 seconds

NOTICE OF NEW GRADUATION REQUIREMENT

Please note the new graduation requirement that will take effect next year. Starting in September, all students must complete a quarter–long internship in their major field of study. Whereas in the past the internship requirement applied only to business majors, it now applies to students in all departments. Only in cases where a student has been accepted into a graduate program by December 1 will the requirement be waived. Please note that many year–long courses in the social sciences and the performing arts already have an experiential learning option that will provide enough hours of work experience to fulfill the internship requirement.

Now cover the passage and listen to the conversation. You may take notes, and you may use your notes to help you answer the question. After you hear the question, begin preparing your response. You may look at the question, but NOT at the passage. You have 30 seconds to prepare your response and 60 seconds to speak.

 Audio Track 25

> The woman expresses her opinion about the new graduation requirement. State her opinion, and explain the reasons she gives for holding that opinion.

 Stop

Preparation Time – 30 seconds
Response Time – 60 seconds

Answers to Exercises 16–A through 16–D are on pages 269–270.

EXTENSION

1. **Sentence Analysis.** In reading done outside class, look for examples of sentences with special word order. Bring examples to share in class. Write some of the sentences on the board. With your teacher and classmates, discuss why each sentence has special word order.

2. **Oral Exercise.** Practice using the following structures to describe situations you know.

adjective + *enough* + infinitive	*too* + adjective + infinitive

Examples: I'm hungry enough to eat a bear.   It's too late to catch the bus.

3. **Sentence Writing.** Practice writing sentences with the following modifiers. Make sure to use correct word order.

hardly any	not all	not until
hardly ever	not many	only
never	not much	only if
no	not often	rarely

UNIT 16

UNIT 17 PARALLEL STRUCTURE

1. Parallelism
2. Lists
3. Correlative Conjunctions
4. Comparative Structures

 FOCUS

Read the following sentences. Which sentence is better?

> The beaver is a large rodent with dark brown fur and a scaly black tail, and the beaver also has large front teeth.
>
> The beaver is a large rodent with dark brown fur, a scaly black tail, and large front teeth.

Both sentences list characteristics of the beaver: *dark brown fur*, *a scaly black tail*, and *large front teeth*. However, the first sentence is less balanced than the second sentence. In the first sentence, *the beaver also has large front teeth* disrupts the statement's rhythm. The second sentence is better because it has parallel phrases:

The beaver is a large rodent with **dark brown fur, a scaly black tail,** and **large front teeth**.

Now read another pair of sentences. Which sentence is better?

> The Civil War changed the physical environment of the South, and not just that, but the social structure of the South was also changed.
>
> The Civil War changed not only the physical environment but also the social structure of the South.

Both sentences state ways that the Civil War changed the South. However, the first sentence is less effective because it repeats words unnecessarily. The second sentence is better because it avoids unnecessary words and has parallel phrases:

The Civil War changed not only **the physical environment** but also **the social structure** of the South.

 STUDY

1. Parallelism

Parallelism means similarity in value, construction, and position. A sentence with *parallel structure* contains structures that are *parallel*, or similar in form and function. Various types of structures can be parallel: words, phrases, and clauses. Sentences with parallel structure are balanced and easy to read.

Structure	Examples
Words	Dolphins, seals, and whales are all marine mammals.
	Traditional methods of food preservation include drying, smoking, and pickling.
Phrases	In North America it is colder in January than in July.
	When the beaver fells a tree, it either eats the bark or stores it for winter use.
Clauses	Psychologists study both how we think and why we act.
	Textile mills were first built in Great Britain, but they were quickly copied in the United States.

Independent clauses that are related in meaning should be parallel in structure whenever possible.

The wolf is highly social, but the fox is relatively solitary.
Single life offers more freedom of choice; marriage provides more security.

2. Lists

The structures in a list should be parallel. A *list* is a series of two or more words, phrases, or clauses that are joined by a conjunction. The structures in a list are usually joined by *and*, *or*, or *but*.

Structure	Examples
Nouns	Inertia is the resistance to motion, exertion, *or* change.
	Wolves have a graceful body, slender legs, *and* a long bushy tail.
Gerunds	Writing, editing, *and* proofreading involve skills that can be improved by training.
	Societies have rules for obeying authority *and* treating others with respect.
Infinitives	Thunderstorms tend to transform the local weather *or* to affect a much wider area.
	Animals use behavioral strategies to promote heat loss *and* to conserve body heat.
Verb Phrases	The liver produces bile, stores glucose, *and* digests proteins.
	Even an expert gardener may have plants that become misshapen *or* remain sparse.

UNIT 17

Structure	Examples
Adjectives	Mosaics are <u>strong</u>, <u>colorful</u>, *and* <u>resistant</u> to moisture. The best buys are <u>low in price</u> *but* <u>high in value</u>.
Adverbs	Please follow the instructions <u>carefully</u> *and* <u>completely</u>. A layer of snow may move <u>slowly</u> *but* <u>continuously</u> down a slope.
Prepositional Phrases	Most football games take place <u>in the evening</u> *or* <u>on the weekend</u>. The great blue heron is frequently seen <u>along harbors</u> *or* <u>near suburban lakes</u>.
Subordinate Clauses	Friction appears <u>when a solid object rubs against another</u> *or* <u>when it moves through a gas or liquid</u>. Contract law determines <u>what contracts are enforceable in court</u> *and* <u>what steps must be taken to comply with a contract</u>.

3. Correlative Conjunctions

Correlative conjunctions, or *paired expressions*, have two parts. The structures that follow each part should be parallel.

and…as well as both…and	either…or neither…nor	not…but not only…but also

> Bob Marley inspired <u>musicians</u> *and* <u>followers</u> in Jamaica *as well as* <u>music lovers</u> all over the world.
>
> The Lumière brothers invented a machine that could *both* <u>photograph</u> *and* <u>project movies</u>.
>
> The yellow warbler makes its home *either* <u>in the forest</u> *or* <u>in city parks</u>.
>
> Tall trees *not only* <u>capture the sunlight</u> *but also* <u>shade the shorter trees</u>.

4. Comparative Structures

In *equative* and *comparative* expressions, the structures that are compared should be parallel.

as…as	-er than	more…than	less…than

> <u>The Olmec art of Yucatan</u> is believed to be *as old as* <u>the Chavin art of Peru</u>.
>
> Today <u>the population of the Nebraska panhandle is</u> *as low as* <u>it was</u> in 1930.
>
> <u>Gold</u> is *softer and more malleable than* <u>other precious metals</u>.
>
> <u>Dry soil</u> is *less dense than* <u>wet soil</u>.
>
> <u>Human error</u> causes *more problems* in the workplace *than* <u>computer malfunction</u> does.

The two things being compared must also be parallel in meaning.

Not Parallel	Parallel
The <u>temperature on Mars</u> is lower than <u>on Earth</u>.	The <u>temperature on Mars</u> is lower than <u>the temperature on Earth</u>. The <u>temperature on Mars</u> is lower than <u>that on Earth</u>.
The <u>wall of a plant cell</u> is generally thicker than <u>an animal cell</u>.	The <u>wall of a plant cell</u> is generally thicker than <u>the wall of an animal cell</u>. The <u>wall of a plant cell</u> is generally thicker than <u>that of an animal cell</u>.

The first sentence compares *the temperature on Mars* and *the temperature on Earth*. Using the pronoun *that* avoids repeating *the temperature* but maintains parallel meaning. The second sentence compares *the wall of a plant cell* and *the wall of an animal cell*. Using *that* avoids repetition and maintains parallel meaning.

 PRACTICE

Exercise 17–A

Parallel Structure.   Underline the parallel structures in each sentence. Identify the type of structure by writing **W** for words, **P** for phrases, or **C** for clauses next to each sentence.

1. _____   Kinetics is the study of the forces that produce, stop, or modify motions of the body.

2. _____   Either riding a bicycle or walking briskly will provide an aerobic workout.

3. _____   After locating prey by scent or sound, the cougar slinks forward slowly and silently.

4. _____   Before they leave home, some travelers like to plan exactly where they will go and what they will do.

5. _____   Humidity not only determines the weather but also regulates our comfort.

6. _____   In small companies, the same human resource workers may interview and hire as well as train employees.

7. _____   Demands for goods and services create bonds both within a society and between different societies.

8. _____   At the north magnetic pole the force of Earth's magnetic field is directed downward; at the south magnetic pole it is directed upward.

Exercise 17–B

Sentence Completion.   Choose the word or phrase that best completes the sentence.

1. Houses come in many styles, -------, and sizes.

   (A) the shaping
   (B) to shape
   (C) of shapes
   (D) shapes

2. The value of hardwood furniture is not -------
   but in its strength.

   (A) the beauty
   (B) in its beauty
   (C) beautiful
   (D) it's beautiful

3. The milk of either the cow or ------- is a
   popular dairy product in most places.

   (A) by the goat
   (B) goat's milk
   (C) the goat
   (D) then the goat

4. Spiders establish separate hunting grounds and
   ------- different strategies for catching food.

   (A) had used
   (B) use
   (C) to use
   (D) using

5. Neither ------- nor the middle layer of the
   atmosphere contains cumulus clouds.

   (A) in the upper layer
   (B) it's the upper layer
   (C) the upper layer
   (D) does the upper layer

6. Nuclear fusion not only powers the sun -------
   in thermonuclear weapons.

   (A) but also occurs
   (B) also does it occur
   (C) but also it occurs
   (D) it also has occurred

7. ------- a unicycle usually requires more practice
   than learning to swim does.

   (A) Learn how to ride
   (B) When you learn to ride
   (C) Learning to ride
   (D) It is by learning to ride

8. In the 1980s there was an expansion of the
   Western economies and the emergence -------.

   (A) of a global economy
   (B) the global economy
   (C) an economy that was global
   (D) there was a global economy

9. Blood from the veins, high in carbon dioxide but
   -------, returns to the right atrium of the heart.

   (A) being low in oxygen
   (B) low in oxygen
   (C) lower oxygen
   (D) is low in oxygen

10. Store layout and merchandise presentation, as
    well as -------, help shoppers find items more
    quickly.

    (A) to have appropriate signs
    (B) appropriate signs are necessary
    (C) with appropriate signs
    (D) appropriate signs

Exercise 17–C

Sentence Editing.   One of the underlined parts in each sentence is incorrect. Cross out the incorrect part and write the correction above it.

1. Cold <u>winds</u> carrying ice and <u>sand</u> will kill or <u>cutting</u> new growth on <u>trees</u>.

2. <u>Blind</u> and deaf since <u>birth</u>, Helen Keller eventually <u>learned</u> to read, write, and <u>spoke</u>.

3. Presenting <u>yourself</u> well in a job <u>interview</u> is as important as <u>learn</u> about the <u>organization</u>.

4. Manta rays are <u>able</u> to swim at <u>great</u> speeds and <u>leaping</u> out of the <u>water</u> and into the air.

5. The nerve endings in the skin <u>respond</u> to various <u>stimuli</u>, including pressure, <u>painful</u>, heat, and <u>cold</u>.

6. California <u>has</u> not only the largest <u>population</u> but also the <u>more</u> productive economy of any <u>state</u> in

   the United States.

7. The outer layer of the bark <u>insulating</u> the tree from the <u>weather</u>, protects the tree <u>from</u> animals, and

   <u>forms</u> a barrier against fungi.

8. Every organization that produces <u>goods</u> or services needs a wide <u>variety</u> of people <u>managing</u> the

   operation and to handle the clerical <u>work</u>.

9. Garlic has <u>been</u> hailed for its <u>ability</u> to lower cholesterol, reduce the <u>risk</u> of cancer, and <u>controls</u>

   high blood pressure.

10. <u>When</u> Marconi demonstrated his <u>wireless</u> telegraph, he <u>was thinking</u> not about broadcasting

   <u>but thought</u> about rapid communication.

Exercise 17–D

TOEFL iBT Writing. In this integrated writing task, you will write a response to a question about a reading passage and a lecture. Your response will be scored on the quality of your writing and on how well you connect the points in the lecture with points in the reading. Typically, an effective response will have 150 to 225 words.

Reading Time – 3 minutes

Many anthropologists and linguists have studied storytelling, the accounts of personal experiences that people tell in conversation, because stories reveal a great deal about a person's worldview. In one study, the researcher analyzed twenty–one stories told in conversation by fourteen young men. In all of the stories, the men talked about themselves, mostly in a way that made them look good. For example, two men told about times when their extraordinary performance had won a game for their team.

The men's stories tended to be about competition or contest. Most of the stories had a protagonist, a main character or hero, as well as an antagonist, a character or force opposing the main character. When the storyteller was not the protagonist in his own story, the protagonist was always another man. None of the stories had a woman as the protagonist, although women occasionally appeared as minor characters.

Many of the stories were about contests with other men. There were physical contests, such as fights and sports. There were also social contests, in which the protagonist used verbal or intellectual skill to defend his honor. Some of the stories told of contests with nature, such as hunting, fishing, and mountain climbing. The men talked mostly about events in which they had acted alone. In only four of the stories did the protagonist receive help or advice from another person. The vast majority of men who acted alone achieved a positive outcome.

The researcher concluded that these young men view life as a contest, a struggle against nature and other men. In their world, power comes from an individual acting alone against others in a test of skill and performance.

Now listen to the lecture. You may take notes, and you may use your notes to help you write your response. After you hear the question, you have 20 minutes to plan and write your response. You may look at the reading passage during the writing time.

 Audio Track 26

Summarize the points made in the lecture, explaining how they contrast with points made in the reading.

 Stop

Time – 20 minutes

Exercise 17–E

TOEFL iBT Writing. For this independent writing task, respond to the question by writing an essay in which you state and support your opinion on the topic. Your essay will be scored on the quality of your writing, including how well you organize and develop your ideas and how well you use language to express your ideas. An effective essay will have a minimum of 300 words.

Read the following question and make any notes that will help you plan your response. Then begin writing. You have 30 minutes to plan and write your essay.

Do you agree or disagree with the following statement?

Life is more difficult for children today than it was for children in the past.

Use specific reasons and examples to support your answer.

Time – 30 minutes

Answers to Exercises 17–A through 17–D are on pages 270–271.

Answers to Exercise 17–E will vary.

 EXTENSION

1. **Sentence Analysis.** In reading done outside class, look for examples of sentences with parallel structure. Bring examples to share in class. Write some of the sentences on the board. Your classmates must identify the type of structures that are parallel. Are they words, phrases, or clauses? Are they nouns, verbs, gerunds, adjectives, adverbs, or something else?

2. **Oral Exercise.** Practice using parallel structure with comparative structures and conjunctions. Substitute various words and phrases in the sentences below.

   a. _____ is as much fun as _____.
   b. I like _____ more than _____.
   c. _____ is less _____ than _____.
   d. The _____ is _____, _____, and _____.
   e. Both _____ and _____ are _____.
   f. The _____ not only _____ but also _____.

3. **Sentence Writing.** Practice writing sentences with various types of parallel structures: nouns, verbs, gerunds, adjectives, adverbs, and prepositional phrases. Use the following conjunctions.

and	or	either...or	not...but
but	both...and	neither...nor	not only...but also

QUIZ 5   UNITS 14 – 17

Time – 10 minutes

Choose the word or phrase that best completes the sentence.

1. Heat is transferred from one substance to another by conduction, convection, -------.

   (A) and radiation
   (B) or by radiating
   (C) and it radiates
   (D) also of radiation

2. Not only ------- the fall of the czar, but it also destroyed the provisional government.

   (A) did World War I cause
   (B) World War I caused
   (C) was World War I caused
   (D) World War I to cause

3. Silicon, a nonmetallic element, is ------- abundant element in Earth's crust.

   (A) second more than
   (B) more second the
   (C) second most of
   (D) the second most

4. A lever ------- a rigid bar that can turn around a fixed point called the fulcrum.

   (A) it consists
   (B) consists of
   (C) is consisting
   (D) can consist

5. The booby's brown feathers are ------- its blue feet are bright.

   (A) very dull
   (B) duller
   (C) as dull as
   (D) dull as well

6. Among Italo Calvino's works ------- about World War II, *The Path to the Nest of Spiders*.

   (A) a realistic novel
   (B) it is a realistic novel
   (C) a realistic novel is
   (D) is a realistic novel

7. The chipmunk builds its nest in either an underground burrow -------.

   (A) in a hollow limb
   (B) or a hollow limb
   (C) builds in a hollow limb
   (D) by a hollow limb

8. Of every one hundred new U. S. residents in 2000, ------- sixty–two were born in the United States.

   (A) of only
   (B) only if
   (C) not only
   (D) only

One of the underlined parts in each sentence is incorrect. Cross out the incorrect part and write the correction above it.

9. A comet is a mostly <u>gaseous body</u> of small mass and <u>volume enormous</u> that can be seen <u>from Earth</u> for periods ranging from a few days <u>to several</u> months.

10. The classes <u>of</u> steroids differ <u>by</u> one another <u>only</u> in the additional atoms attached <u>to</u> their central structure.

Answers to Quiz 5 are on page 271.
Record your score on page 301.

UNIT 18 WORD FORM

1. **Word Form and Function**
2. **Noun Suffixes**
3. **Verb Suffixes**
4. **Adjective Suffixes**
5. **Adverb Suffixes**

 FOCUS

What is wrong with this sentence?

> The question of whether computers can have minds is rapid becoming a significant issue.

The sentence contains an incorrect word form: *rapid*, an adjective, which cannot modify a verb. Only an adverb can modify the verb *is becoming*. Therefore, *rapid* must be changed to its adverb form, *rapidly*. The correctly formed sentence is:

> The question of whether computers can have minds is **rapidly** becoming a significant issue.

What is wrong with this sentence?

> Macroeconomics is an important subject today because macroeconomic performance is central to the success or fail of nations.

A word's form must agree with its function in a sentence. The word *fail* is incorrect; it is a verb, where only a noun will correctly complete the phrase *the success or....* The noun form of *fail* is *failure*. The correctly formed sentence is:

> Macroeconomics is an important subject today because macroeconomic performance is central to the success or **failure** of nations.

 STUDY

1. Word Form and Function

A word may have several related forms. The form of a word depends on its ***function***—how it is used in a sentence. A word's function is also called its ***part of speech***. Different parts of speech—*nouns*, *verbs*, *adjectives*, and *adverbs*—take different forms.

A word's form must agree with its function. Its form may change according to its function.

UNIT 18

Function	Examples
Noun	Paul Newman achieved much <u>success</u> throughout his long acting and filmmaking career.
Verb	Paul Newman <u>succeeded</u> in making numerous award–winning films.
Adjective	Paul Newman was a <u>successful</u> American film actor, director, and producer.
Adverb	Paul Newman <u>successfully</u> directed *The Glass Menagerie* and five other films.

The basic, underlying form of a word is called the **stem**. Several words may share the same stem. Words with the same stem are related in meaning but may act as different parts of speech. Adding various endings to a stem will change its part of speech. Word endings are called **suffixes**. Different suffixes give a word its form and thereby indicate its function.

2. Noun Suffixes

A **noun** names a person, place, thing, state, quality, or idea. Various suffixes indicate that a word is a noun.

Suffix	Meaning	Examples
-acy, -cy	state, condition, or quality	democracy, literacy, sufficiency
-age	action, condition, or result	breakage, parentage, postage
-al	action or process	denial, rehearsal, retrieval
-an	one relating to or belonging to	librarian, musician, technician
-ance, -ence	action, process, or quality	appearance, evidence, science
-ant, -ent	one that does something	assistant, correspondent, resident
-ate	state, possession, quality, or office	climate, consulate, protectorate
-dom	state or condition	boredom, kingdom, stardom
-ee	one that receives or possesses	addressee, employee
-er, -or	one that does something	driver, speaker, actor, professor
-ery, -ry, -y	place, condition, practice, or quality	bakery, chemistry, photography
-hood	state, condition, or quality	childhood, falsehood, neighborhood
-ics	art, science, knowledge, or skill	graphics, mathematics, athletics
-ide	group of chemical compounds	chloride, cyanide, oxide
-ing	action or result of action	building, marketing, meeting
-ism	action, process, belief, quality	terrorism, socialism, racism
-ist	one that does or believes something	artist, biologist, capitalist, stylist
-ity, -ty	state or quality	activity, equality, similarity
-ment	action, process, or result	establishment, government
-ness	state or condition	darkness, kindness, sadness
-ship	state or quality	friendship, kinship, relationship
-tion, -sion	action or result	invention, erosion, session
-ure	action, process, or product	failure, moisture, picture

Some nouns identify people, while others name activities, things, qualities, or ideas.

People	Activities, Things, Qualities, Ideas
artist, artisan	art, artistry
banker	bank, banking
chemist	chemistry, chemical
employer, employee	employment, employability
inventor	invention, inventiveness
photographer	photograph, photography
president	presidency
realist	reality, realism

A <u>banker</u> is a person who is an officer or owner of a <u>bank</u>.

A professional <u>photographer</u> is skilled in the techniques of <u>photography</u>.

3. Verb Suffixes

A *verb* expresses action, possession, or state of being. Various suffixes indicate that a word is a verb.

Suffix	Meaning	Examples
-ate	to cause, to become	compensate, indicate, motivate
-ed	past tense: to do in the past	investigated, started, walked
-en	to make, to give a quality to	darken, liken, quicken, sadden
-ify	to cause, to make into something	justify, specify, unify, verify
-ing	progressive tense: to do continuously	discussing, experiencing, studying
-ize	to become	formalize, generalize, standardize

4. Adjective Suffixes

An *adjective* modifies a noun or other noun structure. Adjectives describe, define, qualify, or specify nouns by answering the question *what kind of?* Various suffixes indicate that a word is an adjective.

Suffix	Meaning	Examples
-able, -ible	having a particular quality	affordable, valuable, edible
-al, -ial, -ical	characterized by, relating to	final, terrestrial, physical, tropical
-an, -ian, -ean	belonging to, relating to	African, avian, Canadian
-ant, -ent	causing, promoting	relevant, absorbent, evident
-ar	resembling, relating to	solar, familiar, spectacular
-ate	having, characterized by	corporate, literate, passionate
-ed	resulting from an action	excited, recommended, satisfied
-en	resembling, made of	frozen, golden, wooden
-ese	relating to, originating in	Japanese, Vietnamese

UNIT 18

Suffix	Meaning	Examples
-ful	full of	beautiful, careful, plentiful
-ic	characterized by, relating to	economic, heroic, sulfuric, toxic
-ile	relating to, capable of	mobile, tactile, volatile
-ing	causing something	boring, captivating, interesting
-ish	having qualities of	reddish, selfish, Swedish
-ive	having a particular quality	active, expensive, productive
-less	without something	endless, hairless, soundless
-like	resembling, characteristic of	childlike, lifelike
-ly	resembling, relating to	deadly, friendly, costly, weekly
-ous, -eous, -ious	having qualities of	numerous, gaseous, anxious
-some	characterized by	bothersome, lonesome, wholesome
-th	number in a specified order	fifth, twentieth, thousandth
-y	characterized by, made of	salty, sunny, tricky, windy

The suffix -ly is used with both adjectives and adverbs. Adjectives with -ly usually come from nouns or other adjectives: *friend/friendly*, *sick/sickly*.

Except for *first*, *second*, and *third*, adjectives made from numbers take the suffix -th.

5. Adverb Suffixes

An **adverb** modifies a verb, an adjective, a main clause, or another adverb. Adverbs express *how*, *when*, *where*, or *how often*. Various suffixes indicate that a word is an adverb.

Suffix	Meaning	Examples
-ly	in a specified manner or interval of time	precisely, silently, daily, monthly
-ward	in a specified direction	downward, forward, skyward
-wise	in a specified manner or direction	clockwise, likewise, otherwise

Adverbs with -ly that express manner usually come from adjectives: *common/commonly*, *clear/clearly*.

Some words have the same form whether they function as adjectives or adverbs. The following words can be adjectives or adverbs.

early	fast	high	low
far	hard	late	much

Adjective	The only seats left were in the <u>far</u> corner of the auditorium.
Adverb	The cows had broken the fence and strayed <u>far</u> from the pasture.
Adjective	A diamond is so <u>hard</u> that it will scratch glass and all other stones.
Adverb	If you work <u>hard</u> and play by the rules, you will succeed in life.
Adjective	The announcement caused <u>much</u> confusion in the lecture hall.
Adverb	We were <u>much</u> better informed after listening to the debate.

 PRACTICE

Exercise 18–A

Word Form and Function. In the following sentences, identify the function of each underlined word. Above the word, write **N** for noun, **V** for verb, **ADJ** for adjective, or **ADV** for adverb.

1. <u>Digging</u> by pocket gophers causes <u>much</u> damage to plants, but it also <u>aerates</u> the soil, which helps prevent <u>erosion</u>.

2. The <u>influence</u> of the Sumerians <u>eventually</u> spread to lands as <u>far</u> as Egypt in <u>Mediterranean</u> Africa and the Indus River in the <u>Indian</u> subcontinent.

3. The <u>introduction</u> of new <u>building</u> materials and mass–production techniques <u>changed</u> <u>architecture</u> <u>significantly</u> in the first quarter of the <u>twentieth</u> century.

Exercise 18–B

Sentence Completion. Choose the word or phrase that best completes the sentence.

1. An orange is less ------- than a pineapple.

   - (A) expense
   - (B) expensive
   - (C) expensiveness
   - (D) expensively

2. The flavor of coffee will ------- on the characteristics of the bean.

   - (A) depend
   - (B) dependence
   - (C) dependent
   - (D) dependable

3. There is a ------- between income and wealth; people can have a large income and no wealth.

   - (A) differ
   - (B) different
   - (C) differently
   - (D) difference

4. In a research laboratory, teams of workers ------- investigate a problem.

   - (A) systemize
   - (B) systematic
   - (C) systematically
   - (D) system

5. During an economic depression, business activity and ------- are at a very low level.

   - (A) employ
   - (B) employable
   - (C) employment
   - (D) employee

6. The industrial sector centers on the processing of agricultural ------- such as rice, peanuts, and tobacco.

   - (A) products
   - (B) productive
   - (C) produced
   - (D) producers

UNIT 18

7. Many animals can maintain ------- constant conditions in their internal environment.

    Ⓐ relate
    Ⓑ relative
    Ⓒ relativity
    Ⓓ relatively

8. When farmers ------- their crops with chemicals, excess phosphorus can wash into rivers and lakes.

    Ⓐ fertile
    Ⓑ fertilize
    Ⓒ fertilization
    Ⓓ fertility

Exercise 18–C

Sentence Editing. One of the underlined parts in each sentence is incorrect. Cross out the incorrect part and write the correction above it.

1. The radiator <u>removes</u> heat from the <u>cooling</u> water that <u>circulation</u> through a car's <u>engine</u>.

2. The largest <u>technically</u> <u>occupation</u> in the United States, <u>engineering</u>, has twenty–five <u>professional</u> societies.

3. Business law <u>includs</u> the branches of law that <u>affect</u> the formation, <u>operate</u>, and termination of a <u>business</u> firm.

4. The soles of the <u>polar</u> bear's feet are <u>covered</u> with fur, which <u>provides</u> stability on slippery, <u>freeze</u> ground.

5. Business and labor <u>leaders</u> sometimes <u>join</u> in a <u>cooperatively</u> effort to improve job <u>training</u>.

6. The modern skyscraper <u>originated</u> in the nineteenth century, and many <u>technological</u> improvements <u>contributed</u> to its <u>develop</u>.

7. A group of <u>historians</u> judged the <u>computer</u> to be the most <u>influence</u> invention of the <u>twentieth</u> century.

8. The flares that are <u>used</u> as distress <u>signals</u> contain <u>chemists</u> that produce intense <u>colors</u>.

9. An autistic child usually <u>appearance</u> to go through his <u>early</u> development <u>normally</u>, but a break usually <u>occurs</u> by the age of three.

10. Raoul Dufy is an <u>artist</u> whose <u>paintings</u> are easily recognized: a few colors <u>skillful</u> applied, combined with free, <u>evocative</u> drawing.

Exercise 18–D

TOEFL iBT Reading.   Read the passages and choose the best answer to each question.

QUESTIONS 1–5

1   Because a diamond is made of pure carbon, it has an immensely strong crystal structure, making it the hardest of all minerals. Evidence suggests that diamonds were formed deep within the earth, and some stones may be three billion years old. Alluvial diamonds, those recovered from river gravel, can be carried long distances in rough water with other rocks. Diamond–bearing gravel is the result of one of nature's sorting processes. Many of the diamonds found in gravel are of gem quality because flawed or fractured stones are more likely to be broken up and eroded away.

2   A diamond shines with great luster and fire, properties that are best revealed in the cut known as "brilliant." The brilliant cut dates from the seventeenth century and remains the most popular cut today because it enhances the brilliance of the gem with the least possible sacrifice of weight. It typically has 58 facets, but sometimes up to 104, and resembles two pyramids set base to base.

3   Most natural diamonds are nearly colorless, but truly colorless diamonds are rare. A few stones are found of all colors in the spectrum, and good–quality ones are known as "fancies." Diamonds of exceptional beauty and rarity are highly prized. Some have long, recorded histories, and others have inspired fantastic legends. The deep blue Hope diamond has a reputation for bringing bad luck; however, the sinister stories about it are untrue. At more than 45 carats, the Hope is one of the world's largest diamonds and is apparently flawless.

1. The passage mentions all of the following about diamonds EXCEPT their

   (A) hardness
   (B) formation
   (C) appearance
   (D) price

2. In stating in paragraph 1 that diamond–bearing gravel is the result of one of nature's sorting processes, the author means that

   (A) the least desirable stones have been removed
   (B) diamonds travel long distances in rivers
   (C) the gravel is a mixture of different kinds of rock
   (D) diamonds are among the oldest stones on Earth

3. The word brilliance in paragraph 2 is closest in meaning to

   (A) brightness
   (B) rarity
   (C) softness
   (D) fragility

4. Which sentence below best expresses the essential information in the highlighted sentence in paragraph 3?

   (A) Only a few diamonds are extraordinarily beautiful.
   (B) Because diamonds are rare, we consider them beautiful.
   (C) The rarest and most beautiful diamonds are very valuable.
   (D) Diamonds are the most precious minerals on Earth.

5. The word flawless in paragraph 3 is closest in meaning to

   (A) expensive
   (B) unlucky
   (C) colorless
   (D) perfect

UNIT 18

QUESTIONS 6–7

    The measure of excellence for systems designers is the simplicity of their concepts. Simplicity comes from conceptual unity, when every part of the system reflects the same philosophy and uses the same techniques. If a computer system is going to be easy to use, the design must have conceptual unity. To achieve unity, a design must proceed from the mind of one person, or from the minds of a small number of people who share a way of thinking about the project. Just as a large building is most successful when it comes from the vision of one architect, a software design is most successful when it is unified under the vision of one lead designer. When a system is simple, functional, and conceptually unified, it is a beautiful work of architecture.

6. The author argues that a high–quality computer system must have

    (A) simple instructions
    (B) an experienced designer
    (C) philosophical unity
    (D) innovative thinking

7. Which sentence below best expresses the essential information in the highlighted sentence in the passage?

    (A) Large buildings require the unity of a small team under a lead architect.
    (B) Both architecture and software design are best when based on a single vision.
    (C) An architect and a software designer must share a vision when working together.
    (D) Successful architects and software designers have many qualities in common.

Exercise 18–E

TOEFL iBT Writing.   For this independent writing task, respond to the question by writing an essay in which you state and support your opinion on the topic. Your essay will be scored on the quality of your writing, including how well you organize and develop your ideas and how well you use language to express your ideas. An effective essay will have a minimum of 300 words.

Read the following question and make any notes that will help you plan your response. Then begin writing. You have 30 minutes to plan and write your essay.

Do you agree or disagree with the following statement?

It is always better to speak truthfully, even if the truth may not be pleasant.

Use specific reasons and examples to support your answer.

Time – 30 minutes

Answers to Exercises 18–A through 18–D are on pages 271–272.

Answers to Exercise 18–E will vary.

EXTENSION

1. **Word Forms.** Work with a partner or in a small group. Fill in each row of the chart with related forms of the given word. Use a dictionary or the suffixes on pages 220 through 222. For some parts of speech, there may be more than one word. Share your results with the whole class.

Noun	Verb	Adjective	Adverb
	act		
analysis			
beauty			
		clear	
	comfort		
comparison			
	consider		
			decisively
	divide		
		easy	
economy			
	explode		
identity			
			locally
		political	
	possess		
protection			
	respond		
		vocal	
			vitally

UNIT 19 COMMON WORD ERRORS

1. Words Similar in Sound
2. Words Similar in Meaning
3. Expressions of Quantity

 FOCUS

What is wrong with this sentence?

> Almost earthquakes are a direct result of the natural processes taking place within the earth.

The sentence has an incorrect word, *almost*, an adverb where an adjective is needed before the noun *earthquakes*. The correct word is *most*. The correctly formed sentence is:

Most earthquakes are a direct result of the natural processes taking place within the earth.

What is wrong with this sentence?

> Unusual and severe dust storms frequently arise on the Great Plains while periods of drought.

The sentence has an incorrect word, *while*, an adverb where a preposition is needed before the noun *periods*. The correct preposition is *during*. The correctly formed sentence is:

Unusual and severe dust storms frequently arise on the Great Plains **during** periods of drought.

 STUDY

1. Words Similar in Sound

Some words are confusing because they sound similar to other words. Errors in word choice often occur when two words are similar in sound.

Words	Explanation	Examples
advice	*Advice* is an uncountable noun.	When starting a business, one should seek the <u>advice</u> of other people.
advise	*Advise* is a verb.	Counselors <u>advise</u> their clients in how to cope with life changes.

Words	Explanation	Examples
alike	*Alike* can be an adjective that shows similarity between two or more nouns. It comes after the verb *be*.	Wheat, rye, and oats are <u>alike</u> in their widespread cultivation as cereal crops.
	Alike can be an adverb that means *in the same way*.	Identical twins look <u>alike</u> and sometimes even talk <u>alike</u>.
like	The preposition *like* comes before its noun object.	<u>Like</u> wheat, rye has been cultivated for thousands of years.
almost	The adverb *almost* means *nearly*. It modifies an adjective, a verb, or another adverb.	<u>Almost</u> all beverages get their flavor from plants. The children had <u>almost</u> finished their juice. Summer days are <u>almost</u> always warm.
most	*Most* means *greatest in number* or *amount*. It can be an adjective or a pronoun.	<u>Most</u> soft drinks contain a sweetener. <u>Most</u> contain sugar or corn syrup.
	Most can be part of the superlative form of a long adjective or adverb.	Dogs are the <u>most</u> popular pets in Japan. <u>Most</u> importantly, global warming will cause sea levels to rise.
beside	The preposition *beside*, which means *next to*, comes before its noun object.	Many small towns have a wooded park <u>beside</u> a lake or stream.
besides	The preposition *besides*, which means *in addition to*, comes before its noun object.	There are other types of precipitation <u>besides</u> rain and snow.
	The conjunctive adverb *besides*, which means *also* or *in addition*, joins two independent clauses.	Inflation is hard on the individual; <u>besides</u>, it can be a serious threat to a nation's economic health.
especially	The adverb *especially* modifies an adjective.	Some people are <u>especially</u> sensitive to dust and pollen.
special	The adjective *special* modifies a noun.	In early agricultural societies, the solstices held a <u>special</u> significance.

UNIT 19

Words	Explanation	Examples
hard	*Hard* can be an adjective.	Obsidian, a <u>hard</u> volcanic glass, was used for making arrowheads.
	Hard can be an adverb. The adverb *hard* comes after the verb.	When rain or hail falls <u>hard</u>, crops can be damaged.
hardly	The adverb *hardly* comes before the verb.	Some couples <u>hardly</u> know each other before they are married.
lay	*Lay*, which means *put* or *set* (*lay, laid, laid, laying*), must have a direct object.	At the end of some card games, the players must <u>lay</u> their cards on the table.
lie	*Lie* cannot have a direct object. *Lie* can mean *rest* or *recline* (*lie, lay, lain, lying*), or it can mean *tell a falsehood* (*lie, lied, lied, lying*).	People suffering from insomnia may <u>lie</u> awake all night.
		Children sometimes <u>lie</u> to avoid punishment.
near	The preposition *near* comes before its noun object.	Most settlements thrived only if they were <u>near</u> a source of water.
nearly	The adverb *nearly* means *almost*. It modifies an adjective.	There are <u>nearly</u> enough people present to start the meeting.
raise	*Raise*, which means *move up, cause to exist*, or *grow*, must have a direct object.	Please <u>raise</u> your hand if you want to speak.
		The development of cloning <u>raises</u> several moral and ethical questions.
rise	*Rise*, which means *move up* or *get up*, cannot have a direct object.	If fog <u>rises</u> above the surface of the earth, it forms a cloud.
arise	*Arise*, which means *move up* or *originate*, cannot have a direct object.	Misunderstanding can <u>arise</u> from cultural differences.
set	*Set*, which means *put* or *place*, must have a direct object.	The technician <u>set</u> all of the equipment on the table.
		Shakespeare <u>set</u> *Romeo and Juliet* in Italy.
sit	*Sit*, which means *rest in a chair*, cannot have a direct object.	Workers who <u>sit</u> at a desk all day often develop back and neck pain.
than	*Than* is a conjunction used in comparative structures.	The Lena River is only slightly longer <u>than</u> the Mackenzie River.
then	*Then* is an adverb indicating time order or result.	Beat six eggs; <u>then</u> add them to the mixture.
		If two angles of a triangle are equal, <u>then</u> the sides opposite them are also equal.

Words	Explanation	Examples
their	*Their* is a possessive adjective.	Babies get <u>their</u> first teeth at the age of six months.
there	*There* is a pronoun when it acts as a subject.	In 1789, <u>there</u> were only thirteen states in the United States.
	There can also be an adverb indicating place.	If a bird is frightened off its nest, it may not go <u>there</u> again.

2. Words Similar in Meaning

The following words are often confusing because they are similar in meaning.

Words	Explanation	Examples
and	*And* is a conjunction.	Rubber is composed chiefly of carbon <u>and</u> hydrogen.
also	*Also* is an adverb, unless it is part of the correlative conjunction *not only...but also*.	Sapporo is a food–processing center; it is <u>also</u> a tourist destination. Birds <u>not only</u> live in trees <u>but also</u> eat the fruits of trees.
as	The preposition *as* means *in the role or function of*.	Ernest Hemingway served <u>as</u> an ambulance driver during World War I.
like	The preposition *like* means *similar to*.	<u>Like</u> other members of his generation, Hemingway wrote about the loss of hope.
do	*Do* means *perform* or *finish*.	A study showed that most people would rather play sports than <u>do</u> housework.
make	*Make* means *create*, *produce*, or *cause*.	The ability to <u>make</u> decisions is a necessary skill for managers.
during	The preposition *during* comes before its noun object.	Food shortages may occur <u>during</u> extended periods of drought.
while	The adverb *while* introduces a subordinate clause.	Many students have part–time jobs <u>while</u> they are attending college.
instead of	The preposition *instead of* comes before its noun object.	Some teachers write on an overhead projector <u>instead of</u> a chalkboard.
rather than	The conjunction *rather than* joins words or phrases of the same value.	Some painters mix their own pigments <u>rather than</u> use synthetic products.

Words	Explanation	Examples
too	*Too* usually expresses a negative result caused by something excessive.	If a person's body temperature drops <u>too</u> low, he will get hypothermia.
very	*Very* means *extremely* or *excessively* but does not express a cause–result relationship.	Daytime temperatures on the surface of Mercury are <u>very</u> hot.

3. Expressions of Quantity

Different expressions of quantity are used with countable and uncountable nouns. **Countable nouns** can be singular or plural. **Uncountable nouns** have only one form, instead of different forms for singular and plural. The following expressions of quantity are often confusing.

Words	Explanation	Examples
amount of	*Amount of* is used with uncountable nouns.	Paris and London have almost the same <u>amount of</u> rain each year.
number of	*Number of* is used with countable nouns.	An increasing <u>number of</u> women are choosing to attend law school.
quantity of	*Quantity of* is used with countable or uncountable nouns.	The shipment included a large <u>quantity of</u> toys. Our project requires a small <u>quantity of</u> red paint.
another	*Another*, which means *one more*, can be an adjective or a pronoun. It is used only with singular nouns.	One type of thunderstorm is caused by local conditions; <u>another</u> type is caused by the arrival of a cold front. <u>Another</u> is caused by the arrival of a cold front.
other	The adjective *other*, which means *some more*, can be used with plural or uncountable nouns.	An oak tree provides a home for many <u>other</u> plants. <u>Other</u> equipment will be necessary to complete the job.
others	The pronoun *others*, which means *some more*, replaces a plural noun.	Some birds perch on branches, while <u>others</u> cling to tree trunks.
the other	*The other*, which means *the last of a group*, can be an adjective or a singular pronoun.	The city's <u>other</u> university is much larger. Some of these flowers are cultivated; <u>the other</u> ones are wild. One spouse gets up early; <u>the other</u> stays up late.
the others	The plural pronoun *the others* means *the last of a group*.	Some of these flowers are cultivated; <u>the others</u> are wild.

Words	Explanation	Examples
fewer	The comparative *fewer* can be an adjective or a pronoun. It is used only with countable nouns.	Every day there are <u>fewer</u> students in class. <u>Fewer</u> come to class every day.
less	The comparative *less* can be an adjective or a pronoun. It is used with uncountable nouns.	There was <u>less</u> rainfall recorded this year than in the previous year. <u>Less</u> was recorded this year.
	Less can be part of the comparative form of a long adjective or adverb.	Ferrets are <u>less</u> popular than dogs and cats. Some strategies work <u>less</u> effectively than others do.
lesser	The comparative adjective *lesser* means *lower in value* or *smaller in size*. It is used with countable nouns.	*Titus Andronicus* is considered one of Shakespeare's <u>lesser</u> plays.
the lesser	The pronoun *the lesser* replaces a singular noun.	Sometimes voters choose <u>the lesser</u> of two evils.

 PRACTICE

Exercise 19–A

Similar Words. Circle the one underlined word that correctly completes each sentence.

1. Many animals hibernate <u>during/while</u> the winter.

2. Animals live off their fat stores <u>during/while</u> they are hibernating.

3. Some plants store water in their stems, while <u>another/others</u> store it in their roots.

4. A variety of species will thrive <u>near/nearly</u> a source of fresh water.

5. <u>Near/Nearly</u> all tundra plants grow very close to the ground.

6. The gray jay and Steller's jay are <u>alike/like</u> in their camp–robbing behavior.

7. <u>Alike/Like</u> the gray jay, the Steller's jay steals food from campsites.

8. Sometimes a cat will not allow <u>another/other</u> cat to share its territory.

9. <u>Almost/Most</u> all sports clothing is designed for a specific activity.

10. There is a mass transportation system in <u>almost/most</u> large cities.

Exercise 19–B

Sentence Editing. One of the underlined parts in each sentence is incorrect. Cross out the incorrect part and write the correction above it.

1. <u>Beside</u> killing and <u>eating</u> prairie dogs, the ferret occupies <u>its</u> victim's <u>home</u>.

2. Air <u>heated</u> on the surface of the earth tends to <u>raise</u> as an <u>invisible</u> column through surrounding <u>cooler</u> air.

3. Sometimes <u>lying</u> is an <u>essential</u> weapon for self–protection, and this may be <u>especially</u> true <u>while</u> war.

4. <u>Some</u> birds use rocks <u>as</u> nest sites, <u>other</u> burrow in the soil, and a <u>few</u> build nests on top of cliffs.

5. <u>Near</u> every house contains at least some wood, <u>but</u> in places where trees are <u>plentiful</u>, houses are often <u>made</u> entirely of wood.

6. Tax accountants have to <u>enjoy</u> contact with the public <u>because</u> an important aspect of <u>there</u> work involves <u>meeting</u> with clients face to face.

7. A snowstorm consists of a <u>nearly</u> infinite <u>amount</u> of ice crystals formed in the <u>frozen</u> environment of the middle <u>and</u> upper atmosphere.

8. <u>Many</u> pens work by capillary action in <u>too</u> narrow tubes in <u>which</u> the liquid flows upward when the <u>pressure</u> inside is lowered.

9. If ice were denser <u>then</u> water, it <u>would</u> sink, and if ice did not float, <u>very</u> large bodies of water might <u>freeze</u> over completely.

10. Securities brokers <u>advice</u> customers who want to <u>make</u> financial investments and arrange for the <u>purchase</u> or sale of stocks, bonds, and <u>other</u> securities.

Exercise 19–C

TOEFL iBT Listening.   Listen to the recording. You may take notes as you listen. Do not look at the questions until the conversation has ended. When you hear the questions, look at the questions and choose the best answer to each.

 Audio Track 27

1. Why does the student go to see his professor?

   (A) He is concerned about his grade for the course.
   (B) He needs more time to finish writing his paper.
   (C) He wants her opinion of his idea for a paper.
   (D) He would like to make up work that he missed.

2. How does the student probably feel when he says this: 🎧

   (A) Proud of how hard he works in the course
   (B) Confused because the reading is very difficult
   (C) Frustrated that he is not doing better in the course
   (D) Annoyed because he does not like philosophy

3. What does the professor advise the student to do?

   Choose two answers.

   [A] Rewrite his paper before next week
   [B] Form a study group with other students
   [C] Spend more time on the reading
   [D] Get someone to help with his writing

4. What does the professor mean when she says this: 🎧

   (A) Studying with others is valuable because you hear other points of view.
   (B) It is nearly impossible to find a group of people who all think alike.
   (C) Some interpretations are correct, while others are very misleading.
   (D) Having a tutor does not guarantee that you will get a higher grade.

5. Why does the student say this: 🎧

   (A) To thank the professor for promising to raise his grade
   (B) To express pleasure at how much he learned in the course
   (C) To express relief that the course is almost over
   (D) To show his willingness to follow the professor's advice

Exercise 19–D

TOEFL iBT Speaking. In this integrated speaking task, you will listen to a conversation. You will then be asked to talk about the information in the conversation and to give your opinion about the ideas presented.

Cover the question while the conversation is playing. You may take notes, and you may use your notes to help you answer the question. After you hear the question, you may look at the question and prepare your response. You have 20 seconds to prepare your response and 60 seconds to speak.

 Audio Track 28

> The students discuss possible solutions to the woman's problem. Describe the problem. Then state what you think the woman should do, and explain why.

 Stop

Preparation Time – 20 seconds
Response Time – 60 seconds

Answers to Exercises 19–A through 19–D are on page 272.

 EXTENSION

1. With your teacher and classmates, discuss why word errors occur. Why are some words easily confused with others? In what way are the problem words similar? How are they different? What strategies can help you remember to use problem words correctly?

2. What words or word pairs do you find confusing? Start a journal of your problem words. As you become more proficient in English, what strategies help you avoid word errors?

UNIT 20 PUNCTUATION

1. **Sentence Breaks**
2. **Comma**
3. **Semicolon**
4. **Colon**
5. **Dash and Parentheses**
6. **Apostrophe**
7. **Hyphen**
8. **Quotation Marks**

 FOCUS

What is wrong with this sentence?

> As Earths gravity grew more powerful it pulled in orbiting space rocks which crashed into the planets surface created huge craters and released massive amounts of heat

The sentence lacks punctuation, so it is difficult to read. The sentence is not separated into parts that can easily be understood. **Punctuation** is the use of standard marks to separate text into sentences, clauses, and phrases in order to clarify meaning. The correctly punctuated sentence is:

> As Earth's gravity grew more powerful, it pulled in orbiting space rocks, which crashed into the planet's surface, created huge craters, and released massive amounts of heat.

What does this sentence need?

> Migratory birds feed in the mudflats ------- the bay is a permanent home to 150 species of fish.
>
> ○ ,
> ○ ; moreover,
> ○ : but also
> ○ . And

The sentence has two independent clauses. The clauses must be joined with punctuation and a transition. Only the second answer is a correct combination of punctuation and transition. The correctly formed sentence is:

> Migratory birds feed in the mudflats; **moreover,** the bay is a permanent home to 150 species of fish.

UNIT 20

STUDY

1. Sentence Breaks   .   ?   !

A *sentence* is the basic grammatical unit because it expresses a complete thought. The end of a sentence must have a punctuation mark to indicate a break between that sentence and the next one. Most sentence breaks are marked with a period. Others are marked with a question mark or an exclamation point.

A *period* indicates a full stop at the end of a *declarative sentence*, a statement of fact or opinion.

> A creole is a pidgin that has become the native language of a community.
>
> The best films are those that explore human nature and the human condition.

A period is used at the end of an *imperative sentence*, an expression of command or request.

> Give examples from three phyla of animals that humans use for food.
>
> Please reply to this message by Friday.

A *question mark*, or *interrogation point*, indicates a direct question.

> Do you think I should buy a smaller car?
>
> How does the wind affect transpiration in plants?

An *exclamation point* indicates excitement or emotion.

> Global warming is happening even faster than we think!
>
> Let's rally in front of the library to protest the new rule!

The exclamation point is often used after short exclamations in informal writing.

> What an exciting game!
>
> How nice of you to remember my birthday!

2. Comma   ,

A *comma* indicates a pause in thought or a separation of ideas within a sentence.

In lists of three or more items, a comma is placed after every item except the last one.

> Red, yellow, and blue are the primary colors.
>
> Potassium deficiency often occurs in soils that are sandy, acidic, or low in organic matter.

A comma separates two independent clauses that are joined by a conjunction.

> Leo wants to succeed in college, so he studies six hours a day.
>
> Isotopes have different atomic weights, and some are unstable or radioactive.
>
> Not only was the play well written, but it was also beautifully performed.

A comma separates an adverb clause from a main clause when the adverb clause comes first.

> As the climate becomes warmer, there will be more moisture in the air.
>
> Because we got in line at dawn, we were able to get tickets for the concert.

A comma follows a conjunctive adverb that acts as a transition between two independent clauses.

> Inflation is hard on workers; moreover, it threatens a nation's economic health.
>
> Birds do not have sweat glands. However, they can keep cool by panting.

A comma indicates a pause after an introductory phrase.

> Looking up in the sky, we saw a huge black cloud moving toward us.
>
> In early adulthood, many men give work as high a priority as family.

If the introductory phrase is short, the comma can be omitted.

> In February the nighttime temperatures reach twenty degrees below zero.

A comma or commas separate structures that interrupt the flow of thought, such as unnecessary adjective clauses, unnecessary adjective phrases, appositives, and other structures that convey extra information.

> Alchemy, which reached Europe in the twelfth century, aimed to change base metals into gold.
>
> The children used the old car, rusted from disuse, as a backyard clubhouse.
>
> My brother, a sports nut, owns over five thousand baseball cards.
>
> A cell organizes small organic molecules into polymers, such as proteins and DNA.

A comma or commas set off a contrasted expression.

> The mother, not the father, is the head of many households.
>
> I always drove on the back roads, never the highway.

A comma separates a direct quotation from the rest of a sentence.

> "Can anyone remember," wrote Emerson, "when the times were not hard and money not scarce?"

A comma separates the name of a person who is being addressed.

> Professor Navarro, may I speak with you for a moment?

A comma is used with certain everyday material.

Dates	The first boat went through the Panama Canal on January 7, 1914.
Numbers	The dishonest dealer turned the car's odometer from 98,170 miles to 38,170 miles.
Cities, States, Provinces, Countries	My family has lived in Houston, Texas, and Barcelona, Spain. Halifax, Nova Scotia, was founded in 1749.
Closings of Letters	Sincerely yours, Yours truly, Best regards,

3. Semicolon   ;

A *semicolon* connects two independent clauses and indicates a closer relationship between the clauses than a period does. A semicolon signals a pause longer than that of a comma, but shorter than that of a period.

> My grades are very good this semester; my social life rates only a C.
>
> A baby's knowledge is of objects in the external world; the baby later develops the ability to act upon these objects.

A conjunctive adverb may follow the semicolon and act as a transition to the second clause.

> There is much moisture in the air; as a result, more snow is expected to fall.
>
> A scientific advance came in 1913 with Niels Bohr's theory of atomic structure; meanwhile, there were developments in the structure of literature and music.

Whether to use a semicolon or a period between two independent clauses is the writer's choice. The decision depends on how closely the writer wants to link the two ideas. Both of the following sentences are correct.

> Many professional men are concerned with their appearance; they have their hair styled and use cosmetics.
>
> Many professional men are concerned with their appearance. They have their hair styled and use cosmetics.

A semicolon separates items in a list when the items contain commas.

> My film instructor recommends that we watch *To Catch a Thief*, starring Cary Grant and Grace Kelly; *Animal Crackers*, with the Marx brothers; and *The Wizard of Oz*, with Judy Garland.

4. Colon   :

A *colon* introduces a list or an illustration.

> The following plants grow well in the shade: hosta, primrose, and columbine.
>
> There are two ways to train a dog: with food or with praise.

A colon may introduce an explanation or the restatement of an idea.

> My father accomplished what no one in his family had ever done: at the age of twenty–four, he earned degrees in both history and law.
>
> Pidgins and creoles are two stages in a single process of development: a pidgin becomes a creole when it is the first language that children learn.

5. Dash and Parentheses   —   ( )

A *dash* signals a pause longer than that of a comma, but shorter than that of a period. Dashes separate extra information from the rest of a sentence. The extra information defines, describes, or illustrates whatever came before the first dash.

> An object is symmetrical—the same on both sides—along an imaginary line or plane that passes through its center.
>
> The Northwest Ordinance of 1787—perhaps the first important declaration of national policy—openly encouraged migration into the Northwest Territory.

In the first sentence above, *the same on both sides* defines *symmetrical*. In the second sentence, *perhaps the first important declaration of national policy* describes *the Northwest Ordinance of 1787*.

Dashes also set off words for emphasis or dramatic effect.

> We never went to the Rough Road Cafe again—once was more than enough.
>
> Some of you—I won't mention you by name—owe Martha an apology.

Parentheses, like dashes, separate extra information from the rest of a sentence. The information inside the parentheses defines, describes, or illustrates whatever came before the parentheses.

> The publisher needs to update the section on the medical dangers of tobacco (pages 55 to 71).
>
> Some people learn best by listening (to lectures or recordings), while others learn best by seeing (reading books, the board, or charts).

UNIT 20

6. Apostrophe   '

An *apostrophe* indicates ownership or possession when it is followed by *s*.

Tom's jacket	the bear's footprints	nobody's fault
Aesop's fables	the piccolo's sound	someone else's turn

The possessive form of a singular noun is apostrophe + *s*, even when the final consonant is *s* or has a sound similar to that of *s*.

Charles's speech	the hostess's gift	the fish's eyes

The possessive form of a plural noun takes only an apostrophe after the plural *s*.

parents' obligation	neighbors' gossip	puppies' tails

Possessive adjectives and possessive pronouns do not take an apostrophe.

> Until Barry was twelve years old, he had never met <u>his</u> father.
>
> Shamans were seldom envied because <u>theirs</u> was a difficult role to play.

The possessive form of *it* is *its*, with no apostrophe. *Its* should not be confused with *it's*, which is a contraction of *it is*.

> <u>It's</u> a wise dog that makes <u>its</u> own bed.

An apostrophe indicates omission of one or more letters in a ***contraction***, the shortened form of a phrase. Below are some common contractions.

can't = can not	I'm = I am	they'd = they had/would
didn't = did not	isn't = is not	we've = we have
don't = do not	it's = it is/has	who'll = who will
haven't = have not	let's = let us	who's = who is/has
he'll = he will	o'clock = of the clock	won't = will not
I'd = I had/would	there's = there is	wouldn't = would not

Tip: Contractions are common in everyday speech and in written dialogue, but they are usually considered too informal for academic writing. It is best to avoid using contractions when writing academic papers.

7. Hyphen   –

A *hyphen* joins two or more words that act as a single unit in describing a noun.

> Frederick Douglass became a leader in the anti–slavery movement.
>
> High–flying jets and gear–grinding trucks are sources of noise pollution.
>
> A two–week–old baby is already able to recognize some facial expressions.

8. Quotation Marks " "

Quotation marks enclose direct quotations, text quoted from spoken or written sources.

> "Never let anyone tell you that black is white," my grandfather warned me.
>
> According to the article, "Osteoarthritis affects the daily activities of between 30 and 50 percent of all adults."

The punctuation mark at the end of a sentence comes inside the quotation marks.

> Professor Williams asked, "What is the purpose of culture?"

Quotation marks may set off a word or phrase for emphasis.

> Insomnia is usually defined as a "complaint" rather than a disease.
>
> The skin of a shark is made up of a tough "carpet weave" of fibrous tissue.

 PRACTICE

Exercise 20–A

Sentence Completion.   Choose the word or phrase that best completes the sentence.

1. If chronic hepatitis ------- can cause cirrhosis or liver failure.

   (A) progresses. It
   (B) progresses, it
   (C) progresses; it
   (D) progresses it

2. Elizabeth Cady Stanton ------- proposed that women should have the right to vote.

   (A) , an early feminist. She
   (B) ; an early feminist
   (C) , an early feminist,
   (D) an early feminist

3. The relationship between dance and sound varies widely ------- the right sound is important for creating the mood.

   (A) ,
   (B) . But
   (C) : but
   (D) , but

4. The traditional American breakfast is loaded with fatty foods -------.

   (A) : butter, bacon, and fried potatoes
   (B) , butter, bacon; and fried potatoes
   (C) —butter, bacon—fried potatoes
   (D) ; butter and bacon; and fried potatoes

5. Regulated change is often a reaction to a problem ------- the human body reacts to certain infections by raising its temperature.

   (A) , such as
   (B) . Such as
   (C) , for example
   (D) ; for example,

6. Hydropower is the leading source of renewable energy ------- more than 97 percent of all electricity generated by renewable sources.

   (A) : it provides
   (B) . And it provides
   (C) , it provides
   (D) ; it provides:

UNIT 20

Exercise 20–B

Sentence Editing. In the following sentences, add punctuation marks where necessary.

1. Oscar Peterson was born in Montreal Quebec on August 15 1925

2. Because snowshoes are much larger than the bottom of your foot you must adjust how you walk

3. The waiter asked Would you like milk lemon or honey with your tea

4. Hero an engineer of ancient Greece invented the first steam engine but it was of no practical use

5. How do patterns of production land use and ownership produce certain political family and

   religious systems

6. The plant nutrients that are needed in the largest quantities are nitrogen phosphorus and potassium

7. On the one hand dogs are friendly companions on the other hand they are savage predators that hunt

   in packs

8. For a very long time humans have been thinking about trees in two very different ways the scientific

   and the mythological

9. Mount Vernon George Washingtons mansion has wide lawns fine gardens and several smaller

   buildings all restored with attention to Washingtons detailed notes

10. The following books are required reading for the course *The Color Purple* by Alice Walker *In Our

    Time* by Ernest Hemingway and *Mans Search for Meaning* by Viktor Frankl

Exercise 20–C

TOEFL iBT Reading. Read the passages and choose the best answer to each question.

QUESTIONS 1–2

Cardiovascular diseases, which involve the heart and blood vessels, are the leading cause of death in many developed nations. Atherosclerosis, a chronic cardiovascular disease, involves the gradual buildup of growths called plaques on the inner smooth muscle wall of blood vessels. As atherosclerosis progresses, the risk of heart attack or stroke increases because a blood clot is more likely to become trapped in an artery that has been narrowed by plaques. Hypertension—high blood pressure—also increases the risk of heart attack or stroke. Sometimes called the silent killer, it may cause no symptoms until a heart attack or stroke occurs. Fortunately, hypertension is simple to diagnose and can usually be treated by medication, diet, exercise, or a combination of these.

1. What is atherosclerosis?

   (A) A disease of the heart and blood vessels
   (B) Smooth muscle inside blood vessels
   (C) The inability of blood to clot
   (D) High blood pressure

2. All of the following names describe the same disease EXCEPT

   (A) hypertension
   (B) high blood pressure
   (C) heart attack
   (D) the silent killer

QUESTIONS 3–4

Because so much of culture is learned implicitly, we may be unaware that certain "invisible" aspects of our culture exist: how long we can be late before being impolite, what topics we should avoid in conversation, or how we show attention through listening behavior. Differences in invisible culture can cause problems when we are unable to recognize behavioral differences as cultural rather than personal. Formal institutions— schools, hospitals, the legal system, and so on—are places where invisible cultural differences come together, and where we may misinterpret the behavior of others or misjudge their intentions. For example, when we see someone wearing exotic clothes and speaking a language other than ours, we do not assume that we understand that person or that he understands us. However, when someone is dressed like us and speaks our language, we may fail to recognize invisible cultural differences. If that person spoke "too loudly" or stood "too close" to us, we might interpret his behavior as rude rather than culturally different.

3. Which of the following is an example of invisible culture?

   (A) Wearing exotic clothes at school
   (B) How long we wait to board an airplane
   (C) How we show that we are listening
   (D) Speaking a foreign language in a hospital

4. Why does the author use the phrases "too loudly" and "too close" in the passage?

   (A) To describe the atmosphere in formal institutions
   (B) To identify impolite behavior
   (C) To argue that culture should be taught in schools
   (D) To illustrate invisible cultural differences

Exercise 20–D

TOEFL iBT Writing. In this integrated writing task, you will write a response to a question about a reading passage and a lecture. Your response will be scored on the quality of your writing and on how well you connect the points in the lecture with points in the reading. Typically, an effective response will have 150 to 225 words.

Reading Time – 3 minutes

Business revolves around making decisions, and good decisions are based on good intelligence. Creating useful intelligence involves the following steps: asking appropriate questions, carefully interpreting the answers, and gathering sufficient information to make a decision.

The intelligence–gathering process can be seen in the experience of a greeting card company. The company wanted to attract more of their core customers into their stores, so they considered expanding their product line by selling fresh flowers. The company rarely dedicated resources to a new idea without first doing a considerable amount of market research, planning, and preparation. They began collecting the information needed for the decision to sell flowers.

They set up a number of focus groups composed of their core customers (women aged thirty to fifty). In these groups, the company asked relevant questions, for example, "If fresh flowers were available in our stores, would you be inclined to buy them?" The response from participants was extremely positive, with 78 percent saying "yes." The company also decided to get answers from flower producers, so they interviewed botanists and investigated facilities. They identified personnel and equipment needs and estimated costs, concluding that the venture was feasible. The extensive information that the company gathered supported their belief that the flower business would be successful.

The project was approved, and a fresh flower facility opened in the central region. The company's major stores were equipped with refrigeration units to keep the flowers fresh. A team of botanical experts ensured that the flowers were handled with care during the distribution process. As the stores began receiving shipments of flowers, the company felt optimistic, knowing their decision was based on extensive planning and good intelligence.

Now listen to the lecture. You may take notes, and you may use your notes to help you write your response. After you hear the question, you have 20 minutes to plan and write your response. You may look at the reading passage during the writing time.

 Audio Track 29

Summarize the points made in the lecture, explaining how they cast doubt on points made in the reading.

 Stop

Time – 20 minutes

Exercise 20–E

TOEFL iBT Writing. For this independent writing task, respond to the question by writing an essay in which you state and support your opinion on the topic. Your essay will be scored on the quality of your writing, including how well you organize and develop your ideas and how well you use language to express your ideas. An effective essay will have a minimum of 300 words.

Read the following question and make any notes that will help you plan your response. Then begin writing. You have 30 minutes to plan and write your essay.

Do you agree or disagree with the following statement?

It is better to follow the advice of family members than to take the advice of friends.

Use specific reasons and examples to support your answer.

Time – 30 minutes

Answers to Exercises 20–A through 20–D are on page 273.

Answers to Exercise 20–E will vary.

 EXTENSION

1. In reading done outside class, look for examples of sentences with various punctuation marks. Bring five examples to share in class. Write some of the sentences on the board, but omit all of the punctuation. Your classmates must add appropriate punctuation marks. With your teacher and classmates, answer the following questions.

    a. Would only a particular punctuation mark be correct in each place?
    b. Would a different punctuation mark also be correct?
    c. Compare your classmates' punctuation with that in the original sentence. Are there any differences? Which sentence do you think is better?
    d. Which punctuation is necessary? Which is a matter of the writer's intention?

2. **Sentence Writing.** Practice different ways of using punctuation and transitions to connect independent clauses:

    comma and conjunction

    semicolon and conjunctive adverb

    period and sentence break

Use the conjunctions and conjunctive adverbs in the list below.

and	consequently	in addition
but	for example	in contrast
or	furthermore	meanwhile
so	however	moreover

QUIZ 6   UNITS 18 – 20

Time – 10 minutes

Choose the word or phrase that best completes the sentence.

1. Radio was tremendously ------- for many years before the arrival of television.

   (A) popular
   (B) popularity
   (C) popularize
   (D) popularly

2. The ------- of the steam engine occurred before the development of the railroad.

   (A) invent
   (B) inventive
   (C) inventor
   (D) invention

3. A caricature is a portrait in art or ------- that makes its subject appear ridiculous.

   (A) literate
   (B) literary
   (C) literature
   (D) literally

4. When one restaurant is as good as ------- difficult to choose a favorite.

   (A) another; its
   (B) another, it is
   (C) another. It's
   (D) another—is it

One of the underlined parts in each sentence is incorrect. Cross out the incorrect part and write the correction above it.

5. Many <u>drives</u> use cellular phones <u>during</u> their commute, and this is <u>very</u> dangerous to <u>others</u> on the road.

6. The orca is an <u>extremely</u> intelligent and <u>efficient</u> predator that is <u>special</u> skilled at finding and <u>catching</u> harbor seals.

7. Speeding stars <u>near</u> the center of the Milky Way <u>suggestion</u> that a huge black hole is acting <u>like</u> an anchor at the <u>center</u> of the galaxy.

8. The tower <u>crane, unlike</u> the mobile crane, <u>does</u> not expand like a <u>telescope, instead</u> it extends <u>itself</u> section by section.

9. Range managers must <u>constantly</u> deal with ranch owners, government <u>officers,</u> and people who <u>specialize</u> in <u>others</u> areas of conservation.

10. <u>Alike</u> those of bald eagles, the nests of ospreys are <u>less</u> successful in areas where <u>their</u> food is contaminated with toxic <u>chemicals.</u>

Answers to Quiz 6 are on page 273.
Record your score on page 301.

REVIEW TEST

Time – 30 minutes

Choose the word or phrase that best completes the sentence.

1. On some sailboats ------- a tiller instead of a wheel for steering.

   (A) having
   (B) in which
   (C) there is
   (D) with

2. Scott Joplin ------- composed several works in the style known as ragtime.

   (A) was an excellent piano player,
   (B) , an excellent piano player,
   (C) an excellent piano player, he
   (D) , an excellent piano player who

3. The St. Lawrence Seaway allows large ships to sail from the Atlantic Ocean ------- on the Great Lakes.

   (A) with ports
   (B) but also ports
   (C) and ports are
   (D) to ports

4. Although sunlight appears white, ------- actually a combination of all the colors of the spectrum.

   (A) it is
   (B) he is
   (C) which is
   (D) but it is

5. The piccolo is the smallest woodwind instrument and ------- of the woodwind family.

   (A) of a voice as high
   (B) its voice is higher
   (C) the highest voice
   (D) the higher the voice

6. On moonless nights, it is ------- without some form of artificial light.

   (A) too dark to see
   (B) dark only to see
   (C) very dark to see
   (D) so dark that to see

7. Not often ------- fatal, but immediate medical attention is essential.

   (A) a rattlesnake bite is
   (B) the bite of a rattlesnake
   (C) rattlesnake's bite
   (D) is a rattlesnake bite

8. If bank deposits had been insured in 1930, fewer people ------- their life savings.

   (A) had lost
   (B) had been lost
   (C) will have lost
   (D) would have lost

9. The guide wheels of a roller coaster are used for ------- on straight–aways and hills.

   (A) as gliding
   (B) to glide
   (C) gliding
   (D) glided

10. The Aztecs underwent a period of training under the Toltecs, ------- the agricultural practices of the other culture.

    (A) were learning
    (B) which learning
    (C) in which they learned
    (D) they learned

11. No one who lived during the nineteenth century ------- the changes that would take place in the next century.

    (A) can predict
    (B) predicted that
    (C) has been predicted
    (D) could have predicted

12. The enormous size of mammoths meant that ------- to attack them.

    (A) the fearless men only dared most
    (B) only the most fearless men dared
    (C) to dare the most fearless men only
    (D) dared only the most fearless men

13. Ten years ago the peregrine falcon was endangered ------- the upland sandpiper.

    (A) ; as well as
    (B) —also was
    (C) , and so was
    (D) . In addition,

14. ------- opportunities for irrigation are scarce in New Mexico, most farmland is used for the grazing of cattle and sheep.

    (A) Because
    (B) Neither
    (C) That
    (D) Instead

15. The tasks of preparing project budgets and marketing plans can have disastrous effects on the program ------- done well.

    (A) are they not
    (B) if they are not
    (C) they may not be
    (D) but also not

16. ------- rain falls in Seattle per year than in any city on the East Coast.

    (A) Less
    (B) Lesser
    (C) Fewer
    (D) A little

17. The world's largest deserts lie in regions where mountains block the trade winds, creating a condition where there is ------- precipitation.

    (A) hardly a
    (B) not hardly
    (C) hardly any
    (D) hardly none

18. Niels Bohr's atomic theory ------- the hydrogen atom consisted of a positive nucleus and an electron traveling around it.

    (A) stating
    (B) stated that
    (C) that
    (D) it stated

One of the underlined parts in each sentence is incorrect. Cross out the incorrect part and write the correction above it.

19. In a survey of suburban homeowners, the lawn mower was rated one of the most important equipments.

20. Composing a picture includes choosing its shape and size, deciding what to put in it, and to arrange colors.

21. All astronauts carry a passport during they are traveling in space because they may need it upon returning to Earth.

22. In 1841 America's best–known novelist, James Fenimore Cooper, he published The Deerslayer, the last of the five "Leatherstocking Tales."

23. On the one hand, the use of synthetic chemical products is increasing; on the contrast, vegetable oils are rising in value and importance.

24. Langston Hughes <u>was an</u> American writer <u>who</u> poetry, stories, and drama <u>were</u> important contributions <u>to the</u> Harlem Renaissance.

25. <u>In the</u> liquid–fuel rocket, the purpose of the valves <u>is control</u> the flow of the propellants, enabling the engine <u>to work</u> at different degrees <u>of power</u>.

26. Archimedes, <u>the first</u> person to make a <u>scientific</u> study of simple <u>machines, was</u> one of the greatest <u>engineering</u> in ancient Greece.

27. It is necessary that dental <u>technicians</u> and others <u>working</u> with X–rays limit <u>their</u> exposure to <u>this</u> highly penetrating rays.

28. Between five and six <u>thousand</u> years ago, humans <u>developed</u> the first writing and began <u>to work</u> in metal—first in copper, then in <u>the bronze</u>.

29. Role changes, such as <u>marriage</u>, the birth of a child, <u>and</u> a change in job, <u>causes</u> the stress that all adults experience in <u>their</u> lives.

30. Nine out of ten Americans recognized a man's <u>expression</u> in a photograph as <u>fear, yet</u> six out of ten Japanese <u>thought</u> the man was sad or <u>surprise</u>.

Answers to the Review Test are on page 274.

Record your score on page 300.

REVIEW TEST

ANSWER KEY

Diagnostic Test (p. 4)

1. D   2 – Verbs
2. D   1 – Nouns; 4 – Clauses and Sentences
3. B   1 – Nouns
4. C   7 – Adjective Clauses
5. B   4 – Clauses and Sentences; 5 – Conjunctions
6. B   1 – Nouns; 15 – Prepositions
7. C   5 – Conjunctions; 17 – Parallel Structure
8. A   9 – Conditional Sentences
9. A   2 – Verbs
10. D   11 – Articles
11. C   4 – Clauses and Sentences; 6 – Adverb Clauses
12. B   8 – Noun Clauses
13. B   5 – Conjunctions; 20 – Punctuation
14. C   14 – Comparison; 17 – Parallel Structure
15. D   3 – Infinitives and Gerunds
16. A   4 – Clauses and Sentences; 6 – Adverb Clauses
17. A   14 – Comparison; 18 – Word Form
18. B   1 – Nouns; 16 – Word Order
19. C   Correction: *which.* 7 – Adjective Clauses; 13 – Pronoun Agreement
20. D   Correction: *sun.* 17 – Parallel Structure; 18 – Word Form
21. D   Correction: *and.* 5 – Conjunctions; 19 – Common Word Errors
22. D   Correction: *to produce.* 3 – Infinitives and Gerunds; 16 – Word Order
23. A   Correction: *or.* 5 – Conjunctions
24. C   Correction: *assisted.* 2 – Verbs; 17 – Parallel Structure; 18 – Word Form
25. A   Correction: *divided in* or *divided into.* 15 – Prepositions
26. B   Correction: *are when.* 12 – Subject–Verb Agreement
27. A   Correction: *chemist.* 18 – Word Form
28. B   Correction: *carnivores.* 10 – Singular and Plural
29. C   Correction: *one.* 13 – Pronoun Agreement
30. A   Correction: *Like.* 19 – Common Word Errors

Unit 1 – Nouns

EXERCISE 1–A   (P. 13)

1. DO   *Heat* is the direct object of *absorbs.*
2. S   *How cells grow*, a noun clause, is the subject of the sentence.
3. OP   *Full capacity*, a noun phrase, is the object of *at.*
4. SC   *The highest mountain in the world*, a noun phrase, is the complement of *Mount Everest.*
5. S   *They*, a pronoun, is the subject of the second clause.
6. IO   *Students* is the indirect object of *offers.*
7. OP   *Reality and imagination*, a noun phrase, is the object of *between.*
8. S   *The fingers* is the subject of the sentence.

EXERCISE 1–B   (P. 13)

1. The appositive, *a Montreal artist*, identifies *A. Y. Jackson.*
2. The appositive, *super supermarkets*, identifies *bigger stores.*
3. The appositive, *the ability of paint to remain attached to the canvas*, defines *adhesion.*
4. The appositive, *an organ for breathing and smelling*, defines *the elephant's trunk.*
5. The appositive, *the problem solvers of the world*, describes *engineers.*
6. The appositive, *Jupiter, Saturn, Uranus, and Neptune*, identifies *the gas giants.*

EXERCISE 1–C   (P. 14)

1. B   The noun phrase *the movement of water* is the object of the preposition *for.*
2. A   The noun *nitroglycerin* is the subject of the main clause.
3. D   The appositive *the first college* identifies *Harvard.*
4. C   The pronoun *they* is the subject of the second clause.
5. C   The noun phrase *the sense of smell* is the true subject of the sentence; *it* is the false subject.
6. D   The noun phrase *several precautions* is the true subject of the second clause; *there* is the false subject.
7. A   The pronoun *it* is the subject of the second clause.
8. C   The noun phrase *a constant inflow of moisture* is the true subject of the second clause; *there* is the false subject.
9. C   The appositive *the son of actors* describes *Edgar Allan Poe.*
10. B   The noun phrase *excellent reasons* is the true subject of the second clause; *there* is the false subject.

EXERCISE 1–D   (P. 15)

1. Omit *she*, an incorrect duplicate subject. The subject is *Rosa Bonheur.*
2. Omit *how*, a subordinator, which is incorrect at the beginning of an independent clause.
3. Omit *they*, an incorrect duplicate subject. The subject is *bayberries.*
4. Omit *because*, a subordinator, which is incorrect at the beginning of an independent clause.
5. Omit *it*, an incorrect duplicate subject. The subject is *the digital camera.*
6. Omit *with*, a preposition, which is incorrect before the subject, *a sore throat.*
7. Omit *they*, an incorrect duplicate subject. The subject of the second clause is *Puerto Ricans.*
8. Omit *is*, a verb, which is incorrect before a noun structure that is an appositive.
9. Omit *by*, a preposition, which is incorrect before the true subject, *the failure.*
10. Omit *they*, an incorrect duplicate subject. The subject of the first clause is *heat, water, or pressure.*

EXERCISE 1–E (P. 16)

1. D   *Impairment* means *loss* in this context. Clue: *…a general decrease in intellectual abilities….*

2. B   The passage does not list heart attack as a cause of dementia. All of the other answers are given: *…it can also be caused by depression,…alcohol abuse,… and advanced stages of AIDS.*

3. B   The purpose of the paragraph is to give rates of dementia in older adults. Clues: *…between 3 and 6 percent of all adults over age 65…; …as many as 47 percent of all adults 85 and older…the rate of dementia is highest in adults over 85.*

4. A   The author mainly explains Alzheimer's disease as the result of tangling of the fibers in brain cells. Clue: *…Alzheimer's disease involves specific processes in the brain, most prominently a kind of tangling of the fibers in the nerve cell bodies.*

5. B   Tangling affects areas of the brain that control memory. Clue: *This tangling…occurs mostly in the areas of the brain that regulate new learning and memory.*

6. C   The author's purpose is to give examples of skills affected by Alzheimer's disease. Clues: *…those that show symptoms of Alzheimer's disease…; …interfering with the person's ability to remember even well–learned skills, such as….*

7. B   Big Band: A strong, driving dance rhythm: *Big band jazz was first and foremost dance music; …a style of playing with a strong, driving rhythm.*

   E   Big Band: Musical arrangements on charts: *…highly arranged: prepared in advance and written on charts.*

   A   Bebop: A band with five musicians: *A typical band consisted of five instruments….*

   C   Bebop: Emphasis on harmonic structure: *…based on harmonic structure rather than melody.*

   G   Bebop: Jazz as a form of art: *…viewed jazz not as dance music but as a form of art; …bebop as an art form….*

      Answers (D) and (F) characterize neither big band nor bebop.

EXERCISE 1–F (P. 18)

1. B   The student needs advice about an assignment. She says *What I'd like to do for my survey project is interview three people. Would that be OK?*

2. D   The student would like to do a comparison of opinions. She says *My idea is to interview three people…; …a grandmother who has a lot of opinions…; I want to compare what she says with what the mother says, and also the fourteen–year–old daughter.*

3. A   The student should prepare a list of possible questions. The professor says *Here's my suggestion. Why don't you prepare a list of questions—maybe five, six—no more than ten possible ideas for your interviews.*

4. C   The main idea of the lecture is that children have a culture in which play is central. The professor says *Research on the play of young children has revealed that children have a culture of their own; We find it wherever two or more children are together and reveal their private code of rules in their play.* Most of the lecture discusses the role of play in child culture.

5. C   The professor implies that children learn child culture from other children. The professor says *Younger children eagerly pick up the rules of play from older children.*

6. A   The professor's purpose is to list important elements of child culture: *body language, spoken language, humor, songs….*

7. A, D   Physical activity characterizes the play of preschool children: *In preschool, children are extremely active. They have good control of their bodies, and they enjoy activity for its own sake.* Also, open games characterize their play: *Just as important, however, are the open games, which are mostly created by the children themselves. These open games can be changed at will—kind of like improvisation on a theme.*

8. D   The games are more structured by rules. The professor says *Around the age of five, children start caring about the rules, and the games of five–year–olds tend to be more structured than the games of preschool children; At age six or seven, children like organized games in small groups, but they can be overly concerned with rules….*

EXERCISE 1–G (P. 19)

Key points:
- A bird's wing design provides lift, which pushes the bird up. Different wing types provide the ability to soar, the ability to maneuver, and reduced turbulence during flight.
- A bird's tail helps the bird to steer. The tail allows the bird to brake as it lands and to make sudden stops.
- A bird's strong muscles allow it to flap its wings to take off.
- A bird's large heart beats fast and provides oxygen to the breast muscles.
- A bird's feathers and bones are hollow, which makes them light. The bones have struts, which adds strength without much weight.

EXERCISE 1–H (P. 19)

Responses will vary.

Unit 2 – Verbs

EXERCISE 2–A (P. 31)

1. has experienced
2. can store
3. was formed; erupted violently
4. did not fully understand; had originated
5. have presumably accompanied
6. blocked; permanently altered
7. think; might occur
8. helped…understand; work

EXERCISE 2–B (P. 31)

1. have built
2. do not build
3. will build, will be building
4. built
5. had already built
6. are now building
7. will probably build
8. were still building

ANSWER KEY

Exercise 2–C (p. 32)

1. Accidents involving tankers or pipelines cause most oil spills.
2. The United States annexed the state of Texas in 1845.
3. (We) use a wrench for turning nuts and bolts.
4. (Schools) are teaching foreign languages to children as young as five.
5. Stress management may alleviate some health problems.
6. (We) can dry peas, eggs, and other foods.
7. A dense atmosphere covers Venus, the second planet from the sun.
8. (Someone) has recently developed new marketing techniques.
9. The ancient Greeks first studied the idea that elements make up everything.
10. (Someone) should have taken steps to control the pests before they damaged the plants.

Exercise 2–D (p. 33)

1. A   The simple present verb *prevents* agrees with the verb in the first clause, *occurs*.
2. D   The sentence needs a passive–voice verb; *are named* is the correct form.
3. C   The simple past verb *developed* is the only answer that fits the meaning of the sentence.
4. C   The simple present verb *can inspect* agrees with the other verb in the sentence, *compare*.
5. A   The present perfect verb *have brought* is the only answer that fits the meaning of the sentence.
6. B   The sentence needs a passive–voice verb; *be stored* is the correct form after the modal *must*.
7. D   The sentence needs a passive–voice verb; *was used* agrees in tense with the other verb in the sentence, *made*, and the time marker *1876*.
8. C   The simple past verb *was* agrees with the time marker *the 1960s*.
9. D   The sentence needs a passive–voice verb; *be taught* is the correct form after the modal *may*.
10. B   The simple past verb *took place* agrees with the other verb in the sentence, *was developed*, and the time marker *the first decade of the twentieth century*.

Exercise 2–E (p. 34)

1. *Creation* is a noun where a verb is needed. Correction: *creates*.
2. *Is* is present tense where a past tense verb is needed with the time marker *1800*. Correction: *was*.
3. *Call* is incorrect after *are often* because it is not the passive form. Correction: *called*.
4. *Flew* is past tense where a present tense verb is needed with the other verb, *begins*. Correction: *flies*.
5. *Belief* is a noun where a verb is needed. Correction: *believe*.
6. *Were* is past tense where a present tense verb is needed with *is, determine*, and *fits*. Correction: *are*.
7. *Reach* is present tense where a past tense verb is needed with the time marker *180 million to 135 million years ago*. Correction: *reached*.
8. *Define* is incorrect after *are* because it is not the passive form. Correction: *defined*.
9. *Become* is present tense where a past tense verb is needed with *was living* and *published*. Correction: *became*.
10. *Been* is the past participle where the base form is needed after the modal *had to*. Correction: *be*.

Exercise 2–F (p. 35)

1. A   The passage does not state that real estate agents own car rental agencies. All of the other answers are given: *...sell or rent property or manage, appraise, or develop real estate; ...specialize in undeveloped land sites for commercial...use.*
2. C   *Specialize in* means *focus on* in this context. Clues: *...sell or rent property or manage, appraise, or develop...; ...spend a great deal of time...locating property for sale.*
3. B   *Investigate* means *examine* in this context. Clues: *...locating property for sale...; ...spend time in the field, where they look for...new properties....*
4. D   The author states that the seller may initially ask a price that is too high. Clues: *Many sellers begin by asking more...than buyers are willing to pay....*
5. C   *The agent must make the buyer see...* is a paraphrase of *The agent has to convince the buyer....* *...the purchase as fair and desirable* is a paraphrase of *...that the property suits his needs and is a good buy.*
6. B   You can infer that a real estate agent must persuade the buyer and the seller to agree. Clues: *The agent must persuade the seller to set a realistic price; Buyers generally offer less for a property than the seller asks. The agent helps negotiate the final price....*
7. B   The nebula condensed, grew very hot, flattened into a disk, and started to spin: *As it collapsed...it became hotter, it started to spin, and it flattened into a disk.*
   C   In the nebula's center was a hot, dense protostar that eventually became the sun: *At its core was a hot, dense protostar...; ...the protostar "turned on" and became the sun....*
   E   Nebular material formed the rocky inner planets and the outer gas giants: *The planets formed from the gas and dust left over...; The inner planets...; ...collided...to form larger bodies and eventually, rocky planets. The outer planets...are mainly composed of gases; ...are known as the gas giants....* Answers (A) and (D) are minor ideas; answer (F) is not mentioned.

Exercise 2–G (p. 37)

1. A, D   The professor compares the instruments in the violin family: *...four instruments that are very different in size and range of pitches; Each member of the violin family has four strings that are stretched across a wooden box.* She also explains how a violin creates sound: *Let's take a closer look at the violin and how it produces sound.*
2. D   The professor says *...all the members of the violin family are built and played in basically the same manner; You play all of these instruments by scraping the strings with the bow....*
3. B   The other members of the family play a lower range of notes. The professor says *...four instruments that are very different in size and range of pitches; ...they play lower notes than the violin does.*

4. C   The professor's purpose is to explain how sound increases inside the violin. The professor compares the violin's shape to the mirrored room, saying *In the same way, the violin's specially shaped sound box reflects the sound waves back and forth, making them stronger and louder.*

5. ✓   Yes: The strings vibrate, causing the bridge to vibrate: *When the violin is played, the vibrating strings cause the bridge to vibrate.*

   ✓   No: A piston valve is pressed to lower the pitch of the sound: Not supported by the information in the lecture.

   ✓   Yes: The sound increases as the air inside the instrument vibrates: *The sound grows because the wood makes the air inside the violin vibrate.*

   ✓   No: The instrument's bell shape projects sound outward: Not supported by the information in the lecture.

   ✓   Yes: Sound comes out through two f–shaped holes in the belly: *Finally, the vibrations emerge even louder through the two f–shaped sound holes in the belly.*

EXERCISE 2–H   (P. 38)
Responses will vary.

EXERCISE 2–I   (P. 38)
Key points:
- The man's problem is that his study partner has not contributed much to their project. The study partner has a lot of ideas but does not help with the research.
- The woman suggests that the man talk to his partner and make him help. She thinks the man should divide the research equally and write down a list.
- The woman suggests that the man tell his professor that he is doing most of the work.
- Opinions about the solution will vary.

EXERCISE 2–J   (P. 39)
Key points:
- The lecture states that when fertilizers are used excessively, they wash into lakes, streams, and oceans, with harmful effects. This casts doubt on the point in the reading that chemical nutrients must be replenished often.
- The lecture states that nitrogen quickly washes into our water supply, and that nitrates in our drinking water can be poisonous. This casts doubt on the point in the reading that a high level of nitrogen is beneficial. Nitrogen helps plants but harms human health.
- The lecture states that phosphorus in lakes promotes the growth of algae, which hastens the natural aging of the lake. This casts doubt on the point in the reading that phosphorus is beneficial. Phosphorus makes plants grow faster, but this is not always good.
- The lecture states that excess potassium from fertilizers can damage a plant's metabolism. This casts doubt on the point in the reading that potassium is necessary for plant metabolism.
- The lecture states that different soils need nutrients in different amounts, and that a 20–20–20 fertilizer is not ideal for every garden. This contradicts the point in the reading that a 20–20–20 fertilizer is best for all types of soils.

Unit 3 – Infinitives and Gerunds

EXERCISE 3–A   (P. 48)
1. The gerund phrase *buying a home* is the complement of the subject *one of the biggest decisions we ever make* (SC).
2. The infinitive phrase *to predict* is the complement of the adjective *able* (AC).
3. The gerund phrase *treating mental illness* is the subject of the sentence (S).
4. The gerund phrase *cutting down trees* is the object of the preposition *by* (OP).
5. The infinitive phrase *to keep seafood from spoiling* is an adverb that modifies the clause *it should be refrigerated* (ADV). The gerund *spoiling* is the object of the preposition *from* (OP).
6. The infinitive phrase *to discourage squirrels* is the complement of the adjective *possible* (AC). The gerund phrase *eating food* is the object of the preposition *from* (OP).
7. The infinitive phrases *to hunt in groups* and *to use stone axes* are the direct objects (DO) of *learned* (DO). The infinitive phrase *to dominate the other creatures on Earth* is the direct object of *started* (DO).
8. The infinitive phrases *to flow through a conductor in an electrical current* and *(to) move through a vacuum in an electron beam* are adverbs that modify *may be freed* (ADV).

EXERCISE 3–B   (P. 48)
1. to cut; for cutting
2. for analyzing; to analyze
3. to make; for making
4. for converting; to convert
5. to obtain; for obtaining
6. for providing; to provide

EXERCISE 3–C   (P. 49)
1. B   The preposition *by* needs a gerund as its object: *mixing*.
2. C   The verb *are used* is followed by an infinitive: *to control*.
3. A   The causative *help* is followed by an infinitive, in this case, with *to* omitted: *convey*.
4. B   The infinitive phrase *to form words* is an adverb that modifies the verb phrase *puts a number of sounds together*.
5. C   The verb *permits* needs an infinitive as its direct object: *to move*.
6. D   The verb *began* needs either an infinitive or a gerund as its direct object; *testing* is a gerund.
7. A   The infinitive phrase beginning with *to convert* is an adjective that modifies *machines*.
8. D   The infinitive *to analyze* is an adjective that modifies *subject*.
9. A   The causative *helped* is followed by an infinitive: *to find*.
10. C   The preposition *without* needs a gerund as its object: *having knowledge*.

EXERCISE 3–D (P. 50)

1. *Build* is an incorrect form where a gerund is needed after the preposition *for*. Correction: *building*.
2. *Make* is an incorrect form where a gerund is needed after the preposition *in*. Correction: *making*.
3. *Shaping* is an incorrect form where an infinitive is needed after the causative *helps*. Correction: *shape* or *to shape*.
4. *Develop* is an incorrect form where a gerund is needed after the preposition *of*. Correction: *developing*.
5. *Change* is a verb where a noun is needed with the other nouns in the list: *regulation, spending,* and *taxing*. Correction: *changing*.
6. *The keeping* is incorrect. The gerund *keeping* does not need an article. Correction: *keeping*.
7. *Soar* is an incorrect form where an infinitive or a gerund is needed after the verb *begin*. Correction: *to soar* or *soaring*.
8. *Creating* is incorrect where a base–form verb is needed after *to* in an infinitive structure. Correction: *create*.
9. *For* is incorrect where *to* is needed in an infinitive structure. Correction: *to*.
10. *Enable* is an incorrect form where an infinitive is needed as the subject complement after *is*. Correction: *to enable*.

EXERCISE 3–E (P. 51)

Responses will vary.

EXERCISE 3–F (P. 51)

Responses will vary.

Quiz 1 (p. 53)

1. B The verb *throw* needs a direct object; *hot rocks* is a noun structure. (1)
2. A *A type of grass* is a noun structure, an appositive that defines *papyrus*. (1)
3. C *Spend* is a correctly formed simple present verb. (2)
4. A The subordinate clause needs a subject; *it* is a subject pronoun. (1)
5. B *Were probably written* is a correctly formed simple past verb in the passive voice. (2)
6. D The preposition *to* needs a noun object; *half* is a noun. (1)
7. *Producing* is a gerund where an infinitive is needed after *not unusual for rabbits*. Correction: *to produce*. (3)
8. *Had* is past tense; a present–tense verb is needed with the simple present verb *is* in the second clause. Correction: *has*. (2)
9. *Could* expresses past ability; a modal for present ability is needed with the simple present verb *can communicate* in the first clause. Correction: *can*. (2)
10. *Invest* is a verb where a noun structure is needed as the subject. Correction: *Investing*. (3)

Unit 4 – Clauses and Sentences

EXERCISE 4–A (P. 57)

1. complex
2. simple
3. compound
4. complex
5. complex
6. compound

EXERCISE 4–B (P. 58)

1. Subordinate clause: *because they filter light*; subordinator: *because*.
2. Subordinate clause: *Whenever you use oil paints*; subordinator: *Whenever*.
3. Subordinate clause: *that each hiker carry extra food and clothing*; subordinator: *that*. Subordinate clause: *even if only a day hike is planned*; subordinator: *even if*.
4. Subordinate clause: *who speak to animals*; subordinator: *who*. Subordinate clause: *that the animal understands*; subordinator: *that*. Subordinate clause: *what is being said*; subordinator: *what*.
5. Subordinate clause: *Because its young are vulnerable*; subordinator: *Because*. Subordinate clause: *so that predators cannot reach it*; subordinator: *so that*.
6. Subordinate clause: *when tidal currents are unable to disperse all of the sediment*; subordinator: *when*. Subordinate clause: *that reaches the river mouth*; subordinator: *that*.
7. Subordinate clause: *After a spill has occurred*; subordinator: *After*. Subordinate clause: *when they try to clean themselves*; subordinator: *when*. Subordinate clause: *which can poison them*; subordinator: *which*.
8. Subordinate clause: *that investment takes place*; subordinator: *that*. Subordinate clause: *when investors decide*; subordinator: *when*. Subordinate clause: *that the economy will have more consumption tomorrow*; subordinator: *that*. Subordinate clause: *if it sacrifices consumption today*; subordinator: *if*.

EXERCISE 4–C (P. 58)

1. B The sentence has two clauses; *but they* is the only answer that correctly joins the clauses, forming a compound sentence.
2. C The sentence needs a subject and a verb: *dinosaurs were*.
3. D The sentence needs a subject and a verb: *Flight is*.
4. B The third clause needs a subject and a verb: *they produce*.
5. A The first clause needs a subordinator; *When* correctly forms an adverb clause.
6. C The sentence needs a subject and a verb: *There are*.
7. D The sentence has two clauses; *while movable bridges* is the only answer that correctly joins the clauses, forming a complex sentence.
8. B *After he had returned to power* is the only answer that correctly completes the sentence, forming a complex sentence.
9. A The main clause needs a subject and a verb: *there is*.
10. D The main clause needs a verb: *brings*. The subject is *the Harvest Moon*.

EXERCISE 4–D (P. 59)

1. D   The first clause of the added sentence, *although these scientists believed that the planet was very old*, summarizes ideas in the previous sentences. The second clause, *they had no means of determining its exact age*, introduces the topic of *exact age*, which leads to *modern dating methods* in the following sentence.

2. A   *Pulsates* means *pumps* in this context. Clues: *...slide past each other as the heart...; When the heart beats....*

3. C   The left ventricle has thick walls because it pumps blood through the body. Clues: *The ventricles have thicker walls...especially the left ventricle, which must pump blood to all organs of the body.*

4. B   During the cardiac cycle, the heart contracts and relaxes. Clues: *When the heart beats, the ventricles contract...; As the heart relaxes after a contraction...; One complete sequence...is called the cardiac cycle.*

5. D   The added sentence defines *pulse*, which develops the phrase *taking the pulse,* introduced in the previous sentence.

6. B   Parents play an essential role in teaching children language: *Communication between children and parents starts very early; ...parent's voice helps a baby interpret the strange sounds of language; ...it is beneficial for parents to narrate what happens around a baby; ...parents help children...identifying sounds with experience.*

    C   Young children are proficient language learners: *Babies are extraordinary language generalists and can easily pick up two or three languages.*

    F   Children go through stages as they develop language ability: *At around six months old, they start to babble...; ...earliest age that children start to speak is ten months; ..."one word equals one sentence" stage. Between 18 and 24 months...; After that, they quickly learn....*

    Answer (A) is not mentioned; answers (D) and (E) are minor ideas.

EXERCISE 4–E (P. 62)

Key points:
- A unidirectional microphone picks up sounds that come from one direction. It picks up sounds from the performers, but it keeps out sounds coming from other directions, such as audience noise and echoes. These characteristics make unidirectional microphones good for recording bands in a studio, performers in concert halls and nightclubs, and speech.
- An omnidirectional microphone picks up sounds equally from all directions. It picks up sounds from the performers and sounds reflected from the walls and ceiling. It creates a feeling of space, of being in a large room. For these reasons, omnidirectional microphones are good for the pipe organ or bass drum in an orchestra or symphonic band.

EXERCISE 4–F (P. 63)

Responses will vary.

Unit 5 – Conjunctions

EXERCISE 5–A (P. 69)

1. W   The conjunction *and* connects words: *ice, rocks, dust.*

2. C   The conjunction *so* connects clauses: *The exterior of Hagia Sophia is not elaborately decorated; nothing distracts from the building's basic form.*

3. W   The conjunction *both...and* connects words: *material, spiritual.*

4. P   The conjunction *neither...nor* connects phrases: *the cat's teeth; its digestive system.*

5. P   The conjunction *not...but* connects phrases: *in its bite; in the sting of its tail.*

6. C   The conjunction *furthermore* connects clauses: *Global warming will interfere with the North Atlantic currents; it may disrupt the entire system of ocean currents.*

EXERCISE 5–B (P. 70)

1. B   The paired expression *both...and* connects two nouns: *both light and heat.*

2. C   The paired expression *either...or* connects two adjectives: *either semiarid or desert.*

3. A   The paired expression *not only...but also* connects two verb phrases: *not only bring song, color, and activity to a garden but also are vitally needed by plants.*

4. D   The subordinator *while* introduces a subordinate clause and shows contrast between the ideas in the two clauses.

5. C   The paired expression *both...and* connects two nouns: *Both Mother Teresa and Martin Luther King.*

6. B   The conjunctive adverb *however* connects the two independent clauses and shows contrast between the ideas in them.

7. D   The paired expression *neither...nor* connects two nouns: *Neither Millard Fillmore nor Franklin Pierce.*

8. C   The paired expression *and...as well as* connects noun phrases: *schools of journalism, mining, and international affairs, as well as a geological laboratory.*

9. B   The subordinator *so...that* introduces a subordinate clause and shows a cause–result relationship between the two clauses.

10. A   The paired expression *not...but* connects two prepositional phrases: *not on superior agricultural lands but on superior location for trade.*

EXERCISE 5–C (P. 71)

1. *And* is incorrect in the paired expression *not only...but also.* Correction: *but.*
2. *Nor* is incorrect in the sentence because the alternative is not negative. Correction: *or.*
3. *Instead* expresses contrast where a conjunctive adverb expressing cause–result is needed. Correction: *accordingly, hence, therefore,* or *thus.*
4. *Either* is incorrect in the paired expression *both...and.* Correction: *both.*
5. *Otherwise* is incorrect in the paired expression *on the one hand...on the other hand.* Correction: *on the other hand.*
6. *Neither* is incorrect in the paired expression *either...or.* Correction: *either.*
7. *Also* is incorrect where a conjunction is needed to connect two nouns. Correction: *and.*

ANSWER KEY

8. *Therefore* expresses cause–result where a conjunctive adverb expressing contrast is needed. Correction: *however* or *in contrast*.

EXERCISE 5–D (P. 72)

1. B   Insects live in a wide variety of places. Clues: *Insects live in almost every habitat on land...in fresh water...in the air; ...in the frozen extremes of the Arctic and Antarctic....*

2. D   *Sacrificing* means *using* in this context. Clues: *The wings are not true legs; therefore, insects can fly without...any walking legs. In contrast, the wings of birds are...walking legs modified for flight.*

3. A   *One view is that...* is a paraphrase of *Still others hypothesize that.... ...the first wings enabled insects...* is a paraphrase of *...wings first evolved.... ...to swim rather than to fly* is a paraphrase of *...not for flying but for swimming.*

4. C   In the added sentence, *moreover* is a transition showing addition between *insects that eat plant leaves* in the previous sentence and *insects that eat crops* in the added sentence. The following sentence further develops the topic of *crops* by stating that *in some parts of the world, insects claim over half of the grain crops.*

5. A   The ability to fly is an important factor in the variety and abundance of insects: *...when insect flight evolved...there was a rapid expansion in insect variety; The evolution of flight is one key to the tremendous success of insects.*

   D   The preeminence of insects greatly influences humans and other organisms: *Because insects are so numerous, diverse, and widespread, they affect the lives of all other terrestrial organisms, including humans.*

   E   Global warming will benefit insects and negatively impact humans: *...global warming will lead to an increase in the number of insects worldwide, with serious consequences for humans.*

   Answers (B) and (C) are minor ideas; answer (F) is not mentioned.

EXERCISE 5–E (P. 74)

Key points:

• The lecture gives three examples to support the point in the reading that invasive species have an adverse effect on their new environment.

• The lecture states that the zebra mussel arrived in North America in a cargo ship and invaded a river system. This illustrates two points in the reading: invasive species are associated with human activity; and invasive species outcompete native species.

• The lecture states that the brown tree snake traveled by air cargo to Guam, where it destroyed the native bird populations. This illustrates two points in the reading: invasive species are associated with human activity; and ecosystems are prone to invasion if they have open niches or if their native species have faced few predators.

• The lecture states that the kudzu vine became invasive after it was introduced in the United States. This illustrates two points in the reading: invasive species are associated with human activity; and invasive species proliferate quickly in a new ecosystem with favorable conditions, especially if there are no natural predators.

EXERCISE 5–F (P. 75)

Responses will vary.

Unit 6 – Adverb Clauses

EXERCISE 6–A (P. 81)

1. Adverb clause: *because they are sturdy and lightweight*; subordinator: *because*.

2. Adverb clause: *Before he was cast in his first film*; subordinator: *before*.

3. Adverb clause: *in case there is a natural disaster*; subordinator: *in case*.

4. Adverb clause: *as his father and grandfather had done before him*; subordinator: *as*.

5. Adverb clause: *so that the right brush is always on hand*; subordinator: *so that*.

6. Adverb clause: *in spite of the fact that all seats were taken*; subordinator: *in spite of the fact that*.

EXERCISE 6–B (P. 81)

1. when you drive ⇒ when driving
2. since he immigrated ⇒ since immigrating
3. While we were walking ⇒ While walking
4. before he became ⇒ before becoming
5. Until they reach ⇒ Until reaching
6. As technicians build ⇒ Building
7. After fruit is infected ⇒ After being infected
8. Because they are encouraged ⇒ Encouraged
   when they are given ⇒ when given

EXERCISE 6–C (P. 82)

1. C   *When a cell eats* is an adverb clause that modifies the main clause.

2. B   *Before* is a subordinator that introduces an adverb clause.

3. D   *When lips vibrate* is a subordinator + subject + verb structure, which forms the beginning of an adverb clause.

4. D   *As long as they* is a subordinator + subject structure, which forms the beginning of an adverb clause.

5. A   *Feeding on* introduces an active–voice adverb phrase.

6. D   *Although it has gained* is a subordinator + subject + verb structure, which forms the beginning of an adverb clause.

7. A   *Following* introduces an active–voice adverb phrase.

8. B   *As* is a subordinator that introduces an adverb clause, expressing the time relationship between the two clauses.

9. B   *Apprenticed* introduces a passive–voice adverb phrase.

10. C   *Putting* introduces an active–voice adverb phrase.

EXERCISE 6–D (P. 83)

1. D   *Wrens use much energy for maintenance, so...* is a paraphrase of *Because their maintenance costs are so high.... ...they have little for other purposes* is a paraphrase of *...wrens have little energy for allocating to other functions, such as growth and reproduction.*

2. A   The added sentence gives an example, *the herding of cattle*, to illustrate the topic of *culture trait* introduced in the previous sentence. The second clause of the added sentence, *although different cultures view cattle differently*, introduces an idea that the rest of the paragraph develops with examples of cattle in different cultures.

3. C   The first clause of the added sentence, *after the flower has bloomed*, must follow the previous two sentences in time order. The second clause, *the leaves gradually die back*, introduces an idea that the following sentence develops in *the plant gathers nutrients from the fading leaves....*

4. B   Graham's attempt to be truthful had roots in her childhood. Clues: *...her father warned her never to lie...; She tried to tell the truth in her dances....*

5. C   An attempt to appear effortless did not characterize Graham's work, but it did characterize ballet: *...classical ballet attempted to conceal effort.* All of the other answers are given: *Inventing a new language of movement...; ...it was aligned with a fundamental fact of life: breathing; Graham's characteristic percussive style enabled her to express emotional extremes.*

6. D   *Enthralled* means *fascinated* in this context. Clues: *...both praise and controversy; Although critics faulted her...Graham's audiences were enthralled.* The subordinator *although* shows contrast between *faulted* and *enthralled*; therefore, *enthralled* has a positive meaning.

7. A   *Graham's later dances...* is a paraphrase of *Her later productions.... ...amazed audiences because...* is a paraphrase of *...that they left audiences spellbound. ...they were so elaborate* is a paraphrase of *...were so rich in terms of music and design....*

EXERCISE 6–E (P. 85)

1. B   The main idea of the lecture is that positive and negative emotions are linked to different sides of the brain. The professor says *...the two halves of the brain specialize in different behaviors; ...the left brain is associated with positive emotions...; The right brain, in contrast, is associated with... negative emotions...; ...emotions associated with one side of the brain are expressed in the opposite side of the body.*

2. D   The professor says *It's important to remember that each side of the brain controls the opposite side of the brain. The left brain controls the right side of the body, while the right brain controls the left side of the body.*

3. C   The professor's purpose is to give an example of left–right bias in an animal brain. After discussing left and right biases in the human brain, the professor says *these same biases are showing up in the brains of animals*, citing examples in chimpanzees, birds, and dogs.

4. A   The professor implies that a dog has negative feelings when it sees an unfriendly dog. The bias of the dog's tail toward the left reflects control by the right side of the brain, which is linked to negative emotions.

5. ✓   Right Brain: A bird uses its left eye to watch for predators: *...because their right brain controls danger, they watch for predators with their left eye.*

✓   Left Brain: A dog's tail wags to the right side of its rump: *The left brain controls the right side of the body...; When dogs feel positive about something... they wag their tails more to the right side of their rumps.*

✓   Left Brain: The muscles in a person's face express happiness: *...the muscles on the right side of our face tend to reflect happiness—a positive emotion controlled by the left brain....*

✓   Right Brain: An animal runs away because it senses danger: *...information that tells an animal to run, fight, or watch out for danger is biased toward the right brain.*

EXERCISE 6–F (P. 86)

Key points:
- People who live in Arctic regions must move around in a landscape that looks bare and uniform. They need a highly developed understanding of space.
- A young girl who was born blind was able to find the right path between two toys after she walked to each of these toys only from a third location. This example shows that spatial intelligence does not depend on the ability to see. Spatial intelligence involves the ability to recall distances and angular relationships, and the ability to create and use mental imagery.
- The same girl was able to use a map to find a toy in the room. This example illustrates the spatial skill of working with maps and symbols.

EXERCISE 6–G (P. 87)

Key points:
- The lecture states that some generalizations about the family are myths (not true).
- The lecture states that families are not more rootless than they used to be. Families have always relocated. This contradicts the point in the reading that the family is more rootless than it was a century ago.
- Second, it is a myth that nuclear families lack connections with their extended families. More people know their grandparents than they did in the past. This contradicts the point in the reading that nuclear families have lost touch with extended family networks.
- Third, the bonds between parents and children are not weaker today than in the past. A majority of adults are in touch with their parents, and most children live with at least one parent. This contradicts the point in the reading that parent–child bonds have lapsed so much that parents have little control over their children.

Quiz 2 (p. 89)

1. A   The subordinate clause beginning with *where* needs a subject and a verb: *it forms*. (4)
2. B   The main clause needs a subject and a verb: *There may be*. (4)
3. B   The second clause needs a beginning; *while the oil is* a subordinator + subject structure, which forms the beginning of an adverb clause. (4, 5, 6)
4. D   The paired expression *not...but* connects two prepositional phrases: *not in air but in water*. (5)
5. B   The second clause needs a beginning; *so it is* has a subject and a verb and forms the beginning of a compound sentence joined by the conjunction *so*. (4, 5)
6. D   The first clause needs a beginning. *When viruses enter* is a subordinator + subject + verb structure, which forms the beginning of an adverb clause. (4, 5, 6)
7. A   *Pounding the piano and singing* forms the beginning of an active–voice adverb phrase that modifies the main clause. (6)
8. D   The first clause needs a subject and a verb: *The wood duck builds*. (4)
9. *As well in* is an incomplete conjunction. Correction: *as well as in*. (5)
10. *Determine* is a base–form verb where the present participle is needed in an active–voice adjective phrase. Correction: *determining*. (6)

Unit 7 – Adjective Clauses

Exercise 7–A (p. 97)

1. The adjective clause *who wrote the popular Adagio for Strings* modifies *Samuel Barber*.
2. The adjective clause *which severely restricted immigration* modifies *the Johnson–Reed Act*.
3. The adjective clause *whose purpose is to restrict competition* modifies *organization*.
4. The adjective clause *toward which many lending institutions direct their message* modifies *group*.
5. The adjective clause *in which there are interesting objects* modifies *areas*. The adjective clause *that await our observation* modifies *objects*.
6. The adjective clause *which upgrade the lenses in our eyes* modifies *microscopes*. The adjective clause *that actually is present in light rays* modifies *detail*.
7. The adjective clause *where people who give information are higher in status than those who need information* modifies *situations*. The adjective clause *who give information* modifies *people*. The adjective clause *who need information* modifies *those*.
8. The adjective clause *who study the South Pacific* modifies *biologists*. The adjective clause *that huge snails...feed off the metal–rich compounds that surround hydrothermal vents* modifies *discovery*. The adjective clause *which are aided by bacteria in their gills* modifies *snails*. The adjective clause *that surround hydrothermal vents* modifies *compounds*.

Exercise 7–B (p. 98)

1. who live ⇒ living
2. that falls ⇒ falling
3. which are driven ⇒ driven
4. that impacts ⇒ impacting
5. that is attached ⇒ attached
6. that make up ⇒ making up
7. which are usually made ⇒ usually made
8. which means ⇒ meaning
   that enables ⇒ enabling

Exercise 7–C (p. 99)

1. A   *That come* introduces an adjective clause that modifies *winds*.
2. C   *Which carry* introduces an adjective clause that modifies *molecules*.
3. D   *Who had* introduces an adjective clause that modifies *Hammurabi*.
4. B   *Found* introduces a passive–voice adjective phrase that modifies *instructions*.
5. D   *Entering the labor force* forms an active–voice adjective phrase that modifies *people*.
6. C   *Which are used* introduces an adjective clause that modifies *leaves*. The comma after *leaves* indicates an unnecessary adjective clause.
7. A   *Carried* introduces a passive–voice adjective phrase that modifies *principles*.
8. D   *That can be toxic* is an adjective clause that modifies *quantities*.
9. B   The preposition *of* needs a noun structure as its object. *Information obtained* is a noun + past participle structure. The past participle *obtained* introduces a passive–voice adjective phrase that modifies *information*.
10. C   *To which* introduces an adjective clause that modifies *scales*.

Exercise 7–D (p. 100)

1. *What* is not a relative pronoun. A relative pronoun is needed to introduce an adjective clause. Correction: *which*.
2. *Traveled* is the past participle. The present participle is needed in an active–voice adjective phrase. Correction: *traveling*.
3. *Whose* is a possessive form and is incorrect before the verb *thrive*. Correction: *which*.
4. *Where* cannot follow a preposition in an adjective clause. Correction: *which*.
5. *Which* refers only to things and cannot refer to *innovator* and *one*. A relative pronoun for people is needed. Correction: *who* or *that*.
6. *Specialize* is an incorrect form. The past participle is needed as a passive participial adjective before *role*. Correction: *specialized*.
7. *They* is not a relative pronoun. A relative pronoun is needed to introduce an adjective clause. Correction: *who*.
8. *That* cannot introduce an unnecessary adjective clause with commas around it. Correction: *which*.
9. *Praising* is the present participle. The past participle is needed as a passive participial adjective before *architectural projects*. Correction: *praised*.
10. *Who* refers only to people and cannot refer to *belief*, a thing. Correction: *that*.

EXERCISE 7–E (P. 101)

1. A You can infer that Rivera's expedition did not find gold and other riches. Clues: *...the Spanish, who sought gold...and other riches; Rivera found little of commercial value that would interest his superiors....*
2. C Spanish names for places remain as a sign of the Spanish exploration. Clue: *...left an abundance of Spanish place names, which are the only evidence we have today that the Spanish once explored the region.*
3. B *Permafrost* describes ground that remains frozen. Clues: *...occurs in areas where the mean annual temperature is at or below minus nine degrees Celsius; ...where over fifty percent of the land area is permanently frozen...; ...ground ice....*
4. A You can infer that a large area of Canada has an annual temperature at or below minus nine degrees because over fifty percent of the land is permafrost, permanently frozen ground. Permafrost occurs *in areas where the mean annual temperature is at or below minus nine degrees Celsius.*
5. B Plants and animals face soil moisture in the form of ice. Clue: *Almost all of the soil moisture occurs in the form of ground ice, which creates a challenge for the plants and animals....*
6. D The deep layers of ground remain frozen because vegetation insulates them from surface temperatures. Clues: *...deep layers...remain insulated from current surface conditions; ...sparse vegetation, which acts as an insulating layer for the lower levels, keeping them frozen.*

EXERCISE 7–F (P. 103)

1. B Most of the discussion is about factors that make meetings successful. The professor says *It's up to the person who calls the meeting to make sure the discussion is successful; ...what are some factors that go into planning a meeting; If the meeting is successful, it should achieve a result.*
2. D The professor says *It's up to the person who calls the meeting to make sure the discussion is successful.*
3. A, C The students say *You also need to know how many people are coming...; ...and the equipment you need, like videos and slides, or a projector and screen; You need a room that fits the size of your group....*
4. A The professor means that it is appropriate for the leader to have help in planning a meeting. When the professor says, *this doesn't mean he or she shouldn't get help with the details,* he implies the opposite: the leader *should* get help with the details.
5. B The professor's purpose is to introduce the sequence of events in a typical meeting. The professor says *follows a pattern that goes like this,* and then discusses the pattern of a typical meeting.

6. D The leader calls attention to a current problem: *First, the leader makes a brief preliminary statement calling attention to the issue.*
A Participants state relevant facts and opinions: *They contribute relevant information, facts, and opinions.*
C A decision is made about the best solution: *The participants should discuss possible solutions and decide on the one that's best.*
B The group plans how to put the solution into action: *They need a plan that puts the solution into action, for example, the next steps they should take.*

EXERCISE 7–G (P. 104)

Key points:
- Qualitative research aims to provide a complete picture of an organization. It documents the processes and the products of the organization.
- The key methods of qualitative research are observation and interviewing.
- The talk uses an example of qualitative research in a large urban high school, where the researcher would observe school activities and interview people who study and work there.
- The researcher might observe learning experiences, the social atmosphere, and people's reactions to others of different ethnic groups. The researcher might interview different people about the rules of the school.
- The data collected is in the form of words and pictures. Examples might include detailed descriptions, student work, video recordings, and flowcharts of class discussions.

EXERCISE 7–H (P. 104)

Responses will vary.

Unit 8 – Noun Clauses

EXERCISE 8–A (P. 110)

1. DO The noun clause *what nutrients are present in the soil* is the direct object of *determine.*
2. S The noun clause *whoever arrives early* is the subject of the sentence.
3. DO The noun clause *how many people will be coming to your party* is the direct object of *let...know.*
4. OP The noun clause *who really wrote some of Shakespeare's sonnets* is the object of *over.*
5. SC The noun clause *why its numbers are decreasing* is the complement of *the biggest question.*
6. DO The noun clause *where they can find resources in the community* is the direct object of *will tell.*
7. OP The noun clause *what our instructor required us to do last semester* is the object of *from.*
8. S The noun clause *that standardized tests discriminate against certain types of students* is the subject of the sentence.

ANSWER KEY

EXERCISE 8–B (P. 111)

1. where I might look ⇒ where to look
2. how much ointment should be applied ⇒ how much ointment to apply
3. what I should read ⇒ what to read
4. what they would change ⇒ what to change
5. how we will control ⇒ how to control
6. whom they ought to blame ⇒ whom to blame

EXERCISE 8–C (P. 111)

1. C The sentence needs noun structure as its subject. *How fish swim* is a noun clause.
2. D The verb *includes* needs a noun structure as its direct object. *What every student should know* is the beginning of a noun clause.
3. A The noun clause *which lane he is entering* is the direct object of *let...know.*
4. D The noun clause *when they can be planted* is parallel to the other noun clauses in the list: *how vines climb* and *what special needs they have.*
5. B The infinitive phrase *how to improve* is the object of the preposition *about.*
6. C The preposition *on* needs a noun structure as its object; *whatever they* is the beginning of a noun clause.
7. C The sentence needs noun structure as its subject. *It* is the false subject. *That the principal cause* is the beginning of a noun clause.
8. D The verb *did not know* needs a noun structure as its direct object. *What to do* is the beginning of an infinitive phrase.
9. C *That* introduces a noun clause. *That Abraham Lincoln was the greatest American president* is the subject of the sentence.
10. A The verb *is now believed* needs a noun structure as its direct object. *They learn to hunt by experience* is a noun clause with the subordinator *that* omitted.

EXERCISE 8–D (P. 113)

1. C Economics is primarily concerned with how a society allocates scarce resources. Clues: *The underlying assumptions of the field are that resources are scarce...; How to allocate limited resources...is a principal concern of economists.*
2. A Macroeconomics does not deal with what determines the price levels of particular goods. All of the other answers are concerns of macroeconomics: *Macroeconomics is concerned with how a national or regional economy behaves as a whole; Macroeconomists examine how...output, consumption,...and investment influence each other...; ...why any imbalance among them occurs.*
3. B Microeconomics differs from macroeconomics in its emphasis on how individual behavior affects specific markets. Clues: *Microeconomics is mainly focused on economic activity in the individual case...; It is especially interested in what determines the price levels of goods and services in specific markets.*
4. C You can infer that the field of economics looks at patterns in production and consumption. Clues: *... what goods will be produced and for whom they will be produced; ...gross national product...; ...output, consumption...; ...models to explain the interplay of forces...; ...examining where and why markets fail to produce efficient results.*

EXERCISE 8–E (P. 114)

Key points:
- The man's problem is that he cannot decide which part–time job to accept: waiter in a restaurant (more money) or night clerk in the physics lab (more time to study).
- The woman suggests that he decide what is more important to him: money or time to study. She suggests that he think about how a job would affect his studies and his health.
- Opinions about the solution will vary.

Unit 9 – Conditional Sentences

EXERCISE 9–A (P. 121)

1. D In this future real conditional sentence, *must have* is the correct verb form in the result clause.
2. B In this present real conditional sentence, *if there is* is the beginning of the condition clause.
3. D In this future real conditional sentence, *even if they* is the beginning of the condition clause.
4. A In this present real conditional sentence, *is certainly* is the correct verb form in the result clause.
5. C *In case* is the subordinator in this present real conditional sentence.
6. B In this present/future unreal conditional sentence, *melted* is the correct verb form in the result clause.
7. B *Unless* is the subordinator in this future real conditional sentence.
8. A In this future real conditional sentence, *will rise* is the correct verb form in the result clause.
9. D In this future real conditional sentence, *are accepted* is the correct passive–voice verb in the condition clause.
10. B *Provided that* is the subordinator in this present real conditional sentence.

EXERCISE 9–B (P. 122)

1. *Were* is an incorrect verb form in the result clause of this present real conditional sentence. Correction: *are.*
2. *As long* is an incomplete subordinator in a conditional sentence. Correction: *as long as.*
3. *Was* is an incorrect auxiliary in the condition clause of this present/future real conditional sentence. Correction: *is.*
4. *Are* is an incorrect auxiliary in the condition clause of this present unreal conditional sentence. Correction: *were.*
5. *Making* is an incorrect verb form in the result clause of this future real conditional sentence. Correction: *make.*
6. *Will make* is an incorrect verb form in the result clause of this past real conditional sentence. Correction: *made* or *would make.*
7. *Could* is an incorrect modal in the result clause of this future real conditional sentence. Correction: *can.*
8. *Will* is an incorrect modal in the result clause of this present/future unreal conditional sentence. Correction: *would.*
9. *Did* is an incorrect auxiliary in the result clause of this future real conditional sentence. Correction: *will, may,* or *might.*
10. *Emigrate* is an incorrect verb form in the result clause of this past unreal conditional sentence. Correction: *have emigrated.*

EXERCISE 9–C (P. 123)

1. D   The main purpose is to advise boaters on what to do in a storm. The future real conditional sentences are used to give advice. Clues: *Boaters will see advance warning of a storm...; ...head for a protected area; ...a bucket or any kind of drag should be attached to the anchor line; ...sit or lie on the bottom of the boat....*

2. B   During a storm, people should keep low in the boat. The future real conditional sentence gives advice: *As long as the occupants sit or lie on the bottom of the boat, they should be safe.*

3. D   The author's purpose is to show that advertisers have changed what they do. The present unreal conditional sentence states an untrue condition, *if advertisers still focused on that segment of the population*, meaning that advertisers do *not* still focus on the same population.

4. A   The author does not believe that advertisers should focus on the traditional family. All of the other answers are given: *...it has to identify the potential users of a product...; ...only if it conducts market research...; Unless the agency obtains detailed data and marketing expertise....*

5. C   *Advertisers must know their potential buyers...* is a paraphrase of *...only if it conducts market research to understand who they are. ...in order to reach them effectively* is a paraphrase of *An advertising agency can decide on the best way of reaching potential buyers....*

EXERCISE 9–D (P. 124)

1. B   The student wants to take a course and its prerequisite at the same time. He says *I'd like to take oceanography, but I don't have the prerequisite...; ...if I took the math course at the same time as oceanography....*

2. A   The adviser means that the oceanography course requires a strong background in mathematics. She makes a future real conditional statement, meaning that if he does not have a good foundation in mathematics, he will find the oceanography course very difficult.

3. C   The adviser implies that the professor will not allow him to take both courses. The student's question is in the future unreal: *Would it help if I talked to the professor?* The adviser's reply is also in the future unreal: *You could try, but I wouldn't get my hopes up if I were you.* She means that he should not get his hopes up (expect success) because the professor is not likely to permit him to take both courses at the same time.

EXERCISE 9–E (P. 125)

Key points:
- The university is offering a linked course in Greek drama and philosophy. The man's opinion is that the woman should take the linked course.
- One reason he gives is that she would have a better schedule. She would never have two papers due at the same time or two tests on the same day.
- Another reason is that she would learn more in a linked course than in two separate courses.
- Another reason is that she would earn two units, which would take care of the entire humanities requirement.

EXERCISE 9–F (P. 126)

Key points:
- The woman's problem is that she cannot attend an internship fair because she must take a make–up test on the same day.
- The man suggests that she talk to her professor and try to reschedule the test.
- The woman suggests that the man help her by taking notes and picking up handouts at the fair.
- Opinions about the solution will vary.

Quiz 3 (p. 128)

1. C   *That does not* introduces an adjective clause that modifies *muscle*. (7)

2. D   *In which* introduces an adjective clause that modifies *chamber*. (7)

3. B   In this present real conditional sentence, *may appear* is the correct verb form in the result clause. (9)

4. A   *Finding out* must have a noun structure as its direct object; *who was best informed* forms part of a noun clause. (8)

5. A   The first clause, a noun clause, needs a subject; *living material* is a noun phrase with an active–voice participial adjective. (7, 8)

6. D   *Learn* must have a noun structure as its direct object; *how to find more of them* is an infinitive phrase. (8)

7. C   In this past unreal conditional sentence, *had not plowed* is the correct verb form in the condition clause. (9)

8. A   *Held* introduces a passive–voice adjective phrase that modifies *the Montreux International Jazz Festival*. (7)

9.   *Do* is an incorrect auxiliary in the condition clause this present/future unreal conditional sentence. Correction: *did*. (9)

10.   *What* is not a relative pronoun. A relative pronoun is needed to introduce an adjective clause. Correction: *which* (7)

Unit 10 – Singular and Plural

EXERCISE 10–A (P. 134)
1. theses
2. phenomena
3. crisis
4. species
5. criteria
6. analyses

EXERCISE 10–B (P. 135)
1. B   The singular noun *ring* needs a singular expression of quantity: *Each*.
2. C   The plural numeric term *thousands* is correct before the *of* + plural noun structure *of bird species*.
3. A   The singular noun *state* needs a singular expression of quantity: *Every*.
4. A   The singular noun *soft white stone* is correct after *a kind of*, a singular expression of class.
5. C   The uncountable noun *news* needs an uncountable expression of quantity: *much*.
6. B   *Million years* is correct after the numbers *25 to 11*. The noun *years* is plural, but the numeric term *million* after a number does not have a plural form.
7. D   The uncountable noun *light* needs an uncountable expression of quantity: *amount of*.
8. C   The superlative expression *the first of the* must be followed by a plural noun: *satirical stories*.
9. D   The singular noun *word* needs a singular expression of quantity: *every*.
10. C   The uncountable noun *traffic* needs an uncountable expression of quantity: *less*.

EXERCISE 10–C (P. 136)
1. *Tooth* is singular where a plural noun is needed. Correction: *teeth*.
2. *Function* is singular where a plural noun is needed after the superlative structure *one of the most important*. Correction: *functions*.
3. *Every* is a singular expression of quantity and is therefore incorrect before the uncountable noun *furniture*. Correction: *All*.
4. *Country* is singular where a plural noun is needed after *different*. Correction: *countries*.
5. *Sceneries* is not a proper word; *scenery* is an uncountable noun and therefore has no plural form. Correction: *scenery*.
6. *Animal* is singular where a plural noun is needed after the superlative structure *some of North America's largest*. Correction: *animals*.
7. *Few* is used only with plural countable nouns and is incorrect before *increase*. Correction: *little*.
8. *Hazard* is singular where a plural noun is needed after *other*. Correction: *hazards*.
9. *Less* is used only with uncountable nouns and is therefore incorrect before the plural countable noun *boys*. Correction: *fewer*.
10. *Much* is used only with uncountable nouns and is therefore incorrect before the plural countable noun *storms*. Correction: *Many*.

EXERCISE 10–D (P. 137)
Responses will vary.

EXERCISE 10–E (P. 137)
Responses will vary.

Unit 11 – Articles

EXERCISE 11–A (P. 143)
1. The blue whale is the largest of the marine mammals.
2. John Steinbeck, an American writer, won the Nobel Prize for (X) literature in 1962.
3. Economics is the study of (X) money, (X) capital, and (X) wealth.
4. A/The huge release of energy from a large star at the end of its life is called a supernova.
5. A/The woodchuck has traditionally been called a/the "groundhog" because it lives in an underground den.
6. James Cotton began playing the blues harmonica after leaving (X) home at the age of nine.
7. Because so much news is available on the Internet, some experts predict a decrease in the number of (X) newspapers.
8. The remains of buildings are (X) our principal sources of (X) information about (X) many early cultures.
9. Soybeans are a valuable subsistence crop, and they are used as a source of protein for (X) humans and animals.
10. The number of hair cells that are stimulated in the ear depends on the loudness of a sound.

EXERCISE 11–B (P. 144)
1. C   The noun phrase *outdoor job* is non–specific and begins with a vowel sound. Therefore, it takes the indefinite article *an*.
2. D   *This stamp* refers to the singular definite noun *the first gummed postage stamp*. It is the only answer that correctly precedes a *"lick–and–stick."*
3. C   *Uniformly* begins with consonant sound and therefore takes the indefinite article *a*. The noun phrase *a uniformly dark color* is parallel to *a shapeless appearance*.
4. D   In this general statement, *electronic equipment* is an indefinite uncountable noun. Therefore, it takes no article.
5. B   *The ink sac* is a body part, and *the octopus* is a species of animal. Therefore, both nouns take the definite article.
6. C   The gerund *hunting* is uncountable. Therefore, it takes no article.
7. B   *One of the first* is correct before the plural noun *major composers*.
8. A   In this general statement, the plural nouns are indefinite. Therefore, *identical blood types* takes no article.

EXERCISE 11–C (P. 145)

1. *The computers* is incorrect because *computers* is plural and indefinite in this general statement. Therefore, it takes no article. Correction: *computers*.
2. *Most* is part of a superlative structure and therefore needs the definite article. Correction: *the most*.
3. *Plow* is an invention and therefore needs the definite article. Correction: *the plow*.
4. *A largest* is an incorrectly formed superlative structure. The definite article is needed. Correction: *the largest*.
5. *Snake River* is a large body of water and therefore needs the definite article. Correction: *the Snake River*.
6. *Star* is an indefinite singular countable noun that needs an article. Correction: *a star*.
7. *Greatest* is an incorrectly formed superlative structure. The definite article is needed. Correction: *the greatest*.
8. *A seawater* is incorrect because *seawater* is definite before the limiting modifier *from which our ancestors first emerged*. Correction: *the seawater*.
9. The expression of class *the kind of* comes before *cheese*. Therefore, *cheese* takes no article. Correction: *cheese*.
10. *An evidence* is incorrect because *evidence* is uncountable and indefinite in this general statement. Therefore, it takes no article. Correction: *evidence*.

EXERCISE 11–D (P. 146)

Key points:
- Mutualism is an interaction between two species in which both species benefit. Both the acacia tree and the singing ant benefit from living together.
- The acacia tree provides a place for the ants to live. The ants live in the tree's hollow thorns.
- The acacia tree provides food for the ants. The ants eat the sugar and protein produced by the tree.
- The ants protect the tree from harmful influences. The ants attack anything that touches the tree. The ants sting other insects and chase away animals that eat plants. The ants clip all vegetation that grows close to the acacia and competes with the tree for sunlight.

EXERCISE 11–E (P. 147)

Responses will vary.

Unit 12 – Subject–Verb Agreement

EXERCISE 12–A (P. 155)

1. Plural: *Both Latvia and Lithuania are*
2. Plural: *Chemical oceanographers search*
3. Singular: *A sensor detects...and...measures*
4. Plural: *There are* (*many types* is the true subject)
   Plural: *that grow* (*that* refers to *many types*)
5. Plural: *Studies have linked*
   Singular: *it triggers*
6. Plural: *Some grizzly bears are*
   Plural: *others are*
   Plural: *still others have*
7. Singular: *what will be produced*
   Singular: *what will be produced is determined*
   Singular: *which is considered* (*which* refers to *the marketplace*)
8. Singular: *the descending half (of the stairs) acts*
   Singular: *the motor moves*
   Plural: *who are riding* (*who* refers to *people*)

EXERCISE 12–B (P. 155)

1. C The singular subject *physics* needs a singular verb: *deals with*.
2. D The singular subject *Washington* needs a singular verb: *has been*. The present perfect tense fits with the time marker *for more than two centuries*.
3. C The plural subject *many* needs a plural verb: *are disappearing*.
4. B The singular subject *The Book of Changes* needs a singular verb: *consists*.
5. A The singular subject *finch family* needs a singular, active–voice verb: *includes*.
6. D The singular subject *physical environment* needs a singular, present–tense verb: *affects*.
7. A The subject, the noun clause *why a person has no friendships*, needs a singular verb: *is*.
8. A The compound subject *both strip mining and quarrying* needs a plural verb: *maintain*.
9. C The subject, the indefinite pronoun *everyone*, needs a singular verb: *knows*.
10. B The subject is *none*; a plural noun after *none* needs a plural verb. The plural noun *poisonous snakes* needs a plural verb: *are*.

EXERCISE 12–C (P. 156)

1. *Contributes* is a singular verb. The compound subject *ocean currents, wind, and air temperature* needs a plural verb. Correction: *contribute*.
2. *Are* is a plural verb. The relative pronoun *which* refers to *a bank*, which needs a singular verb. Correction: *is more*.
3. *Have* is a plural auxiliary. The uncountable subject *information* needs a singular verb. Correction: *has*.
4. *Shows* is a singular verb. The relative pronoun *that* refers to *records*, which needs a plural verb. Correction: *show*.
5. *Qualify* is a plural verb. The singular subject, *a college graduate*, needs a singular verb. Correction: *qualifies*.
6. *Help* is a plural verb. The relative pronoun *that* refers to *testing*, an uncountable noun that needs a singular verb. Correction: *helps*.
7. *Have* is a plural auxiliary. The subject, *the number of women*, needs a singular verb. Correction: *has*.
8. *Are* is a plural verb. With the compound subject *either aerobics or cycling*, the verb must agree with the closer noun, *cycling*, an uncountable noun that needs a singular verb. Correction: *is*.
9. *Consumes* is a singular verb. After *recommend that*, a verb of importance, the subject takes a base–form verb, even though the subject is singular. Correction: *consume*.
10. *Cause* is a plural verb. The uncountable subject *adding extra passengers* needs a singular verb. Correction: *causes*.

EXERCISE 12–D (P. 157)

Responses will vary.

ANSWER KEY

EXERCISE 12–E (P. 158)

Key points:

- The lecture states that the growth of the suburbs has led to dependence on the automobile, as well as traffic problems and pollution. This differs from the point in the reading that the private automobile is convenient.
- The lecture states that urban villages are transit–friendly, so residents do not need a car. This differs from the point in the reading that the private automobile made public transit unnecessary.
- The lecture states that suburban life is predictable, boring, unbalanced, isolated and unfriendly, and that suburbs are cultural deserts. This differs from the points in the reading that the suburban lifestyle is appealing and that many suburbs are attractive because they are built around a single purpose.
- The lecture states that urban villages are multiple–use, coherent, balanced, and diverse neighborhoods. This differs from the point in the reading that living conditions in the city are crowded and deteriorating.

EXERCISE 12–F (P. 159)

Responses will vary.

Unit 13 – Pronoun Agreement

EXERCISE 13–A (P. 166)

1. *Itself* refers to *the cat*. *Its* refers to *the cat*.
2. *Their* refers to *rivers*. *Our* refers to *humans* (implied).
3. *This* refers to *driving while intoxicated is illegal*. *It* refers to *driving while intoxicated*.
4. *Those* refers to *the stories of Mark Twain*. *His* refers to *Mark Twain*.
5. *Others* refers to *people who are not creative*. *They* refers to *creative people*.
6. *Its* refers to *the vampire bat*. *That* refers to *body*. *This* modifies *blood–sucking creature*.
7. *Who* refers to *men*. *Their* refers to *men*. *Those* refers to *men*. *Who (are less successful)* refers to *those* and *men*.
8. *Its* refers to *the bassoon*. *That* refers to *tonal quality*. *That (of the oboe)* refers to *tonal quality*.

EXERCISE 13–B (P. 167)

1. A *Their* agrees with its referent, *desert trees*.
2. B *Others* agrees with its referent, *people*.
3. D *Which* agrees with its referent, *the thymus gland*.
4. A *That* agrees with its referent, *the composition*.
5. B *Who* agrees with its referent, *John Marin*.
6. D *Their* agrees with its referent, *bicycle messengers*.
7. D *Those* agrees with its referent, *plays*.
8. C *You* agrees with the pronoun in the condition clause, *you*.
9. C *Which* agrees with its referent, *telescope*.
10. B *Nothing* refers only to things or ideas. *Nothing* is the only answer that can correctly come before *in the grammar and vocabulary*.

EXERCISE 13–C (P. 168)

1. *He* does not agree in number with *people*, the noun it refers to. Correction: *they*.
2. *Yours* is a possessive pronoun. A possessive adjective is needed before *salads*. Correction: *your*.

3. *That* does not agree in number with *population, industrial capacity, and financial resources*, the nouns it replaces. Correction: *those*.
4. *His* does not agree in gender with *Mary Pickford* and *actress*, the nouns it refers to. Another gender clue is *The Poor Little Rich Girl*. Correction: *her*.
5. *Their* does not agree in number with *a child*, the noun it refers to. Correction: *his* or *her*.
6. *His* is a personal pronoun. An adjective clause must begin with a relative pronoun, in this case, the possessive form. Correction: *whose*.
7. *Ours* is a possessive pronoun. The object form is needed after the verb *reassures*. Correction: *us*.
8. *Your* does not agree in person with *students*, the noun it refers to. Correction: *their*.
9. *Whom* is an object–form relative pronoun. The subject form is needed before the verb *numbered*. Correction: *who*.
10. *Those* does not agree in number with *coat*, the noun it replaces. Correction: *that*.

EXERCISE 13–D (P. 169)

1. D The subject of the previous sentence is *some bulbs*. Logic tells you that *others* refers to *bulbs*.
2. C The main clause states that parasites, viruses, and bacteria all specialize in breaking into cells. The object of the action is *cells*. Logic tells you that the object pronoun *them* refers to *cells*.
3. A The subject of the previous sentence is *parasites*. Logic tells you that the subject pronoun *they* refers to *parasites*.
4. B In the first clause, the indirect object of the verb *help recognize* is *people*. Logic tells you that the object pronoun *them* refers to *people*.
5. D The previous sentence states that manufacturers want their customers to make repeated purchases. Logic tells you that *this* refers to *making repeated purchases*.
6. A The subject of the first clause is *Saturn*. Logic tells you that *its* refers to *Saturn*.
7. C The subject of the sentence is *atmosphere*. Logic tells you that *that* refers to *atmosphere*.
8. C *About which* introduces an adjective clause that modifies *an abundance of natural wealth*. Logic tells you that *which* refers to *an abundance of natural wealth*.
9. D *Who* introduces an adjective clause that modifies *Sacajawea, the Shoshone "Bird Woman."* Logic tells you that *who* refers to *Sacajawea*.
10. A *The antelope walked up to the men...* is a paraphrase of *...they tamely approached the men. ... because they did not fear humans* is a paraphrase of *They encountered antelope so innocent of human contact that....*
11. D In the added sentence, *many* refers to *stone arch bridges* in the previous sentence and in the following sentence.
12. B In the added sentence, *they* refers to *tourists*, the subject of the previous sentence. In the added sentence, *those* refers to *natural wonders* in the previous sentence.
13. D In the added sentence, *it* refers to *social support*, which the previous sentence defines. The added sentence develops the definition by showing how social support is measured.

EXERCISE 13–E (P. 172)
Responses will vary.

EXERCISE 13–F (P. 173)
Key points:
- The center will be open only three days a week, and students must pay a fee for workshops that used to be free.
- The woman thinks that the changes are not fair to students. One reason is that it will be difficult for her to go to the center because it will be closed on Friday, the only day she has free time.
- Another reason is that the new workshop fee is too high for something that used to be free. It is unfair because their tuition has also increased.

EXERCISE 13–G (P. 174)
Responses will vary.

Quiz 4 (p. 175)

1. D   *Is an* correctly completes the sentence. The uncountable noun *water* takes the singular verb *is*. The noun phrase *invisible vapor* is non–specific and begins with a vowel sound. Therefore, it takes the indefinite article *an*. (10, 11, 12)
2. B   *A few* is correct before the plural countable noun *job changes*. (10)
3. C   *Comes from a* correctly completes the sentence. The singular subject *a demonstration* takes the singular verb *comes*. Because *demonstration* is an indefinite noun, *study* is also indefinite and therefore takes the indefinite article. (11, 12)
4. A   The gerund phrase *oil refining* is indefinite and uncountable, and therefore takes no article. (11)
5. *Whom* refers only to people and does not agree with *storm*, the thing it refers to. Correction: *which*. (13)
6. *He* is a subject pronoun. The object form is needed after the preposition *before*. Correction: *him*. (13)
7. *That* does not agree in number with *films*, the noun it replaces. Correction: *those*. (13)
8. *Collapses* is a singular verb. The plural subject *leaves* needs a plural verb. Correction: *collapse*. (12)
9. *Which* refers only to things and cannot refer to *people*. Correction: *who* or *that*. (13)
10. *Are* is a plural verb. The gerund subject, *enforcing minimum wages*, needs a singular verb. Correction: *is*. (12)

Unit 14 – Comparison

EXERCISE 14–A (P. 181)
1. S   Superlative: *the most visible*
2. E   Equative: *not as large as*
3. C   Comparative: *faster than*
4. E   Equative: *just as damaging as*
5. S   Superlative: *the earliest*
6. C   Comparative: *more likely...than*

EXERCISE 14–B (P. 181)
1. D   *Less dense than* is a correctly formed comparative structure.
2. B   The equative structure *as tall as* correctly compares two things.
3. A   *More likely* correctly completes the comparative structure *more likely to be built...than....*
4. A   *Less* correctly completes the comparative structure *have changed less in design...than have....*
5. B   The equative structure *as popular as* correctly compares two things.
6. C   The comparative structure *the warmer* completes a double comparative: *the more...the warmer*.
7. D   The equative structure *as the bulldog is ugly* completes a complex equality: *the collie is as beautiful as the bulldog is ugly*.
8. C   *Much more* completes the comparative structure *much more complex than*.
9. A   The comparative structure *less valuable than* correctly compares two things.
10. D   *The largest* after *one of* correctly completes the superlative structure: *one of the largest*.

EXERCISE 14–C (P. 182)
1. *Dry* is a base–form adjective. The superlative form is needed with the other superlatives in the sentence: *flattest*, *oldest*, and *most isolated*. Correction: *driest*.
2. *High* is a base–form adverb. The comparative form is needed before *than*. Correction: *higher*.
3. *Least* is a superlative form. A comparative form is needed with *smaller* and before *than*. Correction: *less*.
4. *Than* is a comparative form. An equative form is needed after *almost as large and just as powerful*. Correction: *as*.
5. *Hottest* is a superlative adjective. A comparative form is needed with *the faster* in the double comparative structure. Correction: *hotter*.
6. *Formalest* is not a proper form. *Formal* is a long adjective (with two or more syllables) that takes the long–form superlative. Correction: *most formal*.
7. *More* is incorrect before *greater* because *great* is a short adjective that takes the short–form comparative. Correction: omit *more*.
8. *Most* is an incomplete superlative form before *successful of the*. Correction: *the most*.
9. *As if* is an incorrect equative form after *just as well*. Correction: omit *if*.
10. *Lesser* is an incorrect comparative form before *direct*. Correction: *less*.

ANSWER KEY

EXERCISE 14–D (P. 183)

1. D   You can infer that foods high in protein are less energy–dense than foods high in fat. Clues: ...*a gram of protein...about four kilocalories of energy. A gram of fat yields nine kilocalories....; ...fat has a greater energy density than...protein....*

2. B   *The high–protein, less energy–dense breakfast...* is a paraphrase of *However, the first breakfast, which is higher in protein, has a lower energy density than the doughnuts.... ...provides three times as much energy as the doughnuts* is a paraphrase of *...and supplies three times as much food energy.*

3. D   Satiation is lower in energy–dense foods. Clues: ...*fat has a greater energy density...; Foods low in energy density are more satiating than foods high in energy density; ...fat is the least satiating.*

4. A   The passage supports the statement that the nutrients in food determine its energy yield and level of satiation. In fact, these are major ideas in the passage. Clues: *The amount of energy a food provides depends on how much of each nutrient it contains; The nutrient composition of a meal affects the level of satiation the meal provides.*

5. C   You can infer that one's perception of social support is stronger when one feels a sense of security. Clues: *Our perception...is related to our attachment to other people. The more secure the attachment, the greater the sense of social support.*

6. A   *Depression after a major change was four times as likely...* is a paraphrase of *...were four times as likely to become depressed after a major change as were those who had a close confidant. ...in women without close social support* is a paraphrase of *The women who had no close relationship....*

EXERCISE 14–E (P. 184)

1. D   The professor means that we know relatively little about deep–water circulation. We know *much less about the deep ocean*, in relation to the *fair amount* we know about water circulation in the shallow ocean.

2. A, D   One factor that influences the movement of ocean water is wind blowing across the surface: *The wind has a major impact on surface water currents. In fact, water circulation at the surface is driven mainly by the wind.* Another factor is a change in the water's density: *The movement of the deep water is driven by gravity and caused primarily by changes in the density of seawater.*

3. C   The ocean's deep water is colder, heavier, and slower moving. The speakers say ...*water movement in the deep ocean is slow, compared to how it is at the surface; ...the deep water is so much colder and so much heavier than the water at the surface; This colder, heavier water moves much more slowly.*

4. B   The professor's purpose is to emphasize a property of the ocean's lower layers. As the water gets deeper, it becomes denser. The professor also says *The deepest water has the greatest density.*

EXERCISE 14–F (P. 185)

Responses will vary.

EXERCISE 14–G (P. 185)

Key points:
- Mudflow is a fast, sudden process, while creep is slower and more gradual. Creep is the slowest type of mass wasting.
- Mudflow is catastrophic and dramatic. Creep is less dramatic, but moves more material than mudflow does. Creep is more widespread.
- Mudflow occurs on steep slopes, while creep occurs on gentler slopes.
- The evidence of mudflow is obvious (downed trees, buried roads and buildings), while the evidence of creep is less obvious (bent trees, dips in roads and fences, leaning poles).

Unit 15 – Prepositions

EXERCISE 15–A (P. 192)

	Preposition:	Noun object:
1.	by	William Shakespeare
	around	1595
2.	(based) on	decades
	of	research
	into	using vitamins and minerals
	as	immunity boosters
3.	before	1779
	about	photosynthesis
	by	which
4.	through	the use
	of	a simple genre
	like	the folktale
	(point) out	ways to solve moral problems
5.	in	the distribution
	of	organisms
	because of	its effect
	on	biological processes
6.	for	the study
	of	older adults
	to	younger adults
	in	dental samples
	from	successive time periods

EXERCISE 15–B (P. 193)

1. A   The preposition *during* expresses time: *during the early years.*

2. B   *Because of* is a compound preposition with the object *the nature of rock.*

3. A   *Respond to* is a verb + preposition structure. *Respond* must be followed by *to* because there is a noun object, *impulses.*

4. C   *Through and* joins two preposition with a conjunction, forming *through and around*, to express direction.

5. C   The adjective + preposition structure *different from* expresses a relationship between women and men: *not very different from.*

6. D   The verb + preposition structure *consists of* expresses the correct relationship between *flower* and *many tiny parts.*

7. B   The sentence contains *from...to*, a paired expression: *from Hawaii to California.*

8. B   *Into a* expresses a relationship of direction between *insights* and *variety of diseases.*

9. D *By determining* is the beginning of a prepositional phrase that functions as an adverb.
10. C *At the height of* is the only answer with prepositions that correctly link parts of the clause *A man of twenty is at the height of his physical vigor.*

EXERCISE 15–C (P. 194)

1. *To* is incorrect in the paired expression *between...and.* Correction: *and.*
2. *Next* is an incomplete compound preposition. Correction: *next to.*
3. *For* does not show the correct relationship between *mountains* and *Europe, Asia, and South America.* Correction: *of.*
4. *Similar* is an incomplete adjective + preposition structure. Correction: *similar to.*
5. *For* does not show the correct relationship between *breakup of Vietnam* and *several smaller states.* Correction: *into.*
6. *From* does not show the correct relationship between the passive–voice verb *was founded* and *the psychiatrists.* Correction: *by.*
7. *Down* is incorrect because objects cannot fall *down* the ground. Objects fall from the sky *to* the ground. Correction: *to.*
8. *To* does not show the correct relationship between *found* and *the northeastern part.* Correction: *in.*
9. *Of* is incorrect before the adverb *there.* Only a noun can follow a preposition. Correction: omit *of.*
10. *Of* is incorrect after *deal. Deal with* is a common phrasal verb. Correction: *with.*

EXERCISE 15–D (P. 195)

1. B The number of working married women in the United States increased after 1900. Clues: *...married women in the United States did not work outside the home in great numbers until the twentieth century. Between 1900 and 1930 there was a steady rise in the employment of married women.*
2. A The author's purpose is to distinguish "women's" and "men's" jobs. *Instead of taking men's jobs in industry* means that women did *not* take men's jobs in industry. Women took jobs as domestics, typists, and clerks, which are different from jobs *in industry.*
3. C *Due to* means *caused by* in this context. Clues: ... *difference in male and female earnings...; ...business policies that tried to bind male employees to the company through pay raises and promotions but excluded women from advancement....* The difference in male and female earnings was caused by policies that favored men but excluded women.
4. C The passage does not state that women faced unsafe working conditions. All of the other answers are given: *Federal laws discouraged the hiring of married women...; ...laws prohibiting the employment of married women...; ...gender stereotypes in pay and promotion; ...difference in male and female earnings increased from 20 percent...to 55 percent...; ...excluded women from advancement....*

5. B The passage does not state that palpitations may result from a change in occupation. All of the other answers are given: *A person may experience palpitations during times of stress, such as... before a test...; ...medications such as cold tablets may be factors...; ...a sudden change of position, such as getting out of bed too quickly....*
6. D The author compares the heartbeat regulator to the motor of a car. Clues: *...the heartbeat regulator has trouble adjusting to the quick switch from a circulatory system that is horizontal to one that is vertical; ...the heart may skip a few beats, similar to the way in which a car motor misses a beat as it goes from driving on a flat road to climbing a hill.*

EXERCISE 15–E (P. 196)

Key points:
- The government studies the labor force and unemployment by collecting statistics every month. Researchers use a procedure called random sampling, in which part of the population is chosen at random and interviewed about their work patterns.
- The government divides the population into three groups: employed, unemployed, and outside the labor force. The employed are people with jobs. The unemployed are people without jobs who are looking for work. People outside the labor force do not have jobs but are not looking for work.
- The total labor force consists of people who have jobs and people who are looking for jobs. The unemployment rate is the number of unemployed people divided by the total labor force, or the percentage of people who are out of work but looking for work.

Unit 16 – Word Order

EXERCISE 16–A (P. 205)

1. C *A very fine spray* is a noun phrase with correct word order.
2. D The second clause needs a subject and a verb. After *and so,* the subject and verb are inverted: *does the leopard.*
3. B The sentence needs a subject and a verb. After the prepositional phrase of location, *in the very center,* the subject and verb are inverted: *is the pistil.*
4. A The sentence needs a subject and a verb. After the introductory negative *nowhere,* the subject and verb are inverted: *are there more.*
5. D The second clause needs a subject and a verb. After the introductory negative *seldom,* the subject and verb are inverted: *does it bloom.*
6. C *Large enough to carry* is an adjective + *enough* + infinitive structure that expresses cause and result.
7. A The sentence needs a subject and a verb. *Only Earth is* has correct word order.
8. A After the introductory negative *under no circumstances,* the subject and verb are inverted: *should one back up a motor vehicle.*
9. D The verb *had* needs a direct object. *Hardly any flavor* is a noun phrase with correct word order.
10. C A noun structure must follow *there is. No warning* is an adjective + noun structure that correctly completes the sentence.

EXERCISE 16–B (P. 206)

1. *Side opposite* has incorrect word order. Correction: *opposite side.*
2. *Walls very thick* has incorrect word order. Correction: *very thick walls.*
3. *Tashkent is* has incorrect word order. After the prepositional phrase of location, *among central Asia's oldest cities,* the subject and verb are inverted. Correction: *is Tashkent.*
4. *Enough heavy* has incorrect word order before the infinitive *to fall.* Correction: *heavy enough.*
5. *Lincoln issued* has incorrect word order. When an introductory subordinate clause begins with *only after,* the main clause has question word order. Correction: *did Lincoln issue.*
6. *Skits humorous* has incorrect word order. Correction: *humorous skits.*
7. *Half live* has incorrect word order. After the prepositional phrase of location, *on the Galapagos Islands,* the subject and verb are inverted. Correction: *live half.*
8. *So weak* is incorrect before the infinitive *to resist.* Correction: *too weak.*

EXERCISE 16–C (P. 207)

1. B   The student does not understand something on her bill. She says *I need to talk to someone about my bill; ...there's a charge for eighty–seven dollars, and nowhere does it say what it's for.*
2. C   The student denies that anything happened in her room. After the man tells her that the charge on her bill was for *the repair of a broken closet door,* the student says *no way did that ever happen,* meaning that the closet door in her room was never broken.
3. A   The student implies that she and her roommate would not damage university property. *I respect university property, and so does my roommate* means that they both respect university property. The student denies that the closet door was broken and believes that they are *too careful for something like that to happen.*
4. D   The man suggests that the student describe the problem on a complaint form. He says *You can appeal the charge by filling out a complaint form; Below that is a place to explain the problem.*
5. D   The student means that she hopes the charge will be removed from her bill. The man says *I hope you get the problem cleared up.* She replies *So do I,* meaning that she agrees with him.

EXERCISE 16–D (P. 208)

Key points:
- The new graduation requirement is that all students must complete an internship in their major field of study.
- The woman thinks that the new requirement is a good idea (*not a bad idea*). One reason is that an internship will provide valuable training.
- An internship will give her an advantage when she looks for a job after graduation. She will have work experience that will look nice on her résumé.
- She will meet people who will be good mentors, teach essential skills, and recommend her for jobs.
- Also, the internship requirement links the college to the community.

Unit 17 – Parallel Structure

EXERCISE 17–A (P. 213)

1. W   Parallel words: *produce, stop, modify*
2. P   Parallel phrases: *riding a bicycle; walking briskly*
3. W   Parallel words: *scent, sound; slowly, silently*
4. C   Parallel clauses: *where they will go; what they will do*
5. P   Parallel phrases: *determines the weather; regulates our comfort*
6. W   Parallel words: *interview, hire, train*
7. P   Parallel phrases: *within a society; between different societies*
8. C   Parallel clauses: *At the north magnetic pole the force of Earth's magnetic field is directed downward; at the south magnetic pole it is directed upward*

EXERCISE 17–B (P. 214)

1. D   *Shapes* is parallel to the other nouns in the list, *styles* and *sizes.*
2. B   *In its beauty* is parallel to *in its strength,* to which it is joined by *not...but.*
3. C   *The goat* is parallel to *the cow,* to which it is joined by *either...or.*
4. B   *Use* completes the list of two parallel verb phrases: *establish separate hunting grounds* and *use different strategies.*
5. C   *The upper layer* is parallel to *the middle layer,* to which it is joined by *neither...nor.*
6. A   *But also occurs* is parallel to *not only powers.* The paired expression *not only...but also* connects parallel verb phrases: *not only powers the sun but also occurs in thermonuclear weapons.*
7. C   *Learning to ride* is parallel to *learning to swim* in the comparative structure joined by *more...than.*
8. A   *Of a global economy* completes the list of two parallel noun phrases: *an expansion of the Western economies* and *the emergence of a global economy.*
9. B   *Low in oxygen* is parallel to *high in carbon dioxide,* to which it is joined by *but.*
10. D   *Appropriate signs* is parallel to *store layout* and *merchandise presentation,* the other noun phrases to which it is joined by *and...as well as.*

EXERCISE 17–C (P. 215)

1. *Cutting* is not parallel to *kill,* the other verb in the list. Correction: *cut.*
2. *Spoke* is not parallel to *(to) read* and *write,* the other base–form verbs in the list of infinitives. Correction: *speak.*
3. *Learn* is not parallel to *presenting* in the equative structure joined by *as important as.* Correction: *learning.*
4. *Leaping* is not parallel to *to swim,* the infinitive to which it is joined by *and.* Correction: *to leap* or *leap.*
5. *Painful,* an adjective, is not parallel to the nouns in the list: *pressure, heat,* and *cold.* Correction: *pain.*
6. *More* is a comparative word. *The more productive* is not parallel to *the largest population,* the superlative structure to which it is joined by *not only...but also.* Correction: *most.*
7. *Insulating* is not parallel to the other verbs in the list, *protects* and *forms.* Correction: *insulates.*
8. *Managing* is not parallel to *to handle,* the infinitive to which it is joined by *and.* Correction: *to manage.*

9. *Controls* is not parallel to *(to) lower* and *reduce*, the other base–form verbs in the list of infinitives. Correction: *control*.

10. *But thought* disrupts parallelism. The paired expression *not...but* joins two prepositional phrases: *about broadcasting* and *about rapid communication*. Correction: omit *thought*.

EXERCISE 17–D   (P. 216)

Key points:
- The lecture is about stories told by women; the reading is about stories told by men.
- The lecture states that the women's stories focused on community and social norms. In contrast, the men's stories were mainly about contest or competition. The men's stories usually had a protagonist and an antagonist.
- The women told stories about themselves, about other women, and about men. In contrast, all of the men's stories were about themselves.
- Women often told stories that made them look foolish, while men told stories that made them look good.
- The women's stories were about people helping others, while the men's stories were about people acting alone.
- The women's stories reveal community as the source of power. In contrast, the men's stories reveal the individual as the source of power.

EXERCISE 17–E   (P. 217)

Responses will vary.

Quiz 5   (p. 218)

1. A   *And radiation* completes the list of three parallel nouns: *conduction, convection, and radiation*. (17)
2. A   The first clause needs a subject and a verb. After the introductory negative *not only*, question word order is used: *did World War I cause*. (16)
3. D   *The second most* correctly completes the superlative structure *the second most abundant*. (14)
4. B   The verb + preposition structure *consist of* must come before the object *a rigid bar*. (15)
5. C   The equative structure *as dull as* completes a complex equality: *brown feathers are as dull as... blue feet are bright*. (14)
6. D   The sentence needs a subject and a verb. After the prepositional phrase of location, *among Italo Calvino's works*, the subject and verb are inverted: *is a realistic novel*. (16)
7. B   *Or a hollow limb* is parallel to *either an underground burrow*. The paired expression *either...or* connects parallel noun phrases: *either an underground burrow or a hollow limb*. (17)
8. D   The adjective *only* modifies *sixty–two*, the subject of the sentence. (16)
9. *Volume enormous* has incorrect word order. Correction: *enormous volume*. (16)
10. *By* is the incorrect preposition after *differ* in this sentence. Correction: *from*. (15)

Unit 18 – Word Form

EXERCISE 18–A   (P. 223)

1. Digging—N. much—ADJ. aerates—V. erosion—N.
2. influence—N. eventually—ADV. far—ADJ. Mediterranean—ADJ. Indian—ADJ.
3. introduction—N. building—ADJ. changed—V. architecture—N. significantly—ADV. twentieth—ADJ.

EXERCISE 18–B   (P. 223)

1. B   The adjective *expensive* is correct after *less*. The comparative adjective *less expensive* modifies *an orange*.
2. A   The sentence needs a verb: *depend*.
3. D   The noun *difference* is the true subject. *There* is the false subject.
4. C   The adverb *systematically* modifies the verb *investigate*.
5. C   The noun *employment* names an act, state, or process.
6. A   The noun *products* names things: *rice, peanuts, and tobacco*.
7. D   The adverb *relatively* is correct before the adjective *constant*.
8. B   The first clause needs a verb: *fertilize*.

EXERCISE 18–C   (P. 224)

1. *Circulation* is a noun where a verb is needed. Correction: *circulates*.
2. *Technically* is an adverb. An adjective is needed before the noun *occupation*. Correction: *technical*.
3. *Operate* is a verb. A noun is needed in the list of nouns, with *formation* and *termination*. Correction: *operation*.
4. *Freeze* is a verb. An adjective is needed before the noun *ground*. Correction: *frozen*.
5. *Cooperatively* is an adverb. An adjective is needed before the noun *effort*. Correction: *cooperative*.
6. *Develop* is a verb. A noun is needed after the possessive adjective *its*. Correction: *development*.
7. *Influence* is a verb or a noun. An adjective is needed before the noun *invention*. Correction: *influential*.
8. *Chemists* is a noun for people. A noun for things is needed. Correction: *chemicals*.
9. *Appearance* is a noun where a verb is needed. Correction: *appears*.
10. *Skillful* is an adjective. An adverb is needed before the verb participle *applied*. Correction: *skillfully*.

EXERCISE 18–D   (P. 225)

1. D   The passage does not mention the price of diamonds. All of the other answers are mentioned: *...the hardest of all minerals; ...diamonds were formed deep within the earth...; ...great luster and fire...; ...brilliance...; ...nearly colorless...; ...exceptional beauty....*
2. A   The author means that the least desirable stones have been removed. *Sort* means separate by type; a *sorting process* is an act of separation. During the long river journey, *flawed or fractured stones are more likely to be broken up and eroded away*, leaving diamonds *of gem quality* in the gravel.
3. A   *Brilliance* means *brightness* in this context. Clues: *...shines with great luster and fire....*

ANSWER KEY

4. C   *The rarest and most beautiful diamonds...* is a paraphrase of *Diamonds of exceptional beauty and rarity.... ...are very valuable* is a paraphrase of *...are highly prized.*

5. D   *Flawless* means *perfect* in this context. Clue: *Many of the diamonds found in gravel are of gem quality because flawed or fractured stones are more likely to be broken up and eroded away* (paragraph 1). A *flaw* is a defect or imperfection; the suffix *–less* means *without*.

6. C   The author argues that a high–quality computer system must have philosophical unity. Clues: *...conceptual unity, when every part of the system reflects the same philosophy...; ...from the mind of one person, or from the minds of a small number of people who share a way of thinking ...; ...unified under the vision....*

7. B   *Both architecture and software design are best...* is a paraphrase of *Just as a large building is most successful..., a software design is most successful.... ...when based on a single vision* is a paraphrase of *...when it comes from the vision of one architect... when it is unified under the vision of one lead designer.*

Exercise 18–E   (p. 226)

Responses will vary.

Unit 19 – Common Word Errors

Exercise 19–A   (p. 233)

1. during
2. while
3. others
4. near
5. Nearly
6. alike
7. Like
8. another
9. Almost
10. most

Exercise 19–B   (p. 234)

1. *Beside*, which means *next to*, is incorrect in this sentence, where the meaning is *in addition to*. Correction: *besides*.
2. *Raise* must have a direct object. This sentence has no direct object. Correction: *rise*.
3. *While* is an adverb. A preposition is needed before the noun *war*. Correction: *during*.
4. *Other* is an adjective. A plural pronoun is needed to replace the plural noun *birds*. Correction: *others*.
5. *Near* is a preposition. An adverb is needed to modify the adjective *every* in this sentence. Correction: *Nearly*.
6. *There* is incorrect before *work*, where a possessive adjective is needed. Correction: *their*.
7. *Amount* is used only with uncountable nouns. *Ice crystals* is countable. Correction: *number*.
8. *Too* is incorrect because the sentence does not express cause and result. Correction: *very*.
9. *Then* is an adverb. A conjunction is needed after the comparative adjective *denser*. Correction: *than*.
10. *Advice* is a noun where a verb is needed. Correction: *advise*.

Exercise 19–C   (p. 235)

1. A   The student is concerned about his grade for the course. He says *It's about the grade on my paper. Um, the grade is too low...so I was wondering if I could rewrite it to raise my grade; ...is there anything I can do for extra credit to raise my grade?*

2. C   You can infer that the student feels frustrated that he is not doing better in the course. He is concerned about the grade on his paper. He is convinced that he already studies hard because he reads for nearly three hours daily. He probably feels that he should be doing better than he currently is.

3. B, D   The professor advises the student to form a study group with other students: *...I advise you to study with other people. Organize a study group with other people from the class.* She also advises him to get someone to help with his writing: *...for help with your papers, my advice is to find a tutor or go to the Writing Center.*

4. A   The professor means that studying with others is valuable because you hear other points of view. She has encouraged him to organize a study group with other students. She says *You get to hear how others interpret the material*, meaning he will hear other points of view. She says *that's often the best way to learn* and *it's an especially good way to test your own interpretation*, conveying the value of studying with others.

5. D   The student shows his willingness to follow the professor's advice. The professor has advised him to find a tutor or go to the Writing Center for help with his papers. She tells him about *teaching aides that will read your paper and suggest ways to improve it*. The student says *Sounds good*, showing his desire to follow her suggestion, adding *If it helps raise my grade, I'd be very happy.*

Exercise 19–D   (p. 236)

Key points:

- The woman's problem is that she is too busy with basketball and debate club. She must give up one or the other. Quitting either one would have consequences.
- If she quits basketball, she will have more time for debate, but she will disappoint the team and get less exercise.
- If she quits debate, she might hurt her chance at getting a debate scholarship.
- Opinions about the solution will vary.

Unit 20 – Punctuation

EXERCISE 20–A (P. 243)

1. B The sentence has two clauses. The first clause is an adverb clause. A comma separates the adverb clause from the main clause.
2. C *An early feminist* is an appositive. Commas separate the appositive from the rest of the sentence.
3. D The sentence has two independent clauses joined by a conjunction. A comma follows the first clause.
4. A A colon introduces the list of *fatty foods*.
5. D The sentence has two independent clauses. A semicolon follows the first clause, and a comma follows the transition *for example*.
6. A A colon introduces an explanation of the idea that *hydropower is the leading source of renewable energy.*

EXERCISE 20–B (P. 244)

1. Oscar Peterson was born in Montreal, Quebec, on August 15, 1925.
2. Because snowshoes are much larger than the bottom of your foot, you must adjust how you walk.
3. The waiter asked, "Would you like milk, lemon, or honey with your tea?"
4. Hero, an engineer of ancient Greece, invented the first steam engine, but it was of no practical use.
5. How do patterns of production, land use, and ownership produce certain political, family, and religious systems?
6. The plant nutrients that are needed in the largest quantities are nitrogen, phosphorus, and potassium.
7. On the one hand, dogs are friendly companions; on the other hand, they are savage predators that hunt in packs.
8. For a very long time, humans have been thinking about trees in two very different ways: the scientific and the mythological.
9. Mount Vernon, George Washington's mansion, has wide lawns, fine gardens, and several smaller buildings—all restored with attention to Washington's detailed notes. Mount Vernon—George Washington's mansion—has wide lawns, fine gardens, and several smaller buildings, all restored with attention to Washington's detailed notes.
10. The following books are required reading for the course: *The Color Purple*, by Alice Walker; *In Our Time*, by Ernest Hemingway; and *Man's Search for Meaning*, by Viktor Frankl.

EXERCISE 20–C (P. 245)

1. A Atherosclerosis is a disease of the heart and blood vessels. Commas and appositives provide clues: *Cardiovascular diseases, which involve the heart and blood vessels...; Atherosclerosis, a chronic cardiovascular disease....*
2. C Heart attack is not the same disease as the others; it is a possible effect of the disease. *Hypertension, high blood pressure,* and *the silent killer* are all names for the same disease. Dashes and a comma provide clues: *Hypertension—high blood pressure—...; Sometimes called the silent killer, it may cause no symptoms until a heart attack...occurs.*
3. C How we show that we are listening is an example of invisible culture. Clue: *...we may be unaware that certain "invisible" aspects of our culture exist: ... how we show attention through listening behavior.*

4. D The author's purpose is to illustrate invisible cultural differences. Quotation marks emphasize that "too loudly" and "too close" are misinterpretations related to invisible culture. Clues: *...we may fail to recognize invisible cultural differences; ...we might interpret his behavior as rude rather than culturally different.*

EXERCISE 20–D (P. 246)

Key points:
• The lecture states that the company's flower venture failed because of bias in the gathering and interpretation of information. This casts doubt on the point in the reading that the intelligence–gathering process can be seen in the experience of a greeting card company. The company's experience is not a good example of intelligence gathering.
• The lecture states that the company had been excessively optimistic. They had been confident in their idea, and this bias caused them to interpret information positively. This casts doubt on the point in the reading that creating useful intelligence involves asking appropriate questions and carefully interpreting answers.
• Bias caused the company to gather information that supported their belief. They did not ask their customers the right questions about their shopping habits. This casts doubt on the point in the reading that the company asked relevant questions in the focus groups.
• Bias caused the company to stop researching too soon; they did not realize that their information was incomplete. This casts doubt on the point in the reading that creating useful intelligence involves gathering sufficient information to make a decision.

EXERCISE 20–E (P. 247)

Responses will vary.

Quiz 6 (p. 248)

1. A The adjective *popular* is correct after the adverb *tremendously*. (18)
2. D A noun must follow *the*. The noun *invention* is the subject of the sentence. (18)
3. C The noun *literature* is joined to the noun *art* by the conjunction *or*. (18)
4. B The sentence has two clauses. The first clause is an adverb clause. A comma separates the adverb clause from the main clause. (20)
5. *Drives* is a verb. A noun for people is needed. Correction: *drivers*. (18)
6. *Special* is an adjective. An adverb is needed before the adjective *skilled*. Correction: *especially*. (19)
7. *Suggestion* is a noun where a verb is needed. Correction: *suggest*. (18)
8. *Telescope, instead* lacks correct punctuation. A semicolon is needed to join the two independent clauses. A comma is needed after the transition *instead*. Correction: *telescope; instead*, (20)
9. *Others* is incorrect before the plural noun *areas*. Correction: *other*. (19)
10. *Alike* is an adjective. A preposition is needed before *those*. Correction: *Like*. (19)

ANSWER KEY

Review Test (p. 249)

1. C   The sentence needs a subject and a verb: *there is*. (1, 4)

2. B   The answer, *an excellent piano player*, is an appositive that identifies the subject, *Scott Joplin*. Commas separate an appositive from the rest of the sentence. (1, 20)

3. D   The sentence contains *from...to*, a paired expression: *from the Atlantic Ocean to ports on the Great Lakes*. (15)

4. A   The main clause needs a subject and a verb: *it is*. The neuter subject pronoun *it* refers to *sunlight*. (1, 4, 13)

5. C   The superlative structure *the highest voice* is parallel to *the smallest woodwind instrument*. (14, 17)

6. A   *Too dark to see* is a too + adjective + infinitive structure that expresses cause and result. (16, 19)

7. D   The first clause needs a subject and verb. After the introductory negative *not often*, the subject and verb are inverted: *is a rattlesnake bite*. (16)

8. D   The sentence is a past unreal conditional sentence; *would have lost* is the correct verb form in the result clause. (9)

9. C   The sentence needs a noun structure as the object of the preposition *for*. The answer, *gliding*, is a gerund. (3)

10. C   The sentence needs an adjective structure to modify *a period of training under the Toltecs*. The answer, *in which they learned*, is the beginning of an adjective clause. (7)

11. D   The sentence needs a verb that fits with the time marker *during the nineteenth century* and the past–tense verb *would take place*. The answer, *could have predicted*, is a past–tense modal + verb. (2)

12. B   The noun clause starting with *that* needs a subject and a verb. *Only the most fearless men dared* is a subject + verb structure with the correct word order. (8, 16)

13. C   The sentence needs a conjunction to join *the peregrine falcon was endangered* with *the upland sandpiper*. The answer, *and so was*, has the correct conjunction, word order, and punctuation. (16, 20)

14. A   The first clause needs a subordinator. *Because* correctly introduces the adverb clause. (6)

15. B   The sentence is a present/future real conditional sentence in the passive voice; *if they are not* introduces the condition clause. (9)

16. A   *Less* is the correct comparative adjective before *rain*, an uncountable noun. (10, 14, 19)

17. C   The sentence needs a modifier before *precipitation*. The answer, *hardly any*, is an adverb + adjective structure. (16)

18. B   The answer is the main verb *stated* and the subordinator *that*, which introduces a noun clause, the direct object of *stated*. (4, 8)

19. *Equipments* is not a proper word. *Equipment* is an uncountable noun and therefore has no plural form. Correction: *pieces of equipment*. (10)

20. *To arrange* is not parallel to the other gerunds in the list, *choosing* and *deciding*. Correction: *arranging*. (3, 17)

21. *During* is a preposition where an adverb is needed to introduce a subordinate clause. Correction: *while*. (6, 19)

22. *He published* is incorrect; *he* is a duplicate subject. The subject is *novelist*. Correction: omit *he*. (1)

23. *Contrast* is incorrect in the paired expression *on the one hand...on the other hand*. Correction: *other hand*. (5)

24. *Who* is a subject pronoun. The possessive form is needed before *poetry, stories, and drama*. Correction: *whose*. (13)

25. *Is control* is an incorrect structure. An infinitive is needed after *the purpose of the valves is*. Correction: *is to control*. (3)

26. *Engineering* is the noun for a field of study. The sentence needs a noun for people. Correction: *engineers*. (18)

27. *This* is a singular demonstrative. The plural form is needed before *highly penetrating rays*. Correction: *these*. (13)

28. *The bronze* is incorrect. The definite article is incorrect before *bronze*, an indefinite uncountable noun. Correction: omit *the*. (11)

29. *Causes* is a singular verb. The plural subject *role changes* needs a plural verb. Correction: *cause*. (12)

30. *Surprise* is a verb. An adjective is needed after the adjective *sad* and the conjunction *or*. Correction: *surprised*. (17, 18)

AUDIO SCRIPTS

EXERCISE 1–F (P. 18)

Audio Track 1

Questions 1 through 3. Listen to a conversation between a student and a professor.

W: Professor Wilson, can I ask you something?
M: Sure.
W: What I'd like to do for my survey project is interview three people. Would that be OK? Because in class you said a survey is usually done with a large number of people.
M: That's right, it is. But tell me about your idea.
W: My idea is to interview three people in my host family. There's a grandmother who has a lot of opinions—oh, about everything. I want to compare what she says with what the mother says, and also the fourteen–year–old daughter. Would that be all right?
M: It's a start, but what would your focus be? You said the grandmother has opinions about everything—opinions about what?
W: It's a philosophy of life, I guess.
M: Here's my suggestion. Why don't you prepare a list of questions—maybe five, six—no more than ten possible ideas for your interviews. When you've done that, show me the list, and we'll go from there.
W: All right. I'll work on it tonight. Thanks for the advice.
M: You're welcome.

1. Why does the student speak to her professor?
2. What is the student's idea for her project?
3. What does the professor suggest the student do?

Audio Track 2

Questions 4 through 8. Listen to part of a lecture in an anthropology class.

Research on the play of young children has revealed that children have a culture of their own. Where do we find this culture? We find it in the sandbox and at the daycare center. We find it in the schoolyard. We find it wherever two or more children are together and reveal their private code of rules in their play.

Games and play are the realities of child culture. At the age of three, children are initiated into the secrets of child culture. Younger children eagerly pick up the rules of play from older children. Older children are the leaders of play activities because, of course, older children are experienced players. At age three, the ability to learn is enormous. There are so many skills to be mastered, including body language, spoken language, humor, songs, and so on. All of these are like keys that open the door to the fellowship of child culture. It's a culture preserved in an oral tradition of songs and rhymes.

In preschool, children are extremely active. They have good control of their bodies, and they enjoy activity for its own sake. They love opportunities to run, climb, and jump. The play of preschool children has a broad range. Traditional games like hopscotch and ring around the rosy are an important part of

their play. Just as important, however, are the open games, which are mostly created by the children themselves. These open games can be changed at will—kind of like improvisation on a theme.

In primary school, children are extreme in their physical activities and tend to express their emotions freely. Around the age of five, children start caring about the rules, and the games of five–year–olds tend to be more structured than the games of preschool children. Games are spontaneous and creative, but they also contain the rules, norms, and values of the group. At age six or seven, children like organized games in small groups, but they can be overly concerned with rules, or get carried away by team spirit. There are frequent quarrels, and many children indulge in punching, shoving, and wrestling.

4. What is the main idea of the lecture?
5. Listen again to part of the lecture. Then answer the question.
    "At the age of three, children are initiated into the secrets of child culture. Younger children eagerly pick up the rules of play from older children. Older children are the leaders of play activities because, of course, older children are experienced players."
    What does the professor imply about child culture?
6. Why does the professor say this:
    "There are so many skills to be mastered, including body language, spoken language, humor, songs, and so on. All of these are like keys that open the door to the fellowship of child culture."
7. What characterizes the play of preschool children?
8. How are the games of older children different from those of younger children?

EXERCISE 1–G (P. 19)

Audio Track 3

Listen to part of a lecture in a biology class.

Birds have many physical features that contribute to their flying ability. Wings are important, but so are adjustable tails, strong muscles, large hearts, and light bones.

A bird's wings are designed so air above the wing is forced to move faster than air below the wing. This creates higher pressure under the wings, called lift, which pushes the bird up. Different wing types evolved for different ways of flying. Birds that fly long distances need long wings and the ability to soar. Other birds need superior maneuverability. Fast birds, like hawks and falcons, have wings with built–in spoilers that reduce turbulence during a speedy flight.

A bird's tail acts like a rudder to help the bird steer. Birds brake by spreading out their tails as they land. This adjustment allows them to make sudden, controlled stops—an essential skill, since most birds need to land on tree branches, or on the prey that will be their dinner.

Flapping the wings to take off requires muscle strength, and strong muscles need oxygen. Birds have large, specialized hearts that beat much faster than the human heart and provide the necessary oxygen to the breast muscles. A bird's breast muscle accounts for 15 percent of its body weight. On some birds, such as pigeons, the breast muscle accounts for one–third of their total body weight.

Birds carry no excess baggage. They have hollow feathers and hollow bones. The bones have struts inside them, like the crossbeams in a bridge, which gives them strength without adding much weight.

Using points and examples from the lecture, explain how a bird's physical features contribute to its ability to fly.

EXERCISE 2–G (P. 37)
Audio Track 4

Questions 1 through 5. Listen to part of a lecture in a music theory class. The professor is talking about the violin family.

The string section of an orchestra is made up of four instruments that are very different in size and range of pitches. These four instruments are the violin, viola, cello, and double bass. They are often grouped together and called the violin family. Think of violas, cellos, and double basses as just larger–sized violins. The strings on these instruments are longer, thicker, or heavier, and they play lower notes than the violin does. However, all the members of the violin family are built and played in basically the same manner.

Reduced to its basics, a stringed instrument of the violin family is simply two bows rubbed together, but one of the bows has a sound box attached. Each member of the violin family has four strings that are stretched across a wooden box. You play all of these instruments by scraping the strings with the bow, which causes the strings to vibrate.

Let's take a closer look at the violin and how it produces sound. Notice that the strings are stretched over this upright piece of light–colored wood. The piece of wood is called the bridge. When the violin is played, the vibrating strings cause the bridge to vibrate. The bridge has a design carved in it, a design that helps the wood to shake back and forth freely in rapid vibrations. The bridge sends the vibrations to the top, or belly, of the violin. Since the belly is much larger than the bridge, it causes more air to vibrate, making the sound louder.

But even the vibrating belly of the violin does not by itself make a very loud sound. The sound grows because the wood makes the air inside the violin vibrate. Imagine you're standing in a room with mirrors on all the walls. Your image is reflected back and forth, and you can see yourself lots of times. In the same way, the violin's specially shaped sound box reflects the sound waves back and forth, making them stronger and louder. The violin's characteristic shape amplifies the sound vibrations. Finally, the vibrations emerge even louder through the two f–shaped sound holes in the belly. By that, I mean they look sort of like lower case letter Fs.

1. How does the professor develop the topic of the violin family?
2. What point does the professor make about the instruments in the violin family?
3. How do the other members of the family differ from the violin?
4. Listen again to part of the lecture. Then answer the question. "Imagine you're standing in a room with mirrors on all the walls. Your image is reflected back and forth, and you can see yourself lots of times. In the same way, the violin's specially shaped sound box reflects the sound waves back and forth, making them stronger and louder."
Why does the professor mention a room with mirrors on all the walls?

5. The professor briefly explains what happens when a violin is played. Indicate whether each sentence below is part of the process.

EXERCISE 2–I (P. 38)
Audio Track 5

Listen to part of a conversation between two students.

W: How's it going in your history class?
M: Not very well, actually. I can't get my study partner to help with the oral report we're doing together. We're getting a joint grade for this project, but so far, he hasn't contributed much.
W: Oh. That is a problem. You'd better talk to him. You need to get him to do his part.
M: The problem is, he has lots of ideas—big ideas—but we need to focus more. We have to limit our topic to something realistic. He can come up with a lot of ideas, but then he doesn't want to actually do the research. He thinks I should do that part.
W: Couldn't you let him know that he has to do more? Make him help you. Divide the research equally. Write down a list and give it to him. Make him responsible for specific things.
M: I could do that, but it may not work.
W: Another thing you could do… You should talk to your professor. Let your professor know that you are the one doing most of the work.
M: I don't know… I could do that.
W: You should. And then, just do the best you can.

The students discuss possible solutions to the man's problem. Describe the problem. Then state which of the solutions you prefer and explain why.

EXERCISE 2–J (P. 39)
Audio Track 6

Now listen to part of a lecture on this topic in a botany class.

Fertilizers improve crop productivity, but whenever they're used excessively, they wash into lakes, streams, and oceans. This is why we need to balance the benefits of fertilizers against their harmful long–term effects.

Nitrogen, a major ingredient of fertilizers, quickly washes out from the soil and into our water supply, where it's converted to nitrates. The increasing nitrate content of our drinking water is a problem because nitrates can be poisonous to humans. Once taken into our bodies, nitrates are converted in a process that interferes with our blood's capacity to carry oxygen, causing serious illness—and sometimes death.

Phosphorus can be equally harmful. While phosphorus promotes the growth of plants in soil, it also promotes their growth in water. If enough phosphates enter lakes and streams, they stimulate the growth of blue–green algae. Consequently, clear water becomes clouded with massive blooms of algae. When the algae die, the oxygen in the water is consumed, and this speeds up the natural aging of the lake. In just a few years, phosphates can turn a lake into a dead zone.

Another plant nutrient, potassium, is important for a plant's production of carbohydrates. It makes vegetables look pretty and taste good, but excess potassium from fertilizers can damage the plant's metabolism, as well as the metabolism of animals that eat the plant.

One final point I'd like to make is that different soils need nutrients in different amounts. A common mistake is using a 20–20–20 fertilizer without first doing a soil analysis to find out what the soil needs. Without doing a soil test, using a balanced fertilizer can be a waste of time and effort because it's not likely to produce ideal conditions in every garden.

Summarize the points in the lecture, explaining how they cast doubt on points made in the reading.

EXERCISE 4–E (P. 62)

Audio Track 7

Now listen to part of a lecture on this topic in a music class.

When you're "micing," you have to consider both the performers and the room. You want to maximize the sound from the performers but reject the unwanted sounds from other sources. This is why polar pattern is so important.

The most popular pattern hears only, or mostly, the sounds coming from one direction. This is the unidirectional microphone, which picks up the signals that arrive in front. Unidirectional microphones are good for recording bands in a studio. You just aim the mic at the instruments you want to pick up. Unidirectional mics are good for performers in concert halls and nightclubs, and also for recording speech. Their chief advantage is that they keep out audience noise, echoes, and other background noise.

In contrast, omnidirectional microphones can hear sound from all directions because their polar pattern is almost a perfect sphere. Omnidirectional microphones will create a feeling of space. Because they hear from all directions, they pick up sounds from the musicians as well as sounds reflected from the walls and ceiling, and this gives the effect of listening in a large room. An omnidirectional mic is great for the pipe organ, or for the bass drum in an orchestra or symphonic band.

The professor describes unidirectional and omnidirectional microphones. Explain how their polar pattern makes these microphones appropriate for recording specific performances.

EXERCISE 5–E (P. 74)

Audio Track 8

Now listen to part of a lecture on this topic in a biology class.

Most invasive species are the result of human activity, either accidental or intentional. Introduced species will quickly take over when they out–compete native species and have no natural predators. A recent invader in North America is the zebra mussel, which arrived in the ballast water of a cargo ship from the Caspian Sea. Within ten years, the mussels spread through the entire Mississippi River system, where they compete with the native shellfish for space, and with the native fish for food.

Some ecosystems are especially likely to be taken over by invasive species. Island ecosystems, for example, are separated from others by distance, and this makes them likely to have open niches, where introduced species might flourish. An example of this is the invasion of Guam by the brown tree snake. Guam had no native snake species, so all of its native birds had adapted to life without these predators. When the brown tree snake arrived—probably in air cargo from another Pacific island—it quickly established itself, feeding on the defenseless birds. The result was a massive invasion of snakes and the decimation of the native bird populations.

A well–known invasive plant is the kudzu vine. Kudzu was introduced into the United States from Asia in the nineteenth century. At first, it was promoted as an ornamental plant and food crop for animals. Then the government encouraged farmers to plant kudzu as a way to reduce soil erosion. The southeastern states have nearly perfect conditions for kudzu to grow out of control: hot, humid summers and mild winters. Furthermore, the plant has no natural predators. For these reasons, the once–promoted plant is now considered a pest weed.

Summarize the points made in the lecture, explaining how they support points made in the reading.

EXERCISE 6–E (P. 85)

Audio Track 9

Questions 1 through 5. Listen to part of a lecture in a biology class.

A growing body of research shows that the two halves of the brain specialize in different behaviors. The left brain controls behaviors involving approach and energy enrichment, while the right brain controls behaviors involving withdrawal and energy expenditure. In humans, the left brain is associated with positive emotions, such as love, and with feelings of safety and calm. The right brain, in contrast, is associated with withdrawal behaviors, such as fleeing, and with negative emotions like fear and depression.

It's important to remember that each side of the brain controls the opposite side of the body. The left brain controls the right side of the body, while the right brain controls the left side of the body. This means that emotions associated with one side of the brain are expressed in the opposite side of the body. For example, the muscles on the right side of our face tend to reflect happiness—a positive emotion controlled by the left brain—whereas the muscles on the left side of our face reflect unhappiness, which is a right–brain emotion.

Now, some researchers have argued that only humans show left and right biases in the brain. However, these same biases are showing up in the brains of animals. When chimpanzees are upset, they tend to scratch themselves on the left side of their bodies, reflecting the right brain's control of strong negative emotions. Birds show the same brain asymmetry. Because their left brain controls nourishment, a lot of birds look for food with their right eye. Similarly, because their right brain controls danger, they watch for predators with their left eye.

A recent study of body language in dogs supports these same left–right biases. The muscles in the right side of the dog's tail reflect positive emotions, while the muscles in the left side express negative ones. When dogs feel positive about something—for example, when they see their owner—they wag their tails more to the right side of their rumps. On the other hand, when dogs see an unfamiliar, aggressive dog, their tails wag more to the left.

The research suggests that an animal's body is hard–wired so that major nerves send certain kinds of information to the preferred side of the brain. Information that prompts an animal to eat, relax, or restore itself is biased toward the left brain. Conversely, information that tells an animal to run, fight, or watch out for danger is biased toward the right brain.

1. What is the main idea of the lecture?
2. What point does the professor make about the two sides of the brain?

3. Why does the professor say this:
"When chimpanzees are upset, they tend to scratch themselves on the left side of their bodies, reflecting the right brain's control of strong negative emotions."
4. What does the professor imply by this statement:
"On the other hand, when dogs see an unfamiliar, aggressive dog, their tails wag more to the left."
5. Indicate whether each behavior is associated with the left brain or the right brain.

EXERCISE 6–F (P. 86)

Audio Track 10

Now listen to part of a lecture on this topic in a psychology class.

Just as early humans needed spatial intelligence as they traveled in search of food, spatial skills are still important for people living in Arctic regions today. Because so much of the northern landscape looks so bare and uniform, every visual detail is important. When you have to cross wide spaces and then return home safely, you need a highly developed sense of space.

However, spatial intelligence doesn't always depend on visual input. Even when people can't see, they may still have spatial intelligence. For example, a two–year–old girl who was born blind showed amazing ability when she found the right path between two toys—after having walked to each of these toys only from a third location. Even though she'd never taken that path before, she found her way because she recalled the distances of the paths she already knew. She understood the angular relationship of the familiar paths and then used that information to move along the new path. When she was four years old, the same girl was able to use a map that she "read" by touch. Although she'd never used a map before, she immediately understood the concept of a map, including its symbols, and was able to use the map to guide her to the location of a toy in the room.

The professor talks about the movement of people through different spaces. Explain how these examples illustrate spatial intelligence.

EXERCISE 6–G (P. 87)

Audio Track 11

Now listen to part of a lecture on this topic in a sociology class.

Some generalizations about the family are pure myth. For example, families today are not more rootless than they used to be. In fact, a century ago, families moved around quite a bit. Around 1900, in most large and small cities, more than 50 percent of the residents—and often up to 75 percent—were no longer there ten years later. So it's just not true that families stayed in one place for generations. Families have always relocated.

Another myth is that nuclear families lack connections with their extended families. In truth, more children than ever before have a grandparent who is still living, and the evidence suggests that ties between grandparents and grandchildren have become stronger. For example, when researchers returned to a town that had been studied sixty years earlier, they found that most of the residents maintained closer kinship networks than had been the case earlier. More people knew their grandparents and reported visiting them than had been the case before.

The bonds between parents and children have not weakened. In fact, a majority of adults today say they see one of their parents at least once a week. Sixty–eight percent say they talk on the telephone with a parent once a week. Furthermore, almost 90 percent of adults describe their relationship with their mother as close, and 78 percent say their relationship with their grandparents is close. Finally, despite all the disruption from divorce, most children today—96 percent—live with at least one of their parents. This is a big difference from a century ago, when ten percent of the children didn't live with either parent, usually because the parents had died.

Summarize the points made in the lecture, explaining how they contradict points made in the reading.

EXERCISE 7–F (P. 103)

Audio Track 12

Questions 1 through 6. Listen to part of a discussion in a business class.

M1: The business meeting, which is part of an average business day, is the logical way to share information and get things done. As a manager, you will call meetings for a lot of reasons. Your company has to make policy, for example, so you might call in a group of people that will help you develop policy. Or you might call a meeting to gather information you need to solve a problem that's come up. It's up to the person who calls the meeting to make sure the discussion is successful. That person, who will probably lead the meeting, should let all participants know the purpose and agenda well in advance. So, what are some factors that go into planning a meeting?

M2: One factor is the length of the meeting, which determines whether you need to have coffee and snacks.

W: You also need to know how many people are coming, which tells you how many handouts you need.

M1: Uh–huh. What else?

M2: You have to plan your facilities, like the room where you're having the meeting, and the equipment you need, like videos and slides, or a projector and screen.

W: You need a room that fits the size of your group, and enough chairs for everyone.

M1: Right. Room size, audiovisual equipment, handouts, coffee—those are all things you need to consider. The skilled leader will check on all of them in advance, but, of course, this doesn't mean he or she shouldn't get help with the details. OK. So, that's what happens before the meeting. Now think about what happens during the meeting. A typical business meeting—one dealing with policy or problems—follows a pattern that goes like this. First, the leader makes a brief preliminary statement calling attention to the issue. Next, the participants discuss the issue—its scope, causes, and effects. They contribute relevant information, facts, and opinions. After that, what should happen?

W: Well, isn't it important to agree on a solution? I mean, if that was the purpose of the meeting.

M1: Absolutely. The participants should discuss possible solutions and decide on the one that's best. Then what?

W: They need a plan that puts the solution into action, for example, the next steps they should take.

M1: Yes, absolutely. If the meeting is successful, it should achieve a result. Of course, maybe the result is the need for another meeting, in which case it's the leader's job to determine the time and place for that.

1. What is the discussion mainly about?
2. What point does the professor make about the person who calls a meeting?
3. According to the discussion, what are some factors that should be considered in planning a meeting?
4. What does the professor mean by this statement: "The skilled leader will check on all of them in advance, but, of course, this doesn't mean he or she shouldn't get help with the details."
5. Why does the professor say this: "A typical business meeting—one dealing with policy or problems—follows a pattern that goes like this."
6. The class talks about what usually happens during a business meeting. Put the events in the order in which they occur.

EXERCISE 7–G (P. 104)
Audio Track 13

Listen to part of a talk given to university students who are majoring in the social sciences.

Researchers who want a complete picture of an organization use several methods that all come under the label "qualitative research." The goal of qualitative research is to document the processes as well as the products of an organization. The key tools of qualitative research are observation and interviewing. Interviewing people is an important way for researchers to check the accuracy of the impressions they gain through observation.

For example, an organization that might be investigated is a large, inner–city high school. The researcher would aim to portray the everyday experiences of the people who study and work at the school. The researcher would visit the school regularly over a long period of time. He would observe classrooms and try to describe everything that happens there. He would interview teachers, students, administrators, and support staff. The researcher might observe the learning experiences of the students and the social atmosphere of the school. He might observe the manner in which students and teachers react to others of different ethnic groups.

In qualitative research, the data collected is in the form of words and pictures rather than numbers. It includes detailed descriptions written by the researcher. In our example, it might include samples of student work and video recordings of classrooms and student–teacher conferences. There might be flowcharts illustrating the direction of comments made during class discussions. All of these would help the researcher to "paint a portrait" of the school.

Using points and examples from the talk, describe qualitative research, explaining some of the methods that researchers use.

EXERCISE 8–E (P. 114)
Audio Track 14

Listen to part of a conversation between two students.

W: How are you, Jim?
M: Busy with school, and looking for a part–time job. I've been offered two jobs, and the hard part is deciding which one to take.
W: Oh, really? What sort of jobs?
M: One is a dinner waiter in a restaurant. I'd have to work until late at night, but I'd make good money in tips. The other is a night clerk in the physics lab, here on campus. It doesn't pay much, but it would be quiet, and I could study at the desk.
W: That's a difficult choice. You have to decide what's more important to you—money or time to study. You need to think about how the job would affect your studies. Didn't you tell me that you were having trouble in some of your classes?
M: Yeah … well, not really, but I should spend more time studying.
W: You need to think about how much stress the job would cause, I mean, how it might affect your health. Would you get enough sleep?
M: I don't know.
W: Well, it's a difficult choice. You have to decide what your priority is.

The students discuss a problem that the man has. Briefly summarize the problem. Then state what you think the man should do, and explain why.

EXERCISE 9–D (P. 124)
Audio Track 15

Questions 1 through 3. Listen to a conversation between a student and his adviser.

M: Could I talk to you about registration?
W: Sure. What can I do for you?
M: I'm, um, I'd like to take oceanography, but I don't have the prerequisite that's listed in the catalog, you know, Math 150.
W: Oh, I see. Well, if you took oceanography, you'd need that mathematics course first. There would be some physics and chemistry, so you'd need a solid grasp of numerical data.
M: That's what I wanted to talk to you about. I thought, if I took the math course at the same time as oceanography, then I could graduate at the end of the year.
W: Sorry, but you need to have the math course first. Unless you have a good foundation in math, you'll find oceanography very difficult.
M: I've taken three math classes already. Isn't that enough?
W: I'm afraid not. The Oceanography Department specifically requires Math 150.
M: I wish I could convince someone! I know I could do both courses! Would it help if I talked to the professor?
W: You could try, but I wouldn't get my hopes up if I were you.

M: Oh, well, in that case, I'd better just take the math course and get it over with.

W: Good idea.

M: But as long as I'm here, can you tell me if oceanography is being taught in the summer?

1. Why does the student talk to his adviser?
2. What does the adviser mean when she says this:
"Unless you have a good foundation in math, you'll find oceanography very difficult."
3. Listen again to part of the conversation. Then answer the question.
"I wish I could convince someone! I know I could do both courses! Would it help if I talked to the professor?"
"You could try, but I wouldn't get my hopes up if I were you."
What does the adviser imply?

EXERCISE 9–E (P. 125)

Audio Track 16

Now listen to two students as they discuss the linked course.

W: Next quarter I need two units in humanities.

M: If I were you, I'd take the Greek philosophy and drama—you know, the linked course.

W: Hmm. I wondered about that.

M: It's really two courses, but the ideas and themes are linked. You have to register for both courses together.

W: Two courses could be a lot of work though.

M: It's not, believe me. If you did it this way, you'd end up with a better schedule. The two professors usually plan the assignments together. That means you'd never have two papers due at the same time or two tests on the same day. Plus, you'd learn a lot more than you would in two separate courses because the readings would all be tied together in class.

W: Really?

M: And you'd also earn two units in humanities because it's a double course. That would take care of your entire humanities requirement all at once.

W: That would be great if I could do that.

M: I took a linked course once, and I'd do it again. I wish the college had more courses like that.

The man expresses his opinion about the linked course. State his opinion and explain the reasons he gives for holding that opinion.

EXERCISE 9–F (P. 126)

Audio Track 17

Listen to part of a conversation between two students.

M: You're going to the internship fair on Wednesday afternoon, right?

W: What? If I'd known about it, I wouldn't have scheduled a make–up test in calculus.

M: But you've got to go to the internship fair! There'll be several people there to talk about engineering internships.

W: Oh, if only I'd known....

M: Can't you re–schedule your test?

W: I wish I could, but it's a make–up for the one I missed last week when I was sick. Dr. Williams gives us just a week to make up a test.

M: But if you went to the fair, you'd have a good chance of getting an internship for the summer.

W: I know, I know. If only I didn't have this test....

M: But if you just explained to your professor... She'd probably want you to go. I'm sure she'd make an exception. At least you should try.

W: Well, as long as you're going to the fair, would you take notes for me? I mean, let me know about anything in civil engineering, and pick up any handouts?

M: Sure, I could do that. But it would be better if you were there in person, in case you wanted to ask questions.

W: I know, but I could still use your help.

The students discuss possible solutions to a problem that the woman has. Describe the problem. Then state what you think the woman should do, and explain why.

EXERCISE 11–D (P. 146)

Audio Track 18

Now listen to part of a lecture on this topic in a biology class.

Mutualism is an interaction between two species, in which both species receive a benefit, such as a higher rate of survival. The relationship between the acacia tree and the stinging ant is mutualistic in this way. The acacia tree has hollow thorns that provide a place for the ants to live. The tree also provides food for the ants. The tree has swollen glands that produce a sugary solution, and the ants feed on this sugar. There are also small structures that grow on the tips of the tree's leaves. These small structures are rich in protein. The ants bite those off and eat them too.

So, the ants get sugar and protein from the acacia tree. And what does the acacia tree get in return? Well, for one thing, it gets protection. Remember that these are stinging ants. They attack anything that touches the tree. They sting other insects and chase off plant–eating animals. They also destroy all plants that try to compete with the acacia for sunlight, by clipping all vegetation that happens to grow close to the acacia. It's an arrangement that's mutually beneficial. The acacia tree feeds and houses the ants, and in return, the ants protect the tree from harmful influences.

The professor describes the relationship between the acacia tree and the stinging ant. Explain how their interaction is an example of mutualism.

EXERCISE 12–E (P. 158)

Audio Track 19

Now listen to part of a lecture on this topic in an urban studies class.

The growth of the suburbs has caused millions of workers to depend on the automobile to get to work, leading to more cars on the highways, more traffic problems, and more air pollution from cars. However, cities are fighting back. Urban planners have developed a new concept, the urban village, a neighborhood that's a distinct community within the greater city—a mix of commercial buildings, public spaces, and housing.

Unlike the automobile–dependent suburbs, urban villages are transit–friendly. Residents in urban villages don't even need a car because buses and trains stop right there. It's hard to build a coherent neighborhood around a suburban highway. But in an urban village, light–rail transit stops are an excellent way to anchor and center the neighborhood. Urban villages are small, dense, and walkable, so a lot of daily trips can be done on foot.

Suburban life is predictable at best, boring at worst. A suburban district is unbalanced because it specializes in a single use. A lot of suburbs are "bedroom communities" because people just go there to sleep. There's not much else there—just residences. A suburb is a cultural desert—isolated and unfriendly—where neighbors are strangers to each other. On the other hand, an urban village is a multiple–use district, with a balance of housing, shops, and recreation—a mix of private and public spaces. This makes an urban village a coherent, balanced, diverse neighborhood, unlike the cultural desert of the suburbs.

Summarize the points made in the lecture, explaining how they differ from points made in the reading.

EXERCISE 13–F (P. 173)

Audio Track 20

Now listen to two students as they discuss the changes at the Counseling Center.

M: Did you see the announcement about the Counseling Center?
W: Yes, I did. They'll be open only three days instead of five. How could they do that to us?
M: Budget cuts—that's how.
W: Well, it's not fair to students, especially those of us who can't get there on the days when it's open. I need to talk to someone about finding a job after graduation, but I have a pretty heavy schedule. The only day I have free time is Friday, but now they're closed on Friday.
M: I see your point.
W: I might be interested in one of the evening workshops, but now there's a fee for those.
M: I saw that—twenty–five dollars!
W: That's too much for something that used to be free. It's unfair to charge us for a class in career planning, especially since our tuition went up this year too. I know they need to make budget cuts, but why cut the Counseling Center? That should be a basic service included in our tuition.
M: I agree.
W: We should complain to someone about this.

The woman expresses her opinion about the changes at the Counseling Center. State her opinion and explain the reasons she gives for holding that opinion.

EXERCISE 14–E (P. 184)

Audio Track 21

Questions 1 through 4. Listen to part of a discussion in an oceanography class.

W1: We know a fair amount about the circulation of water in the shallow ocean, but much less about the deep ocean. The deep ocean is vast—about 90 percent of the total volume of the ocean—and we know very little about it. We do know there's a close relationship between the ocean and the atmosphere. A lot happens at the surface of the ocean, where water meets air, including some of the forces that drive ocean currents, such as … what? What's one thing that happens at the surface?
W2: The wind blows at the surface. The wind has a big effect.
W1: Yes, that's right, it does. The wind has a major impact on surface water currents. In fact, water circulation at the surface is driven mainly by the wind. But what about the water in the middle and lower layers of the ocean? What drives the circulation of deep water?
M: Well, we know there are deep currents in the lower layers and near the bottom. Our book says that water movement in the deep ocean is slow, compared to how it is at the surface. That's because the deep water is so much colder and so much heavier than the water at the surface.
W1: That's right. This colder, heavier water moves much more slowly. The movement of the deep water is driven by gravity and caused primarily by changes in the density of seawater.
W2: So, it's gravity that drives the water circulation in the deep ocean.
W1: That's right. OK. Another thing we know is, what happens at the surface has an impact on what happens in the deep ocean. For example, one change at the surface is an increase in the water's salinity—or saltiness—which can happen when the water evaporates or sea ice forms. And what happens when water gets saltier?
M: It gets heavier and denser. If it gets dense enough, it will sink downward until it reaches a level of equal density, or until it reaches the sea bottom.
W1: Yes, that's right. The deeper you go, the denser it gets. The deepest water has the greatest density. And all of these properties—temperature, density, salinity—all play a crucial role in the ocean's flow.

1. What does the professor mean by this statement: "We know a fair amount about the circulation of water in the shallow ocean, but much less about the deep ocean."
2. According to the discussion, what factors influence the movement of water in the ocean?
3. How is the ocean's deep water different from the water at the surface?
4. Why does the professor say this: "The deeper you go, the denser it gets."

EXERCISE 14–G (P. 185)

Audio Track 22

Listen to part of a talk in a geology class.

An important part of erosion is the phenomenon of mass wasting, the downslope movement of soil and loose rock, mainly due to gravity. Mass wasting moves material from higher elevations to lower elevations. Some types of mass wasting occur very suddenly, while others are more gradual.

One fast type of mass wasting is mudflow, the movement of material containing a large amount of water. Mudflows can move at speeds greater than one kilometer per hour and travel long distances. They usually result from heavy rains in areas with loose sediment. Because they happen so quickly, mudflows are catastrophic. However, mudflow is actually responsible for moving less material than the slower and less obvious action called creep. While mudflow occurs on steep slopes, creep occurs on gentler slopes.

Creep is the slowest type of mass wasting. It may take years for creep to have a noticeable effect. It involves the very gradual movement of soil and rock as a result of alternate freezing and thawing, or wetting and drying, which causes the surface material to expand and contract. Most vegetated slopes in humid climates are subject to creep, but it also occurs in deserts because even dry soil will creep as a result of daily heating and cooling.

Creep is more widespread than mudflow, but much less dramatic. When a mudflow occurs, we see direct evidence in downed trees and buried roads and buildings. With creep, the evidence is less obvious, usually in the form of bent trees, dips in roads and fences, and leaning utility poles. This is because the upper layers of soil move gradually, while the deeper layers stay fixed.

Using points and details from the talk, explain some of the differences between the mass wasting processes of mudflow and creep.

EXERCISE 15–E (P. 196)

Audio Track 23

Listen to part of a lecture in an economics class.

Sometimes unemployment occurs when workers are simply moving between jobs. Sometimes it occurs when the economy suffers a downturn and large numbers of workers are laid off. How do we know how many people are unemployed? We mainly know through statistics on the labor force, which the government collects every month in a procedure known as random sampling of the population. Random sampling consists of choosing a part of the population at random and then surveying the selected group. Each month, researchers interview 60,000 households and ask questions about their recent work patterns.

The government divides the population—that is, men and women age 16 years and older—and puts them into three groups: employed, unemployed, and outside the labor force. The employed are people with jobs and people who performed any paid work, and also people with jobs but absent from work because of illness, vacations, or strikes. The unemployed are the people without jobs but who are actively looking for work or waiting to return to work after a layoff. People outside the labor force are those who don't have jobs but are not looking for

work. They might be going to school, caring for children, retired, or too sick to work. This last group also includes people without jobs who have stopped looking for work.

The total labor force consists of the first two groups, the employed and the unemployed—people with jobs and people looking for jobs. The government calculates the unemployment rate by taking the number of unemployed and dividing it by the total labor force. So the unemployment rate is the percentage of people who are out of work but looking for work.

Using points and examples from the lecture, explain how the government studies the labor force and unemployment.

EXERCISE 16–C (P. 207)

Audio Track 24

Questions 1 through 5. Listen to a conversation between a student and an employee in a university business office.

W: Hello. I need to talk to someone about my bill.

M: I can help you. What's the problem?

W: Well, there's a charge for eighty–seven dollars, and nowhere does it say what it's for.

M: All right. Let's have a look.

W: Thanks.

M: OK. Uh, this charge is from the Housing Office. Let's see what the computer says. Hmm. OK… There's an eighty–seven–dollar repair charge.

W: A repair charge? There must be some mistake.

M: It's for the repair of a broken closet door.

W: Nothing like that—no way did that ever happen—not in my dorm room.

M: Are you sure?

W: I didn't break the closet door, and neither did my roommate.

M: Are you sure about your roommate?

W: I can't be certain. You'd have to ask her. But I don't remember a broken door. I mean, I respect university property, and so does my roommate. We're both too careful for something like that to happen. I'm sure that charge is a mistake.

M: There aren't many mistakes like this. The Housing Office is always very careful. They say they fixed the closet door in your dormitory room.

W: I have no idea why they say that. At no time was there ever a broken door in our room! Maybe Housing got the room number wrong.

M: Well, in that case there is something you can do. You can appeal the charge by filling out a complaint form. The Housing Director will look at it, and if there was a mistake, they'll remove the charge.

W: All right. May I have the form?

M: Sure. You need to fill out all the personal information on the top. Below that is a place to explain the problem.

W: OK, and what do I do after I've filled it out?

M: You can take it to the second floor. Across from the elevator is Student Services. You can give it to the person at the counter.

W: All right. I'll do that.

M: I hope you get the problem cleared up.

W: So do I! I've got enough to worry about already.

M: Good luck.

W: Thanks.

1. Why does the student speak with the man?
2. Why does the student say this:
   "Nothing like that—no way did that ever happen—not in my dorm room."
3. What does the student imply when she says this:
   "I mean, I respect university property, and so does my roommate. We're both too careful for something like that to happen."
4. What does the man suggest the student do?
5. Listen again to part of the conversation. Then answer the question.
   "I hope you get the problem cleared up."
   "So do I! I've got enough to worry about already."
   What does the student mean?

EXERCISE 16–D (P. 208)

Audio Track 25

Now listen to two students as they discuss the new graduation requirement.

M: Hey, I just found out about the new internship requirement.
W: So did I. It's not a bad idea, actually. It will be very useful for me because I'm in arts management, and I'd hoped to get an internship in my final year anyway. For me, an internship is really important. Not only will it give me valuable training, but it will also give me an advantage when I look for a job after graduation. I'll have work experience that will look very nice on my résumé.
M: I see what you mean.
W: Even more importantly, I'll meet producers and other people in the arts—hopefully, people who will be good mentors and teach me essential skills, and who will recommend me for interesting jobs that come up.
M: You seem very optimistic. How can you be sure you'll get the right internship?
W: The college will offer more options. They're making this a graduation requirement, so they have to provide enough ways for everyone to do it, right? It's good for the college, too, because it links us more to the community.

The woman expresses her opinion about the new graduation requirement. State her opinion, and explain the reasons she gives for holding that opinion.

EXERCISE 17–D (P. 216)

Audio Track 26

Now listen to part of a lecture on this topic in a linguistics class.

The study about the storytelling of young men reveals themes of individuality and competition. These themes reflect the men's view of themselves and their position in society. When linguists analyzed the stories told by young women, they noticed certain themes common in their stories as well. The first thing they noticed was that the women's stories focused on community rather than contest. For the women, community was the source of power.

In the twenty–six stories that were analyzed, almost all of them centered on the norms of the community and on joint action by groups of people. The women told stories about themselves, about other women, and about men. Half of the stories were about incidents in which they were involved, and half were about things that happened to other people. Some stories were about meeting their boyfriends or about acquiring their pets.

The women told of times when they had departed from social norms and were frightened or embarrassed as a result. They told stories about strange people—people whose behavior violated social norms. In many of the stories, the women made themselves look foolish. For example, one woman told about not realizing she had broken her nose until a doctor told her about it many years later.

A majority of the stories were about people helping other people out of bad situations. In eleven out of the twenty–six stories, the main character received help or advice from others. In fact, when the women told stories about acting alone, the results tended to be negative. Most of the women who acted alone portrayed themselves as suffering a consequence.

Summarize the points made in the lecture, explaining how they contrast with points made in the reading.

EXERCISE 19–C (P. 235)

Audio Track 27

Questions 1 through 5. Listen to a conversation between a student and a professor.

M: Professor Nolan, do you have a few minutes?
W: Sure, Jason. What can I do for you?
M: It's about the grade on my paper. Um, the grade is too low, I mean, it's lower than I expected, so I was wondering if I could rewrite it to raise my grade.
W: I'm afraid it's too late for that. In fact, it's nearly time for the next paper, which is due at the end of next week. Instead of worrying about just one paper, I think it would be better if you focused on the rest of the semester. Study hard and concentrate on what you can do during the remaining eight weeks.
M: I already study hard for this class. I spend almost three hours a day on the reading. What's your advice—I mean, is there anything I can do for extra credit to raise my grade?
W: You're doing the reading, and that's good, but maybe you need to do something different, to make the most of your study time. Instead of always reading alone, I advise you to study with other people. Organize a study group with other people from the class. Reading and discussing philosophy with others can help everyone understand the most challenging material. You won't always think alike, but that's often the best way to learn. You get to hear how others interpret the material, and it's an especially good way to test your own interpretation.
M: It would be like trying out my ideas on other people.
W: Yes, you could say so.
M: That might help me with my papers—lay out my ideas and see what other people think.
W: Sure, discussing ideas with your classmates is always stimulating. I strongly recommend it. However, for help with your papers, my advice is to find a tutor or go to the Writing Center.
M: Are there tutors at the Writing Center?
W: There are teaching aides that will read your paper and suggest ways to improve it.

M: Sounds good. If it helps raise my grade, I'd be very happy. Thanks, Professor. I appreciate your advice.

W: You're very welcome. I'm glad you came to see me.

1. Why does the student go to see his professor?
2. How does the student probably feel when he says this: "I already study hard for this class. I spend almost three hours a day on the reading."
3. What does the professor advise the student to do?
4. What does the professor mean when she says this: "You won't always think alike, but that's often the best way to learn. You get to hear how others interpret the material, and it's an especially good way to test your own interpretation."
5. Why does the student say this: "Sounds good. If it helps raise my grade, I'd be very happy."

EXERCISE 19–D (P. 236)

Audio Track 28

Listen to part of a conversation between two students.

M: Hi, Lisa! How are you?

W: Very busy—too busy, actually.

M: How's basketball going?

W: Great—the team is doing very well this year. Unfortunately, though, I may have to quit the team.

M: Quit? Why?

W: I love playing, but basketball takes too much of my time, and I have less time for the debate club, my other activity. I have to make a decision soon, and it's very hard. I have to give up one or the other.

M: Don't give up basketball! You're one of the best players, and it would hurt the team.

W: If I quit basketball, I'd have more time for debate, but I'd disappoint the team. Besides, I'd get less exercise. On the other hand, quitting the debate club might hurt my chance at getting a debate scholarship, which I'm almost certain to get, according to the debate coach.

M: It's a tough choice, but maybe the scholarship is more important. You can always play basketball next year, or just play a little for exercise. Besides, don't you want to go to law school? Debate is good preparation for that.

W: I do want to go to law school, but I also love basketball. My problem is, which is less essential now?

The students discuss possible solutions to the woman's problem. Describe the problem. Then state what you think the woman should do, and explain why.

EXERCISE 20–D (P. 246)

Audio Track 29

Now listen to part of a lecture on this topic in a business management class.

You've read about the greeting card company's decision to sell flowers. The company did a great deal of research, including focus groups with customers. Yet, in spite of all that, the flower venture failed. Flowers literally died on the shelves, and before long the flower operation was shut down. Why? Why did it fail, when all the research pointed to success?

Well, the company's biggest mistake was bias—both in the information they gathered and in how it was interpreted. They had been confident that fresh flowers would be a great addition to their product line. This bias caused them to interpret the available information positively. They didn't ask enough questions that would have proved their theory wrong. They didn't realize that the information they had was incomplete. They stopped researching too soon.

They felt certain that the venture would succeed, and all the information they gathered supported this belief. In the focus groups, for example, they asked if people would buy flowers from the company's stores. Of course the answer was "yes." However, the company neglected to ask when and how customers usually bought flowers. Only later did they learn that people usually buy flowers at the end of their shopping routine. The company's stores, however, were usually the first or second stop on their list. Furthermore, people don't like going to malls, where the company's stores are located, if flowers are the only thing they want. At those times, their neighborhood florist shop is much more convenient.

The company failed because they had been excessively optimistic, and this distorted their intelligence. The lesson here is that decision–makers have to avoid bias when they are collecting and evaluating information.

Summarize the points made in the lecture, explaining how they cast doubt on points made in the reading.

INDEX

A

a 132, 139–140
a few 132, 153, 166
a little 132
a lot of 132
a number of 154
a single 132
ability 26
able 45
-able 221
about 189
above 189, 203
abstractions 131, 163, 165
academic nouns 130
according to 191
accordingly 67
across 189, 190, 203
across from 191
active participial adjective 96
active voice 28, 30, 80, 96
activities, nouns for 131, 221
-acy 220
addition 65, 66, 67
adjective clause(s). . . 56, 90–96, 154,
           164, 199, 239
adjective complement 42, 43, 45
adjective phrase(s) ...90, 91, 95–96,
           199, 239
adjective suffixes 221–222
adjective(s) 91, 133–134, 199,
           202, 221–222
   base form 177, 178
   comparative 141, 176, 177,
             179, 233
   demonstrative 142, 164–165
   equative...................178
   form....... 177–179, 180, 219,
           220, 221–222
   function 91, 188, 219,
           220, 221, 222
   in a list 212
   infinitive as............ 42, 43
   irregular 177
   long............ 178, 179, 180
   no plural form....... 133–134
   numeric............ 133–134
   of importance 154
   participial 91, 96–97
   possessive 142, 161,
           162, 163, 180, 242
   prepositional phrase as 188
   short 178, 179, 180

   superlative 141, 176,
             177, 180
   with infinitive........ 45, 201
   with noun 199
   with preposition 192
   word order 198, 199,
             200–202
admit 46
adverb clause(s)   56, 76–80,
           116, 202, 239
adverb phrase(s) 76, 79–80
adverb suffixes 222
adverb(s) 23, 77, 200–201, 222
   almost negative....... 201, 204
   base form 177, 178
   comparative.......... 177, 179
   conjunctive 66–68, 239, 240
   equative.................178
   form 177–179, 180,
             219, 220, 222
   function 23, 77, 189,
             200, 219, 220, 222
   in a list 212
   infinitive as............ 42, 43
   irregular 177
   long............ 178, 179, 180
   negative..... 200–201, 203, 204
   prepositional
     phrase as 188, 189
   short 178, 179, 180
   superlative........... 177, 180
   word order 23, 30,
             200–201, 202
advice 116, 118, 119
advice 131, 228
advisability 26, 27
advise 44, 46, 228
affirmative verb 117
afford 44
afraid 45
after 56, 69, 77, 189
afterward 68
against 189
-age 220
ago 25
agree 44
agreement 149
   pronoun............ 160–166
   subject–verb 148–150
   word form
     and function........ 219–220
ahead of 191
aid in 46

-al 220, 221
alike 229
all 132, 153, 166
allow 28
allow 44, 46
allude to 191, 192
almost 178, 229
almost negative adverb 201, 204
almost negative expression .201, 204
along 189, 203
along with 191
also 66, 67, 231
alternative 65
although 55, 56, 68, 78
amazed 45
among 189, 190, 203
amount of 132, 232
an 132, 139–140
-an 220, 221
-ance 220
and 11, 55, 64, 65, 66, 149,
           152, 178, 211, 212, 231
and...as well as 65, 66, 212
animals
   irregular plurals for........ 130
   pronouns for......... 92, 160,
             163, 164, 166
   species of 141
another 132, 166, 232
-ant 220, 221
antecedent 161
anticipate 46
any 132, 153, 166
anybody 151, 165
anyone 151, 165
anything 151, 165
apostrophe 242
appear 44
appoint 44
apposition, noun in 10
appositive 10–11, 95, 239
appreciate 46
approve of 46, 191
-ar 221
arise 230
around 189, 203
arrange 44
article(s) 139–142, 199, 200
   definite 46, 139, 140–142
   indefinite............ 139–140
as 56, 68, 69, 77, 78,
             79, 178, 189, 231
as a result 67
as a result of 191
as if 56, 78

as long as 77, 78, 117
as soon as 77
as though 78
as well 66
as well as 66
as...as 178, 212
aside from 191
ask 44, 154
associated with 192
at 189, 203
at no time 204
at present 25
-ate 220, 221
attempt 44, 46
attitude 26
attractive to 192
auxiliary 23, 24, 29, 119,
        150, 152, 200, 203, 204
auxiliary verb 22, 23, 26, 202
aware of 192
avoid 46

B

bad .177
badly 177
barely any 201
base form
        of adjective 177, 178
        of adverb 111, 178
        of verb . . . 8, 22, 23, 26, 28, 154
based on 192
be 9, 11, 23, 24, 26, 29, 30,
        44, 57, 91, 95, 96, 107, 119,
        150, 152, 154, 199, 200, 203
be going to 26
because 56, 68, 78, 79, 191
because of 191
become 96, 199, 200
before 55, 56, 69, 77, 189
beforehand 68
beg .44
begin 46
behind 189, 203
believe in 46
below 189, 203
beneath 189, 203
bent .97
beside 189, 190, 203, 229
besides 67, 229
between 189, 190, 203
between...and 190
beyond 189, 203
big .177
-body 165
body parts 130, 141
both 132, 153, 166
both...and 65, 66, 152, 212

bring about 191
British English 151
broken 97
build .23
but 55, 65, 211, 212
by 189, 190
by the time 77

C

call 22
call for 46
can 26, 30, 118
can't 242
capable of 192
care .44
careful 45
category of 133
causative 28, 43
cause 44
cause 67, 68, 77, 78, 179, 201
cause and result 65, 66, 67,
        68, 179, 201
certainty 26
challenge 44
choose 44
chosen 97
cities 240
claim .44
class 131, 132, 133, 139, 142
class of 133
clause marker 56
clause(s) 54–57
        adjective 56, 90–96, 154,
                164, 199, 239
        adverb 56, 76–80, 116,
                202, 239
        condition 116, 117, 118,
                119, 120
        dependent 55, 56
        if- 117
        in a list 212
        independent 9, 55, 65, 66,
                116, 200, 202,
                211, 237, 239, 240
        joined by a conjunction 55,
                65, 66, 211, 212, 239
        main 56, 57, 68, 77, 78,
                79, 80, 92, 108, 109,
                116, 204, 239
        necessary 94
        nonrestrictive 94
        noun 8, 56, 106–110,
                150, 154, 188
        of similar value 211
        parallel 211
        reduced 79–80, 95,
                96, 109–110

relative 92
restrictive 94
result 116, 117, 118,
        119, 120, 121
subordinate 8, 9, 55, 56,
        57, 68, 77, 91, 106,
        107, 116, 202, 204, 212
unnecessary 94, 239
wish 121
clauses and sentences 54–57
closing of letter 240
collection 151
collection of 151
collective noun 151
colon 241
colony of 151
come 23, 44
come up with 191
comma 10, 66, 78, 79, 94,
        95, 116, 199, 238–240
command 238
command 44
common 45
common in 192
common noun 12, 161
common to 192
comparative adjective 141, 176,
        177, 179, 233
comparative adverb 177, 179
comparative degree . . .176, 177, 179
comparative form 179
comparative, double 179–180
comparative, parallel 212–213
compare 204
comparison 176–180
compel 44
complement
        adjective 42, 43, 45
        object 10
        subject 9, 43, 45, 107
complete 46
complete sentence 55, 77, 116
complex equalities 178
complex sentence 55, 116
composed of 192
compound prepositions 191
compound sentence 55
compound subject 11, 152, 153
compound verb 149
condition . . .66, 68, 77, 78, 115, 116
condition clause 116, 117,
        118, 119, 120
conditional sentence(s) .78, 115–121
        future real 118
        future unreal 119
        past real 118
        past unreal 120
        present real 117–118
        present unreal 119

real 117–118
unreal 119–121
conditions, nouns for 131
confined to 192
confused about 192
conjunction(s)   55, 64–69,
                              152, 153, 239
coordinating 65
correlative 65–66, 212
subordinating 56, 68–69,
                         77–78, 92, 107
two–part 64, 65–66
conjunctive adverb . .66–68, 239, 240
conscious of 192
consent .44
consequently 67
consider 46
consist of 191
consonant 140
consonant sound 140
construction, similar 211
content .45
content word 8, 22
continue 46
continuous action 24, 26
continuous tenses 24
contraction 242
contrary to 191
contrast . . .65, 66, 67, 68, 77, 78, 79
convince 44
coordinating conjunction 65
coordination 65
correlation 65–66
correlative conjunction . .65–66, 212
could 26, 118, 119, 120, 121
count nouns 129
count on .46
countable noun(s) 129–130, 131,
                  132, 133, 139, 140,
                  142, 154, 232, 233
countries 240
cry 22
currently 25
-cy 220

D

dangerous 45
dare 44
dark 177
dash 10, 241
dates 240
deal with 191
decide .44
declarative sentence 238
definite article 46, 139, 140–142
definite noun(s) 140, 141
definite pronoun(s) 161, 166

definite quantity 154
degree .177
comparative. 176, 177, 179
equative. 178
positive 177
superlative. 176, 177, 180
delay 46
delighted 45
demand 44, 154
demonstrative adjective 142, 164–165
demonstrative pronoun 164–165
deny 46
depend on 46, 187, 191
dependent clause 55, 56
deserve .44
desire .120
despite 189, 190
despite the fact that 78, 190
determined 45
didn't 242
die 22
differ from 191, 192
different from 192
difficult .45
direct 44
direct object 7, 10, 106, 107
of infinitive 42
gerund as. 45, 46–47
in adjective clause. 93
infinitive as. 43, 44, 46–47
noun clause as. . . . 106, 107, 109
direct question 238
direct quotation 239, 243
direction 189
disappointed 45
discuss 46
dislike 46
divide in 191
divide into 191
do .23, 231
-dom 220
don't 242
double comparative(s) 179
down 189
down from 191
dramatic effect 241
dreams 116, 120
due to .191
duplicate subjects 11
during. 189, 190, 228, 231

E

each 132, 151, 152, 166
eager 45
-ean 221
early 222
easy 45, 177

eat 23
-ed 22, 80, 96, 97, 221
-ee 220
either 151, 152, 166
either...or 64, 65, 66, 153, 212
emotion 238
emphasis 241, 243
-en 221
enable 28
enable 44
-ence 220
encourage 44
endeavor 44
enjoy 46
enough .201
-ent 220, 221
-eous 222
equal to 192
equality 178
equality, complex 178
equative adjective 178
equative adverb 178
equative degree 178
equative, parallel 212
-er 220
-er than 179, 212
-ery 220
-es 129, 130, 150, 152
-ese 221
especially 229
essential 45, 154
-est 180
even if 56, 78, 117
even though 68, 78
every 132
every time 25
everybody 151, 165
everyone 151, 165
everything 151, 165
except 189, 190
except for 191
excitement 238
exclamation point 238
exclamations 238
exclusion 65, 66, 189
expect 44
expectation 27
explanation 241
expression(s)
almost negative 201, 204
negative. 200, 204
of class 133, 142
of importance 154
of necessity. 154
of quantity. 132, 232–233
of type. 133
paired 65–66, 67, 190, 212

INDEX

F

f sound 130
fact(s) 116, 117, 118, 238
fail 44
fallen 97
false subject 11, 57, 108–109,
153, 203
far 177, 222
farther 177
farthest 177
fast .178, 222
feminine pronouns 161, 162, 163
few 132, 153, 166, 177
fewer 132, 177, 233
fields of study 131
figure out 191
find out .191
finish 46
first 222
first person 161, 162, 163
flock of 151
fly 23
for 41, 45, 47, 189, 201
for example 67
for instance 67
forbid .44, 46
forbidden .97
force 44
forget 46
forgotten .97
fragment .56
from 189, 190
from now .25
from...to .190
frozen .96, 97
-ful 222
function 219–220
further 177
furthermore 67
furthest 177
future perfect 24, 25, 29
future perfect progressive 24, 25
future progressive 24, 25
future real conditional 118
future tense, simple 24, 25, 29
future time 24, 25, 26, 27, 28
future unreal conditional 119

G

gender 161, 162, 163
general statements 142
general truths 116, 117, 118
generic noun(s) 139, 140
genre of 133
genus of 151

geographical regions 141
gerund phrase 42, 45–46, 47, 141
gerund(s) 8, 41, 42, 45–47,
141, 142, 150
after verb 46–47
as direct object 45, 46–47
as object 45, 46–47
as object of a preposition 46,
47, 188
as subject 45, 150
as subject complement 45
in a list 211
with *of*. 46, 141
get 28, 43, 44
give up 46, 191
glad 45
go 23
good .45, 177
grammar topic, by skill area 1
great 177
group of 151

H

habit 27
had better .26
had to 27, 118, 119
hand in 191
happy 45
hard 222, 230
hardly 230
hardly any 201
hardly ever 204
has 150
have   23, 24, 26, 28,
29, 30, 120, 152
have got to 27
have to 27, 118
haven't 242
he 9, 162, 163
he'll 242
help 28, 43, 44
hence 67
her 10, 161, 162, 163
herd of 151
hers 162, 163
herself 161, 162
hesitant 45
hesitate 44
hidden 97
high 222
him 10, 162, 163
himself 162
hire 44
his 142, 162, 163
honored 45
-hood 220
hope 44

hot 177
how 107
how long .107
how many 107
how much 107
how often 107
how soon 107
however 67
hundred .134
hyphen 242

I

I 9, 162
I'd 242
I'm 242
-ial 221
-ian 221
-ible 221
-ic 222
-ical 221
-ics 220
-ide 220
ideas, nouns for 131, 221
ideas, pronouns for 163, 165
idiomatic structure 192
if 56, 78, 107, 117,
118, 119, 120, 121
if I were you 119
if only 121
if- clause 117
-ify 221
-ile 222
illustrate 241
illustration 66, 67, 241
imagine 46
imperative sentence 238
importance 154
important 45, 154
in 187, 189, 190, 203
in addition 67
in addition to 191
in back of 191
in case 78, 117
in case of 191
in contrast 67
in contrast to 191
in fact 67
in favor of 191
in front of 191
in order that 78
in spite of 191
in spite of the fact that 78
inclusion 65, 66, 189
indefinite article(s) 139–140
indefinite noun(s) 139, 140, 142
indefinite pronoun(s) .151–152, 160,
161, 165–166
indefinite quantity 154

DELTA'S KEY TO THE NEXT GENERATION TOEFL® TEST

independent clause 9, 55, 65, 66, 116, 200, 202, 211, 237, 239, 240
indirect object 10, 28, 44
inequality 178
infinitive phrase(s) 42–43, 47, 109–110
infinitive(s) 8, 41, 42–45, 47, 188, 201
   after adjective 45, 201
   after causative. 28, 43
   after verb. 44, 46–47
   as adjective 42, 43
   as adjective complement 42, 43, 45
   as adverb. 42, 43
   as direct object . . . 43, 44, 46–47
   as noun 41, 42
   as object 43, 46–47
   as subject. 43
   as subject complement 43
   direct object of 42
   in a list 43, 211
   negative. 43
   passive voice. 29, 44
   with indirect object. 44
   word order. 201
infinitives and gerunds 41–47
information 131, 139
-*ing* 8, 22, 23, 45, 80, 96, 220, 221, 222
inside 189, 203
insist 154
insist on 46
instead .67
instead of 191, 231
Institutional Testing Program 3
instruct .44
instruments 141
integrated skills 3
intend .44
intention 26
interested in 192
interrogation point 238
into 189
introductory negative adverb 204
introductory phrase 198, 239
introductory prepositional phrase 198, 203
introductory prepositions of location 203
introductory subordinate clause . .204
inventions 141
inverted subject and verb 117, 202–204
invite .44
involve .46
-*ious* 222
irregular adjective 177
irregular adverb 177
irregular past participle 97
irregular plural(s) 130, 152
irregular verb(s) 23, 97, 150
-*ish* 222
islands .141
-*ism* 220
isn't 242
-*ist* 220
it 9, 10, 11, 108, 162, 163, 242
it is 154, 242
it's 242
its 162, 163, 242
itself .162
-*ity* 220
-*ive* 222
-*ize* 221

J

just 178
just as 56, 78

K

keep 46
keep from 191
keep on 46, 191
keep up 191
kept 97
kind of 133
known .97

L

lakes 141
late 222
later 68
lay 230
lay off 191
learn .44
least 177, 180
less 132, 177, 233
-*less* 222
less...than 179, 212
lesser .233
let 28
let's 242
letter, closing of 240
lie 203, 230
like 41, 46, 189, 190, 229, 231
-*like* 222
limited quantity 131
list(s) . . .43, 211–212, 238, 240, 241
listen to 191
listening 1, 3

little 132, 177
live 203
location 198, 203
long adjective 178, 179, 180
long adverb 178, 179, 180
longing 120
look for 191
look forward to 46
look up 191
lost 97
lots of 132
low 222
luggage 129, 131
-*ly* 222

M

machine parts 141
made of 192
made out of 192
main clause . . .56, 57, 68, 77, 78, 79, 80, 92, 108, 109, 116, 204, 239
make 23, 28, 231
manage 44
manner 77, 78
many 132, 153, 166, 177
many of 180
masculine pronouns . . .161, 162, 163
may 26, 30, 118
me 10, 162
mean 44, 46
meaning, parallel 213
meaning, similar 231–232
meanwhile 68
-*ment* .220
mention 46
might 26, 30, 118, 119, 120, 121
million .134
mind 46
mine .162
miss 46
mistaken 97
mistakes 116, 120
modal verb 22, 26–27
modal(s) 26–27, 30, 116, 118, 119, 120, 121, 150
models .141
modifier 42, 90, 91, 107, 149, 178, 188–189, 201, 202
mood 22, 26
more 178
more...than 179, 212
moreover 67
most 132, 153, 166, 177, 180, 228, 229
motivate 44
motivated 45
mountains, groups of 141

much 132, 177, 222
multiple 132
must 27, 30, 118
my 142, 162
myself 162

N

near 189, 203, 230
nearly 230
necessary 45, 154
necessary clause 94
necessity 27, 154
need 44
need to 27
negative adverb . .200–201, 203, 204
negative equality 178
negative expression 200, 204
negative verb 117
negative, introductory 204
neglect 44
neither 151, 152, 166, 203, 204
neither...nor . . .65, 66, 153, 204, 212
-ness 220
neuter pronouns 161, 162, 163
never 200, 204
nevertheless 67
news 131, 150
next 68
next to 191, 203
nice 177
no 132, 199
no one 151, 165
no sooner...than 204
nobody 151, 165
noncount nouns 131
none 153, 166
nonrestrictive clause 94
not 43, 178, 200
not all 200
not any 200
not every 200
not many 200
not much 200
not often 204
not once 204
not one 200
not only...but also 65, 66,
                                153, 204, 212
not until 204
not...but 65, 66, 212
nothing 151, 165
noun 12
noun clause(s) 8, 56,
                        106–110, 150, 154, 188
noun in apposition 10
noun phrase 8, 188
noun referent 92, 93, 161,

162, 163, 164, 166
noun structure . .7, 8, 9, 10, 106, 188
noun suffixes 220–221
noun(s) 7–12, 220–221
    academic 130
    after preposition 10, 188
    as object 10
    as subject. 9
    collective 151
    common 12, 161
    count 129
    countable 129–130, 131,
                132, 133, 139, 140,
                142, 154, 232, 233
    definite 140, 141
    facts about. 12
    for abstractions 131
    for activities 131, 221
    for animals 130, 141
    for body parts 130, 141
    for classes. . . 131, 132, 139, 142
    for conditions 131
    for fields of study 131
    for ideas 131, 221
    for people 130, 221
    for phenomena 131
    for public places 141
    for qualities. 131, 221
    for species. 141
    for substances 131
    for things. 221
    for time periods. 141
    form 219, 220–221
    function . 8, 9, 10, 219, 220–221
    generic 139, 140
    in a list 211
    indefinite. 139, 140, 142
    irregular plural 130
    noncount 131
    non–specific 139, 151
    plural 129–134, 140, 141,
                    142, 152, 153, 154
    possessive 180, 242
    proper 12, 141, 161
    scientific 130
    singular 129–130, 132, 133,
                    139–140, 150, 151, 152
    uncountable 46, 131–133,
                    139, 140, 142, 148,
                    150, 153, 232, 233
    with demonstrative
        adjective. 142
    with no article. 142
    with possessive adjective 142
    word order . . 199, 200, 201, 202
now 25

now that 78
nowhere 204
number 23, 129, 148,
                            149, 161, 162, 165
number of 132, 154, 232
numbers 133–134, 222, 240
numeric terms 133–134

O

o'clock 242
object complement 10
object pronoun(s) 10, 161,
                            162, 163, 164
object to 46, 191
object 10
    direct 7, 10, 42, 43, 44, 45,
            46–47, 93, 106, 107, 109
    gerund as. 45, 46–47
    in adjective clause. 91, 93
    in noun clause. 107
    indirect 10, 28, 44
    infinitive as. 43, 44, 46–47
    noun clause as. 107, 109
    of preposition. . . . 10, 46, 47, 93,
                    107, 188, 189, 190, 191
    word order. 202
of 46, 131, 134, 141,
                            151, 152, 189, 190
off 189, 190
offer 44
old 177
on 189, 203
on no account 204
on the contrary 67
on the one hand...
    on the other hand 67
on the other hand 67
once 56, 77
one 132, 160, 166
-one 165
one of 180
one of the 133, 141, 180
only 202
only after 204
only before 204
only if 78, 117, 203, 204
only one of something 142
only since 204
only when 204
only where 204
open 22
opinion 238
or 65, 149, 211, 212
-or 220
order 44
other 132, 232
others 153, 166, 232

otherwise .68
ought to .27
our 162
ours 162
ourselves 162
-ous 222
out 189
out of 191
outside 189, 203
over 189, 203
ownership 242

P

pair of 151
paired expression 65–66, 67,
190, 212
parallel 211
parallel meaning 213
parallel structure 210–213
parallelism 211
parentheses 10, 241
part of speech 219, 220
participial adjective(s) 91, 96–97
participial phrase(s) 79, 95
participle
    past 22, 23, 24, 26, 29,
79, 80, 95, 96, 97
    present 22, 23, 24, 26,
79, 80, 95, 96
passive participial adjective 97
passive subject 9
passive voice 29–30, 44, 80, 96,
97, 120, 149, 150, 154, 190
past ability 26
past advisability 27
past form 22, 23, 24
past habit 27
past necessity 27
past participle 22, 23, 24, 26,
29, 79, 80, 95, 96, 97
past perfect 24, 25, 29, 118, 120
past perfect progressive 24, 25,
118, 120
past possibility 26
past probability 27
past progressive 24, 25, 29,
118, 119, 149, 150
past real conditional 118
past tense, simple 24, 25, 29,
118, 119, 121
past time 24, 25, 26, 28
past unreal conditional 120
people
    irregular plurals for 130
    nouns for 130, 221
    pronouns for 92, 160, 163,
164, 165, 166

percent .134
perfect progressive tenses 24
perfect tenses 24, 29
period 238
permit 28
permit 44
person 23, 119, 150,
154, 161, 162, 163
personal pronoun(s) 161–162
persuade 28
persuade 44
phenomena, nouns for 131
phrasal verb 191
phrase(s)
    adjective 90, 91,
95–96, 199, 239
    adverb 76, 79–80
    gerund 42, 45–46, 47, 141
    in a list 211, 212
    infinitive . . .42–43, 47, 109–110
    introductory 198, 239
    joined by conjunction . . .65, 66,
211, 212
    noun 8, 188
    of same/
        similar value 65, 66, 211
    parallel 210, 211
    participial 79, 95
    prepositional 188–189,
198, 202, 203, 212
    unnecessary 95, 239
    verb 22, 28, 211
place 77
places, public 141
plan 44
plants 141
pleased .45
pleased with 192
plural 129–134, 232
    irregular 130, 152
    possessive 242
    pronoun 152, 153, 161,
162, 163, 164, 232
    subject 148, 149, 152–153
    verb 148, 149, 152–153
    with the 140, 141
point out 191, 192
position 189, 203
position, similar 211
positive degree 177
possession 242
possessive adjective . .142, 161, 162,
163, 180, 242
possessive noun 180, 242
possessive pronoun . . .92, 161, 162,
163, 164, 242
possibility 26
possible .45

postpone 46
practice .46
predictions 116, 118
prefer 46, 154
preference 26, 27
prejudiced against 192
prepare .44
prepare for 191
prepared 45
prepositional phrase . .188–189, 198,
202, 203, 212
preposition(s) 187–192
    compound 191
    object of 10, 46, 47, 93,
107, 188, 189, 190, 191
    of direction 189
    of exclusion 189
    of inclusion 189
    of location 198, 203
    of position 189
    of space 189, 190
    of status 189, 190
    of time 189, 190
present form 22, 23, 24
present participle 22, 23, 24, 26,
79, 80, 95, 96
present perfect 24, 29, 117,
118, 150, 152
present perfect progressive . .24, 117,
118, 150, 152
present progressive 24, 29,
117, 118, 150
present real conditional 117–118
present tense, simple 24, 29, 117,
118, 150, 152
present time 24, 25, 26
present unreal conditional 119
pretend .44
prevent .46
principal parts 22–23
prior to .191
probability 26, 27
proceed .44
progressive action 26
progressive tenses 24, 29
promise .44
pronoun agreement 160–166
pronoun form 161, 162
pronoun(s) 8, 160–166, 188
    agreement with noun . . 160–166
    agreement with verb . . 151–152,
153, 154
    definite 161, 166
    demonstrative 164–165
    feminine 161, 162, 163
    first person 161, 162, 163
    for abstractions 163, 165
    for animals 92, 160,
163, 164, 166

INDEX

for ideas 163, 165
for people 92, 160, 163,
164, 165, 166
for things 92, 160, 163,
164, 165, 166
indefinite 151–152, 160,
161, 165–166
masculine 161, 162, 163
neuter 161, 162, 163
object . . . 10, 161, 162, 163, 164
personal 161–162
plural 152, 153, 161,
162, 163, 164, 232
possessive 92, 161, 162,
163, 164, 242
reflexive 161, 162
relative 92–94, 95, 154, 164
second person 161, 162, 163
singular 151–152, 161,
162, 163, 164, 165, 232
subject 9, 160, 161,
162, 163, 164
third person 161, 162, 163
with singular verb . 151–152, 153
proper noun 12, 141, 161
propose 154
proud .45
prove .44
provided 117
provided that 78, 117
provinces 240
punctuation 237–243
punctuation mark 238
purpose 77, 78
put off 46

Q

qualified for 192
qualities, nouns for 131, 221
quantity
definite 154
expression of 132, 232–233
indefinite 154
limited 131
plural 131
quantity of 132, 232
question 238
question mark 238
question word 202
question word order 117,
202–203, 204
quotation 239, 243
quotation marks 243

R

raise 230
rarely 204
rather than 231
reading 1, 3
ready 45
real conditional
sentence 117–118, 120
real situation 117
recall .46
recollect 46
recommend 46, 154
recommended 154
reduced clause 79–80, 95,
96, 109–110
refer to 191
referent 92, 93, 161, 162,
163, 164, 165, 166
reflexive pronoun 161, 162
refuse .44
regardless of 191
regret .46
regrets 116, 120
regular occurrence, past 118
regular verbs 22
related to 192
relative clause 92
relative pronoun .92–94, 95, 154, 164
relieved 45
rely on 46, 191, 192
remember 46, 47
remind .44
remove from 191
reply to 191
report .46
request 28, 238
request 154
require .28
require 44, 154
required 154
resent .46
resist .46
respond to 191
restatement 241
restrictive clause 94
result 65, 66, 67, 68,
115, 116, 179, 201
result clause 116, 117, 118,
119, 120, 121
resume .46
rise .230
risk 46
run out of 190, 192
-ry 220

S

-s 129, 130, 150, 152
s sound 242
s, plural 129, 130, 242
s, possessive 242
sad .45
satisfied with 192
scarcely 204
scarcely any 201
scientific facts 116, 117, 118
scientific nouns 130
second 222
second person 161, 162, 163
seem .44
seldom 204
semicolon 66, 240
sentence break 238
sentence(s) 55, 238
active–voice 28, 30
complete 55, 77, 116
complex 55, 116
compound 55
conditional 78, 115–121
declarative 238
imperative 238
passive–voice 28–30
simple 55
subject of 9
serve .44
set 230
several 132, 153, 166
sex .163
shall .26
she 9, 161, 162, 163
-ship 220
shocked 45
short adjective 178, 179, 180
short adverb 178, 179, 180
should 27, 30, 118, 120
-sion 220
similar to 192
simple future 24, 25, 29
simple past 24, 25, 29,
118, 119, 121
simple present 24, 29, 117,
118, 150, 152
simple sentence 55
simple tenses 24, 29
since 56, 68, 69, 77, 78, 189
single 132
singular 129, 162
noun 129–130, 132, 133,
139–140, 150, 151, 152
pronoun 150–152, 161, 162,
163, 164, 165, 232
subject . . 149, 150–152, 153, 154
verb 148, 149, 150–152, 153

singular and plural 129–134
sit 230
small 177
so 55, 65, 203, 204
so that 56, 68, 78
so...that 68, 78
some 132, 153, 166
-some 222
some of .180
somebody 151, 165
someone 151, 165
something 151, 165
sorry 45
sort of 133
sound, similar 228–231
space 189–190
speak 23
speaking 1, 3
special 229
species 141
species of 133
spelling change 130
spoken 97
start 22, 46, 47
statement(s) 202, 238
states 240
status 189, 190, 203
stem 220
stolen 97
stop 46
strange 45
strive 44
Structure and Written Expression . .3
struggle 44
subject 7, 9, 106, 107, 148–154
    agreement
       with verb 148–154
    compound 11, 152, 153
    duplicate 11
    false 11, 57,
        108–109, 153, 203
    gerund as. 45, 150
    indefinite
       pronoun as 151–152
    infinitive as 43
    noun clause as 107,
        108–109, 150
    of adjective clause 91, 93
    of adverb clause 77, 79
    of independent clause 9
    of noun clause. . . . 107, 108, 109
    of sentence 9
    of subordinate clause 9
    passive. 9, 29
    plural 148, 149, 152–153
    singular 149, 150–152,
        153, 154
    third person. 150, 154

true 11, 108–109, 153, 203
subject complement . . .9, 43, 45, 107
subject pronoun(s) 9, 160,
       161, 162, 163, 164
subject–verb agreement 148–154
subject–verb word order . . .202–204
subordinate clause(s) . . .8, 9, 55, 56,
      57, 68, 77, 91, 106,
     107, 116, 202, 204, 212
subordinating conjunction 56, 68–69,
      77–78, 92, 107
subordination 68–69
subordinator 56, 68, 77–78, 91,
    92–94, 107–108, 109, 116, 117
substances, nouns for 131
succeed in 46, 191
such as 191
such...that 68, 78
suffix(es) 12, 30, 220–222
suggest 46, 154
suggestions 119
superlative adjective . .141, 177, 180
superlative adverb 177, 180
superlative degree 176, 177, 180
superlative form 180
superlative structures
    with plural nouns 133
surprised .45

T

take 23
take over 191, 192
teach 44
team of 151
tell 44
tend 44
tense 23, 24–25
    continuous. 24
    future perfect 24, 25, 29
    future
      perfect progressive 24, 25
    future progressive 25
    past perfect. 24, 25,
        29, 118, 120
    past perfect progressive 24,
        25, 118, 120
    past progressive 24, 25, 29,
        118, 119, 149, 150
    perfect. 24, 29
    perfect progressive 24
    present perfect 24, 29, 117,
        118, 150, 152
    present perfect progressive . . 24,
       117, 118, 150, 152
    present progressive 24, 29,
       117, 118, 150

progressive 24, 29
simple 24, 29
simple future. 24, 25, 29
simple past. 24, 25, 29,
      118, 119, 121
simple present 24, 29, 117,
      118, 150, 152
Test of English
  as a Foreign Language 1, 3
-th 222
than 176, 177, 230
that   56, 92, 93, 94, 95, 107,
    109, 142, 154, 164, 165, 213
the 46, 133, 139,
      140–142, 179, 180
the -est .180
the first .166
the former 166
the last .166
the latter 166
the least .180
the lesser 233
the most .180
the number of 154
the other 166, 232
the others 232
their 142, 162, 163, 231
theirs 162, 163
them 10, 162, 163
themselves 162
then 68, 230
there 11, 57, 153, 203, 231
there's 242
therefore .67
these 142, 164, 165
they 9, 160, 162, 163
they'd 242
things, nouns for 221
things, pronouns for . . .92, 160, 163,
      164, 165, 166
think about 46, 191
think of 46, 191
third 222
third person .150, 154, 161, 162, 163
this 142, 164, 165
those 142, 164, 165
though 56, 68, 78
thousand 134
threaten .44
through .189
throughout 189, 190
thus 68
till 189
time 24, 25, 66, 68, 69,
      77, 79, 116, 189, 190
time marker 25
time order 66, 68, 69
time periods 141
-tion 220

to (infinitive) 8, 28, 42, 43, 109, 188
to (preposition) 93, 189
today 25
TOEFL 1, 2, 3
   iBT 1, 2, 3
   Internet–based. 3
   ITP 3
   paper–based 3
   PBT. 1, 3
together with 189
tolerate 46
tomorrow .25
too 66, 201, 232
toward 189, 190
transition 66, 237, 239, 240
transitive verb 29
truths 116, 117, 118
try 44, 46
turn into 191
turn off .191
turn on .191
twice 178
two 132
-ty 220
type 133, 139
type of 133

U

ugly 177
uncountable noun .46, 131–133, 139, 140, 142, 148, 150, 153, 232, 233
under 189, 190, 203
under no circumstances 204
unless 56, 78, 117
unlike 189
unnecessary adjective clause .94, 239
unnecessary adjective phrase .95, 239
unreal conditional sentence .119–121
unreal situation 119
until 56, 77, 189, 190
up 189
upon 189
-ure 220
urge 44, 154
us .10, 162
use 47
use up 191
used to 27
usual 45
usually 25

V

value, same/similar 65, 211
variety of 133
various 132
verb 30
verb phrase 22, 28, 211
verb suffixes 221
verbal 42
verb(s) 21–30, 148–154, 221
   affirmative 117
   agreement with subject 148–154
   auxiliary 22, 23, 24, 26, 202
   base form . 8, 22, 23, 26, 28, 154
   causative 28, 43
   compound 149
   facts about. 30
   form 22–23, 219, 220, 221
   function. 22, 219, 220, 221
   irregular 23, 97, 150
   modal 22, 26–27
   negative. 117
   of importance 154
   passive–voice 9, 190
   phrasal. 191
   plural. 148, 149, 152–153
   principal parts 22–23
   regular. 22
   simple–present . 24, 29, 150, 152
   singular . 148, 149, 150–152, 153
   tenses. 24–25
   transitive 29
   with adverb 23, 30, 200
   with gerund 46–47
   with infinitive 44, 46–47
   with preposition . . 187, 191–192
   word order. . . . 23, 200, 202–204
very 202, 232
voice 28–30
   active. 28, 30, 80, 96
   passive . . . 29–30, 44, 80, 96, 97, 120, 149, 150, 154, 190
vowel 140
vowel sound 140

W

wait 44
walk 22
want 44
-ward 222
warn 44
water, large bodies of 141
we 9, 162

we've .242
well 177
what 107
whatever 107
when 56, 69, 77, 92, 94, 107, 118, 202
whenever 56, 77, 107
where 56, 77, 92, 94, 107, 202
whereas 56, 68, 78
whereby 92
wherever 77, 107
whether 56, 107
whether or not 78, 107, 117
which 56, 92, 93, 94, 95, 107, 160, 164
whichever 107
while 56, 68, 69, 77, 78, 231
who . . .56, 92, 94, 95, 107, 160, 164
who'll 242
who's 242
whoever 107
whom 92, 93, 94, 107, 164
whomever 107
whose 56, 92, 107, 164
why 107, 202
will 24, 25, 26, 30, 118
willing 45
-wise 222
wish 44, 121
wish clause 121
wishes 116, 120–121
with 189
within 189
without .189
won't 242
word ending 12, 30, 220–222
word errors 228–233
word form 219–222
word order 117, 198–204
words
   content 8, 22
   in a list 211, 212
   joined by a
      conjunction 65, 66, 211
   of same/
      similar value 65, 66, 211
   parallel 211
   question. 202
   similar in meaning 231–232
   similar in sound 228–231
work 44
worn 97
worry about 191
would 25, 27, 118, 119, 120, 121
would rather 27
wouldn't 242
write 23
writing 1, 3
written .97

Y

-y 220, 222
yesterday 25
yet 65
you 9, 10, 160, 162
your 162
yours 162
yourself 162
yourselves 162

HOW TO SCORE SPEAKING

	INDEPENDENT SPEAKING Score Levels for Independent Speaking Tasks
4	**A response at this level** ↝ effectively addresses the task and is generally well developed and coherent; and ↝ demonstrates effective use of grammar and vocabulary, but may contain minor language errors that do not interfere with meaning; and ↝ demonstrates clear, fluid speech with high overall intelligibility, but may contain minor problems with pronunciation or intonation.
3	**A response at this level** ↝ conveys ideas and information relevant to the task, but overall development is somewhat limited, and connections among ideas are sometimes unclear; and ↝ demonstrates somewhat effective use of grammar and vocabulary, but may contain language errors that do not seriously interfere with meaning; and ↝ demonstrates generally clear, somewhat fluid speech, but may contain minor problems with pronunciation, intonation, or pacing and may occasionally require some listener effort.
2	**A response at this level** ↝ is related to the task, although the development of ideas is limited, and connections among ideas are unclear; or ↝ demonstrates a limited range and control of grammar and vocabulary; or ↝ demonstrates some clear speech, but contains problems with pronunciation, intonation, or pacing and may require significant listener effort.
1	**A response at this level** ↝ fails to provide much relevant content because ideas that are expressed are inaccurate, limited, or vague; or ↝ demonstrates a limited control of grammar and vocabulary that severely limits expression of ideas and connections among ideas; or ↝ demonstrates fragmented speech with frequent pauses and consistent problems with pronunciation and intonation that obscure meaning and require great listener effort.
0	**A response at this level** ↝ is not related to the topic; or ↝ is absent.

INTEGRATED SPEAKING
Score Levels for Integrated Speaking Tasks

4	**A response at this level** ↬ effectively addresses the task by conveying relevant information and appropriate details from the listening and reading texts; and ↬ demonstrates a coherent expression of ideas, with appropriate grammar and vocabulary, but may contain some minor language errors; and ↬ demonstrates clear, fluid speech with high overall intelligibility, but may contain minor problems with pronunciation or intonation.
3	**A response at this level** ↬ conveys information relevant to the task, but shows some incompleteness, inaccuracy, or lack of detail; and ↬ demonstrates a fairly coherent expression of ideas, but may contain some errors in grammar or vocabulary that do not seriously interfere with meaning; and ↬ demonstrates generally clear, somewhat fluid speech, but may contain minor problems with pronunciation, intonation, or pacing and may occasionally require some listener effort.
2	**A response at this level** ↬ conveys some relevant information but omits key ideas, shows limited development, or shows misunderstanding of key ideas; or ↬ demonstrates a limited expression of ideas, inaccurate or unclear connections among ideas, or limited or inaccurate grammar and vocabulary; or ↬ demonstrates some clear speech, but contains problems with pronunciation, intonation, or pacing and may require significant listener effort.
1	**A response at this level** ↬ fails to provide much relevant content because ideas that are expressed are inaccurate, limited, or vague; or ↬ demonstrates a limited control of grammar and vocabulary that severely limits expression of ideas and connections among ideas; or ↬ demonstrates fragmented speech with frequent pauses and consistent problems with pronunciation and intonation that obscure meaning and require great listener effort.
0	**A response at this level** ↬ is not related to the topic; or ↬ is absent.

HOW TO SCORE WRITING

INDEPENDENT WRITING
Score Levels for Independent Writing Tasks

5	**An essay at this level** ➝ effectively addresses the task by clearly stating an opinion; and ➝ is well organized and well developed with appropriate examples, reasons, or details; and ➝ displays unity and coherence; and ➝ uses language effectively, with sentence variety and appropriate word choice and only occasional minor language errors.
4	**An essay at this level** ➝ addresses the task well, but some points may not be fully supported; and ➝ is generally well organized and sufficiently developed with examples, reasons, or details; and ➝ displays unity and coherence, but may have some redundancy or lack of clarity; and ➝ contains sentence variety and a range of vocabulary, but may have noticeable minor language errors that do not interfere with meaning.
3	**An essay at this level** ➝ addresses the task with some development and some appropriate supporting details; or ➝ displays unity and coherence, but connections among ideas may be occasionally unclear; or ➝ is inconsistent in using language effectively, with errors in grammar and vocabulary that occasionally obscure meaning; or ➝ contains an accurate but limited range of sentence structures and vocabulary.
2	**An essay at this level** ➝ displays limited development in response to the task, with inappropriate or insufficient supporting details; or ➝ contains inadequate organization or connections among ideas; or ➝ contains an accumulation of errors in grammar and usage.
1	**An essay at this level** ➝ is flawed by serious disorganization or underdevelopment; or ➝ contains little or no detail, or details that are irrelevant to the task; or ➝ contains serious and frequent errors in grammar and usage.
0	**An essay at this level** ➝ is not related to the given topic; or ➝ is written in a language other than English; or ➝ is blank.

	INTEGRATED WRITING **Score Levels for Integrated Writing Tasks**
5	**A response at this level** ✎ effectively addresses the task by conveying relevant information from the lecture; and ✎ accurately relates key information from the lecture to information in the reading; and ✎ is well organized and coherent; and ✎ contains appropriate grammar and vocabulary, with only occasional minor language errors.
4	**A response at this level** ✎ generally conveys relevant information from the lecture, but may have minor omissions; and ✎ is generally good in relating information from the lecture to information in the reading, but may have minor inaccuracies or vagueness of some content or connections among ideas; and ✎ is generally well organized; and ✎ contains appropriate grammar and vocabulary, but may have noticeable minor language errors or occasional lack of clarity.
3	**A response at this level** ✎ contains some relevant information from the lecture, but may omit one key point; or ✎ conveys some connections between the lecture and the reading, but some content or connections among ideas may be incomplete, inaccurate, or vague; or ✎ contains errors in grammar or usage that result in vagueness of some content or connections among ideas.
2	**A response at this level** ✎ contains some relevant information from the lecture, but may have significant omissions or inaccuracies of key points; or ✎ omits or largely misrepresents the connections between the lecture and the reading; or ✎ contains language errors that obscure meaning of key ideas or connections among ideas.
1	**A response at this level** ✎ contains little or no relevant content from the lecture; or ✎ fails to connect points from the lecture and reading; or ✎ contains language errors that greatly obscure meaning; or ✎ is too brief to allow evaluation of writing proficiency.
0	**A response at this level** ✎ only copies sentences from the reading; or ✎ is not related to the given topic; or ✎ is written in a language other than English; or ✎ is blank.

SCORE CHARTS

TESTS

Circle the number correct on the
Diagnostic Test and the Review Test.

% Correct	Diagnostic Test	Review Test
100%	30	30
	29	29
	28	28
90%	27	27
	26	26
	25	25
80%	24	24
	23	23
	22	22
70%	21	21
	20	20
	19	19
60%	18	18
	17	17
	16	16
50%	15	15
	14	14
	13	13
40%	12	12
	11	11
	10	10
30%	9	9
	8	8
	7	7
20%	6	6
	5	5
	4	4
10%	3	3
	2	2
	1	1

QUIZZES

Circle the number correct on each quiz.

% Correct	Quiz 1	Quiz 2	Quiz 3	Quiz 4	Quiz 5	Quiz 6
100%	10	10	10	10	10	10
90%	9	9	9	9	9	9
80%	8	8	8	8	8	8
70%	7	7	7	7	7	7
60%	6	6	6	6	6	6
50%	5	5	5	5	5	5
40%	4	4	4	4	4	4
30%	3	3	3	3	3	3
20%	2	2	2	2	2	2
10%	1	1	1	1	1	1
	Units 1–3	Units 4–6	Units 7–9	Units 10–13	Units 14–17	Units 18–20

DELTA'S KEY TO THE NEXT GENERATION TOEFL® TEST

DELTA'S KEY TO THE NEXT GENERATION TOEFL® TEST

DELTA'S KEY TO THE NEXT GENERATION TOEFL® TEST

DISK CONTENTS

TOTAL RUNNING TIME – 73:15

Track	Exercise	Skill	Page	Time
1	Exercise 1–F	Listening	18	2:00
2	Exercise 1–F	Listening	18	4:41
3	Exercise 1–G	Speaking	19	2:11
4	Exercise 2–G	Listening	37	4:40
5	Exercise 2–I	Speaking	38	1:24
6	Exercise 2–J	Writing	39	2:23
7	Exercise 4–E	Speaking	62	1:51
8	Exercise 5–E	Writing	74	2:26
9	Exercise 6–E	Listening	85	4:41
10	Exercise 6–F	Speaking	86	1:49
11	Exercise 6–G	Writing	87	2:16
12	Exercise 7–F	Listening	103	4:42
13	Exercise 7–G	Speaking	104	2:06
14	Exercise 8–E	Speaking	114	1:24
15	Exercise 9–D	Listening	124	2:34
16	Exercise 9–E	Speaking	125	1:20
17	Exercise 9–F	Speaking	126	1:29
18	Exercise 11–D	Speaking	146	1:48
19	Exercise 12–E	Writing	158	2:09
20	Exercise 13–F	Speaking	173	1:19
21	Exercise 14–E	Listening	184	3:47
22	Exercise 14–G	Speaking	185	2:27
23	Exercise 15–E	Speaking	196	2:21
24	Exercise 16–C	Listening	207	3:52
25	Exercise 16–D	Speaking	208	1:21
26	Exercise 17–D	Writing	216	2:11
27	Exercise 19–C	Listening	235	3:58
28	Exercise 19–D	Speaking	236	1:29
29	Exercise 20–D	Writing	246	2:22